TRAVELS
WITH THE
FLEA AND OTHER
ECCENTRIC
JOURNEYS

In his youth Jim Perrin was one of the most notable British rock-climbers, 'the best rock-climber in the world for about six weeks in the summer of 1972', according to the *Observer* editor Roger Alton. Since those days Jim has committed his time and energy to the craft of mountain writing and has taken it to new heights.

His first book, *Menlove* (1985), the biography of John Menlove Edwards, was the first outright winner of the prestigious Boardman Tasker Award for mountain literature. He has subsequently written three collections of essays, another biography, and a best-selling book on Snowdonia, *Visions of Snowdonia* (1997). His collection of essays, *Spirits of Place* (1997) was hailed by Jan Morris in the *Guardian* as 'a remarkable book by a remarkable and undervalued writer ... a sort of rucksack Thoreau', and Professor M Wynn Thomas in the *New Welsh Review* claimed that 'no-one else in contemporary Wales is capable of writing prose of this exceptional quality ... he deserves to be recognised as the most singular, and the most outstanding, prose-writer of present-day Wales'. His most recent book is *River Map* (2001), an essay on love and landscape.

Jim Perrin contributes regularly to the *Daily Telegraph*, the *Guardian*, *The Great Outdoors*, *Climber* magazine and other journals.

TRAVELS WITH THE FLEA

AND OTHER ECCENTRIC JOURNEYS

JIM PERRIN

www.theinpinn.co.uk

The mystery does not get any clearer by repeating the question,
Nor is it bought with going to amazing places.

Rumi

First printed in 2002 by

an imprint of
Neil Wilson Publishing Ltd
303a The Pentagon Centre
36 Washington Street
GLASGOW
G3 8AZ
Tel: 0141-221-1117
Fax: 0141-221-5363
E-mail: info@nwp.sol.co.uk
www.theinpinn.co.uk

Second edition printed November 2003

A catalogue record for this book
is available from the British Library.
ISBN 1-903238-43-9
Typeset in Aldine
Cover design by Belstane

Printed in Finland by WS Bookwell

CONTENTS

ACKNOWLEDGEMENTS

Many of these articles first appeared in the *Daily Telegraph* Travel section, and are reprinted here with its editor Graham Boynton's permission. They were commissioned for the most part by Michael Kerr, to whom I'm indebted not only for his own fine example as a travel writer, but also for the opportunities he's put my way, his encouragement, and the meticulous care and skill that he brings to the handling of other writers' copy. His suggested changes have always been improvements and his queries never less than constructive. No writer could hope for a better editor. I'm also grateful and appreciative of the support offered at the *Telegraph* by Nigel Richardson, Richard Madden, Christopher Gilbert, Graham Boynton and, especially, Lisa Donald.

Other pieces in this collection appear courtesy of John Cleare and Duncan Baird Publishing, Roland Smith and Michael Joseph Ltd, Victor Golightly and the *New Welsh Review*, Roger Alton and the *Guardian*, Mairwen Prys Jones and Gwasg Gomer, and Gwenda Williams.

Many people have helped facilitate these travels. I'd like to single out for special thanks Phil Bloomfield, Glyn Lovell, Jane Harris of the Wales Tourist Board, Hamish McCall of Trips Worldwide in Bristol, Maggi Smit of Windows on the Wild and Mary and Joe King-Nemeth of Freewheel Tours (both in London), guidebook publishers Lonely Planet, trekking specialists Himalayan Kingdoms, John Atkinson of equipment manufacturers Sprayway Ltd, and Nim Singh of the Canadian High Commission in London. The friendship and support of Cameron McNeish over more than 15 years has been one of the pleasures of my life, and to him and his deputy at *TGO*, John Manning, I am particularly grateful. They will recognise the provenance of much of this material.

Without the helpful criticism and comment of many friends, all this writer's confidence would have ebbed away. I'd like therefore to record here my thanks to Roger Alton, Sally Baker, John Beatty, Polly Biven, Dr Ian Gregson, Roger Hubank, Clare Hudson, Nigel Jenkins, Aled Jones, Colin and Annette Mortlock, Bernard Newman, Mary O'Malley, the late Robin Reeves, Tony Shaw, Dermot Somers, Professor M Wynn Thomas, Robert Wilkinson, Gwenda Williams and Ray Wood.

To my publisher, Neil Wilson, thanks for his guidance and energy and the opportunity to gather these pieces together, and to my editor, Morven Dooner, gratitude for her wonderfully sound ear, sharp eye, and acute sense of humour.

To anyone whom I may inadvertently have omitted to mention, I apologise, and assure them that appreciation, if not exposure, is theirs.

Lastly, if through fear of being thought gushing or sentimental I did not mention the bright tints of joy with which a friendship begun in that wonderful decade of the 1960s with the artist Jacquetta Balla has infused my perception of the world, then I would have 'missed my chance with one of the lords/ Of life/ And ... have something to expiate;/ A pettiness.' That my oldest and dearest woman friend should now be my wife leaves me marvelling at undeserved providence and pondering, in the words of the Grateful Dead remembered from acid-illuminated nights we shared 30 years ago, on 'what a long, strange trip it's been'.

So to her, as well as the little dog who enhanced my life in her own ways for 17 years (and has come back, obviously, as a cat), this book, with love, is dedicated.

FOREWORD

BY ROGER HUBANK

'A cultured man,' wrote W J Gruffydd, is 'one who touches life in the greatest number of places'. Touching life is precisely what is on offer in Jim Perrin's latest collection.

He is a rock climber: in his prime, one of the very best. As many of the essays collected in an earlier volume, *Spirits of Place,* testify, he found in climbing a subject that enabled him to tell honestly and directly the things he found to be true. Against the great abstractions he sets solid, tangible things, things he can be sure of, things 'felt in the blood, and felt along the heart', and this is the source of his power as a writer.

He is also a traveller, with the same sharp eye for the immediate and the particular. At the same time, he brings to his travels, whether in cities or wild places, a sense of the mystery and summons of creation. It transfigures almost everything he writes. By bleak Arctic shores, on Himalayan ridges and rock faces, or tropical rain forest, even by the burning ghats of Varanasi, always, whatever its defilements, there is the fullness of life, 'starting out, and astounding', as he puts it: the radiance of sheer presence.

Again and again he is moved by something which seems always to elude his human reaching after it, 'a stranger longing,' Perrin calls it, 'the exact words for which remain fixed only in feeling, refusing ever to succumb to our quest after definition.' There is, perhaps, a German word that might come close: *Heimgang* – that return to the heart-land, which is at the source of all man's yearnings. For Perrin, that *Heimgang* has found its spiritual *locus* in Wales, the length and breadth of which he travelled with The Flea, the little terrier who was for so many years his inseparable companion.

Wales, too, has suffered its defilements: the depredations of the developers, of tourism, of the heritage industry, of the Water Boards and the Ministry of Defence. Add to that the long disease of colonialism and economic exploitation: the deserted villages, the subordination of the language, the long suffering Welsh poor.

'If we know in what way society is unbalanced,' writes Simone Weil, 'we must do what we can to add weight to the lighter scale.' So Perrin places in the scale a counter-reality, the reality that is *his* Wales, a country formed in the imagination but which carries weight because it is so steeped in the literature, the history and the language which has shaped its communities and given them meaning.

In doing so he restores the balance, recovers those human resources which are otherwise continually undermined or threatened by the barbarisms of modernity, celebrating them in a way which transcends the particularities of country or nationality.

To echo the poet Seamus Heaney, 'the place of waste' and 'the place of renewal' have become co-terminous with 'the place of writing'. And because of that we are all in debt to Jim Perrin's affirming art.

Introduction

The Familiar *as* Strange
The Strange *as* Familiar

En la noche dichosa,
En secreto, que nadie me veia,
Ni yo miraba cosa,
Sin otra luz y guia,
Sino la que en el corazón ardia.

(Upon that lucky night, / In secrecy, inscrutable to sight, / I went without discerning,/ And with no other light, / Except for that which in my heart was burning.)   St John of the Cross

I have been out walking in the twilight by the badger wood in Standean Bottom. This walking at nightfall or dawn has been my habit for most of my life. When I was an active climber, I never liked to leave the crags until the violet shadows around them were deepening into misty opacity and the bands of colour across the sky were brilliant in sunset's afterglow. Through the years I was shepherding in Cwm Pennant, there would be periods when I'd be out on the hills for many hours after dark or before daybreak, senses becoming instinctually attuned, vibrant knowledge of the place flooding in on me. Often I'd rise early or delay departure to ensure being out when the earthly powers seemed in process of gathering into expression, at the cusp of darkness and light. Not that it is so sharp a thing as a cusp, more a gradual transition, the characteristics of the one lingering palely long after the assertion of the other.

Here in Standean Bottom, on one of those November evenings when air has the touch of damp, warm velvet, the light has resolved itself, drained out of the sky and become no more than a glimmery quality investing the drilled shoots of winter wheat, the grey tilth, the pebbly long strips of chalk along the field margins, the obsidian facets of cracked flints, and high in the beech trees the luminous remnants of foliage that stubborned out the equinoctial gales.

I am not in love with this landscape of the South Downs as I am with that of Wales, which is the country of my blood and long acquaintance. But still, it appeals, it insists quietly on its own quality as I stand here in the dusk, silently among it. The bend of this valley, the interlockingness of its spurs, the sudden dart of a rabbit from a thicket to its burrow in the ruched banks above, the thorns bent on the windward slope or bushed in the hill's groin, the distant rustle that could be the first bold badger of the night emerging into leaf-drift and shadow, the secretiveness of the place despite the so-called communications masts on the ridge and the glow of Brighton over the hill and the liquid incessant dance of car lights, waltzing in three-quarter time along the winding road to Lewes – all these create a mood that has its own harmony, its own balance, and that will linger in the mind and return at odd moments long after I have left this place which I may not love, but for which already I have a feeling that grows and declares its own validity.

This feeling for landscape is so powerful within us. These are new hills, yesterdays of geological time, their rocks soft, moulded into sensuality of texture and shape, curved, womanly somehow in their swell and recline, intimate, as though inviting you to respond uxoriously, to be fond. Though hills of the earth's youth, associatively they are old. Maybe there were badgers here when villeins tilled the linchets, or when the builders of Cross Dyke, or the tumuli along Jugg's Road, lived. One sett looks as though in recent years it has been dug, and the thought casts a bleak moral shadow:

> ... far more ancient and dark
> The Combe looks since they killed the badger there,
> Dug him out and gave him to the hounds,
> That most ancient Briton of English beasts.

Even here, I feel that thrilling plangency of impermanence with which we respond to the earth's lasting beauty. These scarred and abiding loves of ours turn us strangely from regarding their loveliness to lamenting our own ephemeral being amongst them. Even here, in this still place of geological infancy, what do we look for but stability, eternity, though beyond the mist's blanket the stars wheel round in courses marked in millennia of light years? We project spirit and invest it with charity, omniscience and love, whilst talons of the pale and hush-winged owl fasten on the scurrying mouse and all falls to contradiction again in our mind.

Measured against landscape, our intelligence goes awry. We look, we think, we assume, and yet these states are curiously insubstantial – histories, dates, achievements, yes, and we can catalogue, analyse, chronicle, record, log the data into our acquisitive minds and process it all but it is a blind. We desire nothingness. I first understood this clearly when I read a poem by the Scottish novelist Nan Shepherd, where the realisation is put forth in its primal clarity, unadulterated by knowledge. It's called 'Achiltibuie' and dates from 1950:

> Here on the edge of Europe I stand on the edge of being,
> Floating on light, isle after isle takes wing.
> Burning blue are the peaks, rock that is older than thought,
> And the sea burns blue – or is it the air between? -
> They merge, they take one another upon them,
> I have fallen through time and found the enchanted world,
> Where all is beginning. The obstinate rocks
> Are a fire of blue, a pulse of power, a beat
> In energy, the sea dissolves,
> And I too melt, am timeless, a pulse of light.

I call it nothingness, but really it is self-extinction, it is oneness, it is being a part. Nan Shepherd's poem is a classic description of the mystical experience, purely beheld and without the extension of, the interpretation by, what Wordsworth – rightly for once – termed 'our meddling intellect'. It's a journey through confusion to fusion, and its path is a loving quietism. I recognise its truth, can find parallels. Thirty years ago, for example, the American critic Susan Sontag wrote the following:

> Today the project of interpretation is largely reactionary, stifling. Like

the fumes of the automobile and of heavy industry which befoul the urban atmosphere, the effusion of interpretations today poisons our sensibilitities. Interpretation is the revenge of the intellect upon the world. To interpret is to impoverish, to deplete the world – in order to set up a shadow world of 'meanings'. It is to turn the world into *this* world.

You might justifiably turn round after reading that and say, but it is ineluctably *this* world? How could it be other? Which is exactly the point. The otherness of the world, its strangeness, its sometime magic, is surely the element which holds the traveller enthralled. I am at a loss to find meaning in the rainbow shimmer that follows a hare through the dew or the pulsing colour of bluebells or the whistle of wind through a raven's pinions. I can only feel them as simple wonder, the ache of which stops my heart. They are not of the world we inhabit, but of the world of light, the natural world, the ephemeral world of beauty that we witness but do not inhabit, that is gone from us as soon as we cease looking; and of course the boards and signs and guides requiring that we look ensure that we look only at them, and not at what they attempt to explain. By insisting that we look, they ensure that we do not look, the thing we would otherwise see being the strange. They interpose themselves, come between us and the world, as all prescriptive approaches must, whereas the vital thing is that nothing must come between – our experience of the world must be direct and untempered, unmediated even.

Is there any role, then, for the travel writer?

I don't know if many people read Richard Jefferies these days, or even if his best book, *The Story of My Heart*, is still in print. But time and again in that book he returns to this notion of losing yourself in the directness of experiencing the world:

> ... the constant routine of house-life, the same work, the same thought in the work, the little circumstances regularly recurring, will dull the keenest edge of thought. By my daily pilgrimage, I escaped from it back to the sun.

In summer the leaves of the aspen rustled pleasantly, there was the tinkle of falling water over a hatch, thrushes sang and blackbirds whistled, greenfinches laughed in their talk to each other. The commonplace dusty road was commonplace no longer. In the dust was the mark of the chaffinches' little feet; the white light rendered even the dust brighter to look on. The air came from the south-west – there were distant hills in that direction – over fields of grass and corn. As I visited the spot from day to day the wheat grew from green to yellow, the wild roses flowered, the scarlet poppies appeared, and again the beeches reddened in autumn. In the march of time there fell away from my mind, as the leaves from the trees in autumn, the last traces and relics of superstitions and traditions acquired compulsorily in childhood. Always feebly adhering, they finally disappeared.

There fell away, too, personal bias and prejudices, enabling me to see clearer and with wider sympathies. The glamour of modern science and discoveries faded away ... all the experience of the greatest city in the world could not withhold me. I rejected it wholly. I stood bareheaded before the sun, in the presence of the earth and air, in the presence of the immense forces of the universe.

It is so simple in its directness. Only connect! And from those who have learnt that truth there proceeds a benign sense which comes to us in turn as a kind of benediction. There are writers who, because nothing is interposed, because their attention is so wholly centred on the world they have entered in, bring a sense of joy and peace, a tremulous reverence for the world in all its strangeness.

For most of us, I think, that sense comes through most powerfully not as it did for Richard Jefferies in the numen of the ordinary but in the shock of the exotic, which purges us of preconceptions and startles us into awareness. I don't think the rising popularity of foreign travel is any accident in a society sodden with sensation. The exotic is easy. We can come new-born into these worlds, leave our preconceptions behind here because it is all so new, so clear an assault on our senses. Perhaps in its newness and difference is the same thrill and curiosity that falling in love brings? I often think – particularly when I reread Richard Jefferies, with his capacity for eternally renewable wonder at the natural everyday – what a tragic course Wordsworth's life ran, from the intensity of his initial response to the world, through the realisation that his capacity for wonder had gone ('But yet I know where'er I go / That there hath passed a glory from the Earth'), to the grim and mechanical airings of prejudice that occupied the last half of his life. There is a simple Wordsworth, and there is a hateful one too – a pompous, baleful old man full of animosity, self-importance and prejudice, who has foregone his spiritual gift in acceptance of the world's – this world's – acclaim.

In thinking that, I wonder how it could be so? As he woke in Dove Cottage or the grander, gloomier Fox Howe every morning, what had gone so radically wrong that he could no longer record, as he had once recorded, the radical joy in the commonplace and the everyday around him? Hazlitt, the great essayist whom Wordsworth affected to despise but who is in every way a more lovable character, in one of those tumbling flurries of words shot through with truth's genius, produced a phrase which runs thus:

These bargains are for life!

He was talking about the ideals on which the French Revolution was predicated, and from which he saw Wordsworth, Coleridge and Southey as apostate. But he might as well have been talking of the relationship with nature and the world that Wordsworth expressed in his greatest poetry:

Fair seed-time had my soul, and I grew up
Fostered alike by beauty and by fear.

What happened, then, to the joy? The autumn mist on Grasmere, the light on Loughrigg Fell? 'The things which I have seen / I now can see no more.' And if his Grasmere spirit still wanders, it wouldn't be able to see them anyway for the forests of signs and prohibitions and interpretation boards. I pity Wordsworth for his loss, for his immersion in the rewards of this world which led to his loss of the strangeness, the sense of the other world from which our joy proceeds. But the glimpse he gave into the mystical gives us a clue nonetheless that we can follow to our own happiness. And don't be put off by that word 'mystical', the meaning of which doesn't lie along the vague, shadowy, New Age track many hunt it down, but is more nearly a sense of oneness, an absorption in the world's beauty and mystery. There's a passage from the English nature-mystic of whom I'm most fond that expresses this with great force and clarity. It was written by the son of a shoemaker, born on the Welsh borders in the 17th century and serving for a time as Rector of Credenhill in the Welsh Marches. The text it comes from is called the *Centuries of Meditations*, and its author's name is Thomas Traherne:

> ... you never enjoy the world aright, till you so love the beauty of enjoying it, that you are covetous and earnest to persuade others to enjoy it. And so perfectly hate the abominable corruption of men in despising it, that you had rather suffer the flames of Hell than willingly be guilty of their error. There is so much blindness and ingratitude and damned folly in it. The world is a mirror of infinite beauty, yet no man sees it. It is a Temple of Majesty, yet no man regards it. It is a region of light and peace, did not men disquiet it. It is the Paradise ... more to man since he is fallen than it was before. It is the place of Angels and the Gate of Heaven.

I was lying last week in a drift of leaves above the Dane Valley in Staffordshire, and the following passage of poetry slipped out of memory into my conscious mind to elaborate around the same point:

> After the sesoun of somer with the soft wyndes,
> Quen zeferus syfles hym-self on sedes and erbes;
> Wela-wynne is the wort that waxes ther-oute,
> When the donkande dewe dropeth of the leves,
> To bide a blysful blusch of the bryght sunne.
> But then hyghes hervest, and hardenes hym sone,
> Warneth hym for the wynter to wax ful rype;
> He dryves with droght the dust for to ryse,
> Fro the face of the folde to flyghe ful hyghe;
> Wroth wynde of the welkyn wrasteleth with the sunne,
> The leves lancen fro the lynde and lighten on the grounde,

And al grayes the gres, that grene was ere;
Thenne al rypeth and roteth that ros upon fyrst,
And thus yirneth the yere in yisterdayes mony,
And wynter wyndes agayn as the worlde asketh.

It's from one of my half-dozen favourite poems in any language – the Middle-English alliterative masterpiece, *Sir Gawain and the Green Knight*. It occurs, sets the scene, just before Gawain departs on his perilous quest to find the Green Knight and receive in his turn the blow he struck, severing the Green Knight's head, the previous New Year at King Arthur's court. There is scholarly agreement that the dialect of the 14th-century poem can be identified as being from north-east Staffordshire, and there is also a degree of welcome in the same academic circles to the notion that the latter part of the poem, the descriptions in which have considerable topographical precision, is set in the immediate landscape around Lud's Church. So it inhabits this place, roosts here, amplifies it for the sympathetic imagination.

I like to think of the Gawain Poet dreaming around and adorning and embellishing his old story, rendering it into the dancing chime and sway of incomparably beautiful language, in just such a familiar place, in just some drift of leaves as this. I like to think of him here in an eternal hanging moment, working out his theme that mirrors in a rich way all our lives: of the journey, its challenges and wanderings, its attachments, its potential for loss and sorrow, its threat and danger and allurements. I like to think of him pondering on Gawain's perilous, erotic dalliance with the Green Knight's lady, that so nearly compromises the knight and brings upon him his doom rather than the protection that can only derive from integrity. I like to think of the extraordinary, everyday wonders of the world that make the poet's acute imagination seem not so fanciful after all. How does Christina Rossetti's couplet go: 'Could we but look with seeing eyes, / This very spot might be paradise'?

Thinking of those things, after a while, dreamily and happily I rose to my feet, poured out the last of my flask on to the leaves as libation to the tutelary spirits, and descended into the moss-lined shade of Lud's Church. The clang of the flawed knight Gawain's armour echoed in my ear. Glancing behind from time to time, back up the haunted ravine, I caught in swift and slipping motion on the margins of sight the elusive form of the one who was here before, who watched, whose resonance still endures. Out of his green chapel, I turned down to the river, and walked back along its flooding bank, at peace, and seeing for once, as the lost gospel of Thomas has it, the kingdom of Heaven spread out here on earth before me, resolving into a green thought in a green shade. May our every step on the earth be as prayer, joke or embrace.

I hope you share some joy in the places I've seen.

TRAVELS
with a HARLEY

A few grey Federales say
They could have had him any day,
They only let him go so wrong
Out of kindness, I suppose.

Townes Van Zandt, *Poncho & Lefty*

In my youth, I loved motorbikes and grew up in a climbing culture an integral and
adrenalin-fuelled part of which was the Friday night bike-race down to Snowdonia
from Manchester, where I then lived. When the Daily Telegraph *commissioned me*
to write a series of articles about riding a Harley Davidson through the Rockies and
down the West Coast of America, I was delighted to do it, and revelled in the irony
of visiting for the first time under the aegis of our most venerably Old High Tory
newspaper a country from which my former membership of the Communist Party
had previously excluded me.

Taxi Driver, Easy Rider

Nerves don't come into it. First there was the cab ride from Oakland
Airport. 'Eight dollars,' Felix, the Swiss manager of the bike depot, had
barked over the phone. 'Pay no more. Beware the cabs of San Francisco!' At
30 dollars with the meter still running, Iqbal pulled into a Chicken Shack.
He ordered chicken pieces fried crisp, told the attendant I'd pay: 'An advance
on the fare,' he confided to no-one in particular, and put the box on the seat
beside him. A hundred yards down the road there was an explosion.
Shredded chicken and batter sprayed from between his teeth across the
windscreen. He made a U-turn, raced back. A box of chicken hurtled into
the kiosk, followed by the open palm that had propelled it: 'This chicken ...

1

frozen ... I tell you crispy how I like ... my money!' Dollars were passed across and pocketed. We drove out.

'So, Iqbal,' I simpered from the back after a safe interval, 'where are you from?'

'I am Afghani. I fight in the war, kill many Russians.'

'How many?' I quailed.

'Maybe 50, maybe more. I don't know. In this country I should be hero, but in United States the professional has no place. This is why it is time to bring in socialism here, my friend, like they had in Russia. Now, where are you going ..?'

Felix rescued me. He was five feet five inches in all directions, biceps included. Beneath a smiling, world-weary efficiency that had seen every scam, foible and vanity of the human race and come through unmoved, he was cold steel. I'd rather have crossed Iqbal, whom Felix gave ten dollars for his fare and ordered out of the yard, or a psychotic grizzly bear. Iqbal went quietly, the Swiss not being Russians or socialists. Then I was shown the bike. It was a chromium dream. It had running boards and panniers, a screen, top box and sound system, an armchair on the back, an engine bigger than your average car's. It was painted in glitter-fleck metallic crimson. For three weeks, this was my Electra-glide in scarlet, my own pet hog (all Harley Davidson motorcycles are known by the affectionate generic of 'hogs'). 'Guys on real Harleys won't speak to you, Dad,' my son, who is subtle and had just come back from California, had told me. 'Weekenders they call them, or bankers – something like that.'

The first two hours were nightmarish. I'd borrowed some fluorescent zippy thing from a friend for ten minutes' practise before I left. That was the sum total of my riding experience in the last five years. It's not good preparation for six-lane freeways in the San Francisco rush hour. When Stevenson buys his donkey, he tells how 'one child after another was set upon her back to ride, and one after another went head over heels into the air; until a want of confidence began to reign.' I didn't have such liberty, buffeted in the slipstreams of 50-ton Kenworth rigs – the kind that look like mesozoic wart-hogs – that juddered past, twin vertical chrome exhausts roaring, at 60 mph on either side. Six lanes of those things on either carriageway create turbulence. San Francisco earthquakes, collapsing freeways? It's the trucks, and there I was among them, wrestling with every muscle as The Hog veered this way and that, blasted by contrary winds. You call this the menopausal male's dream?

That's how it was all the way along Highway 880 and on to Interstate 80 heading east, past Sacramento, climbing through the foothills of the Sierras and all the little heartache towns with their yearning names – Weimar, Auburn, Toulon – set into the braided margins of the desert. The cuboid weirdness of Reno rose ahead then receded into the rear-view mirrors. Somewhere out north Silverado was signposted, but maybe it wasn't the place of Stevenson's convalescence. All the while The Hog's lazy pistons stroked out their long rhythm – du-dub-du-dub-du-dub-du-dub – holding us rock-steady on a probably illegal 85, hauling in the slow trucks way ahead over the desert miles, leaving them behind, taking us across the thirsty red rock of Nevada as it sucked up the last light. The moon rose and sailed and glimmered across the salt flats and a light mist resolved into their hollows so that, t-shirted, I shivered a little at its clammy touch, saw the gas needle dipping towards empty, and was looking for a place to stay. At which point Lovelock loomed out of the night, lights of a motel on its outskirts. The Hog skittered down the gravel of its drive, flighty in direction on the rough surface, and we checked in. It was American minimal of a thousand movies – TV, coffee machine, satellite decoder, bed with a single blanket against the frosty desert night. I left The Hog cooling and sighing outside and walked downtown, wondering about the craziness of what lay ahead, pondering all the warnings I'd had about the high passes of the Rocky Mountains so late in the season, hoping The Hog and I would get through but not caring too much anyway because already under the glittering stars it felt like a good time, and the texture of it all was just how I'd hoped it would be. It was America, and I liked it here.

Lovelock's the stopping place before the bleakest stretch of Nevada desert. Come sunrise I filled up The Hog and yawned into La Casita to fill up myself. I was learning to use the film-familiar American lexicon: gas stations, diners, eggs over easy or sunny side up. Every time I looked up, it was half in expectation of seeing Jack Nicolson and Karen Black doing the waitress scene from *Five Easy Pieces*. I was getting the caffeine habit too – burnt-tasting, eternally replenished. La Casita's clientele was stretching over breakfast. Tattooed, goatee'd frontiersmen with long, swept-back hair and expanding bellies kissed their pregnant honeys goodbye before heading out to work. A handwritten sign offered 'house for rent in the country – 2 bed, 1 bath, lonely, cheap'. I climbed on the bike and wobbled down to the Interstate.

'Butch Cassidy got rich here – so can you!' say the hoardings at Winnemucca's city limits, but they didn't quite make me want to stay. 'He didn't see nothin' but road' goes the line from the Springsteen song. Mine turned north, the signs read off in hundreds, the desert highway shimmered. Nevada merged imperceptibly into Oregon somewhere along Highway 95, and somewhere around the same featureless place I entered mountain time. Not that time had any meaning. Occasionally a car or pick-up would pass, heading the other way, the driver waving at me; every 50 miles, a couple of wooden houses, dirt tracks wending out to unthinkable lives, maybe a gas station. It was easy riding, dream-time, drifting on a two-lane-blacktop across the naked geology of America, pastel-new where it breaks the tawny matrix, unstill and ravishing. Every two or three hours I'd stop. In country like this, the diners are the oases, their refreshment more than a matter of food and drink. On its lonely roads you come to understand the longing, the sentiment, of country music. Emmylou Harris on the sound system (the throttle automatically turned up its volume) sobbed out 'I would ride all the way / From Boulder to Birmingham / If I thought I could see you / Could see your face.' I made it to the Rome Café on the banks of the Owyhee River under Big Grassy Mountain. Three young guys came in after me. They were followed by their father, all four talking volubly as if just released about the trip they'd made through the Owyhee Canyon. Deeper than it is wide, they told me, thousand-foot walls with warm springs gushing from them, no human beings, just rattlesnakes, the tracks of river otter and bear. What would you have done if you'd met one, I asked? 'Taken photos I guess – they got the right to be there, not us. We're not hunters.'

I left them there shining with the touch of wilderness, clunked up through The Hog's agricultural gears and breasted more desert ridges, bound for the Snake River and Boise across the Idaho state border. In Jordan Valley four kids on snarling trail-bikes waved me through as if to say, 'Go on, you first grandpa.' By Nampa the land was greening, air heavy with the smell of peaches and apples. 'Red delicious', 'Jonagold' proclaimed the scrawled PYO notices. State number plates boasted of Scenic Idaho's Famous Potatoes. The Hog rumbled cheerfully through orchards into the Snake River Valley, crossed the bridge at Nampa and wove its low-speed way through the broad streets of Idaho's state capital, Boise.

You don't hear much about Idaho apart from filmic private versions. But when you arrive, it hits right, comes over alive and vibrant despite those potatoes. Boise's a clean little city against a backdrop of hills, with wide boulevards, trees, fine neoclassical buildings, pavement cafés. There was a whole squadron of undressed Harleys parked outside one of them. The riders looked at my machine and looked away. Every few minutes one would get up and ride off, unhelmeted, on some brief sortie, echo of exhaust crackling and popping along the street. An extravagant hearse drove by, back door wide open, Black Sabbath thundering out from coffin-sized speakers. The waitress caught my quizzical look: 'I was at High School with that guy. He was weird. I guess he likes driving round in kind of a morbid car and sharing his music.'

'Guess he does,' rejoined a man with a cigar, and then added in the enigmatic American way, 'but he better watch out. You don't know what bad luck tastes like till you get good luck, and that rig of his looks like it might keep it away. Cain't say the same about yours,' he added, with a final nod of approval in The Hog's direction. The Hog basked. Violets and mauves and lengthening shadows crept out from the hills that circle the city. The Rocky Mountains lay beyond them. I felt like a child on the eve of some adventure, and one an adult might tell it not to undertake.

Snow on the Passes

The leafy boulevards of Boise are hard to leave behind. Two days of easy riding through the high deserts of Nevada and Oregon had brought me here. I'd had a balmy long evening on the town with Georgia Smith, who had a lop-sided grin, a good-humoured drawl, and the kind of insouciant intelligence that opens up a cavity in your chest, reaches in and gives your heart an inconsolable squeeze. She'd picked me up from J J Shaw's Bed & Breakfast Hotel on West Franklin in a 70s-vintage compact American car called a Skylark that was only marginally smaller than a London bus. We'd driven out to a bright terrace restaurant on a tree-lined avenue. Georgia had a Hog of her own. It was in pieces for the winter. She'd put it together again in the spring, she told me, looking up from her pudding, maple syrup trickling from her spoon. And then she weighed in: 'You gotta be crazy! Those passes, Galena Summit, The Teton – this late, on two wheels? We bin talkin' about your trip. When you get up into the Dakotas, into Montana – man, that's cold country. You better get lucky with the weather.' With that, she set out on her own reverie: drifting in canoes down rivers, traversing wilderness, wandering among mountains, sleeping out in the woods, wolf-watching, ski-ing, catching trout for breakfast. That, she told me, was hers and Idaho's vision of the American Way of Life. I was getting to like this state more and more, and that's no good when you have to be moving on. You get susceptible on the road. 'The moral?' explained Godard. 'It's the travelling.' Idaho made me long for some immorality, or at least a few days' stasis. And the journey was scarcely begun.

I lingered over breakfast at J J Shaw's. Bed & Breakfast hotels in America are not like their British counterparts. They have a cosy, laced opulence that cossets you. The other guests were doctors, washing down 20 oz T-bones and half-a-dozen eggs with a gallon of hyper-caffeine and discussing their health insurance. I guess they needed it. I was being entertained by Ruthie White, the owner. She told me ghost stories, family histories of wilful women and ill-advised marriages – all stuff to feed the imagination of a lonely rider on the high passes. Ruthie waved me off from her porch for what I took to be a short day's ride along the Ponderosa Pine and Sawtooth Scenic Byways to Sun Valley. It was only 200 miles. I'd barely glanced at the small print on the map that spelt out 'may be closed in winter', hardly noticed the elevations. Georgia had known better. 'Get yourself some coffee in Idaho City before you hit the big time,' she'd advised. 'You'll need it.' The Hog was thirsty too, so the first diner and gas station out of Boise I took her advice.

There was a feeling on me like I'd just been cast out of paradise: 'From dawn to dusk he fell, / From dusk to dewy eve,' and it was still only midmorning. I took my coffee across to a table by the window, looking down into the canyon that was taking us away from the Snake River basin. On the other side, across a continuous line of black columnar cliffs, clouds were scudding past like wreaths of smoke. The waitress came over to refill my cup. 'Those ain't Idaho plates, are they?' she ventured with a glance at The Hog, her inflection half a degree off accusation. I shook my head. 'My husband's a wildlife biologist,' she continued, to explain her perspicacity or maybe just to give her view on out-of-staters, 'but my Pa, he's a rancher,' she concluded with emphasis.

'You've got conflict there, then,' I suggested.

'You are so right, honey, you are just so right. Those two guys, they fight and fight and I don't ever get to hear the last of it, 'cos I'm right in the middle. Take wolves. You know we got plenty wolves here in Idaho with the new ones the gov'ment people brought in. Now my Pa, he cain't stand them, says they're nothin' but vermin an' ever' last one of them should be shot. And then my old man, he's forever tellin' me how cute they are, and sociable. I ain't never seen none of them, so who am I to believe? That's how it is when you're around guys – nothin' but contradictions!'

She gave me a dazzling, inclusive smile and retreated behind her counter. It wasn't that I felt unwelcome. It just seemed like time to leave. When I started up The Hog, even her lazy good nature was tinged with testiness and hesitance. She coughed and hiccuped and with a few explosive detonations from her exhaust as comment on all diners in cold places, thrummed on towards Moore's Summit – at 6,110 feet our first and lowest pass of the day.

You might think that one motorcycle is much like another and they are all equally soulless, dangerous, thrilling. I'm not so sure. A biker would tell you that the motorcycle is the nearest humanity has come to imbuing an artefact with character and soul. A car is simply an envelope in which you are posted more or less efficiently from one place to another (albeit with the usual vagaries attendant on the mail services). With a motorcycle, the biker would argue, you attempt to harmonise, establish some sense of balance and rhythm, even mutual understanding. At this point I want to make clear just how apposite is that terse epithet bestowed upon every two-wheeled product of the Harley-Davidson factory in Milwaukee. A Hog is a Hog is a Hog. In certain situations – on a die-straight desert highway for example, or posing at an agricultural show or stationary at a gas pump, which is its version of the feeding trough – it is perfectly capable of behaving itself and concentrating on the matter in hand. But show a 1340 cc Electra-Glide Classic full-dresser in glitter-fleck metallic crimson two hundred miles of narrow, twisting mountain road with a loose surface, roadworks, instant-180-degree hairpins, radical gradients, ruts and gullies and it transforms into some jittery, darting, groaning monstrous thing with which you wrestle and fight, and the harmonies of those desert highways on which your relationship was founded become a distant dream. Across Banner Summit, through Stanley and Obsidian and over the Galena Summit at 8,701 feet we were travelling through landscape as sublime as any I'd ever seen. The Sawtooth range gnawed at the sky and I thought I'd never glimpsed more mountainy mountains. The White Cloud Peaks floated away to the east; the Salmon River prattled down through Redfish Lake; the back country beyond, ridge upon forest ridge of it, went by intriguing names like the Gospel Hump and Frank Church River of No Return Wildernesses. Lewis and Clark had threaded their way through the region somewhere over there in their epic 1804–5 crossing of America, and from the Sawtooth Scenic Byway you could be vouchsafed an insight into how wild this country is, and how recent has been its exploration and recreational exploitation.

You could have been. I had to content myself with a prolonged bout of hog-wrestling as she veered this way and that, slithered on the ice at Galena Summit, shied at flurries of snow that came gusting in on a violent wind. I made it down through the woods at last to Sun Valley, the American West's glitziest ski resort. The Hog slumped on to her stand in the portico of the Lodge and I sprawled from the saddle, cold as only a biker can know cold. In the vernacular, I was beat.

Sun Valley Lodge is exclusive. It's American neoclassical at its most expansively confident, built in the 1930s by some media multi-billionaire. All the stars, from Mary Pickford to Robert Redford, from the Kennedys to Gary Cooper had stayed here. Ernest Hemingway shot himself just down the road in Ketchum. I was thinking that not even Michael Palin would dare make a joke out of that when I became conscious of someone staring at me.

Odd, I thought. The very rich whose province this is are usually liberal in their attitude towards eccentricity. I glanced back. Or rather, I looked round and down and there was a guy of about five feet two with shoulders maybe a foot wider than that and fists like hams hanging loosely at his side:

'How d'you like the bike, son?' he growled.

At that precise moment I didn't like the bike at all, and the feeling was probably mutual. But this was American soil, the Stars & Stripes was flying, and I was being asked about the other great American icon. Sometimes you just get put on the spot:

'Well ... (long pause, not for emphasis) ... it's got character ... the, er, saddle's very comfortable, I like the riding position, and the way the sound system volume turns up when you twist the throttle's ... amusing. And I love the exhaust note ...'

'Yeah, yeah – offset crank – atmosphere at the expense of performance ...' he responded, a little impatiently.

I'd dried up. He was watching me. 'What the hell,' I thought, and launched in:

'OK. It's got performance half of what that engine size should offer, handles like a tank, steers like a wasp in a jam jar, push it hard on bends and neither you nor it knows where it's going, feed in the gas and it gets the message five minutes later, the gears are borrowed off a tractor ...'

'Hold it right there!'

He held up his hand, reached in his pocket, handed me his card:

C William Gray: Vice-President, Harley-Davidson Motor Company.

'That's me, and you and I are having dinner together tonight to go through this thing in detail. You European riders are just so aggressive. Chill out, man. Get in the hot tub. See ya later.'

Extracting a foot from my mouth, I hobbled away at his command.

The Rocky Mountain Hog-ride

Sometimes you wake in the morning with only the vaguest notion of what might have taken place the night before. I peered out of the windows of Idaho's Sun Valley Lodge, bloodshot eyeballs recoiling from the sight of women skaters absorbed in describing elegant ellipses across sun-reflecting ice. The hiss of their blades cut down into recollection. Last night – what had I done? Held forth drunkenly to assembled delegates for a conference on human resource management on the sensuality of motor-cycling? Told them that balancing a bike – Japanese by preference – through fast bends was the best fun you could have with your clothes on? Do I believe that? I groaned – not just at memory's crass embarrassments, more at the prospect of another freezing day heaving The Hog around hundreds of miles of twisting mountain roads. I skulked out of the hotel to remake her acquaintance, anxious to avoid recognition. I needn't have worried. Sun Valley on a bright morning was all excitability and frenetic loudness. Leisure fanatics displaying corn-fed American physiques, couples clad in identical-patterned fleece, braying and whinnying children by the horde spilled out of lodge and cabin and restaurant to set out across the wide range of all-American activity: hiking, biking, skating, eating, shooting, shopping, eating some more, their energy quivering in its eagerness to get focused, to get it on.

The Hog quivered too when I started her up. She grumbled, she shook, she protested that altitude she did not like, and she conveyed me haltingly down to Ketchum for her breakfast and mine. A regular intake of gasoline is a necessity in the life of a Hog. She will run 140 miles on a tank, at which point the engine cuts out. When this has happened for the third or fourth time, you've learnt the technique to keep going: steer one-handed, grope under the tank, switch on reserve and pray that a gas station turns up within 20 miles. American distances are huge. Twenty miles is nowhere. Gas stations occur at curiously regular 80-mile intervals, though sometimes they come in herds like metropolitan buses. I leave the mathematics to you. Most of southern Idaho, across which I was now bound, is taken up by the Snake River Plain, which is one enormous lava-field and uninhabited by virtue of being uninhabitable. I never saw anywhere that better exemplified Wallace Stegner's maxim, 'to understand the American West, you have to get over the color green.' This volcanic landscape reaches its apogee at the Craters of the Moon National Monument, and The Hog and I duly rolled up there an hour or so after breakfast. 'A desolate and awful waste, where no grass grows nor water runs, and where nothing is to be seen but lava,' is how Washington Irving described it. Yet it's curiously beautiful in its monochrome, far-flung way, with that sense both of space and recent genesis so characteristic of The West. Because the predominant palette here is sombre, you look for relief, and find it in rye-grass and tansy that seek out the few patches of soil; in bitterbrush, sagebrush and rabbitbrush the names of which speak sparseness; in prickly pear and isolated Ponderosa pines gaunt against the backdrop of a plain that stretches to Big Southern Butte and beyond. Its paucity and minimalism bring home the sufferings endured by wagoners on the Oregon Trail as they curved round the butte. That thought made The Hog's saddle feel shamefully comfortable and welcoming as we headed down into Arco.

We didn't linger there. Nor did we opt for a self-guided tour of the now-defunct Experimental Breeder Reactor Number One, eerily appropriate to this moonscape. The town's claim to be the first lit by nuclear power is a testimony that glows in other ways than intended. Beyond Arco the road cuts straight for miles through agricultural country, smells of manured earth and mown hay heavy across it. In KG's Country Diner at Mud Lake the pin-ups on the walls were of tractors. 'You goin' north?' asked the waitress. 'Sure gonna get cold up there.'

At the end of the afternoon The Hog wove her way up four miles of gravel to Jacob's Island Park Ranch. I parked up and sat on a corral fence to talk to Brad. He was sunburnt whipcord in silver spurs, scuffed boots and leather chaps, his talk all of the horses he was grooming. He brushed aside offers of help: 'Last time I did that, guy let go the rope an' I got my leg bust.' With an entirely different inflection, he told of the kindness of 'this fellow here' – a sturdy, glistening American quarter-horse – and of how you rode her with your knees and she just knew. He described how, when his leg was broken, the horse would instinctively back right up to the rails to make it easier for him to mount. All the while he was stroking the mare's flank like a lover. I left them to it and swung back on The Hog. Today's long straights had re-established a degree of affection between us, but it wasn't to last. A dude ranch off-season's a lonely place. The track up to the cabin where I was staying threw the whole offensive repertoire at us: washboard surface, one-in-three gradients, rutted hairpins, loose gravel. The Hog's screen was covered in dust and squashed bugs. We were riding blind into the sunset. Even at two miles an hour I was terrified, spent a hungry, sleepless night not daring to ride back down to town in the dark for food, wondering whether we'd make it in the morning.

I needn't have worried. By the time The Hog was warmed up and I'd shifted her into the sun for the ice to melt off saddle and tank, she crunched phlegmatically down the ruts, scarcely putting a wheel wrong, and we sped down Highway 20 into Ashton, 'seed-potato-growing capital of the world'. The diner was a dark log cabin between grain silos and railway tracks. Its walls were covered in Hallowe'en masks, advertisements for seed-drills, soil technicians, tractors, and animals to shoot. At the table next to me a couple of obviously recent provenance talked about moving a sofa to make way for the boy's bunks, and about growing old:

'Honey, that's what we do together,' the woman purred, 'and then we can, you know ...'

'What? Get married?'

'Yeah, that ... '

'Honey, a log cabin and a big fireplace ..?' he inquired, without warmth.

'Well whaddya expect? A blonde in a Mustang by yourself?'

A suppressed gleam of hope traversed his face. Outside, it looked like snow and we had the Teton Pass to cross. This was the one that had caused all heads to shake. This late in the season? You gotta get lucky! It's only 8,400 feet, I told The Hog, we've been higher than that already. As we coasted through the last of Idaho, the Tetons reared up hooked and hunched and jagged, like Chamonix aiguilles discordantly abutting the Weald of Kent. Their name translates roughly and reductively as 'titties'. The French travellers who gave it to them must have had odd notions of anatomy. The pass turned out wide and easy, snow holding off till we'd descended to Jackson Hole. On the town's outskirts a man and woman clad in identical Levis, gilets and stetsons looked up from hoeing their flower-beds to wave. A bald-headed eagle drifted over the town square. In Harvest Wholefood Emporium a woman filled her basket with foil-packed Back-country Eco-cuisine and confided in a fellow-shopper that her hypertension was making her real cold. On the balcony of the Sundance

Inn opposite, among a dozen flags I did or did not recognise, unfurling on the cold breeze of 5,000 feet and incoming winter was the green-and-red dragon of my own small country. The thrill of belonging flooded in on me, brought with it a sudden understanding of the enclavism and familialism, the state pride and insularity of the human psyche loose, free and frightened in a hostile new world. Lead story in the Jackson Hole News was of two hunters mauled by a grizzly bear, whilst the galleries of this little tourist town paraded a bizarre anthropomorphism of cute wildlife photography, assimilating polar bear and mountain lion into the protective family through captions like 'mother's love', 'taking it easy', and 'friends'.

It was time to run north. The sun shone into birch copses cross-hatched with silver beneath crowns of russet and lemony-green as we paid our 15 dollars on the gate and entered the Grand Teton National Park. Douglas firs looked like children's drawings of trees. The mountain ridges were dusted with snow. A half-moon floated above the Grand Teton itself, high curling wisps of cloud threaded across it and the dry, sweet fragrance of autumn hung on a warm breeze. At the Glacier Turn-out a woman from Bombay and a man from Bangalore engaged an old-timer with a white beard in conversation. Was it safe to walk the paths with bears about? Might they attack?

'Ma'am, I'd say ya stand more chance a' bein' struck by lightnin', an' I don't see too much a' that about either.'

With that, he climbed into a battered Dodge pick-up and turned south. Two ravens above us called metallically, then flew together for the sake of flying. A few miles up the road we glimpsed four moose in the willow flats by a lake, with 50 photographers stalking them through purple sage. Butterflies flitted in the sunshine, some exotically new, some familiar. A soft-tailed Hog with studded leather panniers drew alongside on a straight, cruised amicably with us as far as Snake River, where it turned off up a side road with a wave. At Flagg Ranch we stopped for coffee and gas. A middle-aged woman came over, asked where I was from, told me her mother was from Gwernymynydd, and there in Wyoming, perceived exiles both, we launched into a Welsh conversation that warmed me all the way to Yellowstone's Old Faithful Inn.

Ghost Towns & Biker Chicks

There are days when the devil gets inside you. Maybe it was the surroundings – all that grandiose, varnished log-cabin conservatism of Yellowstone's Old Faithful Inn. Or maybe it was the volcanic huffings, the charcoaled forests, the infernal regions brought to earth and duly itemised as a major tourist attraction. Whatever the explanation, as The Hog wheezed her way out of the park that morning I was looking for trouble. Didn't know quite how much I'd find, but we'll come to that.

West Yellowstone should have calmed me down. There was a bookshop-café with deep chairs, a fire, and a sense from its clients of the quiet, acceptant confederacies of men and women shaping and sorting regular lives across the town's neat grid of streets. But on those streets, The Hog and I were exotics among an everyday throng of pick-ups and big hats. We were eyed askance, nodded to cautiously, grated along the resistance of any community living too close to mass-tourism from which it doesn't itself benefit. We soon quit, headed north and west into Montana, bound for Hebgen Lake and the Madison River Gorge.

If Yellowstone gives vent to the infernal as drama, the Madison Gorge expresses it as gloom, makes Merthyr Tydfil on a wet November afternoon seem cheerful. At the exact crucial point in a narrow valley, a mountainside has slipped. It happened 40 years ago. The matrix is still raw, huge slatey rocks poised crazily above Quake Lake. Dead tree stumps broke the latter's surface, poignant memorials to the dead. Faintly, in the shallows of black water, house-ruins were visible. A gusting wind streaked foam in lines. Dirty-fleece billows of cloud drove past. Survivors of the settlement that was here have moved down-valley, into temporary-looking habitations scattered over alluvial washes. I wanted out of the place and The Hog's plodding ponderousness was getting to me. I twisted the throttle hard round and kept it there.

Nothing happened.

That's not strictly true. The Hog ambled to her habitual cruising speed of 85 miles per hour, the high desert blacktop dipped arrow-straight in front across illimitable shimmering distance. Eventually, that pressure on the twistgrip alerted her to more being required. She groaned. She shuddered violently. The speedometer needle crept up: 87, 88, 89. A few more downhill miles on a brisk following wind and it flicked into the high 90s. The Hog gasped. Her engine made weird, disturbing noises of unbalanced metallic pain. The needle stretched finally and definitively on to 100 and just at that moment The Hog's back end broke free, began waltzing from one side of the blacktop to the other. This, I thought, is death. I cannot accelerate, dare not brake. With a deft flick at the return point of a parabola she will consign me to the air and herself too. With a squelch and a terrible shrieking she will land on top of me. It will be the end. I thought of dead friends waiting on the other side. All the while from side to side we veered on the empty road, and I eased off the throttle as delicately as a frightened man could.

Until suddenly, as the needle dropped to 80, with a final little shake of her rump The Hog came back on line and purred smugly along again as if to say, 'I warned you! Don't try that again.' On the outskirts of Ennis, a sign proudly proclaimed it home to the 1987 World Steer-wrestling Champion. On the wide, empty street of Twin Bridges a diner beckoned, a couple of old-timers conversing leisurely inside:

'Do you reckon the frost is going to get on that rhubarb tonight?'

'Only way it won't is if it's in a can.'

I shivered over the Badger Pass and down to the turning for Bannack – Montana's first territorial capital, and reputedly the 'Grand Ghoul of all ghost towns'. The protesting Hog rattled down four miles of dusty dirt track from the main road. Old mine workings that were the town's brief *raison d'être* in the 1860s stood out around the valley head. A dry croon of wind spiralled ash leaves down to rustle along the sidewalks. Sagebrush was spreading between the houses, tumbleweed rolled through the main street. Its carpentry and blacksmithing, its horse-wagons and mine-trucks, all the evidences of the town's working life were present, but stilled. Wind-noise apart, it was deathly quiet, uncannily preserved. I sat on the steps of the saloon, across from the Masonic Lodge. A lone woman approached. She introduced herself as Cindy, Senior Manager of Bannack Historic State Park. She lived here with her two daughters. Sometimes they'd go out on a full moon night and the town was not so empty then. All the hanged men, the shootings ...

The sun was sinking. I didn't know if the smile on Cindy's face was ironic or just deranged. The Hog and I left fast. A high pass took us over into the Big Hole Valley, light angling low, cattle dotting the plain, haystacks too like glistening yellow boulders. Rich fall colours of creekside willows incandesced against a dark mountain wall. A little town loomed: gas station, diner, tractor showroom, a couple of houses, a log hotel. The Hog and I pulled up outside, both of us dust-rimed. I wrested my bags from the panniers and shambled up to the door. It opened a sliver and a woman peered out. She looked me up and down, stood on tiptoe, glanced past me at The Hog:

'Stick a fork in their ass and turn 'em over – they're done.' she snarled, swinging open the door to a mock-baronial hall. Trophies adorned the walls: moose, elk, a grizzly bear wearing biker goggles. One side of the vast room was a bar. There was a reception desk, a blonde, crew-cut woman in a t-shirt and tight black leather pants behind it. I checked in. 'I am Inge,' she announced, in a clipped German accent. 'Carly will show you to your room.' The woman who'd answered the door came over. She was five feet nothing and any age from 20 to 50. Her face had heard a thousand stories that all ended badly. She'd come through on gales of laughter. I spent a long evening at the bar, talking to one woman, working along the bottles, communicating with the other. Much later, they conferred: 'When you leave you will switch out all lights,' came the order, 'and remember, guests are not allowed in staff bedrooms, and staff are not allowed in those of guests.' I went off alone to my room. It was a good way to end the day I nearly died.

Morning hangovers were beginning to feel like a habit. I slouched out to greet The Hog. She looked sorry for herself, covered in grey dust, a pool of oil under her crankcase. I warmed her up gently, easing the choke in till she thrummed away contentedly. It was bitterly cold, snow on the hills. I clambered into all the warm clothes I could find, stuffed the rest into her panniers, strapped on my helmet and was just pulling gauntlets on when the door of the hotel burst open and Carly hurtled down the path. She wore skin-tight jeans, a t-shirt and a biker jacket, carried a bag that she thrust at me before jumping on to the front of The Hog, revving her, kicking away the stand and rapping a command to get on. I scrambled into the armchair on the back as we took off down the road. Her hair lashed against my face.

We cruised down into Wisdom at 80 mph. I was enjoying the ride. 'Hey,' she screamed into the wind, 'you mind bein' packed by a chick?'

'Not if I knew what it meant,' I screeched back. We turned west. She gestured down at the Big Hole battlefield, where topography wrote its story of brutality and surprise with cruel clarity. On the 7,264 foot Chief Joseph Pass, over which the Nez Perce tribe came in their flight before the Big Hole massacre, snowflakes were whirling in the wind. Robert Pirsig came this way too, describes it in his unpleasant and near-unreadable book *Zen and the Art of Motorcycle Maintenance*. I was thinking about that when my friend upfront cut in:

'I'm fuckin' freezin' man – rub my thighs.' I did just that as she drove 140 miles straight, down into the Bitterroot Valley before the gas needle drooped on to empty and we pulled into a diner.

'Man, that was so cold,' she shivered, grabbing back her bag and putting it down on the table with a thunk.

'What's in your bag, Carly?' I asked.

'What's in my bag? You wanna know what's in a girl's bag? What kinda pervert are you?' She emptied it out on the table: make-up bag, lighter, cigarettes, clean pairs of knickers, a large, chromium-plated pistol.

'What's that?'

'What's that? Whaddya think? Fuckin' .357 magnum, man. Girl needs protection in these parts. This is Montana ...'

We hit The Hunters' Bar in Stevensville sometime that afternoon. It was smoke-wreathed, dark. There was a pool table, several dozen bootleg versions of ZZ Top spectating around it, too doped up to play. Carly and I had a few beers, a few games. I kept winning by default. I'd pot one, maybe two balls. She'd crack down seven like gunfire and then sink the black. Game to me.

'Try a bit harder,' she whispered, 'might not be too healthy round here if I won. They don't like to see a guy beaten by a chick.'

There was a friend of hers at the bar. We went over:

'This is Skeeter. She's gonna talk to you while I go get my bike.'

She was gone. I was sole, vague focus of Skeeter's dilated pupils. Suddenly Carly was back:

'Oh, Skeeter – I just want you to know you ain't screwin' him. You're just making sure he don't go nowhere.' She was gone again. Half an hour passed. Fascinating conversation about bikes and bikers. Roar of an engine came from outside. Carly reappeared, came over.

'OK man – whaddya want?'

She was studying my glass. I asked for a coke. She went off through a door behind the bar, re-emerged ten minutes later.

'C'mon, we're off.'

I followed her out. There was a stripped-down chromium gleam of Harley next to mine in the dusk.

''72 shovelhead,' she explained proudly.

'What're you doing now?' I asked.

'I'm checkin' into your hotel, man. What the fuck d'you think?'

I followed her down to Missoula, racing through traffic. In the hotel room she pulled off her cowboy boots, threw her jacket on to a chair, wriggled out of her jeans, sat on the bed, switched on the TV, slapped a plastic bag on the pillow:

'OK. I got brown heroin, white heroin, opium, coke, crack, dope, speed. What's it to be, man? We can be outta here for a week.'

'I'll just have some beer. Long ride tomorrow ...'

She looked at me, disappointment and incredulity registering:

'Down at the gas station,' she jerked her thumb at the window, 'get a coupla six packs.'

It took me 15 minutes. She was lying on the bed when I got back, smiling at the TV, playing vacantly with a gold bar skewered through her right nipple. Next morning, with a little shake and a sigh, she roused herself, had steak and eggs for breakfast, climbed on her Hog, wiggled its butt through some roadworks and with a wave was gone. I had 600 miles to ride, over the Lookout Pass, the Fourth of July Pass, the Snoqualmie Pass, in driving snow and sub-zero temperatures, all the way to Seattle. I was never so glad to arrive anywhere in my life.

Hogging the Coast

Rain in Seattle, and The Hog slithers across tramlines and cobbles on to the Bainbridge Island ferry. Porpoises arch and splash alongside the boat as we cross Puget Sound. The island itself is interminable, well-heeled, self-satisfied suburbia, every sub-sector announcing itself home to this or that world champion in kayaking, under-eleven basketball, slam-dunking or doughnut-gobbling. The Hog and I – road-grimed, weary, sodden travellers with four thousand miles behind us – feel like aliens until passage of the iron-shod Hood Canal Bridge in a gusting wind disgorges us onto the wilder shores of the Olympic Peninsula. Laden timber trucks pass in a steady stream. Slopes of lodgepole pines disappear into the cloud. Glacial-deep Lake Crescent is sombre, the tourist facilities along its shores shut down for the winter. We make a detour up to Sol Duc Resort, eager to savour the American obsession with thermally-heated water. Salmon are leaping the cascades in the Sol Duc River, speckled-brown, red beneath, vivid against the white water. Five or six in the space of a couple of minutes hurl themselves with astonishing vigour into the air, flailing into pools 20 feet higher. One lands on a slimy rock-face and slithers back into the torrent. A more languid activity's taking place at the hot springs. Overweight bathers displace floods of steaming water as they loll into the pool and swap enigmatic Clinton jokes. I head downriver again and, weary of the downpour, book into the Hungry Bear Motel at Sappho – strange name in this butch territory – where I spend a night in a cedar-clad chalet, listening to rain drumming on the roof and truck tyres hissing along the road.

'You won't be able to ride that Hog up the track to where the trail starts!'

In the Hungry Bear Café at breakfast, a couple of old hunters in a Chevy pickup with a gun-rack in the cab and the corpse of a deer across the hood shake their heads over my fancy bike, quiz about where I'm bound. Cape Flattery, I tell them – northwesternmost point of the United States. They shake their heads even more, offer the advice, conclude that I'm some kind of weird out-of-state vagrant who won't listen to no commonsense, and go back to hunting talk:

'Nothin' but the one buck, an' him so damn scrawny you'd think he'd been eatin' Momma's breakfasts here – no offence, ma'am, but a man gets kinda hungry when he's bin up from two hours 'fore dawn. Any hunters in this place?'

'Hell,' his companion piped up, 'these guys ain't bin hunters for years.' A row of grey heads attached to ample backs swivels round at this and fixes levelling glares on the company I'm keeping. 'Ain't never seen the blood of no animals round these parts save what we let ourselves. Plenty of bullshitters though ...'

The waitress brings across mountainous plates of bacon, sausages, eggs, hash browns, fries, steak, beans, toast:

'Just slap him, Debby,' comes from a back whose owner has turned round again to the bar. 'You done it before, an' he's gonna die early in those woods one night.'

I pay my check and steer The Hog through streaming rain along the coast towards Cape Flattery. Vancouver Island's a vagueness of hill outline smudged by blue moist across the Strait of Juan de Fuca. The last ten miles of track through wild forest of Hemlock and Douglas Fir confirm the hunters' advice. Ruts, bends, hills, streambeds, adverse camber – that track had them all, and The Hog liked none of them. If I dropped her here I'd be in trouble, and the possibility was not remote. Red Electraglide had turned into grey miremobile steered by equally disreputable mudrider. I ease her down on her stand by the bear warnings at the start of the trail, aching in every muscle and relieved in every brain-cell. It was a bad trip.

The sun comes out and I walk through woods and over sections of boardwalk, down to the Cape and my first view of the Pacific Ocean. It's revelation: power and lapidary splendour on the wave-crests, bold memories in the headlands, the hollowed caves, the boom and wash and roar. I sit with my back to a tree, facing west, helmet and gauntlets at my side, and talk to a couple from Austin, Texas, who'd arrived at the trailhead just after me in a Winnebago. They'd come for the rain, they said, lot of water hereabouts, not like southern Texas. I leave them sitting on a bench, holding hands, watching the ocean, and jounce back down to Neah Bay. In the Makah Maiden Café the proprietress, a tall Native American woman, is reading the *Peninsula Daily News*: 'Lack of whales might delay hunt until November' and 'New method could speed tsunami warnings' run the headlines:

'So whaddya think about the boys goin' after a whale?' she raps, and goes on to explain that the men of the Maka'ah, a coastal Indian tribe whose reservation this is, are fasting, have been ready for days to go out in a 32-foot cedarwood canoe called The Hummingbird to catch a grey whale. It's to be the first Maka'ah whale hunt for 70 years. She talks of the cold, rough ocean, the pitching small boat, the huge creature rolling in its agony and fear, the new-generation warrior diving into the waves to attach inflated bladders, sew up its mouth to stop it from sinking.

That was the plan. Looking out of the café windows even at the sheltered strait, you knew it wasn't going to happen. The gap in tradition, the distance from compelling necessity, the stormy season would all subvert this reassertion of cultural potency. But the woman's excitement and indignation give another perspective: the white world was on the collective Maka'ah back, and in a disturbing display of incipient racism, frothing career-conservationists and sentimental tourist whale-watchers were protesting countrywide against a slaughter-that-was-not-to-be of their pets. She shows me the cuttings. I leave feeling chastened by association and go south, a blinding sun in my eyes, filmy golden light and glimpses of ocean waves rolling in to the Pacific beaches. The highway twists through mile upon mile of spruce, Hemlock and Douglas Fir. Huge patches of clear-cut with white, skeletal stumps spiking out of the spoiled ground stretch towards Mount Olympus behind, the roseate glow of late afternoon suffusing its snow-covered summit-ridges. Sweeping, smooth-surfaced bends make riding a pleasure. I play the plus game – each bend at 10 or 20 mph more than the signs dictate – and The Hog behaves perfectly, the spell of the sensuous on her, only once wobbling in a tight chicane.

We fetch up at Lake Quinault Lodge with the shadows lengthening. My room's balcony overlooks the water. The last of sunset reflects on its surface. The sky's cleared. Jays are screaming from behind dark curtains of moss that hang from the trees in the surrounding rain-forest. Late tourists down on the shore video each other, self-absorbed, transferring their lives to television. Within the hotel, Indian art decorates the walls: animals, shamanistic figures curl tight amidst white space, contorting into defensive smallness, warily and angrily looking out. Outside the gas station at Neilton next morning I meet young men from the Quinault Indian Reservation. The same expression's on their faces. One, cradling a small-calibre rifle, asks me for a couple of dollars for a beer. I give him five, feeling uneasy and sad, trying to buy absolution for my inculpated whiteness but receiving only a grunt and a scowl as I ride off down the dirt road to Moclips. It's 20 miles of gravel with bumps and gullies and slopes on the bends that have The Hog threatening to pitch me into the ditch unless I slow to walking speed. Time slows to the ticking of miles on the odometer. We arrive at Pacific Beach. Graft Mablethorpe in November on to Les Landes and you'll get the picture. There's a scattering of bungalows and run-down bars, sand and pinewoods, decrepit Oldsmobiles and Dodges, tsunami warnings that tell you to run for high ground if you spot one, but there is no high ground. The weather-fronts roll in to collide with the mountains far behind. In the Surfhouse Tavern the bartender's in the middle of a story: 'Lisa was in Trudi's Bar, 'bout three a.m., and Bob – that's her husband – comes hammerin' on the window sayin' for her to come on home. She just ignores him and he goes off lookin' real mean. Well, half-hour later the cops are hammerin' on the door so I grab the drinks and pour them down the sink, let 'em in an' this kid cop says "I got reason to believe there's late-night drinkin' goin' on here."

"We was just talkin' about gettin' a pool table," I tell him, and off he goes. He's done his job. It was Bob, sneakin' 'cos he was pissed at us. But next day I have to go get this ol' pool table and what's the use o' that when none o' the guys round here can see straight, they drink so damn much. Not much else to do round here, I guess.'

When the saga's finished and finally they notice me, I'm told they have chicken soup with potatoes, and week-old cheesecake that they decide after a discussion they'd better not sell me. I leave. Ten miles down the road is Larry's Copalis Beach Café. Inside, things brighten up. Larry's chaffing his customers. His wife's fussing over them. Old men and women discuss their sex lives and the decline of innocence. They both fix on me and work on where I'm from, shake their heads like there was a Martian in their midst when they find out. 'Wales? Wales? Where in hell's that?' Larry delivers the *coup de grâce*:

'This is Copalis Beach. The folks from Seattle, they bring their dogs out here to go shit down by the river. I guess I should take mine to do the same in their backyard, but we don't do that in Copalis Beach. This is absolute nowhere – downtown-metropolitan-absolute-nowhere. And I'm tellin' you this, son ...'

He pauses for emphasis, rattles another scoop of fries onto my already laden plate.

'... there's no finer place on this earth. Ain't that right?'

His eyes scan Sunday-crowded tables. Every bowed grey head in the place looks up with a shining, righteous expression, meets them and nods assent.

Ocean Boulevards

The Shiloh Inn at Ocean Shores, Washington State, looks out over dunes covered with marram grass to a beach where waves curl and plume from a dark and hazy ocean. I take a shower, sit out on the balcony with a beer to watch ravens glide along the foreshore, pick up shellfish, soar above the car-park, drop them on to concrete and tumble down to eat, heads curved intently towards grasping feet. Pangs of homesickness, of *hiraeth* consume me. The foreground could be Braunton Burrows or Newborough Warren, could be any western British coast. Suddenly disconsolate, I get up to go inside. A gust of ocean wind slams the door and it self-locks. I'm on a first-floor balcony of a three-quarters-empty hotel, naked except for a barely adequate towel. Explaining the situation at reception in the hotel's lobby a few minutes later produces a demand for identification. In my room, I plead. But how do we know you're the guy whose belongings are in that room, the receptionist sweetly and reasonably enquires, enjoying the situation. I rack my brains. Photo in my passport, I venture. 'OK – I'll come with you and check this out.' She peers over the desk, sizes up the situation. 'On second thoughts, you're not entirely decent. Guess I'd better just give you the key.' I make it back to my room and – from behind the safety of glass this time – watch skeins of Canada geese fly up-coast in ragged vee-formation that's echoed by stunt kites soaring line-bound from the beach. Beyond them, even off a calm sea wavecrests break the horizon of this powerful, cold, capricious ocean. 'What do people like to do round here?' I ask the receptionist as I check out. 'Oh, storm-watchin' mostly,' she giggles, 'it's kinda orgasmic. Goes on a long time too ...'

So does America's Pacific Coast, and I had all of Oregon and some of Washington and California before I got The Hog safely back into the hands of Felix. The Washington coast, elemental at Cape Flattery to the north, fades out southwards in a confusion of inlets and sandspits above the Columbia River estuary. Cape Flattery's southern counterpart is Cape Disappointment. I park The Hog and walk up to its lighthouse. A snake, four feet long, slender, brown with vivid green stripes down the length of its body on either side, crosses my path and rustles away into dead leaves. Across the river-mouth sandbars and breakwaters and a continual surge of surf about them mark its mergence with the ocean: 'The men appear much Satisfied with their trip beholding with estonishment the high waves dashing against the rocks and this emence ocean,' wrote Captain Clark in his journal for 18 November, 1805, looking on the same scene at the end of his and Meriwether Lewis' great exploratory journey across the American West.

My exploratory instincts only went as far as persuading me, the day being hot, to head north up the Long Beach peninsula in search of an ice-cream parlour. I found one in Ocean Park, hidden among a gaggle of churches, motels, car factors, 2-4-1 bookstores, diners and 'NO public access to the beach' signs. 'We were in Salt Lake City, but we ain't Mormons so we just packed up, set out travellin' an' this is where we ended up,' Mavis related as she served me with a blueberry delight. 'It's kinda quiet here. We ain't slowed right down to it yet – still speedier than most of the folks around.' Another version of the same story came from Susie Goldsmith in Boreas Bed & Breakfast Inn next morning over my best-ever American breakfast. She was an analyst, married an English lawyer, lived in Chelsea, soon tired of the way Brits put Americans and their culture down, split, and ended up here with Bill Verner, her 'significant other'. Bill's a chunky, pony-tailed Vietnam vet. He talks over the breakfast he's cooked about the crackheads and heavy dope-users in 'Nam, the guys on whom you couldn't rely to cover your back, their eyes bloodshot, their attention wandering. Bill's a Hog enthusiast, has a '79 Y-glide on which he and Susie escort me to the Astoria Bridge that crosses into Oregon. I wave goodbye and pick up Highway 101. It runs right down the coast for 350 miles to the California state line, and for the same distance beyond that to San Francisco. Straight it is not. Every headland, bay and gully puts a kink or a knot into it and The Hog's getting tired. She needs a service and a bath. We pull into a gas station in Manzanita:

'You picked up a lotta bugs on that screen,' remarks the attendant with a pitying look.

'We've come a lot of miles.'

'Well, the more miles, the more bugs – Yup!'

In Lincoln City, sun-tanned Oregonians sit out in late-October 70-degree sunshine, sip Californian merlot and discuss their sins whilst the surf rolls out an unceasing counterpoint to their muttered disclosures. A stream of Recreational Vehicles driven by leathery retirees chases past southwards in pursuit of the sun. And I follow. In Newport I lean over the harbour rails to watch sea-lions loll and bark on floating wharves. My neighbour catches my eye, gestures down:

'Those fellows, they're just guys hangin' out. They get to be a nuisance. Same old story. Guess we cain't shoot 'em or lock 'em up 'cos the tourists seem to like them ...'

She pauses, ponders.

'... an' I guess I do too. They're pretty much like our guys – bit ornery, bit whiskery, bit fat. If you wanna see a real crowd, get along to the Sea Lion Caves.'

A young guy with a biker helmet tells me he's going there. He'll show me the way. The Hog and I hare after him as he flings his old Honda through bends, arrive a little ruffled from the experience. The elevator ride down a 208-foot shaft in a headland doesn't help, lands us on a viewing platform 50 feet above the sea, looking into the meeting of two vast, hollowed rift-caves that run out at right angles through shadowy yellow volcanic rock to the ocean. Everything's cacophony and confusion. Waves crash in, collide, rear onto the boulder beach at the back. Herds of Steller's sea-lions growl and roar. Even more are on the adjoining headland, playing tag with the rollers. It's one of the weirdest and most atmospheric tourist attractions I've ever seen. Old Louis, the guide, tells me he's worked here for 13 years, since he retired from his proper job. He drove a truck. Did he have favourite characters?

'All look the same to me – just one big, wet, happy family.'

I press on south. The roadside maples are crimson with autumn. In the creek behind the Travellers' Cove Café in Florence, a sternwheeler's moored up for the winter between fishing boats that have seen too much of the Pacific. Two ancients nurse Mexican beers and try to decipher the name of a lovely 30-foot ketch:

'Is that an 'i'?'

'Sure it's an 'i'. If you got yourself an eye job done, you could see that.'

'Well, whatever, but I sure hope they run on outta here and get back to Seattle OK. There's storms comin' this weekend.'

A white-haired man and a much younger woman with long, dark hair climb off the boat and walk to the end of a floating jetty, carrying what look like bicycle wheels. He unwinds yellow cord from them as she sits cross-legged in the sun. They're hooped nets. He baits them with fishheads and throws them into the ebb-tide. I move on. Coos Bay, once the World's largest timber-port, is industrial, down-home, a scent of resin on the air from pyramids of logs ready for loading on the wharves. I have a date there with a woman in Benetti's Italian seafood restaurant. She brings her baby, the baby screams, the staff dote. It's warm, relaxed, small-town America. She tells me Oregon's biggest export now is not timber but cranberry juice: 'The one sure-fire cure for cystitis, so you see, it's Oregon and not California that's benefited from the sexual revolution. This state helps women throughout the world.' Outside, we cross the road to the 30s-kitsch Egyptian Movie Theatre. In the foyer is a gigantic, gilded mummy. She puts the baby in its lap. The baby screams. A wide-eyed little girl with bunches and a lollipop points out the obvious: 'He wants his real mommy.'

Out of town, emerging from a sea-fret into bright sunshine, I stop to shed a few layers. A traffic cop eyes me, does a U-turn, pulls up behind: 'Do you know it's a state offence to step on the highway in a situation like this?' I plead ignorance, explain that I'm from Wales where there are no cars, only sheep, and you can walk down highways. 'Wales,' she repeats, 'my husband's folks came from there, way back. Maybe we're kin, by marriage that is.' We sit in her car for half-an-hour over a flask of coffee and talk racial antecedents before I put my brain into drive mode, cross the California state line, cruise on down under towering redwoods that I remember from photographs, little black cars driving through holes in them, in childhood books. Eureka, Fort Bragg, Mendocino pass in an oceanside dream. In a Santa Rosa gas station I pull The Hog up alongside the pumps. A beat-up white Mercury's circling the plinth, comes to rest with an offside back wheel on the corner. A fat guy in a dirty t-shirt climbs out clasping a can of beer, sees me watching, puts the can on the car roof, reaches inside, backs out with a large gun in his hand that he waves in my direction: 'Just go, man – just fuckin' go,' he yells.

I don't argue. The Hog limps back into her Oakland depot. She weeps oil. Scales of mud crack and flake from her. She whispers abuse as she cools. Felix the manager mutters something about hard travelling and tots up excess mileage. I make the airport ten minutes before take-off. They let me on the plane.

SMALL WORLDS

Some places, often very small, are so completely of themselves they seem like separate worlds. Whether the reason stems from geographical isolation, cultural antecedents or industrial history, they have an unfailing attraction. Here are three of my favourites:

1: Green Gables, Red Earth

As I stood on the kerb in Water Street two cars heading in different directions along it pulled gently to a halt. I went through a mime-routine, finger pointing at my own chest, a shrug, a wave. The drivers smiled and spread their hands wide, gestured me over. I crossed, thinking it a joke. Then the same thing happened on Grafton Street, and that's pretty well Charlottetown's main thoroughfare, so I turned round and crossed right back over again just to check this thing out. It was true. In Charlottetown, drivers stop to let you cross the road.

Charlottetown's the capital of Prince Edward Island. I'd wanted to go to this cradle of land that lies in the Gulf of St Lawrence, separated from mainland Canada by the Northumberland Strait, since I'd had one of those intense in-plane conversations about home place with a lovely, wholesome young woman whose skin had a cream-and-strawberries tone, whose hair was vibrant red, and whose voice was the calmest thing that ever insinuated itself osmotically into a susceptible traveller's world-view. Why was she going back, I'd asked? Because if you're brought up on PEI you don't ever want to be no place else for too long was the reply. I had to see what she meant. Besides, she'd given me a book of Milton Acorn's poems and her address. I'd loved the one and lost the other, but I don't believe in looking people up that you meet in these circumstances anyway. Milton Acorn, PEI's home-grown bard, was enough: 'To be born on an island's to be sure / You are native with a habitat. / Growing up on one's good training / For living in a country, on a planet. / Shall I tell you the soil's red / As a flag? Sand a pink flesh gleam / You could use to tone a precious stone? / All its colours are the colours of dreams.' So as soon as the opportunity arrived, I was on my way to Acorn's red-flag, pink-flesh, heavenly island. Besides, I was a bookish child. You create from that time your idylls. *Anne of Green Gables* had a part to play in mine (maybe it was her I'd met on that plane – maybe she was a dream?):

> A huge cherry-tree grew outside, so close that its boughs tapped against the house, and it was so thickset with blossoms that hardly a leaf was to be seen. On both sides was a big orchard, one of apple-trees and one of cherry-trees, also showered over with blossoms; and their grass was all sprinkled with dandelions. In the garden below were lilac-trees purple with flowers, and their dizzily sweet fragrance drifted up to the window on the morning wind. Below the garden was a green field lush with clover ...

... and on and on, and that's still the eternal-summery way it is in PEI. In Charlottetown, on Queen Street by the Grafton Street crossing one night at a quarter to eleven under a bright gibbous moon, I saw the reflection of it gleaming out from the hordes who were crowding on to the sidewalks from the subterranean Confederation Centre for the Performing Arts, where they'd just seen a stage production of Anne: beaming Bostonians, leathery Nova Scotian retirees, hieratic Japanese (there is an Anne cult in Japan), still applauding and chattering happily, with a childhood delight thrilling out from them.

I was heading for the Old Dublin Pub ('established 1983') on Sydney Street, to have a beer or two with Grant MacRae and Jack MacKinnon, and hear The Boys in the Band belting out old West Coast hippy favourites like *The Weight* and *Love the One You're With*. Charlottetown's broad church in its appeal, and techno's not yet hit the place. Jack and Grant are discussing a ladies' golf tournament that's being held on the island – golf's an obsession here, and they round on me about how golf clubs treat women in Britain:

'They wouldn't take that here,' Grant growls.

'Besides,' adds Jack, 'they need their business, and you know what Milton Acorn said about England ..?'

I do, but some readers might not like it. By now I've got talking to Marilyn. Most people here, as you'll have guessed from Grant's and Jack's surnames, have Scottish antecedents, so laments are the thing. Marilyn's was about the lack of men on PEI: 'I used to be picky, but now, you know, so long as it's a he, taller than me and can read, he'll do – and even the reading's negotiable.'

With every beer, this island was getting to seem more like heaven. Even the hotel I was staying in, the Fairholm Historic Inn, a couple of leafy blocks away from downtown Charlottetown, was maybe the most perfect I'd ever set eyes upon – small, comfortable and exquisite in every way, the proprietors wonderfully matter-of-fact about the detail of the place: '... these parquet floor-blocks were little mothers to sand!' Marilyn walked me back there, to keep me out of mischief: 'Mischief's about as bad as it gets hereabouts,' she confided, as we watched a police car stop by an old white-haired man and the officer inside lean out and talk to him in a friendly way. I ask her what all that's about and she tells me, 'Oh, he's an old guy, he's had kind of a hard life, drinks too much, everybody knows him. I guess the policeman's just asking if he's OK or if he needs a ride anywhere.'

I spend a morning walking round Charlottetown before driving off to see the island. There may have been an increase in tourism here since the astonishing, sinuous, eight-mile-long Confederation Bridge was opened to connect PEI with New Brunswick on the mainland, but the island, at 175 miles long, is big enough to absorb it. It doesn't much show, either, on these quiet, wide streets, shady with chestnut and lime, sycamore and maple, the leaf-tines of the latter tinged with the first fire of autumn. The buildings are of wood and warm red stone and mellow brick. They add to the peaceful atmosphere. Conducted groups of Japanese sightseers amble around, old men along the waterfront watch the boats, end-of-season Anne dolls are going for 9.95 Canadian dollars apiece. I trip in and out of St Dunstan's Basilica, dominant, triple-spired and the island's cathedral, and visit the classically balanced and austere Province House, where the Dominion of Canada came into being in 1867, before heading on out of town.

I'm looking for some clue, some explanation of the tranquility that belongs so uniquely to PEI. There's plenty of suggestion towards it in the texture of the landscape. It is extraordinarily lovely in an understated way. Tracks of red-baked earth lead secretively through glades brilliant with the berries of the rowan; glimpses of blue sea flash from between copses, the gentle swell and heave of the land gives it an intimacy, an unthreatening secrecy. Little combine harvesters drone about their work among fields of barley and rye, a warm fall wind husking and rattling through them. Old John Deere farm machinery and tiny grey Ferguson TVO tractors bring to mind an English countryside that disappeared half a century ago. Their continuing practical use echoes a resourcefulness that's apparent everywhere in these maritime provinces of Canada, peopled by good men and women of their hands. Salients of golden corn or sage-leaved fields of cabbages thrust in among the dark green spruce or the silver trunks of the birch, 'upspringing airily out of an undergrowth suggestive of delightful possibilities in ferns and mosses and woodsy things generally'. If you were a simple, outdoor child – if you were some latter-day Anne or Bevis – you would want to live in a place like this. I drive down to the sea. Shy herons, legs trailing, flap on stiff wings along the margins of saltwater lagoons. At Red Point, along several miles of beach, three people walk in the distance and a woman paddles in the shallows nearer at hand, her footprints and those of her dog the only ones in this white and squeaking sand. Low red cliffs with pinewoods where the jays scream rise above it, and Nova Scotia is a haze of land away to the east. In the Inn at St Peter's, looking out across water where the path of sunset glitters and ripples, I eat grilled Arctic Char – the most delicious of all fish – with roasted island sweetcorn fritters and lemon butter sauce and muse on the question still: why is PEI so at peace with itself?

The answer suddenly presents itself on my last day. I've driven down a flower-verged lane and arrived at the white-shingle-walled church of St John's, Belfast, that's stood here since 1824. Its rich simplicity of honeyed wood and lancet window, scrollwork and spire, are calming, satisfying. I drift among the graves. There's a memorial to Thomas Douglas Selkirk, fifth Earl, who 'believed that the hardships of the Highland peasantry could only be alleviated by settlement'. Walter Scott said of him that 'I never knew a man of more generous distinction.' He shipped his tenants out here at his own expense, into a cricket-chirruped countryside like the Sussex Weald from the rough, bitter coasts of Skye, Mull, Colonsay, Argyll – the MacRaes and MacTavishes, MacEacharans and MacDonalds, McLeods, McLennans and MacNabs. They lie here in the soft ground, having died in their 80s and 90s. For them this was, simply, the paradise place. Among their descendants, the belief still holds.

2: *Landing sheep on Caher Island*

This desire to go to Inishturk took root years ago in a conversation I had one night with Leo Hallissey in Veldon's Bar in Letterfrack. Leo's the National School headmaster there, patriarch-white-bearded and himself a Connemara institution with an ear for the gossip onshore or offshore for miles around and a good eloquent Irish tongue for spreading it too.

What he'd related was a story of surveyors having secretly landed on the island, reported back favourably on prospects for gold-mining, and been followed by a group intent on buying up mineral rights and drilling there. Shades of *Local Hero*, but these are the wild western shores and we're not talking Burt Lancaster. In Leo's tale, they were called to account by the community, told to clear off the island and not come back. Told summarily. You don't argue in places like this.

I was staying in Leo's house out on the Renvyle peninsula. On the way back there that night, mist quicksilvering down off Mweelrea and the sea all gleaming phosphorescence under a full, bright moon, he gestured into the Atlantic. Lights glimmered from amidst the dark whale-bulk of an island miles out: 'That's it, Inishturk – they've got electricity out there now! They're the best boatmen in Ireland, but a wild lot, mind, a wild tribe. There's no ferry, and how you'd get across is anyone's guess.'

Leo's talent for exaggeration is calculated to entice. I did my homework. Inishturk is the most remote inhabited island off the west coast of Ireland, ten miles out from the bleak little quay at Roonagh by Louisburgh, or 15 from the more sheltered Cleggan. Until last year, when one of the islandmen, Jack Heanue, bought a boat for the purpose, there was no passenger service. The island hovered in the map's blank, teasing at imagination, little-known and with scarcely anything to be found out about it. Sure, Robert Lloyd Praeger's *The Way that I Went* (Hodges, Figgis 1937 – the classic of Irish topographical writing) had brought him and his wife here, but that was in 1906:

> Ordovician strata form alternate ribs and hollows running across the island, so that the surface resembles corrugated iron on a large scale. It has a greater diversity of wild-flowers than either Bofin or Clare Island and the cliff scenery of its western coast is imposing. There is no inn

there, but ... we secured the use of a shed belonging to the Congested Districts Board, perched on a low rock with deep water half surrounding it. In the early morning we stepped out of the door and head first into twenty feet of Atlantic water, and all day long we explored the hills and hollows and lakelets and caves ... It was an ideal existence.

Getting to most of the islands off Ireland's west coast is easy enough these days. In high season it's almost harder to avoid being dragooned on to Inishmore or Inishbofin, Clare Island or Inisheer by coach-and-boat-tour touts, enthusiastic hoteliers or commission-crazed hostel-proprietors. Even the abandoned Great Blasket or the bare rocks of the Skelligs have, weather permitting, their bobbing, circumnavigatory, licensed flotillas. Islands have allure. However peripheral their existence may be in fact, they thrive in another dimension, are crucial to Ireland's post-colonial notions of identity, nationhood and cultural resistance: *Riders to the Sea* and the Gaelic summer schools, Peig Sayers' egotistical maunderings on every Irish school's syllabus, the lean profile of pithy old Tomas O'Crohan (best by far of the Blasket writers) adorning all the tourist posters. This *mythos* of a small nation, in a world whose every culture is increasingly beleaguered by global communication, assumes ever more urgent resonance. Take a scrap of land, skirt it with sea, add in some literary, filmic or ethnographic reference and you're in business – paradoxically big business these days.

But little Inishturk is different. For a start, there may be Jack Heanue's new (relative term!) ferry, the *Caher Star*, with a licence for a dozen passengers, but weather has the last word. Inishturk is a long way out. When I finally tracked down a place to stay on the island – Mrs Phylomena Heaney's Tranaun House – and phoned her from Wales, these were the directions:

'If you'll phone me from Ballinasloe on your way across on Friday, I can tell you whether my husband will be picking you up from Roonagh Quay, but if the wind's blowing, which it will be, it might be better if you head for Cleggan because Roonagh's so exposed and he'll not make the landing, though of course you could come over from Clare Island, and you'll get there easily enough, in the priest's boat with him saying Mass but he'll not be coming either if it's blowing and the lay ministers of the

Eucharist will be taking the Mass then but we'll see. And either way we'll
be looking forward to having you with us ...'

Perfectly clear, if a little contingent! As it happened, more messages
flashed between us, there was an epic night-time dash across Ireland in the
Easter snow for a boat the storm denied, and when I finally caught up with
Phylomena's husband Bernard, it was at Westport Quay 36 hours later. I
was discovering the elasticity of island time. The boat was a tiny orange
twin-diesel-engined fishing craft newly arrived from South Wales, and it
had three Heaneys on it, all of them peering into the engine hatch. (If you
live on Inishturk, your name's Heaney, Heanue or O'Toole and there's an
end of it.) The repetition of name didn't worry me. The sight of Bernard,
Dessie and Dominic peering into the engine of a new (to them) boat with
a force eight gale blowing itself out in Clew Bay and my life to be entrusted
did. But they were calm and competent men, there were crates of vodka
and barrels of Guinness on the quay ready to be loaded in, they told me to
be at Roonagh by five and off I went.

At Roonagh Quay I watched and waited. The fat tub that ferries the
hordes across to Clare Island wallowed in, and then its cowboy-booted
crew wallowed it out again. At seven the Heaney boat streaked in from
among the waves. A few cars arrived mysteriously, disgorged women,
young children and babies who were handed down along with boxes of
shopping. All were packed into the wheelhouse, I tumbled aboard, and
with no more ado we battered out into mountainy seas. I braced myself
across a corner of the leaping deck. Spray showered over. From time to
time a child was handed out to Dominic or Dessie, who hung it over the
side to empty it of fluorescent vomit before passing it back to a mother in
the wheelhouse. The men were exulting in their sea-craft and the new craft
alike, the ride exhilarating, the cans of lager circulating. We passed a low,
rocky island and gained some shelter from the northerlies:

'Caher Island,' gestured Dessie, crossing himself, 'see the monastery?
Say a prayer for Saint Patrick.'

I was praying anyway. Ten minutes later we were running in calm
water along the lee of Inishturk, its glaciated slate slabs gleaming like the
scales of an armadillo, a bonfire burning on the quay and the whole
population gathered to greet the new boat. Most of them, after it had been

unloaded, went out for a quick spin in it too. There are only 90 of them. I was whisked off to Phylomena's house, reeling.

In a recent book about Ireland, Jan Morris writes about the country's hazed allure, and any frequent visitor there knows exactly what she means. Again, Inishturk is different. There's an intense clarity of purpose here to match the turquoise water that surrounds it. The population is young, urgent and committed. Over 50 per cent of school-leavers return to live on the island – an extraordinary statistic for the west of Ireland.

They know what they have to be of value, and they want to preserve it. On my first night with the Heaneys – the ones at Tranaun House, that is – the conversation round the turf fire, flesh of its English utterance hanging lightly on the skeleton of Irish syntax, drifted round to the Blasket Island literature. Yes, Peig, Moiris, Tomas had their effect, Bernard agreed, but there had been more changes in the last 15 years than Peig maybe had witnessed in a lifetime, and one other difference – a crucial one. The Great Blasket had died. That wasn't going to happen to Inishturk. It hadn't died in the Great Famine. It wasn't going to die now. The Blasket was a harder landscape. This is a good little island. I thought as he spoke of those haunting, roofless westerly villages: on Finis Island, out to which you can wade; on Mason Island, that I once watched an old man watching for most of a day from the nearest point on Mweenish, watching as though for signs of the old life; on Inishshark, only evacuated in 1960, the islanders finally giving up after two of their young men were drowned on their way to mass on Bofin.

To lift that sombre mood Phylomena, heavily pregnant with their first child, chimed in to tell me of Mary Roche, the new teacher at St Columba's National School, and the vibrancy she'd brought, the trust won of the parents. How many children? It varied between 16 and 25 but they'd be adding their clutch in time, she hoped. And the Island Development Officer, Dave FitzGibbon, was pressing for an extension to the quay, a cold-store on it for the fishermen, a health clinic, all canvassed in a three-year-plan the islanders had put forward. In the season, too, they were hoping for visitors – not in hordes but a few, for special-interest weeks based at the community centre, or anglers Bernard and his brothers could take out after the cod, the pollock and the shark, or walkers and naturalists and painters, for whom the island could be an enthralling, heavenly place.

It is. From the sheer, cleaving edges of its western cliffs to the iris-bordered streams, narrow coves and silver strands of the lee shore, it is magical. But more magical even than these was a chance occurrence on my last day on Inishturk. Over one of her capacious breakfasts – you do not go hungry here, and Phylomena's cooking of fish, lamb, island-grown potatoes is excellent – she mentioned that Jack Heanue was taking some sheep over to Caher that morning, where the islanders all have commonage. Would I like to go? Apart from the stormy passing glimpse and a vague memory of folk-traditions concerning the *Leac na Naomh*, the Saint's Stone, on its oratory altar that could pass on curses or conjure up storms, I'd gleaned a little about Caher from Michael Gibbons, the Connemara archaeologist whose walking holidays out of Clifden are the best introduction to the West of Ireland: 'Get there if you can,' he'd urged, with a gnomic shake of his head, 'there's a completely undisturbed Celtic Christian monastic site, the last point on the Croagh Patrick pilgrimage route, that is breathtaking. Look out for what's on the altar. But you're unlikely to make it. You can only land on rocks in flat calm and the Inishturk men guard access to it jealously.'

I ran down to the harbour. The afterdeck of the *Caher Star* was filling up with sheepdogs and children and sturdy, corkscrew-horned Blackface ewes. A *currach* was tied on behind and we nosed out into the sound, Mweelrea snow-streaked and cloud-capped ahead of us. I'd been looking at the rows of *currachai* round the harbour on Inishturk. Bernard Heaney and his uncle make them to the distinctive island design, nose more uptilted than their Kerry or Aran counterparts to breast the bigger seas round this island, the outer skin of fibreglass mat now rather than the old tarred canvas. They filled my mind with memories of Synge's doom-laden focus on them; of the wreck in Robert O'Flaherty's film *Man of Aran*; of Tomas O'Crohan's accounts of Blasket fatalities; of Richard Murphy's poem on the Cleggan disaster when 31 men drowned on a November afternoon in 1927; of the old *Sean-nos* laments sung by Joe Heaney. As we drifted in to Caher I was joking to Jack Heanue that I thought the moment you stepped into a *currach* you drowned. One of the boys had untied it and brought it alongside as we talked. Jack flung a couple of dogs and eight of the ewes in, gestured me over the side, instructed me to hang on to their horns, gave over the wheel, jumped in himself, started the outboard and we steered in to the rocks:

'You've got an hour,' he said, 'the monastery's that way.'

There are rare times when fragility of subject lacerates the writer-on-landscape's desire to communicate it. I can scarcely bear to tell you of what I saw on Caher Island – its carved crosses, oratory, altar, all standing there beneath the sky and against time, a thrilling, aching plangency in their silent notation. Landing sheep to graze on Caher Island is one thing, bringing people here another. Of course difficulty of access is defence against abuse, but atmosphere and holiness are so tenuous, a near-inevitability about their destruction by management and interpretation and other of our modern ills.

There was a religious dreamer landed here last year. Because of the sea he couldn't be brought off for three weeks. When they did reach him, he was near starvation. Could he not have lived off the seaweed and the shellfish, I asked Jack Heanue? Of course he could, came the reply, but he was the sort of fellow wouldn't think to look after himself that way. And by the way, he added with a grin, that Saint's Stone on the altar, do you know it floats?

When Jack landed me at Roonagh next day, I asked him about the gold prospectors. Oh yes, they'd been told: 'You're off this island today, and you'll not be back!' I thought in that instant that he had the coldest sea-green eyes that ever looked straight into mine; and then a sparkle of light glinted across them, he folded my hand into his huge one as if into a mangle, and added firmly, 'but we'll be seeing you again, I suppose.'

3: A Place Apart

You see them best from the ferry returning from Ireland or the wide beaches along the western seaboard of Anglesey: the low hills of Lleyn, long ridges of Eifionydd, the rough peaks of Arfon stretched out against the sun or under the moon, away on the starboard side. 'Bro sêr hefin' – 'Land of summer stars' – is how the sixth-century poet Taliesin described them. They are so obviously old, worn down, picked bare. None of the plum-pudding inelegant richness of the English Lake District, nor Pennine bleakness nor even the winding impenetrability of Scottish peaks and glens. They are ancient, bald, entrenched in their own being, lived-in. At dusk orange skeins of neon braid their shadows; in daylight cloud swathes them reverently; nowhere is more beautiful.

In one of Krishnamurti's dialogues there is a poignant exchange on beauty. A bewildered engineer confesses to the sage that though he is told a tree is beautiful, he cannot feel it so. In reply he's instructed in the watchful quietude from which appreciation stems, in which sensitivity intensifies. I'm reminded of a line from the Welsh poet T H Parry-Williams: *'Mae lleisiau a drychiolaethau ar hyd y lle'* – 'There are voices and phantoms throughout the place.' Everywhere among these hills, even within the smallest compass, the range of reference is extraordinary. To many visitors, unacquainted with the culture, inattentive to the signs, it is often obscurely inaccessible.

On an autumn afternoon I went to Dyffryn Nantlle, the valley that runs up to Parry-Williams' birthplace. My memories of the village here from the 1960s centre around characters like Dafydd Nantlle, with his white hair and piercing blue eyes, cycling off before daybreak on an upright black bicycle with a long, single-barreled shotgun slung over his back, and returning at noon with a couple of foxes and a rabbit or two dangling from the crossbar. Or Mrs Myfanwy Williams of Nantlle Terrace, garrulous and hospitable octogenarian in her back kitchen, who would tell you what she'd learnt as a young woman in the 1930s on WEA courses run by the poet Robert Williams Parry. She'd heard from him of Richard Wilson, whose two paintings of Snowdon from Llyn Nantlle date from 1765. The version in Liverpool's Walker Art Gallery is the more delicate, suffused with a hazy, russet, glowing light, exquisitely composed, the natural contours of the hills accentuated for harmony and balance. A group of rustics – a white-shawled woman and two men fishing – stand in the foreground, framed by a dome of light reflected in the still lake that leads the eye up from this scene of Arcadian contentment to the peak of Snowdon, elegant and benignly grand.

So idealised a picture of peasantry peacefully coexisting with nature at the lower margin of an orderly universe appealed to the artistic patrons of the time. To regain the reality, my eye travels up to the commons above the lake, with their scattered communities and relict former industry, and the memorial to a woman whose enduring testimony of experience constitutes one of the profound achievements of Welsh literature. 'If Kate Roberts had written in English,' an academic once told me, 'she would single-handedly have sustained women's literary studies courses and the Virago backlist for decades.' She is one of the crucial keys to an understanding of the former life of these communities of the slate hills. When I look out from her memorial, Golygfa Lôn Wen, a line resounds from one of her finest short stories, *Y Condemniedig* (*The Condemned*) in which she comments of her quarryman subject, a victim of illness and repression who at the last comes to appreciate the small, everyday acts of the wife whom he had never allowed himself to know, that *Pan oedd ar fin colli peth, dechreuodd ei fwynhau*. ('When he was on the point of losing a thing, he began to enjoy it'). That grave, typical, concise moral, in its universality shouldn't be lost on those who view this land. Far too little of her work has been translated into English, and even less translated well – the common fate of Welsh literature. Nantlle is associated with another key achievement of European literature, *Math fab Mathonwy*, the final story of the *Mabinogion*. It's a long and complex bundle of themes, embodying many folk-tale motifs, handled by its final anonymous redactor with remarkable skill and fluency and rooted in the features and place-names of Dyffryn Nantlle.

This obscure valley, away from the tourist centres, unvisited by the coach tours from the coastal resorts, has yet another masterpiece of an entirely different kind. A piece of fine carving, it used to stand half-a-mile above the village on a terrace of the abandoned Penyrorsedd quarry – a fitting, desolate shrine, looking out to Drws y Coed and Snowdon. Perhaps it was feared that up there it would be vandalised, for now it shelters discreet and unknown in the garden of Baladeulyn Welsh Presbyterian Church. It's a Great War memorial. What makes this four-foot-square slab of slate, with its minimal text and 18 names, unique is the frieze surrounding the Roll of Honour. Incised with painstaking delicacy into the single slab are four scenes: of quarry rock-men in a pit with a Blondin (a carrying-cradle running on wire cables) above them; of work in a cutting shed; of an incline and wagons (on one of which, quite reverently, some wag has added a CND sign); and finally, across the bottom, a war scene: dead trees, ruins, hunched soldiers, huge guns. The images revolve, echo, run into each other disturbingly; their design's stark, naive, lived-through. In their medium-dictated tautness of line they have something of the quality of those marvellous drawings by Henri Gaudier-Brzeska in Manchester Art Gallery. No-one seems to know whose work it is. Its craftsmanship and clear record speak volumes about the culture that produced it.

All this exists in the space of a mile, and yet there is more. A back road from the end of Nantlle Terrace leads through the old Dorothea quarry workings to Talysarn. Two of this village's former inhabitants generate an interesting tension. The first is John Jones, Victorian Calvinistic Methodist preacher (the Reverend Ian Paisley proclaims him his hero), whose self-denying ordinances thundered out thrice every Sunday from the pulpit of Capel Mawr. The second is another great modern Welsh poet, and one who, despite the small total of his poetic output, touches unforgettably on the emotions of his readers. A blocky little memorial to him at the village crossroads reads 'Robert Williams Parry 1884-1956'. Dissent between preacher and poet is well illustrated by the last couplet from one of the latter's sonnets, cast in the form of question and response between a visitor who's heard the Mabinogion story mentioned above and a resident:

> *Clywsant am ferch a wnaeth o flodau'r banadl*
> *Heb fawr gydwybod ganddi, dim ond anadl.*
> (They've heard – of a woman he made from flowers of the broom, /
> Without much conscience in her, only breath.)

41

What's crucial here is the word *cydwybod* – 'conscience' – the target at which John Jones' strictures were unerringly aimed from Capel Mawr pulpit, in the hard light of which the beautiful reduced at best to the merely moral, more often to the dubious and immoral. The opposition between poet's sympathies and pulpit strictures is made more plain as you climb to the watershed ridge that bounds Dyffryn Nantlle to the south, beneath which is Cwm Pennant. Here's Williams-Parry again in his most famous sonnet, after chapel, in fleeting encounter with a fox up here on this sublime ridge a hundred yards from the hill summit, seeing him as I have seen him so often, caught in poised surprise with one paw hesitantly held up, keen muzzled and the fires of his eyes upon me:

> *Llwybreiddiodd ei ryfeddod prin o'n blaen.*
> (the rare wonder of it appeared before us)

This – the sonnet itself – is the watershed. It looks anew not on the return on investment in God, which message thundered out from the pulpit below, but on – if you like to phrase it thus – the work of God that is nature. *'Ei ryfeddod prin'* – the rare wonder of it! Through the years I lived in Cwm Pennant that sense of wonder grew on me: here was a landscape where every field-corner was thick with ghosts, where generations had played some cosmic chess-game, arranged and rearranged stones into the temporary shapes of 200 or 300 years, borrowed from here to build there, let frost and wind collapse and the grass wipe clean. It is one of the half-dozen valleys that can claim to be loveliest in this most lovely of all countries, and vibrant with the life of nature. The peregrines in Cwm Trwsgl – I've seen so often the tiercel attract the falcon from her nest, she flying under him and upside down to catch the pigeon he dropped to her, then breaking away and back to the inaccessible ledge as he sported round her. And the foxes, supposed to be so alert, yet one passed me among the summit rocks of Moel Hebog one morning, coat glistening rich chestnut in the just-risen sun, my dog and I quite still and he not ten feet away so that his acrid stink had her quivering in excitement.

Hawk and fox were not the only hunters here. There were summer nights on the river when the foxglove bloomed and Owen John Cwt-y-

Bugail and I patrolled our favourite water, where I held the lamp and carried the heavy battery as he poised, *trifar* in hand, fiercely intent, eyes flaring-cold as any soldier's hewing limbs at Pilleth or Mortimer's Cross five hundred years before; then the shaft's plunge into dark pool, thrash and gleam of the stricken fish. Once the bailiff came along, two women with us that night and no chance of escape. Two of us hid behind a bush, fish and lamp among the roots of a tree. Owen John and his friend were on the grass, she wriggling out of her knickers and pulling him down on top of her when the bailiff flashed his lamp: 'Oh, sorry mate, have one for me while you're at it!' And away he went.

The people were as much a part of the spirit of the place as river or hills: old faces, lingering conversations, the companionable crises of the farmer's year – the frenetic sweat and itch of stacking hay in a barn, pandemonious sadism at the sheep-dipping, the shepherding – that time in the late snow, the sheep tired with long labour and no option but to bare your arm to the elbow, push the breech lamb up and round before pulling it out, the lamb and your arm both marbled bloody and yellow against the white ground, and a few days later, in a field which the warming sun had now patched with green, a hare reared up to box with this same lamb. I remember the young man from the 'hippy' colony at Tanygraig who, desiring to live off the land's bounty, gathered the roots of a riverside plant and grated them into his salad. It was hemlock water dropwort. Within an hour he died in agony. His ashes were buried in the churchyard of Llanfihangel y Pennant, on the left as you enter the gate, under a painted slate. I remember talking with old Mr Morus of Gilfach, asking him why sheeps' heads hung in the trees above the stream by his house:

'*Duw*, it's cure for the *pendro*. When the sheeps die, I cut off his head and hang it there. Blowfly lays eggs, maggots eat the brain, fall into the stream, and the sickness is washed from the land.'

You will not find beliefs like that current if you go to Cwm Pennant these days. It has changed. A stiff knot of baling twine secures the rusting chapel-gate. Acre-millionaires and seekers of subsidies bought into the valley. My old friends no longer farm their land, now fenced around with wire. Grey wintering sheds of corrugated iron dominate. It is made to work to repay investment in it. Rather than this exploitation, I am not sure that

I do not prefer the old unease at its beauty, which spoke at least of the mystery of the place, and of a certain reverence.

I go elsewhere now – down over the shoulder of Moelfre, for example, on a dull February afternoon to the chapel in Cwm Nantcol, gleaming against the bare ribs of the Rhinog mountain from which it came. A sudden ray of sunlight slants through the clouds to light upon a bank of the small, frilled early daffodils of Wales, the flanks of the hills a sombre blue-grey behind. Even in their abandonment, the stones remain as statements of core value and belief. These places, with their beached, lonely resonance, their sense of community and aspiration, of hardship and endurance, are scattered throughout the Welsh hills. This is the land of summer stars, yes, but also of the stony pasture and the rough hills, the ravens' guttural cry and joyful play in the rage of the wind, the ermined stoat stuttering across the scree, the peregrine's stoop. In the afterlight beyond sunset when the colours glow at their fiercest there is the emerald cushion of moss, on it a pearl-grey corona of feather and down, splash of bright blood at its centre still sticky to the touch and the falcon chattering against nightfall from her rock. All in so small a space. Only in Wales.

CITYSCAPES

My local overgrown village of Bangor – a city in no more than name – apart, I spend
very little time in cities. Perhaps because of that, when I do visit them they seem to me
infinitely exuberant and entertaining. These are some of the more intriguing from
among those I've visited.

1: That's the way it is when you're in Seattle

At the corner of Third Avenue and Bell, heading down into Belltown, I halt
in momentary amazement opposite the Regrade Park. Behind me, an olive-
green doorway in a dusky pink building bursts open and a black woman
dances out into the street, stops in front of me, hands on hips. Maybe she's
30, very dark, exquisite features. She bestows a quick glance, a wry twitch
lifts a corner of her mouth:

'You looking at the guys in the park?'

She answers her own question, continues in a brisk undertone, maybe
directed at me, maybe not:

'Those guys, hey man, that's a mental map of the union. Insanity,
profanity, stupidity, religiosity, gluttony, lechery, pride – all goin' on over
there, honey.'

She graces me, the street, the park with a seraphic smile and
disappears back through the dusky pink wall as summarily as she came. I
stand transfixed, watch the human marionettes on the triangle of
shrubbed concrete opposite strut, pace, twirl, gesticulate, recline, shriek at
no-one in particular until making them the object of my attention makes
me the object of theirs so I hurry off downhill, down to the waterfront of
this oddest, most observed, maybe most geographically blessed of all
American cities.

Seattle! It's farthest north and west, top left of the States, four thousand miles from New York, just down over the border from Vancouver, up in Washington State and along the shores of Puget Sound, into which, by way of the Strait of Juan de Fuca, the waters of the Pacific leak a hundred miles inland. My first night in town, at Kell's Irish Pub along Post Alley, after I've been served by a flame-haired, green-eyed waitress all the way from Chicago, I listen to old Emmett Watson, mock-curmudgeonly Seattle press institution, holding forth. He's the man who suggested, ten years ago when the Berlin Wall was coming down, that in order to keep the Californians out it be bought and rebuilt around his town. His town! That's the key. If you live in Seattle, it's your town and urban brand-loyalty, strong wherever you go in the States, is potent as a Starbuck's double espresso or a Redhook microbrew in this demesne.

Watson's jibe is as post-modern and ironic as Seattle itself. The place doesn't need walls. Eastwards, it has natural ones on the grandest scale – the Bitterroot Mountains, the Northern Cascades. I rode in on a Harley-Davidson one day from Montana – 600 miles straight, snow on the Lookout and Fourth of July Passes, on the Snoqualmie Pass – descended into Seattle on its spit of land between Washington Lake and Puget Sound, moated and turreted and against the sunset like any fantasy medieval fortress, Mount Rainier glowing pink away to the left, a clashing and screeching mist of traffic swirling about the freeways and boulevards, half-a-dozen skyscrapers creating their own clouds, the Space Needle – built for the 1962 World Fair and still prefiguring the future in its design – glittering on the launch pad as though ready for take-off. 'Seattle reigns', punned *Newsweek* when it ran a feature on the town; it has the look of a place that feels about itself that perhaps it should.

But it's not just the things you commonly hear about – Microsoft and Boeing, Hendrix and Nirvana, rain, Pearl Jam and Pacific Northwest Lifestyle versions of the American Dream – that come on strong. Sure, the city's energy and commercial acumen in selling itself are immense. Their counterparts down at street level, the texture, are also unique. That natural setting out-grands at times any other city I know, and the Seattle residents know it too as they dream along Pike Place at sunset to gaze across a chaos of cars on the Alaskan Way and yearn after the green-and-white Washington State ferries crossing to the quiet islands in the sound. They stand there, stilled somehow, and they're rewarded as the famous rain relents, sky clears from the west, scraps of washed blue unfurl slowly between the piled clouds, a brightness slips in, intensifies along the fantastically serrated skyline of the Olympic Peninsula as it saws a bloody wound in the sky.

Maybe some of these watchers are among the people dining an hour or two later in the revolving restaurant 500 feet up the Space Needle, dominant wonder that it is, barely noticing their food or the *maitre d 's* obsequy as the whole sublime landscape of city, mountain and sea aches imperceptibly past at one revolution per hour. Jonathan Raban settled here for the sailing. Half an hour across Puget Sound and I was sea-kayaking alongside otters in the waves one morning. The focus in Seattle is different – its orientation out here in the farthest west geographically different too. The cranes on the container wharves stand like skeletal red giraffes, dipping to lift the ship-borne foliage of the east on which the port grazes. In El Gaucho's restaurant a table of Japanese businessmen to a man order tuna steaks extremely rare and carry the substantial remains back to their hotel in doggy bags. 'That's the way it is when you're in Seattle!' my companion observes, with the referentiality of the true Seattle native, 'West Coast food – too much of it, and maybe too much choice too!'

Drifting around Pike Place Market next morning I could see her point. It's not only the varieties of cuisine – sushi joints, Chinese pastry cooks, Bolivian restaurants, Greek salad-bars, Italian sandwich-makers, French patisseries, *mitteleuropäisch* establishments selling borscht and Pirogi, cantinas, bistros, farm bakeries, country stores. It's the diversity, too, in the market itself. I stand next to a cheese stall and pick up on the arcane name tags scattered among its veined and marbled produce: Linburger, Muenster, Asiago, Fontina, Provolone, Finnish Lappi, Myzithra, Mozzarella, Roquefort, Parmagiano Reggiano and Oregon Rogue River Blue. The proprietor catches my eye:

'You wanna buy something?'

'Just looking,' I shrug.

'Cain't make your mind up, heh? Well, that's the way it is when you're in Seattle.'

Alongside us a busker with a hiccuping, tear-stained voice sings how he loved his dear old daddy and guesses he always will as the passers-by turn their backs on his lament and cross to the livelier side of the street where an *a cappella* trio of black men, the one in the middle playing a guitar from his wheelchair, ring out animated close harmonies and a street-woman in aztec-print pants dances in front of them to the accompaniment of her own maracas. A passer-by tells me the man with the spoons – an undisputed genius with his chosen instrument – has played with the Seattle Symphony Orchestra: 'Social mobility – that's the way it is in Seattle!' my commentator glosses complacently. Right now the spoon man's part of the soundtrack to the ongoing comedy at the fish-market, where front-of-stall assistants pluck the chosen halibut, ocean perch, yellowfish tuna, chinook and silver and sockeye salmon, buffalo fish, tilapia and Moses Lake carp by the gills from their beds of crushed ice and hurl them flashing silver to be caught expertly in wrapping paper at back-of-stall or, to raucous cheers, dropped flapping across the stone flags by excited invitees from among the customers. The fliers pinned to the market noticeboard provide an apt counterpoint to the hubbub of the place: 'clairvoyance for beginners', 'organic land for sale', 'Stone Soup Theatre', 'Palmistry, Astrology and Tarot by Sita', 'Reptiles Around the World' or 'The Journey from Ignorance to Bliss'. My own journey takes me to a lesbian espresso and sandwich bar back on Post Alley to sit at a sunny pavement table over a latte and ciabatta: old frail men jag through in electric wheelchairs; Vietnam vets with eyepatches and crutches limp by; rag-kneed, safety-pinned and peroxided grunge survivors bear shaven, quiffed heads like inverted keels to keep them to their idiosyncratic course through a bulky waddle of strollers; down-and-outs with angry eyes and St Vitus limbs drag on chewed roll-ups and beg for change; a graceful, slight girl sits on the back steps of a restaurant and weeps.

Any city? No! Walk downtown from here along Second Avenue, over roaring grilles and steaming vents, and a monumental cityscape rears up around you. Redbrick and brownstone glow warm in the sun streaming over Puget Sound. A one per cent tithe on construction allows for sculpture and artwork everywhere, whilst the buildings are themselves sculpted art. The 1930s Smith Tower's a Gatsbyesque wedding-cake for over-reachers. The Alaska and Lyon Buildings hunch stunted and magpie-bricked against cloud-reflective monsters of scooped blue glass that gather their own atmospheres. The place is obsessively architectonic, right the way through to the up-town post-modern melted-guitar joke of the new multi-million-dollar Experience Music Project, founded by Microsoft's other philanthropic multi-billionaire Paul Allen, where you can view that green velvet jacket Jimi Hendrix wore, hear bands in the Sky Church or just musically interact.

But that's peripheral stuff. The heart of this city is right downtown in Pioneer Square. Here, between the massive Richardsonian Romanesque apartment blocks of white brick and salmon-pink stucco, light refracting into it from the glass-and-pastel, scoop-simple geometries of the new, pigeons march and bob and the maple leaves drift down to settle their spikey carmines and ochres across grey cobblestones. Each bench among the rhododendrons is a sort of home to those for whom even the Merchants' and Bohemian Cafés right at hand are forever out of reach, and who, displaced, are watched over by the hook-nosed bird-totem with its queer, splayed frog. Maybe they're spoken for, too, by the little bronze of Chief Sealth, who lived in the former land, gave Seattle a version of his name, and famously proclaimed that 'there is no quiet place in the white man's cities, no place to hear the leaves of spring'. He's addressed here under the autumn maples by his statue's own inscription, replete with the laid-back ironies of the Pacific Northwest:

'Chief Seattle, now the streets are your home'.

2: Pièce de Résistance

There is a kind of relaxed gaiety about Quebec that is utterly disarming. It first crept up on me from the springy soft tread of the wooden boardwalks along the Terrasses Dufferin & des Gouverneurs at sunset. I was idling through the throng of accordion and flute players, chansonniers, puppeteers, escapologists, fire-eaters and clowns that inhabits the place. Slanting low from upriver, the sun was gilding and mellowing their frenetic performances, glinting off copper rooftops and stepped and painted gables. The hills that surround the city were purpling down into shadow. All along this high vantage point above the cliffs of Cap Diamant, the townspeople were out promenading, chattering away in a Quebecois French that is somehow less emphatic, less excitable than its European counterpart, the rolls and trills and posturing exaggerations of the parent language rather occluded, or fined down to an amused, sly drawl that defaults quickly to mirth.

Which latter found its focus in the animals. A woman strolled past with a Burmese cat lolling from her shoulder-bag; a gay couple hand-in-hand walked a ferret on a lead; distracted by this, three miniature dachshunds in a complex harness looped round the legs of a young labrador, two poodles pranced into the melee, a chow barked encouragement, a beagle's tail waved a frantic introduction from the ringside and a Cardiganshire corgi hustled through snarling, causing a West Highland terrier that hitherto had been bustling amiably past the bench from which I was observing this brouhaha to cock his leg and assert himself in the usual canine fashion upon the trousers of my second-best suit:

'*Oh! Qu'a-t-il fait?*' exclaimed his owner, an exceptionally elegant woman of a certain age, proffering a handkerchief and torn between embarrassment and hilarity, her fine-drawn eyebrows arching irrepressibly upwards.

'*Rien que pisser, Madame,*' I replied, with all the dismissive cool I could muster, and by-standers and passers-by took the phrase up and bore it aloft on shouts of laughter and a dozen more handkerchiefs came to my rescue. There are times when, whatever the indignity, the warmth of a place's people impels you not to mind.

Quebec City is one of the great historic settlements from the colonial epoch in the Americas. European explorers first landed at this point in the narrows of the Saint Lawrence River in 1534, and a Frenchman, Samuel de Champlain, founded a city here, and a fort on the towering limestone bluff of Cap Diamant, between 1608 and 1620. For a century-and-a-half thereafter this centre of New France and outlet from a vast hinterland for the lucrative fur trade was skirmished over by French, British and American forces. In that long period when the teaching of history was obsessed with dates, every schoolchild knew of 1759 and the fatal victory of General Wolfe on the Heights of Abraham over the Marquis de Montcalm in the concluding battle of the Seven Years' War. Today, the longer war has been won, cultural resistance has carried the day and the character of Vieux Quebec is inalienably and quite wonderfully French.

It is also an extraordinarily attractive and interesting city – the only walled one in North America, and since 1985 one of only two cities on the subcontinent to be designated a World Heritage Site. So it attracts on that account its quota of coach-tours and tour-groups and guides and horse-drawn trams and traps and be-shorted, be-sandalled, be-stockinged video-wielding, memento-therapy-fixated endomorphs of either sex and from as far afield as Cincinatti and St Louis. Yet unlike all those other designated fellow-sites from the Aran Islands to Buda to the Taj Mahal, Quebec steps quietly aside from all this into the self-containment of its own story.

Simply, you don't get hassled here. The *citoyens* are both acute and relaxed enough to recognise that the drama of their city and its otherness is brought into play by their own continuing presence (which they reinforce by an understated refinement in the matter of interpretation). So the spectators here, witnessing that drama's tacit or overt re-enactment, applaud by their very attendance, and can thus be left safely to their own devices. This is the observers' city par excellence. There are a few cities I would as gladly visit, but none in which I would rather live. Let Jonathan Raban coast in to Seattle and Jan Morris stick to Trieste; my choice would be Quebec.

You get a sense of Quebec's sheer physical presence from the sky-blue-and-white ferries that tick-tock from their pier on the waterfront across the Saint Lawrence every 20 minutes to the town of Lévis on the southern shore. Above the great river down which the grainships and the long, low freighters glide, high over the derricks, gantries and silos of the port, there rises a compact townscape of fairytale texture. From swathes of ancient, cliff-clinging woodland rear massive, cannon-embrasured fortifications; rears also a jumble of copper and tin and tiled and wood-shingled, baguetted, big-dormered, small-dormered, fire-walled and laddered, pink-and-blue-painted and verdigrised roofs that mingle in with Loire-chateau-ornate-and-spikey, with Moorish and neoclassical and steepled and cross-bearing, with barrack-like official buildings and muted skyscrapers with telecommunicational addenda, with the aspiring and the flat-topped and the augmented and the pent-housed that have sprung up here over four centuries and against all odds have gelled and stayed to give an entirely individual character to this green and clean and leisurely city, the text of which stands plain for deciphering from them.

Penetrate its labyrinth by alleys and stairs that lead up from Vieux Port and Lower Town to zig-zag through the walls, or by the brief *funiculaire* that mounts the cliff above Place Royale, and two conflicting impressions strike you. The first is that this lived-in little town – Quebec somehow has the feel of an overgrown village about it – goes about its uncrowded business with an air of laconic enjoyment. The second·is that the whole city is the most exquisitely mounted historical exhibition. Its story is entirely on show: coincidentally in small details like a shining cannonball casually entwined among the roots of a tree on the corner of the Rue du Corps de Garde and the Rue St Louis; deliberately in the grander set-pieces such as the Ursuline Convent where the Marquis de Montcalm, mortally wounded on the battlefield beyond, came to die. He's commemorated here by grand inscription in the chapel (*'Honneur à Montcalm. Le destin en lui derolant La Victoire l'a recompensé par une Mort Glorieuse'*), among a plethora of gilded lambs and gleaming ladders and golden crowns of the Queen of Heaven.

Yet even in the death-place of its last French commander, that finely-held Quebecois tension between the heroic and the everyday exists, and comically. In a piece of exquisite embroidery in gold and silver thread on silk, its impeccable needlework and formal design of sunflowers and roses and baskets of fruit the work of some nameless 18th-century sister, a playful caterpillar crawls across a fig. Perhaps not to take things too seriously, but to take them just seriously enough, has been the key to Quebec's long survival and adaptation? Here, in a glass case, are the letters of Sister Marie de l'Incarnation – telling of how, at the building of the convent in 1642 she went up and down the scaffolding to help the masons without feeling the least afraid; or again, gently teasing at some of her fellow-nuns' cradling wax images of the infant Jesus. The sardonic-humorous liveliness of the Quebec temperament was obviously present over 300 years ago.

There is another palpable tension in Quebec. It is between the safe, alley-wayed, elegant, stone and labyrinthine town within the walls, and the park – surprisingly large for so small a city – that stretches out to the south-west beyond them, parallel to the river and above the cliffs and bluffs to which the city clings. Parc des Champs de Bataille it's called, for these are the Heights of Abraham, and they seem to breathe to themselves Quebec's motto – *'Je me souviens'* – I remember..! Walk here in a sea-fret at dawn and you can almost hear the wash of Wolfe's boat as it drifts downriver with the tide in the dim light from the last quarter of the moon; you can still catch at his consumptive whispering of the quotation – 'The paths of glory lead but to the grave' – from Gray's *Elegy* to his fellow officers, and his telling them he would rather have written those lines than capture Quebec; your nerves still clench to the scrape of a boot on rock, the dull tap of a musket against a branch as the British redcoats scale the cliff-path from l'Anse aux Foulons.

The park's wooded and undulating country at Quebec *citadelle's* vulnerable back door still tells its tale of brutal skirmishing; a granite block here marks where Wolfe died; at another a few hundred yards away Montcalm received his mortal wound. In the Jardin des Gouverneurs close by, a steely-grey and correct limestone ashlar column erected by the Earl of Dalhousie looks down on the river and the lower town. Its Latin inscription praises both generals. In the evening I walk along to it, leaving behind those genial crowds on the high terraces. The last joggers and roller-bladers have left the park. The air is breathy and heavy and warm tonight. Down there along the Rue St Paul and the Rue Dalhousie people sit out at pavement cafés, drink wine, laugh and converse in soft and sibillant French. Lights reflect silkily from the polished setts, the St Lawrence ripples beneath the wharves, ebbing oceanwards. Up here by the monument two huge moths circle the lamps soundlessly. I imagine them to be the spirits of Wolfe and Montcalm, the Marquis with a grave, polite humour asking of the younger man who vanquished him two-and-a-half centuries ago, 'To whom, now, is the victory, my English friend?'

3: *Varanasi in Darkness & Light*

Is Varanasi the holiest of Indian cities? At the source of the Ganges two years ago Sanjay, the sexual healing monk, insisted that it was, and that I go there. Over tea with Mark Tully in one of the leafier suburbs of New Delhi this year, I was warned against ever thinking in terms of the ultimate or prizing singularity as a virtue in India. 'Just observe,' he'd advised, 'and eventually a pattern will emerge.' Then he began speaking of Varanasi with such fervour that I questioned again if this was the holiest place? He repeated his warning, told of the holiness of so much in India, but still, there was a gleam about his expression and his talk. He too ended by urging that I go there, and directed me to the hotel of his friend Shashank Singh on Asi Ghat.

Fourteen hours on the Purshottan Express – second-class air-conditioned, overnight: quiet attendants, patched and threadbare linen, clay cups of hot, sweet *chai* from wayside stations, friendly Indians returning on leave from the Gulf States sitting on your bunk – and a tight-knuckled hour in an auto-rickshaw brought me to Shashank's hotel. 'The best vegetarian food in UP,' Mark had promised. It was so good that throughout the weeks of my stay I felt disinclined to eat elsewhere: bowls of lady's fingers, of potatoes, of spinach, of squashes and pulses and other vegetables the names of which no amount of questioning would gain agreement on came delicately sauced and spiced, with curds and breads and puffy, crisp puris. The hotel used to be the palace in Varanasi for the ruling family of Bihar, and with its portraits and cool marble still feels that way. Best of all about it is the situation, looking out over the Ganga from the southernmost of Varanasi's ghats – the landing and bathing places of which there are more than 70 along the four-mile river-front.

But this is not a tourist town. Getting here is too arduous, the nature of the place too odd for that. Not that there aren't tourist attractions and the inevitable hustlers who accompany them. In terms of art and architecture, too, there is much to see. The moody smallness of temple interiors belies their external splendour. If you must have museums, go to Bharat Kala Bhavan in Banaras Hindu University at the southern end of town, which has a marvellous collection of Indian art and sculpture: one 18th-century miniature from Rajasthan, 'Opium takers hunting a rat,' has all the energetic tomfoolery of Rowlandson and a much kinder eye. Upstairs there is the Alice Boner room, dedicated to the Swiss artist and sculptor who lived for 40 years on Asi Ghat. Her sensuous bronzes of Indian dancers are lyrically expressive. Her house at Asi is poignant in its testimony to her will to continue there into old age – concrete intersteps on the steep, winding stair to the rooftop from which the life of the river spreads out before – the bathers, the devout, the musicians and marriage processions, the holy and the hustlers, the bereft, the cows and children and buffalos and poor, the spice-smell and rich raucousness of sound that are and could be of no other place but here. At Sarnath, on the city's periphery, the Buddha preached his first sermon, the stupa marking the spot now standing in a deer park where hoopoes flit, mongooses scutter through the bushes, and western Buddhist women with cropped grey hair project their serious benignity. The nearby museum is devoted to carvings in the local Chunar sandstone as fine and sharp as though chiselled and polished last year rather than 15 centuries ago. At the other end of town, Ramnagar Fort houses a ramshackle collection of opulence and brutality: ivory howdahs, astrological clocks, gold-plated ambarees, nailed clubs, elephant traps, palanquins still stained with sweat from the bearers' shoulders, imperial fripperies and citations: 'Order of Leopold II with citation presented to His Highness Maharaja Sir Prabhu Narain Singh December 1926 for his prowess in shooting tossed-up coins with a rifle.' With its flaking sandstone and stucco peeling to reveal decayed brick beneath, its scuffed grass, weeds and rust, its begging attendants and vast extent, it's neither more nor less attractive, say, than Toxteth, to which it bears the closest resemblance. But neither Sarnath nor Ramnagar are of the essence of the place. For that, you must walk the ghats.

'I think that the river / Is a strong brown god' wrote T S Eliot. The Ganga is certainly a god – more properly a goddess – and worshipped as such, but brown it is not. At its source, in the ice-caves of Gaumukh high in the mountains of Garhwal, it's milk-white with glacier sediment and roaring. Here at Varanasi, a thousand kilometres on, it's of a colour best described in Ben Jonson's elegant phrase as 'goose-turd green'. But our western response to its apparent pollution shouldn't mask the reverence in which the devout Hindu holds it.

'This water has the property that it never corrupts,' a government official in Delhi asserted to me: 'There are no germs in it. It is always pure.' Nowhere is that insistence on its purity more absolute and striking than in Varanasi. Forget the fact that the bather in the dawn, eyeballs rolled back in his head as he drinks from his brass bowl, is ten yards downstream from a sewage outlet, five yards away from a swollen corpse. Here the weight of history and belief is against the notion of hygiene, the latter almost a blasphemy. On Tulsi Ghat, the laboratory where daily faecal coliform counts – often up to 250,000 times the WHO safe permitted maximum – were posted has been shut down and vandalised. The river is pure, even if only so for a believer. 'For a westerner,' advises Shashank, the genial hotel proprietor, with a little rock of his head and a smile, 'perhaps it is not so pure, but we have known it to be so for a long time, so therefore, for us, it must be.'

The latter's by way of understatement. Varanasi – also known as Kashi, 'the city of light', or Banaras – is one of the oldest living cities, 'older than history, older than tradition, older even than legend, and looks twice as old as all of them put together,' as Mark Twain flippantly put it. I do not know of a more strange or impressive city anywhere in the world. Nowhere more clearly exemplifies Lewis Mumford's brilliant insight that a city is 'energy converted into culture'. Even its form argues the reason for its existence. On the one bank as the river curves in its great northern arc the city is piled up, crowded and teeming along pale sandstone bluffs, alleys and temples, holy sites and markets bewilderingly packed together; on the other, sand, vultures, jungle, emptiness. It is one of the sacred *tirthas*, the crossing-places of the spirit in Hindu cosmology, spiritual fords where heaven and earth meet and where the devout may cross the river of *samsara* – the recurrent cycle of birth and death – to gain the farther shore, which is Nirvana. To die here is to be blessed. The custom, survival, activity of the whole city is thus predicated on death, and it is death that the few western tourists, anxious and apart, come here to see. On the two burning ghats of Harishchandra and Manikarnika – flat, baked aprons of clay slipping into the Ganga – the cremations take place daylong, the pyres smoking on each of them by the dozen. A rim of black, steaming charcoal garish-glittery with scraps of cloth demarcates water and land, attendants raking there for precious melted metal. Downstream, water-buffalo, their glossy black hides slick with wallowing, chew on drifted garlands of marigold by the propped stones where dhobi-wallahs thwack tight-rolled cloths and clothes. On the ghats, the corpses lie wrapped in bright cloth on pallets by the water's edge, so fresh rigor mortis has not set in. (One morning two boys drowned whilst swimming at Asi. Loll-limbed, they were carried without lamentation beneath our balcony; by noon were burning.)

The bodies are dipped in the river, placed on the pyre. The eldest son, shaven-headed with a pigtail tuft, circumambulates the corpse, touches it head and foot with fire from a brand of the sacred kusha grass, lights kindling beneath. The family sit round. There is no overt display of grief. The attendants lever back on to the pyre with greenwood poles the logs that fall from it. They poke the corpses back prone when contraction of muscle and tendon causes them to sit up. When all's over and only ashes and fragments of bone remain, the eldest son fills a bowl with Ganga water, walks one more time round the mound of smoking charcoal, casts the water on to it from over his left shoulder, and steps on his way without looking back.

The wood, of course, brought in by boat and piled in great stacks around the ghats, costs money. Above the ghats are hospices for the terminally aged and ill. They are vast warehouses for the soon-to-be-dead. Smoke and ash drift in from below through open windows, on to emaciated forms lying in rows on the pallets on which they'll soon burn. 'Are they given food, medical assistance?' I ask an attendant. 'They do not come here for those things,' he explains patiently to me, 'they come here to die.' For the poor, there is a charity handout of twigs and sticks. When those are consumed the corpse, lightly charred, is rolled into the water where the packs of dogs home in, tearing at a ribcage, making off with a skull. It seems at times that dogs and brahmins are the only well-fed beings in the city.

Frightful to us as this may seem, and disturbing in the directness of faith as response to social conditions almost medieval in their dispossession, there are worse things for western eyes. Some categories of corpse are not burnt, but rather weighted with stones and thrown into the river: sadhus; snakebite and smallpox victims, who are deemed taken by the goddess Durga; children; pregnant women. After a day they bloat and rise, the turtles having already eaten the flesh from their faces. One morning on the river, downstream from the Dashashvameda Ghat of one of Allen Ginsberg's best-known poems, I saw a woman floating, full-breasted, belly swollen and her sari bloodstained, legs akimbo as though to give birth. Into the eye-sockets of her death's-head the little waves lapped. An old woman on the ghat above pulled her sari across her mouth and looked down with an expression – rare for indifferent India – of utter pity.

It is not all so grim. The city's vitality is immense, its geometries, shrines and architecture continually surprising. Down at the water's edge in the Lolarka Kund – a deep well approached by flights of steps where in August an important fertility rite takes place – I watch a turtle swimming quietly in the noon heat, hear a shrieking, look up, and find myself suddenly being pelted with sticks and buffalo-dung by monkeys on the walls above. When I exit hastily, I'm pounced on – first by a confiding, dangerous youth who invites me back to his brother's house to try 'charas (cannabis), opium, brown heroin, white heroin – all free, you no pay!' I'm rescued from this transaction by a gaggle of even younger boys, who tell me 'this no good man, uncle', and invite me to their brother's silk-shop – merely, of course, to drink tea, in the course of which ceremony the finest silken weaves will be opened with a flourish before me and the proprietor claim that, purchase or not, I am his everlasting friend. Later, as relieved observer, all along the ghats I watch lithe youths play cricket with astonishing grace and agility, their wickets pushed into clots of river clay.

At night-time, the activity of the place transmutes to atmosphere. There is lightning flickering on the far bank of the river, the trees over there backlit in turquoise. Mynahs and the Indian jackdaws that fly open-mouthed and call incessantly are wakened by it. The people on the riverbank talk in subdued voices. Cicadas saw away like worn bearings. From beneath my balcony an old man, one useless limb bent beneath him, crawls across the dirt road, dragging his hindquarters, pushing a steel bowl, shushing and clanking as he goes. A dog – one of the sleek, fawn, black-muzzled dogs of Varanasi – approaches him. From the shadows a watcher emerges to gesture it away. Two Enfields putter up from the ghat, horns blaring. They pass the cripple on either side as, hurriedly, he reaches for his bowl. After they've gone he looks warily up and down, continues a little way to splash water ritually on the shrine of Hanuman the monkey-god under the peepal tree before retreating to his four-foot-square home between two brick pillars by the wall where he shelters daily from the 130-degree noon-time heat. A small girl appears, dances in front of him, stylised, spirited, as a gibbous moon climbs over the Ganga, its silvered path marked in textures of glisten and ripple. More dogs range along the sandy shore, make off in snarling flurries with nameless river-objects dragged from the shallows. The crippled man comes out again, sweeping away dust. There are high scraps of cloud, vultures stretch their wings across the water, and a strange black bird plays on the hot midnight wind. Varanasi by moonlight is eerily beautiful and never quiet. Even in the sleepless small hours when the oppressive heat and mosquitoes of the Gangetic Plain drive me from bed to sit on the balcony in the breeze, the movement's continual. Violent screaming flares up quick as brushfire amongst the riverbank poor. The devout on the Panchatirtha pilgrimage drift past, the white-clad widows like wraiths, heading for the clay bank to bathe, pausing by the sati stones that commemorate wives' burnings on their husbands' pyres, anointing the Shivalinga – the holy shafts of polished and ancient black stone which are found everywhere throughout the city – with vermilion and garlanding them with marigolds. When I leave next morning, it is quickly – torn in that peculiarly Indian way between relief and regret.

4: Propositioned in Portland

The great thing about American cities is their spatial logic. Number and sub-divide a grid – NW 7th, SW 4th. Score a few specifics across it – Jefferson, Broadway – and you've a recipe for perfect orientation. I drove into Portland, Oregon, late one Friday night, made the transition from Interstate to hotel in minutes, and still had surplus energy to sally out for a beer. Maybe, on reflection, that was rash. Or at least, I might have given the choice of bar more thought.

I'd had this impression that Portland, a neat city of half-a-million at the confluence of the Columbia and Willamette Rivers, 100 miles in from the Pacific, 200 south of Seattle, ringed by the volcanic peaks of the Cascades, was a reticent, down-home place. It's good to get rid of illusions. The stubbly, checkshirted man at the bar helped. His eyes slid down me in the mirror. He took a pull on his bottle, swivelled on his stool and let them crawl back up again. 'You take it up the ass?' he briefly enquired, took my speechlessness for a negative, and swivelled back. That was my first proposition in Portland. I didn't know I was starting a collection.

I was staying at The Benson. It's an opulent delight in Italian marble, Austrian crystal and Circassian walnut, lording it like some grand assertion of the social mobility of America over Portland's downtown. Powell's City of Books is a hundred yards behind, the gates of Chinatown are just across Burnside. It's as though the Savoy had moved to Soho. Powell's being so near, open every day as late as an English pub and the biggest single bookshop in the world, that was Saturday morning accounted for. A coffee-shop takes up a corner of the city block the store occupies. I gravitated, to browse acquisitions. The notices were more interesting. One recommended books banned in other American states: *The Scarlet Letter* 'because it conflicts with the values of the community'; *Twelfth Night* because 'it promotes homosexuality'. Conversation from another table drifted through: 'When I was in Eugene, hippie dresses over, like, corduroy pants were really popular. Man, that place was so uncool!' It was a young mother talking to her jammy-faced, cherubic three-year-old, who was spreading sugar-icing across the pages of *Today I feel Silly, and Other Moods That Make My Day*. 'Shall we buy this, Kathy?' her mother asked, perhaps in embarrassment. Kathy shook her head. She was a true exponent of the counter-culture. *Sesame Street*, she insisted. Her mother grimaced. She bit her lip. She raised her eyes. They met mine. I smiled, embarrassed at being caught eavesdropping. I went to the men's room, leaving my stack of books and coffee on the table. When I came back, the mother and child were gone but there was a card on the books: 'Hi, I'm Mary. Kathy and I are free this weekend. Why don't you join us?' The upfront trust of it was staggering. I studied alternatives: 'Civil Disobedience: a three-hour seminar', 'The Soul's Journey Home – an act of meditation', 'Hel Runner – their Portland Debut! Dark noise and percussion', 'Karnal Psychic Kirkus / Fanatic Fuckpriest in concert'. I looked around for guidance. There were flitting eyes at every table. Next time I went for a pee, two more cards nestled on the bookstack: 'Hi, I'm Trudi ...' read one. Was that the 30-something pale, dark-haired woman with the anatomy textbooks and notes spread out in front of her? It surely wasn't any of the three safety-pinned women on the next table, reading Dr Dyke's Column, poring over Girlfriend of the Month, and studying The Tao of Girlrock in *Girlfriend Magazine*. I sidled out, self-conscious, cards in my pocket, and took a walk to Washington Park on the hill above town.

Stelar jays screamed from tall trees. Pine-cones fell and tinked across the path. I found myself in a rose-garden on a sunny high esplanade above the gleaming city, its plan laid out beneath where the rivers forked, forest beyond them and beyond that Mount Hood, snow-capped and glaciered. It's a sublime setting, works on the people up here. They're dreaming. Girls in skirts of shiny chenille bend their heads to snuff the fragrance of roses. Goatee'd young men walk hand-in-hand among petalled beds of Gipsy Dancer, Dublin Bay, Crimson Tide or Angelita. A plump boy frisks under a cuboid stainless steel fountain while his sister smiles wry and sidelong and a musician plays a dulcimer under a red umbrella. On a quiet lawn I think, yes, this is the big easy, this is the good place. A couple appear in front of me, she orange-haired, scarlet-topped, black-skirted, he in grey fedora and waistcoat. They practise, one-two-backstep-hipflick, again and again over the grass. I'm entranced. 'C'mon man, it's the Lindy Hop. She'll show ya ...'

For the next hour they do just that, getting their amusement from my

British accent as well as my ineptitude. Then, with the brief injunction that we're bound for the matinee session in the Crystal Ballroom at Burnside and 14th, we head downtown to mingle with kids in white sneakers, flared skirts, Jimmy Cagney caps, suspenders, suits and ties, and to pace it out on the famous floating floor.

Two hours of one-two-backstep is enough. I'm exhausted, thread down through squares leafy with maple, beech and cherry in the colours of the fall. There are bronze horses, vintage trolley-cars, poets, fountains of every description, jugglers with tasselled sticks, ducks, Irish dancers, little beaver statues, a Laura Ashley shop. 'Shine like thunder, cry like rain' pleads the jacket of a manacled punk. At the corner of 10th and Main an old Lincoln Continental with a VW badge on its bonnet extravagantly avoids my jaywalking, its driver catching my puzzlement: 'That's right, man – it's a squashed-flat Beetle.' The queue for the soup-kitchen in the little park at the back of The Benson is orderly. An old man with a supermarket trolley rearranges his belongings and deposits rubbish in a bin whilst he waits, then sits at a bench and talks amicably to his neighbour who's writing computer programmes on yellow paper that the breeze riffles. A youth tries to leap his skateboard on to a narrow wall. Undiscouraged, he attempts time and again. There's a Monet exhibition at the Art Museum, 'Late Paintings from Giverny'. Inside, rafts of people bump against explosions of colour. I make for the Newmark and Dolores Winningstad Theatres. The building in which they're housed is a soaring, austere version of Ely's Octagon. The woman in front of me at the box office asks about dress for the opera: 'We don't dress up formal here. What I always tell people is wear what you feel comfortable in, and that's fine by us.' I want to see Lilian Hellman's *Little Foxes* at the Winningstad, have a voucher for two tickets, tell the attendant I only need one: 'You alone? Hey, I'll come, if that's OK by you. I'm off at 6.30. See you in the bar?'

It's a repertory performance, spirited, pacey. There's a point at which the character Addie sighs, 'You gotta be mad to be born in the South.' The audience gets to its feet and cheers and claps, halting the play. 'What she means is, you gotta be mad not to be born in Portland,' my companion glosses. She'd been one of the first on her feet. Afterwards, we try draught Guinness in the Ethiopian Restaurant at 3rd Avenue and Oak and she tells me about her pet cause – BADD – bicyclists against dumb drivers. Her bike's at the theatre. I walk her over there. She bestows a brief, friendly kiss on parting and cycles off home. I drift towards Chinatown. There's a footfall along Burnside keeping step with mine. I glance over my shoulder, see a big black guy, get anxious, turn:

'What d'you want?'

'Hey, man, what do you want ..?'

'What d'you mean?' He's non-aggressive, courteous. I'm suspicious but a little confused.

'I mean, whaddya want? You know, whatever ...'

I'm even more confused. He notices.

'I'm gay, man – I'm looking for a date.'

'I'm straight, man – I'm looking for food.' We part on a high five and a brief, laughing embrace. I turn into the Old Town Pizza on NW Davis and 3rd. An exquisite young Chinese woman called Kim pulls herself up to her full four feet ten when I ask for a glass of Merlot: 'No – I think you're intoxicated.'

'I'm intoxicated?'

'Well, you talk funny. Either you're drunk or you're not from Portland.'

We make friends. She tells me about the building, one of the oldest in town. It was once a brothel. She's seen ghosts here, chairs have been hurled.

'By you, at drunks ..?'

'Yeah!' She narrows her eyes. I get my wine. She takes me down into the cellars to see Shanghai tunnels leading down to the river, trapdoors, cages where drunks were kept until there were enough to be sold as crew. 'You got relations, mister?' she leers.

'Oh yes, dozens of them, and they know exactly where I am right now.'

'You can keep your boots, then.'

She escorts me back upstairs, sits me at a table and goes off for food. Across the street, under a lamp, three women perform a slow, intimate ballet against a white wall. A statuesque blonde in a strapless ball-gown slips with three dour escorts into Slaughter's Dance Club, turns briefly in the doorway, haloed, backlit, Adam's apple working as she abuses the doorman.

Two high school girls come into the bar, talk with astonishing sophistication about the techniques of their teachers, discuss Gandhi, dismiss a boyfriend: 'He fucks with my heart.'

The lights strung over the streets of Chinatown dance in a wind streaming off the river up which salmon run. A dark blanket of forest tucks beneath shadowy silhouettes of the mountains gathered round this bright and cradled town. It's the lost traveller's dream under the hill. I was never so sorry to leave a place in my life.

5: *Cool in Montreal*

On the sidewalk of the Boulevard René Levesque I stamp my feet clear of snow and wait for a gap in the flashing traffic. A young woman, elegant in minimal fur, sweeps alongside. Snowflakes alight on exposed cleavage, she rolls her eyes skyward with a wry grin, huddles uninvited under my umbrella. A gap appears in the traffic, she hooks her arm into mine, sashays across the ice of the road on stacked heels, disengages at the other side and with a turn and a wave descends into the underworld. Where else but in Montreal?

The largest French-speaking city in the world after Paris is every bit as scintillating and various as its European cousin, and with an *insouciance* and *élan* all of its own, to encounter which is one of the great and pleasurable surprises of world travel. So the temperature a fortnight before Christmas may be ten below zero; so there may be a foot of snow on the streets, and in the course of a winter more will fall here than in Moscow; does it deter or depress the average Montrealer? Not a bit of it. He or she simply dons a fashionable hat, makes some slight accommodation to the temperature in the matter of dress, performs that perilous dance through the skating traffic (drivers in Montreal are on a most un-Canadian par with those of Delhi or even Corsica for skittish craziness), and with a dismissive gesture disappears – on those few days when the climate is too oppressive even for a Montrealer to loiter on the streets – through one of those mysterious entrances that lead into the subterranean city.

For Montreal is like one of those French cars that may appear inexplicably weird and wonderful to the casual observer, but are based on the soundest engineering principles: 'The winters here are cold. There is much snow. Therefore, we will build our city underground, and you need only emerge to take that bracing air into your lungs on the very finest days!' Imagine being able to walk from the Tate Gallery to the British Museum through a vast subterranean concourse, everywhere provided with shops, restaurants, salons, stations, cinemas, galleries. That's what they have in Montreal. From beneath cathedrals and within the foyers of tower office blocks, from the receptions of hotels and the stops on the

Metro, escalators trundle up and down into a netherworld of pure shopaholic delight. Picture the bloke-and-chick-thing-satisfaction available in a world like this. Ariadne's so caught up in getting kitted out with new threads (and the style of this place is such, she'll be taking her time about it) that she leaves Theseus to figure his own way out; and in the consumerist catacombs of Montreal, fitting the underworld to the street-plan above is no mean task. I have a suspicion you could be lost and wandering here for days, but happily so, with everything you need to survive, and the Canadian dollar being what it is, you're not going to be worrying about how much each of you might spend.

I travesty this city if all I tell you about is the shopping. As a cultural centre, Montreal is ravishingly complete. Gilles Bengle, svelte in a grey fedora, gives me the picture on my first night, over Vodka Martinis in a stylish boutique hotel in Old Montreal and later in a restaurant up on trendy Plateau Mont-Royal – Au Pied de Cochon, where the culinary activity on view around open ranges and wood-fired ovens is frenetic and the food French-Canadian provincial at its robust and delicious best. 'Even the *poutine* here is worth eating,' Gilles tells me, explaining that the Quebecois national dish of French fries doused in gravy and covered in melted cheese – a coronary on a plate – tonight, for the sake of variation, delectation and the boosting of our cholesterol counts, will be augmented with Roquefort and the house-speciality of deep-fried goose-livers. Substantial it may be, but on a cold night it's delicious, and all those anti-oxidants in the red wine that swills it down make you feel better about the health effects. 'You will have no problem in Montreal finding things to do,' Gilles tells me, 'What will be difficult is choosing.' I decide on a Mahler concert – the incomplete F-sharp Tenth, that I've never previously heard. It's given in a gilded, acoustically-perfect, neo-Gothic gem of a suburban parish church up by McGill University. A girl sitting next to me reads Chomsky as the orchestra tunes up. The conductor, Alexis Hauser, delivers a rendition where the tension between the youthful players' *brio* and the Mahlerian *Weltschmerz* seems – the more I see of the city and reflect on the performance – to capture something of the place's essence. The same feeling comes to me when I look down from my hotel window on the Cathedral-Basilica of Mary Queen of the World and Saint James.

It's a scaled-down replica of St Peter's in Rome, built in a dark, silica-rich and delaminating sandstone, and opposite it, Sphinx-like in silvery dressed granite, is the Sun Life Building, grandly expansive, tier piled on tier, formerly the largest building in the British Empire. In Montreal, cultural tensions imbue even the physical fabric of the city. You don't need to have read Tawney to realise what's going on here. Religion and the rise of capitalism were never more clearly exemplified than in the way the city's other basilica, Notre Dame (a neo-Gothic masterpiece the polychromatic wooden interior of which simply takes the breath away – five thousand stars above your head in a turquoise heaven!), faces the Bank of Montreal, which crouches like some malignant spider across the Place d'Armes.

As most Montrealers do, I take a break from all this conflictual high seriousness and make my way to the ice-hockey stadium at the downtown Bell Centre. Montreal Canadiens are playing the Philadelphia Flyers, to an accompaniment of popcorn, strobe-lighting and razzmatazz. The action on the ice is fast and apparently furious – mèlées behind the goal seem the order of the day, and full kevlar body armour looks appropriate for battles between stick-wielding men with blades on their feet. The Philadelphians are black-clad and huge, the Canadiens smaller, nimbler, mostly in white. The commonest tactic seems to be for players to wait for an opponent to crash into the perspex sidescreens, then skate up to him and pin him there, keeping him out of the game. The goals are impossibly small, and the goaltenders' shimmying, cross-legged dance in front of them seems to occlude all possibility of scoring. A long shot occasionally tinks against the post. Amazingly, a puck sneaks through into the Flyers' net. The Canadiens, being Montrealers, thus relax, and so the cartoon baddies score. Thus poised, it goes down to the wire, the Canadiens having the best of the play before the Flyers seize on an error as they're under attack. A lone skater surges down the pitch chased by a Montrealer, who hooks the Flyer's legs from beneath him but not before the puck's been whacked home in the closing seconds of the game. There is much Gallic shrugging, doffing of baseball caps and scratching of heads as the crowd files out.

Feeling the need for a little triumphalism after this defeat – it's amazing how quickly allegiance steals up on you in Montreal – I head for Théâtre Maisonneuve at Place des Arts, to take in a feisty production of

The Vagina Monologues. There are strictly no baseball caps on show up here. In fact, as I look round, there are very few persons of my own gender either. Snatches of extempore monologue from behind drift in as I wait for the play to start: 'My ex-husband's wife's ex-husband's wife's ex-husband – now how in hell do you explain that to the children...?'; 'It's a dance Jewish families do at the marriage of their last child...'; 'Every year around my birthday I make an appointment to go see my doctor and my gynaecologist, whether I need to or not...'; 'Please turn off all beepers, pagers, cellphones and anything else that might vibrate,' requests the announcer, to general and nervous laughter. The actresses file on stage, the lights come up. I settle back for an evening's blissful contemplation of the erstwhile inhabitants of Venus, which is only briefly interrupted by the extraordinary spectacle of thousands of women roaring back to those on stage a single-word response that certainly wouldn't be printed in a respectable newspaper.

Feeling an attack of the vapours coming on after the shock of this, I resolve to spend time in the fresh air, and take the Metro out to the Olympic Stadium east of the town. In the Biodome – the best zoo, if it is that, that I've ever seen – capybaras snuffle and scarlet macaws shriek; a river otter curled up around her cub sleeps and dreams; the Botanical Gardens nearby out-Kew Kew, their complex, watery fernhouse and Chinese-influenced *Jardin Céleste* wholly exquisite; the adjacent Insectarium is living lapidary. My flesh creeps as I watch creatures whose existence I never suspected crawl around their glass cages. Over the whole Olympic complex, the stadium roof suspended by wire hawsers from it, rears the Leaning Tower. The height of a sixty-storey skyscraper, it's a futuristic architectural wonderwork, a long-necked immense creature emerging from the shell of the Biodome. Snowsqualls and sastrugi are bickering across its concrete as the outside funicular rises to the top. From here, the view is among the great sights of the urbanised world, glittering today and simplified under a blue sky and a coverlet of snow. A raven-haired, beautiful woman points down at the Biodome, hugs her companion, and exclaims, 'That is cool! That is just so cool!'. Traffic pulses in and out of the city. Its towers counterbalance but do not dominate the wooded mass of Mont Royal – the city's own mountain and park – above. The two rivers that make Montreal into an island gleam in the sunset and beyond is Canada's endless spread of prairie and forest. I'm captivated. It's like a stay on another planet – one of the truly endearing, sexy, exciting places of the cultured world.

ARCTIC FRACTALS

In 1998 the Daily Telegraph *and the Canadian High Commission sent me on a long trip around the High Arctic to write about aspects of the secession the following April from Canada's North West Territories of the new Inuit homeland of Nunavut. The spare and austere beauty of the Arctic was a revelation and entrancement. These are three of the pieces the experience produced:*

1: Watching narwhal on the Brodeur Peninsula

Simon Karminik tried to sell me a dog. It was a very handsome, friendly dog and it was squatting on its haunches on the gravel shore of Arctic Bay, watching the tide roll a caribou leg-bone with meat attached around in the shallows. I liked this dog, and Simon didn't want much money for it – 300 Canadian dollars, maybe, and at the rate they were falling, if I held out for a day or two that would be the price of a hamster in Britain. But it wasn't viable.

'Come on, Simon,' I asked, 'what use is a husky to me?'

Simon's a hunter as well as a musician and carver. He plays Scottish reels his grandfather learnt from the whalers on his accordion, and shapes whalebone and soapstone into iconic cultural figurines, shamanistic creatures. He had his head on one side, gap-toothed grin and a hunter's narrow-eyed look:

'Husky's a good dog if you get chased by polar bear.'

I pointed out that the nearest polar bear to where I lived was 70 miles away in a zoo. He shook his head. The *qallunaat* – white people – were strange. Wouldn't buy a good dog but kept Nanuq as a pet. One had walked down the main street of Arctic Bay two days before. It had ambled into town and the children, 30 or 40 of them banging lids and hooting and blowing, had chased it right back out again whilst the mothers and fathers looked on with wary smiles from every porch, rifles cradled in their laps.

'No polar bear, hey?'

'No polar bear.'

'Caribou? Seal? Musk-ox?'

My turn to shake my head.

'Hey, what d'you get to eat then where you live?'

He was convulsed with laughter, stopped, became serious again.

'What d'you want to see?'

'Narwhal.'

'Narwhal? You want to eat maqtaaq ? No?'

I grimaced. I'd tried maqtaaq – whale skin with blubber still attached – after the beluga hunt at Resolute Bay. The community were cutting up the carcases on the beach. I was filming. The Inuit eat it raw. It's a delicacy. The man I was filming held out a lump of white hide the size of half a Mars bar and watched as I chewed. It was a challenge, a joke. The Inuit eat it not like that but in thin strips. It was still warm, tasted like fishy hazelnuts fried in industrial grease and is ten times richer in vitamin C than oranges. I know how the anaconda feels when it's swallowed its pig. Simon cut across the memory:

'Esau'll take you out to see narwhal.'

Esau Tatatoapik came round to the hotel later. He was slighter and darker than Simon, with high cheekbones, chiselled features, less given to the wild laughter. He'd been a policemen at the RCMP posts around these arctic communities but the strain had told and now he was in charge of the Hunters' and Trappers' Organisation here, 500 miles above the Arctic Circle at the northernmost settlement on Baffin Island.

'We'll just go out for a drive maybe and look around.'

We climbed into Esau's pickup, drove past Dead Dog Lake and down to the summer camp in Victor Bay. Arctic Bay's a new settlement. In the summer months Inuit families return to the nomadic, go out on the land again. I interviewed Jack Anawak, Chief Minister of the Interim Government of Nunavut a few weeks later. He'd just come back from his holidays. He and his family had been out by boat from Rankin Inlet to Repulse Bay for three weeks, living on the land. The outboard motor had seized. Did he want to be rescued? No way! He'd stripped the engine down, got it started again. Imagine what Tony and Cherie would do if the Galaxy people-carrier broke down in Tuscany?

Here at Victor Bay there were kids playing baseball whilst others stalked seals with .22 rifles and long sights. Women using the traditional scooped *ulu* – the woman's knife – were scraping the fat from the skins of arctic foxes and a smell of boiling seal meat hung round the tents. Scalloped and glistening little icebergs with turquoise meltpools on their tops floated in the sea. We'd been brought here to see the *qamutiq* – the long wooden sled, its 20-foot nylon-faced runners salvaged from Nanisivik Mine timber – that Esau towed behind his skidoo each spring out across the ice of Admiralty Inlet to the floe edge at Cape Crawford. And there you could see polar bear, beluga, walrus as the ice broke up and the thawing margins of Lancaster Sound began to teem with life. Maybe we'd see narwhal tomorrow, Esau thought.

So at some time after midday, which is an artificial concept in a place where there's no summer night, Esau came round to the Enokseot Hotel for coffee. There is always coffee in arctic hotels. Sleep's the variable. In Arctic Bay, the coffee-bar for teenagers opens at midnight. What's time or distance in this place? It's how many gallons of gas it takes to get you out to where the seal or the narwhal are. Would we see narwhal today? Esau was gazing out of the window across the landlocked bay that's called Iqpiarjuq – the pocket – in Inuqtituq. When he spoke, it came out breathy and soft and a little distant:

'It might be OK. Maybe we'll go out for an hour, take a look. Don't know how far we'll get.'

He turned his head, shot me an appraising look, eyebrows raised. Did I understand, it asked, that in this environment the certainties of life in the soft and populous south are put aside and in their place, if you want to survive here as the Inuit have done for centuries, you attune to the tentative, the wary, the provisional? Here, man is both hunter and hunted, and he is infinitely small. We made our way down to the boat. It was a little white Lake Winnipeg boat with twin Yamaha 90s mounted on the back and a hundred-gallon oil drum jammed between plastic fuel containers as the gas tank. Minutes later we nosed out into Adams Sound, its surface unrippled. Beneath the 800-foot-high St George's Society cliffs a boat was drifting. We motored across to it. An old hunter with a rifle at the ready on the gunwale was boiling a kettle for tea. He passed a grimy cup over to us. He and Esau talked. We headed out towards the mouth of the sound. In front was 20 miles of deep, open water – Admiralty Inlet, funnelling every breath of wind from the northern ice, on its farther side the pale bluffs that ringed the Brodeur Peninsula – Baffin's furthermost and uninhabited west. Esau's eye was on them:

'I like it over there.' He spoke with slow emphasis. 'My father used to take me. It's my favourite place.'

He opened the throttle, leaving a creamy arc of wake across turquoise water. That eager crossing took an hour. From time to time Esau would gesture at patches of disturbance maybe a mile, maybe two miles away in the flat calm:

'Narwhal!'

Maybe this was all I was going to see of 'the most extraordinary of all living mammals', the unicorn of the sea, the most magical and legendary of all living things, haunting presence of medieval bestiaries, the corpse-whale – so-called from the colour of its grey and mottled flesh, the creature of the arctic deep, the animal about which Barry Lopez wrote in *Arctic Dreams* that 'we know more about the rings of Saturn than we know about the narwhal'.

We landed on the peninsula, on a beach of splintered and rackety stone beneath the cliffs. All along it were the broken cairns of Inuit meat caches. Esau sat, patient, hands in lap, and watched the water. We talked a little. He told me how the pods of narwhal would sweep past the floe-edge at Cape Crawford at the break-up of the ice on their migration down from the North Water into Lancaster Sound, and I responded by drifting around the European cultural texture: the horn's power to raise the dead, prevail against the devil and poison, subdue epilepsy, cure scurvy, ulcers, dropsy, gout, coughs, consumption, fainting fits, rickets, melancholy, the Green Sickness and obstructions, its capacity to fortify the noble parts and resist injury from an unsound bedfellow, its use by Torquemada and Luther; and then Esau touched a finger to my wrist and to his lips, pointed at the water, and rolling past, a pod of 20 of the small whales, ten yards offshore in the clear sea, the uncanny straight tusk of spiral-patterned ivory pointing skyward as they leapt, clacking like wooden staves as they met in ecstatic, maritime dance. As suddenly as they had come, they were gone and we were alone on the deserted shore again, Esau watching the patterning of ripple and shade across the water, concentrating suddenly and intensely on a dark stain spreading across the inlet from the north:

'Black water! We have to go now. We have to go fast.'

The return crossing took three hours, battling, the wind rising, spray lashing the boat, fuel running out before we were running into the shelter of Adams Sound again. We might not have made it. Visions cost.

2: The Franklin Graves on Beechey Island

We first saw the whales out beyond the point from Resolute Bay. In the translucence of arctic water, grey cloud above and dark gravel below, they were shimmery, an ethereal white, breaking the surface, swirling through the shallows right beneath us, heading for the back of the bay – a pod of beluga maybe 60-strong. We watched entranced.

'Don't get too attached.'

A young Inuit stood behind us. He was dressed in yellow padded jacket and rubber boots, carried a rifle. We'd not heard him approach.

'You *qallunaat* ...' – he gave the Inuqtituq word for white people a nasal edge, as though clearing his sinuses – '... you don't like to see animals die, and most of those guys gonna be dead soon.'

He walked off across the raised beach to his quad bike, started it up and slewed back towards the village from which we'd come. Already, in the back of the bay, the activity was frenetic. Boats were being dragged down shingle into the water, outboards were starting up, a covey of quad bikes raced along the shore. Terry looked at me, shook her head, and we drove slowly back, gunfire already in our ears. The boats trapped the pod close inshore, sped in and out among the little white whales. From boat and beach the shooting was incessant, merciless. Even youngsters of seven or eight lanced round after .303 round into wallowing targets, gouts of dark blood spreading from them into crimson wakes. It takes a lot of bullets to kill a whale, and all the while it cries thinly, like a child in confusion and pain. An hour later there were 20 corpses being flensed and butchered along the shore. I watched one family. The father paused for a moment and, with a hand bloody from groping among the whale's viscera, cut off and handed to me a piece of *maqtaaq*. He gestured me to eat.

Resolute Bay is up above the Barrow Strait on Cornwallis Island at 75 degrees north. The hotel Terry Jesudasen runs here is a haven in a location harsh and barren as anywhere in the polar desert. I'd missed a flight because of fog – an occupational hazard of travelling in the High Arctic – and there wouldn't be another for days, so she was showing me around. We'd been out to a thousand-year-old Thule site by the point, where she'd found a sliver of bone, weathered to the grainy texture of ancient wood, with a hole drilled through it – a needle, maybe, for stitching skins, or an arrowhead. She'd turned it over and over in her hand, speculating on its usage, on the lives of the people of the former time. If the climate for the Thule people a millennium ago was as it is now, there was plenty to wonder at.

There's plenty to wonder at, too, in Resolute's recent history. Inuit families from Baffin Island and Northern Quebec were relocated here in September 1953, in tents at the onset of the High Arctic winter. It was a time when the Canadian government was uneasy both about the openness of its northernmost frontier, and the perceived internal problem of its indigenous peoples. Although never officially admitted, the notion of – as one commentator had it – 'using the Inuit as human flagpoles', and removing them to a place where far greater control over influences upon them could be exercised was, to the government of the time, an attractive one. In those who endured its imposition, it produced a palpable resentment that finds continuing expression in matters like the flaunting of official quotas during the beluga hunt. I could have looked on at that as an eco-tourist, observing the proper pieties, being duly appalled. But to have done so would have been an inadequate response. It would have been to disregard the manner in which ethnic control on such wantonness has itself been destroyed.

None of this makes Resolute Bay an easy place to visit. The High Arctic can be very beautiful, but it's a bleak, inhuman, abstract beauty, best appreciated, maybe, from the distanced comfort of an eco-lodge or a cruise-ship. The only tourists who come here are the wealthy, the curious, or the exceptionally adventurous. People do not seem quite to belong. Even the icily preserved evidence of the Thule site seems temporary, insubstantial. I was glad to escape from the bay settlement to Pete Jess' place out by the airfield. Jess is an arctic enthusiast, with an infectious delight in the history and wildlife of its barrenlands. His current obsession is with the fate of Sir John Franklin's expedition that set sail from Britain in 1845, with two ships and 129 officers and men, to attempt to discover the North West Passage.

The Franklin expedition is one of the great tragic events in the history of exploration. It scarcely ranks as a mystery. Too many fragments of evidence exist for it to attain that status: bones, belongings, equipment, a note found in a cairn, Inuit oral testimony. Even as late as 1993 the skeletal remains of eleven of Franklin's sailors, one of whom would have been no more than a boy when the expedition set sail, were discovered on King William Island. The speculative literature raised on these incomplete foundations is vast, but none of it is conclusive. One of the few things that can be said with certainty is that the story continues to exert as potent an imaginative power now as it did to generations who witnessed the Admiralty and private searches for survivors and proof that were despatched, with huge rewards as their incentive, to the High Arctic in the decades after Franklin's disappearance. Over dinner, Pete Jess talked me through all this and his own theories about where the wrecks of Franklin's two ships, Erebus and Terror, were likely to be found. And then, casually, he suggested that next day if there were a break in the cloud we might fly up to Beechey Island.

Beechey is a craggy promontory on the south-west corner of Devon Island, 60 miles east of Resolute across Wellington Channel. Of all the Franklin sites scattered across the High Arctic – Victory Point, Cape Crozier, The Boat Place, Starvation Cove – it is Beechey that has been focus of most attention in recent years. The first traces of Franklin were found here in 1850, the graves of three of his men included. In the 1980s these graves became briefly famous on the publication of a tendentious and distasteful bestseller that published photographs and described the exhumation and autopsying of perfectly preserved corpses from them. The authors attributed the failure of Franklin's expedition to contamination of its tinned food by lead solder: 'None could have known that inside the tins stored in the ship's hold there ticked a timebomb that helped not only to deny Franklin his victory, but to steal away 129 brave lives.' There was, it should be said, rather more to it than that, and the whole body of evidence provides many contradictions to this assertion. But Beechey was still one place I wanted to see, and next day I was on my way.

The noise and motion of a Twin Otter landing on a shingle strand beggar belief. You break through this sound barrier and step out of the plane into a quiet broken only by wind, wave and your own footsteps. And the latter impel you towards the graves. There are four of them, in a broken row. Three are from the early months of 1846, when Franklin wintered here, and one is that of a seaman from a search expedition of 1854. The weathered wooden headboards have been removed to a Canadian museum and replaced with exact fibreglass replicas. Modern white headstones reiterate their inscriptions ('Sacred to the memory of John Hartnell, AB of HMS Erebus, died January 4th, 1846 aged 25 years. 'Thus saith the Lord of Hosts, consider your ways.' Haggai, i ,7.'). The disturbed graves have been restored. Slabs of shale, orange lichen upon them the only splash of colour in this muted landscape, weight their surfaces. From them I walked the mile along finely graded shingle of a curving beach to the ruins of Northumberland House, built as supply depot by a Franklin search expedition of 1852–4. There are various memorials around it, some decrepit, one from the present Prince of Wales. Scattered around, too, are rusted tins, barrel hoops and staves, coal – the wistful detritus of wasted effort and empty hope. After a while, mindful of the two polar bears heading in this direction that we had flown over, I turned back for the plane. The little white gravestones ahead of me stood out stark from the soft blues and greys, the crouching land-forms of the arctic. Their occupants were the lucky ones; for their companions, loss, hardship, confusion, cannibalism, starvation. The hardiest, tracking to and fro, back and forth in a cruel landscape maybe for as long as five years, made it out of the Arctic Archipelago to the mainland coast four hundred miles to the south before they, too, perished. The echo of that travail amidst this huge and implacable emptiness lends Beechey an unbearable poignancy. The Twin Otter lurched into the air, we banked over the graves, and left them once more to their silence.

3: *Arctic State of Mind*

Three hours and 1,300 miles north of Ottawa, way out beyond the 60th parallel, the FirstAir jet leaves the shield edge of northern Quebec behind and begins its descent. The Hudson Strait beneath is a cold azure that tints and gleams through great drifting blocks of ice. A spit of brown, crumpled land is Meta Incognita – southern peninsula of Baffin Island – its detail entirely textural, its scale inhuman. The plane glides in and touches down on the tarmac at what appears to be a cross between shanty town and industrial estate, set at the back of a long bay. This is Iqaluit, capital of Canada's new territory of Nunavut, that came into being on the first of April, 1999. It's the Inuit homeland, comprises one-fifth of the land-mass of the second-largest country on earth, extends over more than three-quarters-of-a-million square miles – well over half of it within the Arctic Circle – and has a population of under 25,000, of whom 85 per cent are Inuit.

As a tourist destination, Nunavut is hugely problematical. It is difficult of access, expensive, in thrall to the elements, and yet, perhaps because of all these, it is also uniquely appealing. The artist Nature often achieves greatest effect when not working with a full palette. When you've grown weary of the density and mind-clutter of landscapes more or less familiar and want something simpler, more abstract; if you're an ethno-tourist intent on witnessing at first hand the Inuit journey back from subjugation and degradation to self-determination and cultural pride; if you're an eco-tourist seeking out some of the most spectacular – and dangerous – wildlife on the planet; or if you're simply a traveller with a taste for the farthest-flung, here are your Arctic dreams.

The high, brief Arctic summer is the surest time for travel around an archipelago that stretches virtually to the North Pole. Iqaluit, population about 4,000 and growing, two or three decent hotels, Arctic char, musk-ox and inventively-sauced caribou steak on the menu in their restaurants, has most of the amenities that a new administrative capital might require. There are no surfaced roads, but why would they be needed when they'd be under snow for nine or ten months of the year? When I arrived, grubby globes of bog-cotton waved in ditches and the Arctic fireweed flamed across every patch of waste ground. Even the easy wind of summer had a cold crystal edge, and rococo-sculpted little icebergs clustered along the beach where boats with hefty Yamaha-outboard horsepower were heaved up and the dog-teams of winter lay sullen and chained among scraps of seal carcasses. Just back from the shore a copper-sheathed Arctic ketch, that had left Newfoundland in the 1890s and butted its way through the small ice of Frobisher Bay, had been hauled out to fall apart slowly, desiccated planks springing in this cold desert climate.

I flew on to Pangnirtung, a sea-dependent, self-contained community of 1,200 in a steep-sided fjord setting on the east side of Baffin 150 miles north of Iqaluit. The tiny Beechcraft 99 juddered round in the tightest arc on updraughts against thousand-foot cliffs to land on a gravel strip built up through the centre of the town. Up-fjord there was a mist-wreathed suggestion of huge cliffs, snow-peaks. Crated skidoos were piled behind the Northern Store (formerly the Hudson's Bay Company Store), with its Kentucky Fried Chicken and Pizza Hut concessions. Boats rocked at their moorings. Along the shoreline the granite had split off and weathered like stacks of round cakes. In the television lounge of Pangnirtung's single hotel, the Auyuittuq Lodge, the accountants, the construction workers, the conservationists ate their way through mountainous plates of cookies and crowded round the screen as it fed an unremitting diet of Stateside pap, soap and chat. Taking refuge among the merely bodily vices of the smoker's lounge, I talked to Susan Black, daughter of the former Anglican missionary here, educational adviser and fluent Inuqtituq-speaker, and asked about her flight in the previous day:

'Oh, we were all hollerin' and yellin' – it was a real Pangnirtung Screamer.'

I winced at the memory. Next morning Peter Kalebik called for me. He was to take me out to the former whaling station at Kekerten, now preserved as a historic park. But as we nosed out into Cumberland Sound in his Lake Winnipeg boat, the slamming of the waves was as turbulent as the air had been. We turned back, headed inland and up-fjord towards the Auyuittuq National Park. This is Arctic Canada's most obviously spectacular location, its huge granite walls a magnet for the more adventurous rock-climber. At the narrows of the fjord, ten miles from Pangnirtung, Peter gestured across at a tiny wooden cabin no bigger than a modest garden shed, anchored with stone and wire behind a sheltering moraine promontory:

'As a child, I would live there with my parents from October through to December, while my father worked the traplines. He traded fox furs to the Hudson's Bay Company for food, ammunition and clothes. My mother didn't like life in the cabin – too hard for her, too lonely. You see that peak?'

He pointed at a high, rocky peak with a peculiarly hooked profile above the hut:

'It's called "cold peak, bent over with arse sticking out" in Inuqtituq. And the one next to it?'

I nodded.

'That's "cold peak, doubled up like woman with period pain holding belly".'

The grin on Peter's face suggested he was making a cultural point. And they certainly seemed more imaginative and precisely descriptive names than the Thors and Asgards that European mountaineers had bestowed on peaks with no-doubt-equally-good Inuq names beyond. We turned back, an icy wind funnelling down the pass that led through the mountains and over to Broughton Island and chasing us home.

If you want dramatic mountain scenery then, Auyuittuq aside, you don't come to the Arctic. That much is obvious from the four-thousand-mile itinerary of Ottawa–Iqaluit–Nanisivik–Resolute Bay–Cambridge Bay–Yellowknife–Ottawa that FirstAir flies most days, weather permitting (a large proviso, this). You look down, and for hundreds of miles there is only the endless tundra, featureless more or less, frost-textured; there are only the crazed mosaics of ice fracturing out across an inky sea. As you descend across the Barrow Strait to the airstrip at Resolute Bay, the Poles – North and Magnetic – are just over there, for all you know in the scale of things up here. But in a sense there is nothing there: a moving point in an electro-magnetic field; another point fixed only by the determining power of mathematics, and marked by champagne bottles of tourists from commercially-operated, nuclear-powered Russian ice-breakers. In Inuqtituq, this whole region of polar ice is called *Kingmersoriartor-figssuaq* – the place where you only eat dogs. The Inuit do not go there. The poles are only for us, the distanced and uncomprehending, who need to assert the abstract power of number over the flux.

Yet if you come down into the landscape, it has a spare and startling beauty. I set off across the tundra, into the arctic desert, on a borrowed quad-bike from the settlement of Iqaluqtuutiaq – a name that means 'fair fishing place' in Inuqtituq – on Victoria Island, where most of Franklin's men died. The track crossed the river, curved round the cemetery-topped drumlin with its errant white crosses and slabbed and frost-heaved graves, and headed out towards the hill of Uvayok. A white banner of dust trailed behind me and a long-tailed skua (called a parasitic jaeger on this western side of the Atlantic – a sea-bird that thinks it's a hawk) hunted after ground squirrel that the sound of the ATV's engine sent fleeing on either side. There were 20 kilometres of rough track out to the foot of Uvayok. The cabins and camps thinned out and soon the only signs of humanity were the track and an occasional *inuqsuq* – a cairn shaped like a human and traditionally used to herd caribou towards the hunters' blinds. The little ATV bounced and skewed along merrily, its fat tyres sending the gravel skittering. At one point I saw a herd of musk-oxen far out across the tundra to the west and set off towards them for a closer look, dropping down into low ratio to grind across gravel ridges in a landscape where nature has managed only to blur here and there with a ribbon of green, and not mask, the abstraction of geomorphological yesterdays. They saw me coming, continued to graze unconcernedly – shaggy, primitive, great-horned beasts – but at the last moment, when I was 50 yards away, wheeled into defensive formation and I peeled hastily away, wondering what chance an ATV had on this terrain of outstripping a charging musk-ox. I kept to the track after that, and two hours of this jouncing space-time odyssey brought me to the foot of the hill.

A legend attaches to Uvayok and it runs like this: before death arrived on earth a race of immortal giants lived in the north of Qiiliniq. But one summer food was in short supply, the walrus and the bowhead whale had disappeared, so the giants set off towards the south. South took them farther from food, for to giants the caribou and musk-oxen that grazed on the tundra were like rats and mice and ground squirrel, not worth the effort of hunting. And so they starved. Uvayok was the largest of them. In time his body sank into the soil, subsided among the rocks. The sparse arctic grasses and the small flowers grew over him until only a rib showed through here and here and his great prone shape became the hill Uvayok. Lakes formed around it from the liquid that drained from his bladder on his death. So there are stories, even here, and some echoing substance too – a human dimension in those preoccupations with migration, starvation, the animals' changing pattern of presence, of absence. There are even more stories, built on these, more strange facts and resonances, but I didn't want these tales of cannibalism, of skilled hunters, of communities sharing the carcase of a single loon, of caches of carefully disarticulated loon bones. I wanted a naked, unpeopled world, wanted to reach the crest of an arctic hill, and this is how I went about it.

I don't know how high Uvayok is. In this landscape notational height is an absurd irrelevance. This hill is massive, recumbent, alone. I doubt if it's much more than 200 metres above sea-level. It dominates. It is a ribbed and sleeping giant. There is nothing complex here in terms of form – just a whaleback ridge rising out of flat shield country. The complexities are all of scale. And they are oddly contradictory when you first notice them, before their pattern emerges and takes on its own satisfying beauty through the lens of imagination.

I walked to the summit – a long, featureless slog up fractured stony slopes, the ground thawed billowy and summer-soft, surface litter of stone graded into parallel or polygonal abstractions and in among these are the life-tokens of the flashing summer at high latitude: scurry of a pair of snow-buntings, the minimal low plants crouched beneath a dry, harsh wind, a wind the chill of which even now in early August catches sharp in your lungs. The relict arctic-alpine vegetation of my Welsh home hills that I make a pilgrimage to view each spring – the saxifrages and sedums, the roseroot and mountain avens, the cinquefoils and grass-of-Parnassus and fragrant shield fern – shrinks in size, spreads in number here. Versions of other plants I recognise too: bog-cotton ever-moving, the polar willow, slender-shooted, its leaves a muted, dark and unassertive green. Only the lichens flourish, proliferate, their names expressing their contained and exquisite vigour: jewel lichen, map lichen, sunburst lichen. These seamed and flaky growths, slow-colonising, rustling out from dead and hollow centres in ages of infinite patience, these are the arctic hearts. I walked to the top of the hill. It was a long way and when I got there, a memorial reared up. A three-legged steel plinth bore a plaque to an Inuit regiment. Old bone from the caribou herds, honeycombed and grey, mottled, taking on the appearance of bleached and seasoned timber, lies everywhere with the mosses growing over it. Humanity's a stranger, an alien, among all this ice-scoured simplicity of form, this bareness. I'd found what I'd come to find – a place to look out into the ultimate wilderness, where there is no point, no objective, just space and a curiously uplifting sense of nature's design, of the fractal nature of physical earth that asserts matter as echoing, interlocking abstraction. However much your mind, your eye, expanded and roved across space, which here has the appearance of being infinite, always the same cleft and splintered forms you saw there were busily arranging themselves also in the contracted and immediate view, so that the stones at your feet, the lacustrine tundra, became one and the same and process of the slow ages argued both of them in its coherence and humans played no part, were truly an irrelevance among the austere beauty of this fractal universe.

I came down because you cannot live or stay up there, out there, and an Arctic hill is nowhere. The ATV started, careered away, after a mile coughed, stalled, coasted to rest. Ten miles at the very least from town and I was out of gas – that diversion to approach the musk-oxen was promising to cost me dear. I climbed off and searched around, discovered a reserve fuel tank switch, rattled the starter round till the engine fired and puttered into rhythm again and off I went. A couple of hundred yards farther on, round the next bend and over the next low ridge, I first caught sight of Sylvia.

She was standing by the side of the track across an entirely empty tundra, and she was thumbing a lift. I slowed down, mindful suddenly of how far it was to town on foot, superstitiously troubled by the bad karma of leaving her there. She was a small Inuit woman in a fur-trimmed parka, was maybe 30, her eyes distant behind spectacles, and she murmured *qallunaat* in a bemused way before climbing on behind.

All the way into town she clung on – curiously tightly, thighs pleasantly warm against my flanks, arms round my waist, head heavy at the back of my shoulder. Back in Iqaluqtuutiaq she directed me to her wooden house, gestured me inside urgently. 'No,' I said, 'I have to go back to the hotel.' She pulled at me and I gave in, went through the door into a decorous, comfortable room: a sofa, coffee-table, entertainment systems, children's photographs on the walls.

'Yours?' I asked.

'Yeah, three of them.'

She told me. Husband gone with them down to Saskatoon. She had tried it there, had left. But better for the children that they stay. She went to the kitchen, came back with a bottle of clear liquor and two glasses, filled one each, gave me one, clinked it with hers, swallowed hers at a gulp. I sipped and gasped, put down the glass. She had another.

'Kills the pain.'

She giggled the words at the wall, scanned the photographs, became vacant. 'I go out to Uvayok. It's empty there.'

When I went, she was already asleep on the sofa, eyes screwed tightly shut. Another door was ajar by the one through which I left, blinds drawn in the bare room, three small made-up beds on the floor.

In a noisy, radial-engined, pre-war Beaver float-plane I flew down from Iqaluqtuutiaq to land on Elu Inlet south of the Kent Peninsula. One afternoon I took a boat out, landed on a beach of fine sand. There was an old Inuit camp here – meat caches, stone fox-traps on the hill above, hut shelters. The roof of one of these latter was a slab of silvery, fine-grained granite furred with black lichen. Balancing it, locked in place, throwing the slab's weight precisely across the angle of a cliff-edge, was a pebble of rose quartz maybe half-an-inch square. It was so deliberately and poignantly positioned, so redolent of human ingenuity in an exigent landscape, that it lodges in my memory still. A day later I flew south to Yellowknife. In the Cave Bar a band rapped out Country-and-Western standards, couples danced. The men hugged their plump women, who in turn cast fond, forbearing looks over their paunchy, moustachioed Romeos. Outside, it was late August, twilight, this extremity of the earth tilting away from its encounter with the sun, the shadow cascading down, the northern winter clawing back into its long ascendancy.

Changing Places

My emotional allegiance throughout my life having been strongly to the political left, travelling around countries and regions where those beliefs formerly held, or still hold sway, has often been a challenging experience. Whether it's in the perceived gap between ideology and reality; or in the way that former ideologies are supplanted by vaunted freedoms that themselves have darker aspects; or even in the way that an old, enduring nation shrugs off yet another imposed system as though it were an irritant in its pelt, to visit these places is always an absorbing exercise.

1: Cuba: Confronting the Negative

Early morning at Heathrow, with a long and disjointed flight to Cuba in prospect, the thing that captures my attention is the oddity of the check-in queue. A requisite assertive neurotic demands a seat proximous to an exit. There are a very few excited, resort-bound couples, gel-haired, fat-novel-bearing. And there are two other defining categories: beautiful young black women, well-dressed and flashily bejewelled, accompanied by middle-aged and unremarkable white husbands; and lone holidaying men. My antennae quiver.

A few days later, at a table next to me in Havana's Restaurant Hanoi sit two American journalists. One is an assured woman of a certain age, extravagantly coiffured, in a print dress, cardigan and sandals. She talks loudly, incessantly, titters when she mentions bullet holes and evidence of torture from Batista's regime. The other stares blankly ahead, scribbles occasionally in a notebook, chops from time to time at her rice and black beans, uncomfortable as if aware of what it means to be an American in Cuba. They have as guest at their table a government official: 'No, ladies,' he proclaims, 'there is nothing much wrong on the streets of Havana. I assure you our police are not here in response to a crime wave. A few small problems, maybe – too many taxi drivers who take their fares in dollars on which they don't pay their taxes – but there is nothing much else, and certainly nothing for you to worry about.'

He straightens a lapel, lifts his chin, allows an authoritative smile to travel across yellow walls, open rafters, blue woodwork. No challenge rises from the bowed heads of the other diners, no hint of a smirk across averted faces. Sound of children at play in the square outside drifts in upon us. I finish my rice and scrawny chicken, step outside and join them. A pimp standing with two women, one of them days from giving birth, catches my eye, wags a finger from one to the other in quizzical invitation. Havana, I'm rapidly finding out, is no place for this lone male tourist. The door of the church in the Plaza del Cristo is open so I enter for brief sanctuary. Inside a congregation of the halt, the sick and the old process around the Stations of the Cross in pre-Easter Mass. An affable fat priest chews on the Host and joshes his flock. The pillars that decorate either side of the nave are precast concrete pipes from ragged holes in which electrical wires trail. Sacred music's tinning out of a cheap mini-system. Christ's blood barely streams in this firmament. I forego the sacrament, walk back down mean streets towards my hotel on Parque Centrale.

On the way, Heriberto leaps down from the bonnet of a Lada taxi to accost me. He's a dapper little black guy in a white shirt. I lapse into defensive mode. There are at least two policemen observing our encounter, and the word is that visitors and residents must not talk:

'No taxi, no chicas, no cigars ...' I rattle out at him, hand raised. He reaches to slap my open palm in a high five:

'So how about some conversation, man?' he rasps. 'Where you from? What you doin' in Havana ..?'

We sit under the statue of a hero of some forgotten revolution, I breathe easily again, and send to a bar for cans of Mayabe, the malt-rich staple Cuban beer. The policemen lounge in doorways, hands in pockets, eyeing the passing girls, showing not an iota of concern for our dialogue. Which is fortunate, given the part they play in it.

'These police guys, they're just country boys, provincials. They're all from Santiago and they're out of their depth, into every little racket ...'

Heriberto talks on, interrogates me about attitudes towards his country, thirsts for outside knowledge, tells me he earns 12 dollars a month as a teacher in Habana Vieja – 'tough kids, good kids, streetwise!' – in a run-down, under-resourced school with classes of 30 and over. He tells of how, for all the problems brought about in his country by external agencies – the USA's Burton-Helms legislation, its associated effect in the cancellation of Russian subsidies – for him it is the only place, and it's booming. Look at all the new construction and tasteful renovation going on in Havana. Look at the investment in tourism here from Canada and France. He lectures me like a patriot, yet extracts a promise that I should send him British newspapers, American news magazines to leaven the revolutionary propaganda he's fed and recognises and sees a legitimate purpose in but shrugs off amusedly every day. Heriberto provides a counterbalancing positive to a city experience that might seem too entirely predicated on hustlers of all varieties, and the glib and vitiating range of response contact with them allows. He gives me a lot to think about. I'm thinking about it when I run into Jesus in the bookshop on Obispo next morning. He wears Ray-Bans, Levis, a polo shirt, asks for an extempore English lesson, offers to guide me round the city, the country even, says he's a teacher from Matazas, up in town for the Easter vacation to coax some dollars from the tourists and supplement his Government salary. I buy him a couple of Mayabes in a pavement bar with a struggling band:

'Their rhythm,' Jesus informs me, 'is very contentious.'

The rhythm of Jesus' approach is building along with the day's heat. The beat of his story's laid down like a slow waltz: divorce, women's selfishness, his daughter's need for a new pair of shoes. There's a weariness in the presentation, an over-rehearsedness. I lure him on to state of the nation. He briefly holds a line on good things coming from the revolution: education, health care. But communism, he wails, isn't working here. The party officials live in castles, drive round in Mercedes while the people are very poor – very, very poor. This Tocquevillean line he's running sets me thinking of people living on the bank of the Ganges in Varanasi, owning nothing but a cooking pot, dying of TB, without money to pay for medicines even for their children. I scan round the Plaza de la Catedral, see healthy, well-dressed, well-fed Cuban people everywhere, mention it:

'Ah yes, my friend, but teachers are leaving teaching, doctors are leaving the hospitals, professors the universities. Their children go without shoes, like mine. They leave to work in bars and restaurants and hotels for tips that are three or four times their salaries. Maybe a heart-surgeon carried your bag to your room. What you see of our country's wealth is not real. It comes back to Cuba from those who escaped to Miami – 900 million dollars a year. American dollar is what we need.'

I don't query the statistic, give him five dollars instead and slip away. He's tired of working the dollar-face, exasperated at the sense that his chisel's hitting a resistant seam. I've no idea whether his story was true or not. All I know is that he's told it before too many times in a town where everyone has something to sell, whether it be cigars, roses, paper twists of peanuts, sex or their own private sorrow. So many stories, so many demands. Later, I drift up the Prado – the tree-lined, marble-terraced boulevard that runs from Parque Central down to the Malecon and the sea. Two etiolated ducks quack from the balconied, decaying elegance of a neoclassical slum. The house next door has fallen down. Across the next junction an immaculate Chevrolet Bel-Air draws up outside the Palace Matrimonial and a couple emerge, the bride swathed in yards of white tulle, to sweep past another couple – she 16 and pregnant in a faded blue dress – who wait their turn at the foot of the steps. It's ostentation and exigence in one of their habitual Havana conjunctions. The visual impact of this city, ranging from architectural elegance to the most abject decay, is enthralling, overwhelming. But as a tourist you range among it as one of the hunted, as prey, able to glimpse it only in moments of respite, seldom afforded even the slightest view into the lives of the ordinary people who inhabit and for the most part thrive here – new hospitals, immaculately uniformed schoolchildren, impressively high statistics of literacy and continuing education comprise one aspect of Cuba's social reality.

I head on down to Parque Centrale, sit outside the Hotel Inglaterra. Crocodiles of small schoolchildren in bright red skirts and short pants with crossover braces wind by. Around the bulbous silver trunks of the palm trees opposite, under the admonitory white marble finger of Jose Marti, watched by a woman police officer, notebook in hand, a constant hundred or so men swarm, cacophonous, gesticulatory, striking mighty unfocused blows, names drifting out of their discourse and into my recognition: Mark Maguire, Babe Ruth, Joe DiMaggio. Two of them detach, walk across the street, talk to me over the barrier. I shake Julio's hand. He winces. He has an abscess between his fingers, needs a couple of dollars for folk medicine. Rafael is just poor and hungry. His brother's in Miami, but never writes – or at least, it never gets here. How could it? Then Magda arrives, takes a seat. She waves the men away. Her assurance is breathtaking. She gestures to her face, asks if I think her pretty. She is. She slily hoists up her skirt. I look away, sigh, hold up my hand, tap my ring. She smiles, nods, tells me she's married too but no matter. Tonight we shall go dancing at the Café de Paris and she'll arrange it so that afterwards I can stay at her place. I have just met this woman, have given her no encouragement. These are the first words we are exchanging. My notion that she's a prostitute seems mistaken. She tells me she's a secretary. She's just sexually confident, straightforward about what she wants. But it comes across as hustling. And it compounds. The significance of those lone men at Heathrow begins to dawn. I buy Magda coffee. She tells me she's hungry, points to a display of cakes. I give her money for them. She smiles at me engagingly as she puts the change unbidden into her handbag. I turn the conversation to economics:

'Ah, Cuba – mucha problemes!' She laughs gaily, as though whatever those problems were, they do not affect her. I pay the bill, make a polite farewell, break for the safety of my hotel to regain faith and enjoy some privacy. Magda follows. As I'm mounting the stairs I glimpse her by reception. Money passes across. In my room, the phone's ringing. I shut the door again, take the elevator to the rooftop bar, look over the skyline of this strangest, most compulsive, in some ways most repellent of cities.

What can you say about it when your experience as an ordinary tourist here is so pressured, the pleadings of the people who fasten upon you often so apparently desperate? Surely it cannot all be thus, and what you're experiencing is a kind of legislated divorce, born of necessity, from the real population? The cultural texture is vibrant – 'music in the cafés at night and revolution in the air'. The colonial architecture's an inexhaustible fascination. It rears up against a gunmetal sea and a hazed sky, imposes on that plain wash a texture so weird that the tribes of heavenly appearance who throng its streets might have dowsed hell in sunshine to create it. The operative principle is entropy. Everything here is in decay. Shadow it and you might think it was the blackened, molar stumps of Dresden after the firestorm. But there is no shadow here, and the people are gay. Plaques of stucco peel from crumbling brick, sewage weeps into the streets, pneumatic drills sound from every alley as construction imposes its thin new veneer, washing flutters in squalid stairways, wrought iron and ornate plaster rust and crack, Spanish, ecclesiastical-baroque and Soviet-functional styles jumble and the streetlife mills joyfully amongst it. I descend again. I want to see the *Musée de la Revolucion*, because for me all that ideology is what Cuba is about, is what has brought me here.

It's in the former Presidential Palace. On its marble staircase, above impassive busts of Marti, Juarez, Bolivar, Lincoln, bullet-holes pock the wall, date from the attempt by students to assassinate Batista in 1957. Elsewhere, slogans dominate: 'Memories, rejoicing, reflection, courage to continue the work! Let's travel together on the same path – the path of hope, the one that will definitively lead us to victory!' Three young Cubans in dreads and combat fatigues wander among them, brimming with gestural elation. I study old photographs: Che Guevara in all his long-lashed beauty, dead, a uniformed man inspecting his hair; a group of six revolutionaries from 1958, one of them bespectacled, wisp-bearded, reading a dog-eared volume of Jose Marti, another a young woman with the blank gaze of loss. In one room a video's playing Castro delivering the address at the opening of the Santa Clara memorial to Che. The camera lingers on the size of the crowds, on the emphatic, intimate way of speaking. Fidel's in his drabs, grown old, grey in his beard, but the stature impressive, features hewn from granite, flash of the eye still dangerously thrilling. Heads of police and soldiers who pass through the room swivel – particularly those of the women. I'm briefly revisited by that visceral appeal there once was for those of the political left in Britain at mention of Cuba, realise articles of faith are still at play here: Fidel as God the Father, Che the Son, Revolution the Holy Ghost. But it's run short of funds. The dollar's a more potent object of worship now. It buys bread.

Back in Parque Centrale, Caribbean clouds are building. The statue of Marti, so dazzling-white in the morning, has faded to a dull grey.

Raindrops blotch the pavements. Tourists hurry in under awnings, dimly conscious maybe that systems preaching principle and justice can only be undermined by the influx of manifest inequity. Water streams down through thick foliage of laurels above the baseball devotees, quenching their ardour, stilling all the frustration and pride of those extravagant strokes. I watch them disperse, and wonder about the potent, distressing country they inhabit. Its revolutionary fervour seems in its official expression to have dissipated into sloganeering. On the streets, those you are likely as a visitor to meet are both exponents and victims of a grasping material envy. Maybe the ideology of revolutions always peters out thus? It's over 30 years since Che left Cuba, to meet his death at the designings of the CIA. His image is everywhere, on every t-shirt and street corner countrywide. But his example's gone underground in this brave, vulnerable, resourceful little nation where Uncle Sam's subversive greenback's everyone's indiscreet object of desire, poised for the final counter-revolutionary coup. Havana, ultimately, leaves me harassed and depressed. I decide to head up-country to seek out some remnant of Cuba's uncorrupted elsewhere.

But to escape from Havana by road is a version of tasks set in nightmare. There are no signs or apparent thoroughfares. Geographical boundaries conspire to whirl you back into the innermost circle of urban hell. The only consolation is that Cuban drivers for the most part proceed at funereal pace (of necessity, since they drive immediate-post-war Detroit dinosaurs designed to run on seven litres of V8 and now mostly converted to 1200cc's of Lada power). If chance so wills, you pass the Nassau cruise ships towering over old Havana's tenement blocks, craze your way through divers junctions and Caribbean versions of council estates and perhaps eventually emerge on to Autopista One heading east. You know you've arrived by the crowds, and by the policeman who keeps them in check and makes sure they wait their turn. They're hitchhikers. If your car has a 'Particular Cuba' number plate he'll flag you down and fill it up – with people. If it has a 'Turismo' number plate you don't get coercion. You get moral pressure. Go past without stopping and the fists would be waving in the rear-view mirror. This is a communist country. The prevailing ideology says you share. So wherever you go, you have company. It's useful. Those roads – three or four lanes of white concrete in each direction heat-miraged across the endless plains – get lonely. The dark abbreviated crosses, fringed with a dirty white, of the turkey vultures circling overhead give you a sense that they're dangerous, too. There was the Buick Six with flapping wings reversing at speed down the fast lane, for example. The two men in it had decided to return for a particularly attractive hitchhiker a kilometre or so back. She was striking, but then, Cuban women so often are. I was looking at her as well, in the mirror. My newly-acquired passenger brought my attention back to the road. He grabbed the wheel. Just in time. We laughed. He was going to Santa Clara and so was I – 20 miles of midday heat in something called a Daewoo.

You go to Santa Clara out of revolutionary respect. This is *Ciudad Che* – Che City – home to the remains of *El Guerilla Heroica*, site of the decisive battle at which the revolution was won, and the place where Batista's forces surrendered to Guevara on 1 January, 1959. It's a dusty little hot town. I stay in the Hotel Santa Clara Libre. It's a green and poky concrete high-rise pitted with bullet holes from the last days of 1958 and the last stand of Batista's forces. From its rooftop bar you look down, as they must have done, on Parque Vidal. The bandstand's empty. A woman nurses a child and talks to a dreadlocked black youth under trees that shed orange and pink blossoms upon them. Marble pulses with heat. Afternoon bystanders and flower-sellers seek the colonnades of the Teatro La Caridad, where Caruso performed, and the Palacio Provincial. A flock of white doves gleams momentarily white against the tawny aridity and hazy distances of the plains. The hotel's water and electricity are off. In the restaurant Ramon, the old waiter, offers a rare take on the essential decency of the Cuban revolution: 'I never went to school. Before the revolution there were none for the poor people. But now, see, I can read and write.'

Ramon inspires me to visit the two significant memorials in Santa Clara. A rickshaw driver races me along alleys to the first, half a mile east of the town. It's called *Monumento a la Toma del Tren Blindado*. A little river winds beneath laurel trees, the railway cuts in dye-straight from the plain. Between them are five derailed wagons, a bulldozer on a plinth, and one of those assertive concrete memorials, all splayed fins and abstraction. The bulldozer cut the line. The train had 22 wagons, 408 soldiers, arms to reinforce the garrison. Che captured it with 18 men and a few rifles and that was the end for Batista's rule. A guard lazed in the shade and watched me in and out of the wagons. There are more slogans than guns in them now.

The other monument's west of town and it's magnificent. You see it from miles away, a huge statue atop a column, the ultimate expression of the Cuban cult of Che. He's urgent, forward-leaning, shaggy. This is Christ Militant with his hand on a gun and a grenade in his belt, idealism and a secular sanctity gleaming from a corona of beard and black curls. In a vault beneath is an eternal flame, and bas-reliefs of all the young altruists who died with Che in Bolivia: 'This,' my young Cuban guide tells me, 'is Tania!' She glows with pride at the female revolutionary example, and asks me for a dollar. I take the concreted road out of Santa Clara through the Sierra Escambray. Ken Livingstone wrote recently that it matches anything in the Himalayas. It doesn't. It threads through soft, wooded hills of oolite, valleys of rich red soil. The surface is dire, the surrounding jungle benign. You pitch out of the hills into Trinidad.

Most World Heritage Sites become victims of their own popularity. Trinidad hasn't quite suffered that fate yet. Its townscape bespeaks the colonial wealth of 200 years ago, its physical fabric surviving little-changed. It is wrought-ironed, red-tiled, pastel-painted, marble-trimmed, cobble-alleywayed, baroque-towered, and it looks down on to the Caribbean beaches a few miles away. Tourism's come to squat here among the grand and empty habitations on the hill from which the life of the town has drained away. Slowly the flaggings and museumisings and signpostings intrude, the souvenir-street-market of fine lace and crochet, cruder wooden carving, spreads along from the Plaza Mayor. Everyone has a cigar to sell, every cocktail's the most delicious, every palador (the restaurants in private houses which proliferate throughout Cuba) the best at which to eat. In the shade of the Taberna Canchachara the sightseers in for the day from Playa Ancon cosset their lunchtime bottles of Cerveza Nacionale and break into spontaneous applause as the solo drummer concludes each masterclass with a resounding 'cha-cha-cha'. But at five o'clock, a change: the coaches leave, people come out, bands play on the streets, in front of the houses clicking domino-schools gather, a lone saxophonist riffs and trills on his doorstep, doors open to afford glimpses into cool courtyards, the sun bronzes down into the Bay of Mexico, real dark floods through the streets. I eat in Carmen and Marun's palador. Myself and two Frenchwomen sit at an oilcloth-covered table whilst Carmen shuffles pots and frying pans on a small gas stove and serves up exotic fried vegetables, battered mysteries from the sea, on mismatched 1950s jazz-patterned crockery. Marun punctuates the meal with mangoes from a garden tree, flirts with the Frenchwomen. The woman who brought me here asks if I will need a chica – a woman, and by implication a sexually available one – after the meal. I decline. Marun tells her I am greedy, and want the Frenchwomen. They scowl a little wearily at him and harangue Cuban morals. Carmen takes my hand and firmly shows Marun the ring I'm wearing. He's unabashed, fondles one of the Frenchwomen, gets a sharp elbow in his ribs from her and a kick on the ankle from his wife, retreats into the night laughing at the ways of women. I pay eight dollars for lobster, beer, salad, floor-show, then wend back to my hotel. Next morning over leisurely breakfasts two enterprising widows from Esher in prints of muted lime and turquoise discuss quality of coffee and their history of hairdressers before sallying forth into town. I leave for Camaguey.

Cuba's third-largest city is famous for its pots. They're huge, made of terracotta, called *tinajones* and were meant to hold water, for this city of the plains is a dry furnace of a place. Nowadays they lounge about the colonial squares in signal fashion under the more urgent graffiti of the revolution: *'Morir por la Patria es vivir!' 'Confianza en el Futuro!'* – this latter illustrated by a cow, an orange as big as the pots, a factory, a tractor, a guitar. The mottos are no more grating than Harvard Business School mission statements. They just come in bigger, brighter letters. Camaguey itself is an indescribable architectural jumble strewn around courtyards of shadowy silence that hide behind shuttered windows, studded doors. Its main attraction, the Plaza of San Juan de Dios, is 18th-century colonial at its most simply picturesque, all pastels and colonnades and very quiet, for this is not a tourist town.

Nor is Bayamo, to which I drive on next day, and which impresses me more favourably perhaps than anywhere else I see in Cuba. Its centre is focused, elegant, local, river-bounded. The church of Santisimo Salvador on the Plaza del Himno Nacional has huge presence, dates from the 16th Century, is being restored. The custodian introduces me to a guide and refuses my reflex-action proffered dollars; the guide himself at the end of the tour only wants a limonado chico from a street stall. The pressure lifts. In balance, colour, harmony, the Plaza and the adjoining Parque Cespedes come to seem like an expression of the town's spirit instead of the more normal Cuban version of some ruin the 20th century happens to inhabit. Inside the church an apsal frieze – martial, vigorous and quite unspiritual – reminds that this is the place where the Cuban National Anthem was first sung:

> *Al combate corred, Bayameses ...*
> *No temais una muerta gloriosa,*
> *Que morir por la Patria es vivir ...*
> (Hasten to battle, men of Bayamo, / Do not fear a glorious death, /
> For to die for the fatherland is to live ...)

The town's peaceful these days. Mimosa petals drift across plaza and parque. In the cool of evening a stout, elderly black woman sweeps them into mounds with a besom. Girls tilt languorously across the carriers of bicycles, arms draped round the riders' waists. On the terrace of the Hotel Royalton I talk in French with a young black man, Henriques. He's a singer in a café, bestows on a policeman who's observing us a hard, rebellious stare:

'He's from Santiago,' he tells me, 'we take no notice of them here.'

Our conversation's drowned out by the arrival of Bud, a large, slack, loud American. I express surprise at meeting him in Cuba.

'Listen, my friend, there's no – read my lips – NO prejudice against Americans in Cuba. Ain't that right, Chico?'

The little man at his side nods, weight of a large arm round his shoulder.

'You limeys think the Cuban people all worship Che. You're wrong! They worship the mighty American greenback and I got plenty of those for what I want.'

He gives me a significant wink and eases himself behind a table next to a pretty young black man. Henriques, who's been following this with puzzlement, asks me if the American's here for the chicas? I tell him I think not, that his preference seems to be for boys. Henriques cranes round in open-mouthed astonishment, looks at me and laughs. I end up in Santiago next day. In the Taberna Dolores, Emilio and his sister Emilia seize on me, suggest a music club. Lured by her chiselled ebony beauty I say maybe, so long as I end up in my own bed, and then I drift downtown. The cathedral's an impeccable magnolia picked out in white, rests on a stained commercial plinth. The bay glitters down shabby, plunging streets, hills against the sunset beyond. Kids play baseball with scaffolding tubes and bottletops on the Padre Pico steps where Castro blazed off the opening rounds of his first offensive against Batista. A group of men in dirty vests perched all over a 1940s DeSoto hand the circulating rum-bottle down to me outside the municipal market where the plantains are piled high. At a snack bar on the wharves a beggar comes over, very old, very ill. I give him a dollar and the sandwich I've not begun.

'Viva Cuba!' he breathes.

Yes, but for how long ..?

2: *Downtown Hungary*

In the 14th district of Pest I sit in an early evening bar with garish wooden painted furniture. Trams clack through the dusk outside and the damp leaves fall as I talk to Ferencz Gyozo, poet and lecturer at Budapest's university. The waitress taps her pencil on the table, commanding orders:

'Barna,' I request from the menu, enjoying its pouting, plosive 'b', the roll of its 'r'. She smiles incredulously, lets loose a volley of words.

'She's scolding you for wanting peasant beer,' Gyozo explains, 'you're a Westerner – you can afford better.'

I tell him I chose it because I like the sound, receive this response:

'This name, Barna, was on what do you say? Balls for tennis table? When I was at school in the old days they were very strict. I remember the teacher taking one of these from me, her foot coming down. Phut!'

Reshaping the memory, his hands describe a form crumpled as the expression on his face. The beer arrives in tall bottles, the waitress pouring it with a coquettish, disapproving rock of the head.

'It means brown,' Gyozo says as I sample it, malty and porter-like under the froth.

'It means the gap,' I respond, 'in Irish,' and tell him of a place called Barna in the townland of Roundstone in Connemara, and a famine graveyard there with the low sun picking out quartz boulders on children's burial plots. In my memory they are puckered-white and grounded as his ping-pong ball.

'Here's to the birth of hope, then, and not its death,' Gyozo nods, an ache of a look in his eyes, 'and before you go, make sure you visit Lot 301.'

The tourist guides and magazine articles tell you time and again to cross the river, make for Buda, see the sights, but it's bad advice. Buda's overcrowded, over-decorated antiquities, its tour-touts, its neat cobbles, its hustlers and buskers and vendors frantically performing to a susurrus of Japanese video cameras synthesise its atmosphere into an approximation of any tourist destination anywhere in the world: Stonehenge, Inishmore, the Taj Mahal, Athens, Buda – they're all becoming the same commodity now. And in Buda, the distinguishing coordinate of these places has arrived:

interpretation boards, each one of which, wherever it's to be found, like cigarette packets with government health warnings ought to carry Susan Sontag's words from 30 years ago: 'Interpretation is the revenge of intellect upon the world.' From Buda on its sanitised, homogenised hill, what grasps and holds the attention is the street-web of Franz Josef's orderly, mercantile Pest across the yellow river below, fading out into the indistinctness and mystery of Zwischen-Europa – in-between-Europe – the swathe of plain and low hill, birch heath and beech forest which curves round from the Low Countries to follow the Danube down to the Black Sea, separating East from West. Along this arc workaday Pest, and not cryogenic Buda, is one of the great provincial and typical centres.

Also, it is strange. Without the familiarising apparatus of tourism, it lives its own life. The market hall at Fovam Ter by the Freedom Bridge gives a child's-spectrum view into it. Its wrought-iron balconies are crowded with snack-bars. Young mothers and pipe-smoking older women brood together, children of four or five (school doesn't begin until six in Hungary) run up and down or chew watchfully on the stalls' favoured delicacy of bread-and-dripping whilst at ground level, underneath the arch-girder-and-cat-walked ornateness, produce stalls brim with incandescent apples and capsicums, bunched carrots, swollen-fingered hands of maroon or white salami and wheels of yellow-waxed cheese to remind you that, despite the balance-of-trade deficit so obvious around the wealthier boulevards, Hungary's is still an agrarian economy.

The planes here shift disconcertingly: above Vaci Utca's glitter of jewellers and boutiques, grimed ashlar's raked and scarred by bullet and shell. In flashback I see a sardonic joke in Szabo Istvan's film *Dear Emma, Sweet Böbe*, Emma's eyes lighting on a volume of Rosa Luxembourg in the window of a fur shop. This is a version of Bond Street, for heaven's sake, yet it bears the insignia of uprising. In Habsburg coffee-houses Americans bray for iced tea and compare notes on hotel hairdryers whilst lap-topped Western sharp-suits hammer out figures with a flourish. Above bright façades, stone wounds crumble and flake. In courtyards of the Jewish quarter by Astoria children bike and hurl and shrill, and no-one is old. Between tall, hunched buildings which would not be out of place in the centres of Birmingham or Manchester, an extraordinary gaiety's abroad.

Gipsy bands – Andro Drom, Kalyi Jag ('Black Fire') – perform music of furious intensity to dark people; jugglers toss flaming sticks; boisterous gangs of pick-pockets by the Opera bring a sadistic, jostling hilarity to their crime; at night the streets come alive, doors to the subterranean world of cellar restaurant, club and bar open, the ghosts of Patrick Leigh Fermor's phantasmagoria reaffirm themselves: '... the scintillating cave of the most glamorous night-club I have ever seen. Did the floor of the Arizona really revolve?' But not in acrobats and elephants and snowy steeds, as when he visited in 1934; rather in the animation of people who've emerged with his attitude towards life – 'a sea-lion's to the flung bloater'. For all this vivacity is undercut by memory.

In the Fatal – a busy, cheap eating place down an alley off Vaci Utca – noisy parties face down heaped plates of meat, cabbage, fried potatoes, vegetables in batter, and drain deep glasses. Nick Thorpe, the BBC World Service correspondent here, talks about a recording he made the week before. At Lot 301 – the name crops up recurrently – he fell into conversation with a man sitting quietly. Why was he here? The man's in his 40s, a moustache, thick greying hair. It's his father's grave. He last saw him, as a six-year-old, the night before he was executed. For taking part in the uprising? No – he was a medical student – they caught him distributing leaflets. They hanged him – not by the drop, but slowly. Twenty-five thousand dead – the worst European war between 1945 and Bosnia. He and his grandparents would go at night to put flowers on the grave. Next day they'd be scattered. Those who were seen – children, old people, women – were clubbed by the soldiers.

Always with Hungary there's the glimpsed hero at the mind's margin. Cultural resistance could be the country's stereotype. At times the trait's overblown, as in the epic national obsession with statuary, nowhere more grandiose than in Hosok Tere ('Heroes' Square'), where bearded giants (Hungarian statues, excepting the occasional draped and bosomy grace or symbolic figure, are always male) from Magyar history cluster round the base of a 120-foot-high column supporting the Archangel Gabriel. The canvases in the nearby Museum of Fine Arts are often on the same oppressive scale, though in the basement there is an exquisite, tiny, late-period Egyptian cat statuette with topaz eyes and in a side room upstairs, unexpectedly, you come across three luminous, ethereal El Grecos – *The Annunciation, Mary Magdalene, The Agony in the Garden* (this last entirely haunting) – which must surely have been among the ones Patrick Leigh Fermor saw in 1934 when 'Annamaria ... acted as Open Sesame to a private house with a long room which was empty except for half-a-dozen tremendous El Grecos.'

Unexpected, too, are the statues of James Watt and George Stephenson that perch, alien and morose, among the embellishments of the East Station, from which I catch a train out to Eger, 90 miles north-east of Budapest in the northern uplands that march with the Slovakian border (distances are not great in a flat country 200 miles long by 350 wide, with its capital more or less at centre). The scenery along the way is middle-European nondescript – a landscape expressing itself not through form, but through tint and shade: of sky, field, wood. Pale oolites shimmer in cuttings, slow tractors work down rows of green and purple cabbage that converge on villages where baroque flashes from between ten-storey Soviet concrete functional, and complex-cupola'd verdigris churches gleam. Flocks of shy deer by trackside field-hedges peer warily at the train, crested larks scurry along platforms in provincial stations, red wagons full of muddy beet wait in sidings. As the train approaches Eger, the hills swell, striped with terraces of vines. Against the wall of the booking office when we arrive a group of skinheads, who'd mix and mingle in a Millwall crowd, lounge by graffiti which reads 'Welcome to English Jewish Pigs' (during my time in Pest, Jean-Marie Le Pen holds a meagrely-attended rally there). I ask directions of an old woman in a red wool cap. She dismounts deftly from her folding bicycle to answer and offers me a marigold from a blue plastic bag. My hotel is by the minaret and I climb it next morning.

It dates from the 90-year Ottoman occupation of the town in the 17th century. Built of honey, beige and pinky-grey blocks of sandstone with intricate bas relief and cross-hatching to the first taper, it soars. At the base it's perhaps 12 feet in diameter, 14 scalloped facets centering on a crescent moon and star topped by a cross 130 feet above. You pay 30 forints (12p) to climb it by an intra-mural stair which is so close you thrust up sideways, clammy walls amplifying heartbeat and panting breath, to emerge on an 18-

inch-wide balcony with a rail at mid-thigh height 110 feet up. The stonework's crumbling, the rail crudely cemented. Descent's not much less scary, and if you meet others climbing, the result is unwonted intimacy. But the adrenalin sharpens your appreciation of the view over baroque rooftops, the muscular 19th-century cathedral and the even more solid castle – scene of famous resistance to the advance of the Turks in the 16th century. The town's main square, Dobo Istvan Ter, is named after the castle's commander during the siege, and martial statues dominate. The mood changes for the 'Valley of Beautiful Women', a 20-minute walk out of town, and worth it for the wine-vaults. This is where 'Bull's Blood' (*Egri Vikaver*) of teenage first binges comes from. The cellarers seem intent on maintaining the tradition. At dusk on All Souls' Night, not one but was garrulous-drunk. One by one their lamps were extinguished, doors closed, and they came out with candles and children to roll down the road to the cemetery to light up the graves, until the whole scene flickered with light and movement, voices and play.

North of the town are the Bukk Mountains – a national park. They're limestone hills, as high as Snowdon maybe but not so grand, and entirely covered in beechwoods where the flaring of orange against ochre in autumn is enrapturing, as would the paths be to children, knee-deep in drifts of leaves for noisy miles. In their May-green, these woods must be one of the great natural sights of Europe. The area's marred by quarries and spectacular, decrepit cement factories like Mad Max film-sets, but British visitors, used to Bradwell chimney, Trawsfynydd nuclear power station and Lake District tourism in our national parks, won't find much to complain about. They will find a degree of solitude here, an undeveloped rural atmosphere typical of this part of Hungary.

The same can't be said of Pecs (pronounced 'paitch'), 100 miles south of Budapest close to the Croatian border, where a certain cosmopolitanism obtains. Large Mercedes with UNHCR plates are parked outside opulent houses on the hill, looking down on the rout of Skodas and Polski Fiats, Wartburgs, Ladas and Trabants in the streets below. The town's monuments are in turn massive and elegant. Around the cathedral, huge and angular as a municipal building, there's a profusion of things to see: an unkempt early Christian mausoleum which acts as dormitory to hordes of feral cats; a parish church which patently started life as a mosque; the Csontvary museum – overwhelming, brilliantly-coloured canvases by the least-known of the pre-eminent modern European painters, about whom Picasso, after seeing an exhibition of his work in Paris, said 'I did not know there was another great painter in our century besides me.'

The street life of Pecs, too, is a curious mix. There is the Hungarian calm: couples out strolling with the men pushing prams; idle smokers – most here do, to America's delight – on the seats in squares; pavement coffee-shops; weekend people unoppressed by their children or bound for Mass; the ubiquitous dog-walkers (Britain as a nation of dog-lovers pales to insignificance in comparison with Hungary, where they're worn almost as fashion accessories: Pekinese, Kerry Blues, Yorkshire terriers, Dalmations, Dobermans, Shih-tzus, Schipperkes – the streets of any major Hungarian town provide an inventory of canine breeds, every park's provided with a dog toilet area, every wealthy garden has its guardian mastiff). And then there is Western incursion: the John Bull Pub, darts, Guinness, McDonald's (where people queue as for exotic treats) and the Pizza Hut, Shepherd Neames, a froth and scum of sex-tourism in the darker eddies of the town – all this in a sort of Hungarian Oxford, with the fifth-oldest university in the world founded here.

Back in Pest before I leave Hungary, Tomcsanyi Laura brings up the subject of Lot 301 again in a students' coffee bar. This lovely, voluble, edgy young woman offers to take me there because for her it is *the* text in which to read the last half-century of her country's history. A three-quarter-hour tram ride from Blaha Lujza Ter past Lowry factories and shabby apartment blocks brings us to the Ujköztemetö cemetery on the eastern outskirts of town. We enter past flower-sellers and walk down a long road, its margins braided with the funerary culture of Catholic Europe. All Souls' Night has just past, each grave left starred by firmaments of coloured, melted wax where the children, the old people, lit bouquets of candles to flicker against the dark. There are no signposts, but each sector of the enormous cemetery is numbered. As we penetrate further – a mile, a mile-and-a-half – the place becomes progressively more unkempt and overgrown, reverting to the birch heath of middle Europe. Listing monuments catch our eye amongst impenetrable brushwood, the road narrows. We bear left, concrete-lap fencing of the perimeter in front, jag suddenly right and it's ahead.

Prone small slabs among the grass, some bearing names, are flowered with the wax All Souls' Night blooms. The larger grave of Nagy Imre – leader of the uprising – is hung with ribbons, each one for a streetfighter of '56. The ones who didn't escape west, who were executed, were buried here, face down, hands and feet tied, among the zoo animals and the criminals.

In one of Konrad György's essays there is an anecdote that implies the extent of an oppression Hungary now often seems to look away from or revise. In a working-class district of Pest in 1959 he comes across women weeping. They've just been given permission to collect clothes and possessions of children who fought in the uprising, and who the authorities watched and left for three years until they were of an age to arrest and hang. The memorial for these and the rest of the resistance dead is in a clearing among wooded heathland, below the flight-path of jets as they climb and heel over for Paris, Warsaw or Berlin. It's like a passage grave, like a portal-dolmen in form, built from great slabs and blocks of soft, white oolite, preternaturally light in this sombre setting, a chalky deposit adhering in the whorls of your finger when you touch. Underneath a huge capstone, its top elaborated with stone curtain and slender obelisk (the latter veined with incipient cracks), a passage leads to a natural boulder behind, its great weight come to rest. In the boulder is a niche. No names are carved. The monument's stone at front and top is fine-dressed, gives way to coarse-chiselling at its rear, then the rooted, native rock – from show through texture to gravity. Fifty yards away across the grass is a sunken, stone-lined recess like a well, in it a squat hexagonal black marble pillar, polished, worked, oddly threatening and repellent. You stumble across it as afterthought, as reminder. The resonance between cenotaph-dolmen and the pit-phallus is intense. The sculptor has created in them something perfectly expressive of their place, as puzzling as the co-existence in humanity of heroism and brutality. Around the clearing, ash-trees are heavy-keyed, acacia and cotoneaster spread, rooks fly across an autumn sunset and the harsh call of a pheasant comes from the wood. Ordinary people sidle together, sharing stories they – and we – need to hear. Next morning, as my plane banks round, I see it down there again, tiny, pure, and lodged.

3: The Valleys

This framed and riven landscape defies attempts to view it from a single perspective. Call it The Valleys, yes, but even the name implies complexity. You cannot have valleys without intervening ridges, without heads of valleys and the moors lying beyond, that drain down through their own subterranean landscapes into the valleys' streams and rivers. Geography and geology themselves insist that it is useless to look here for straight lines, single viewpoints, shallow perspectives. To come to terms even with this small corner of a small country is a lifetime's work of the imagination. Apparent contradiction, paradox, the co-existence of opposites are matters that immediately confront the traveller passing through. Here's George Borrow, heading towards Neath and leaving vistas worthy of Hieronymus Bosch behind him in the autumn of 1854:

> The scenery soon became very beautiful; not that I had left machinery altogether behind, for I presently came to a place where huge wheels were turning and there was smoke and blast, but there was much that was rural and beautiful to be seen, something like park scenery, and then there were the mountains near and in the distance.

That sense of disparate elements in closest proximity, of the exploiting and the enduring, has long hung over these valleys. To see it clearly, drive up the road, say, from Mountain Ash – Aberpennar – in Cwm Cynon, past the stagger and cling of colliery terraces on either side, to cross the head of Cwm Clydach and climb by a narrow, flycatcher-and-wagtail-flitted lane heading for Twyn y Glog. On this broad spur between Rhondda and Taf, quartered by buzzard and raven, all industry far below, you enter a swallow-thronged loft of memories of the old agrarian Wales.

Here are rickety farms held through generations; field systems and boundaries built on yet more ancient versions of the same; thick-fleeced sheep scuttering and jostling away through a gap of a wall. This is what existed before the ironworks and the collieries came. This is what existed alongside them. (If you doubt that, take a look at Vincent Evans' fine allegorical painting from 1935, *A Welsh Family Idyll*, based surely on some smallholders-and-colliers hamlet on Mynydd Allt-y-grug above his childhood home of Ystalyfera in the Swansea Valley.) This, despite encroachment of the alien conifers from up-ridge, is what has survived them.

That which survives presupposes there was that also which is defunct – or nearly so. The Valleys landscape is one where the former presence of heavy industry is inescapable, its images implanted in our consciousness, whether from school geography for those of a certain age, or from the American-Welsh-accented colliers of the film of *How Green Was My Valley*, or perhaps from Borrow again:

> What shall I say about the Cyfarthfa Fawr? ... I saw enormous furnaces. I saw streams of molten metal. I saw a long ductile piece of red-hot iron being operated upon. I saw millions of sparks flying about. I saw an immense wheel impelled round with frightful velocity by a steam engine of two hundred and forty horse power. I heard all kinds of dreadful sounds ...

Thus it was, and its scattered though often astonishingly subsumed impact was dire until the growth 30 or 40 years ago – after the trauma of Aberfan – of a recognition of the urgent necessity for 'proper handling of the inherited artefacts and residue of two centuries of coal mining, smelting and manufacturing, so that the quality of life is not injured by a senseless, disordered mess of dereliction'. That recognition expressed itself in the landscaping, restoration and 'heritage' that have changed the look of The Valleys. The abscesses raised by mineral extraction and processing on the skin of the land have been lanced and levelled, their poisons drained, their presence now as often a thing of the past and of the mind as of physical reality. In the Lower Swansea Valley, once one of the most polluted regions of Britain, 'a horrid filthy place, part of which was swamp and part pool; the pool black as soot and the swamp of a disgusting leaden colour', the fox and the kestrel range and the planted trees once more signal the seasons' change. Instead of exploitation, there is inward investment in – the word seems in all senses appropriate – 'light' industry. The rivers – Twrch and Tawe and Taf, Rhondda and Rhymney and Neath, Clydach and Cynon,

Afan and Ogwr – begin to run clear, their life returning and replenishing. At their headwaters the dipper creeps over rocks, and trout swim in the pools. Civilisation, its abuses perhaps receding, invents a hopeful grammar of reparation within whose structure the old and simple life thrives – observed, encouraged, emblematic, therapeutic within an exigent world. The Valleys, eternal witnesses to change, witness it again in a new and positive-seeming phase.

As well as change, there is a sort of peace at times, which is that of a thing accomplished, of labour finished and going back, reabsorbing into the silence of the long ages. I feel it when I walk the old quarry tramway from Dowlais Top on the Heads of the Valleys Road, up above Merthyr which was once the largest town of this little nation. The cropped sward, the grazing sheep, the wide views over the dammed and light-reflecting waters of the Taf Fechan to the rounded backs of our highest South Walian hills – all these assert purity and space. Even when you come to Twynau Gwynion – the quarried face of Merthyr Common – and blasted outcrops of white, rough rock on which the mountain ash takes root in cracks appear at the end of green, sheltering bays of turf-cloaked spoil, there is a magic and connection in the close and minute view. In the face of the rock are fossils of tiny creatures from millions of years ago – slender shoals of crinoids, whorled ammonites. They reveal the spent life that rock holds within itself, make me think of the trilobites that start out from interleavings of Silurian rocks to the north of here along the Wye; of the delicate tracery of fern leaves etched into the shaley cleavings of coal, sight of which was everyday to the workers underground. Everything that lives is stilled at last, and the earth takes it back into its own internal landscapes.

That thought in its turn stills my mind. I stand with my back to the quarry face and look out west across the southward-dipping slopes of Fforest Fawr, catch with sudden excitement at a craggy-knolled outline which must be Carreg Cadno, a dozen miles away. I remember walking towards it on a bright day 30 years ago, across a moor pocked with natural shakeholes and swallets at the start of a lovely, mysterious journey into the earth. The limestone uplands between the valleys of Tawe and Usk are where the longest and deepest cave systems in Britain are to be found: Dan yr Ogof, Agen Allwedd (on the cliffs above which the whitebeam, rarest of

British trees, grows), Ogof Ffynnon Ddu. It was into the latter that I was bound. Within its passages are scenes and atmospheres of such exquisite, jewelled splendour that recollection of them still takes my breath away. In Column Hall the floor of pearled, pooled and gleaming calcite glittered in the light of our miners' lamps, and the sheaves of straw stalactites hanging from the roof swayed into barely audible chiming contact through a disturbance of air our mere passing caused. Much deeper within, we dropped into the rushing course of an underground river, followed its foaming descent between black, calcite-veined walls of rock – earth-born, water-carved, elemental counterpart to the contexts of colliers' lives – for three miles, plunging over our heads sometimes in potholes in the floor to bob along in the rapid current, until roof met water and we made our escape up a side passage and through a squirming and perilous choke of muddy boulders to clear daylight again. This hidden, secretive landscape gives so variously of experience and adventure. In Ogof y Ci above Faenor are blind, white trout – how many centuries have they lived underground, to evolve thus? From Llygad Llychwr the River Loughor, whose estuary splits off the Gower Peninsula from the mainland, gushes out, behind its resurgent source a maze of interlinking passages and dark, unknowable lakes. The Afon Mellte below Ystradfellte flows through Porth yr Ogof. The brave or foolhardy can act out their own Orphean myth here, walk in along ledges at the upstream entrance and swim out a quarter-mile downstream through deep and dangerous water where many have drowned. If you try it and survive, walk downriver into the enchanting oakwoods of the waterfall country that stretches to Pontneddfechan. This is water's playground, where it dances as though glad to be released from subterranean thrall: Sgwdiau Clungwyn, Sgwd y Pannwr, Sgwd yr Eira on the Afon Hepste, the latter a bridal veil of water hung from the brow of a recessed rock-face, and white and lacey as the snow of its name.

These intimate delights of The Valleys are matched by a grandeur of framing, a carved high sandstone surround with a flourish of white, marbled rock that is Gower round its lower westernmost corner. From Rhydaman in the west to Abergavenny in the east, above Gwaun Cae Gurwen and Gurnos, Hirwaun and Merthyr, Treherbert and Tredegar, the mountains begin a gradual swell towards their great north-facing scarps.

Pen y Fan and Fan Gihirych, Bannau Brycheiniog and Bannau Sir Gaer, ice-gouged and aloof, looking down on their cold, deep, fairy-legended corrie lakes, give a release along their tussocky, wild promenades from the closeness and occasional claustrophobia of valley-side dwelling, as also do the flower-starred, windswept clifftops of Gower. The colouration of these high hills, too, is a thing to marvel at, an ever-changing wash across the canvas, land's illuminated manuscript. Looked at from down-valley, the hills body forth a whole spectrum of blues, violets, mauves. In summer, dense green of the bracken is patched and shaded by a salmon-flesh tinge on new leaves of the bilberry. The heather blazes with circles of fire in the spring, and with scented, bee-hummed, reddish-purple glories in August. Autumn sears a vivid terracotta into the bracken, picked out like flame by a slantwise westering sun.

The hills look out to northward on a pre-industrial and abiding Wales that fed The Valleys with labour and provisions, with Methodism and hymns and poetry. Just across their valley-occluding ridges, just down there, is the country of Howell Harris and Pantycelyn, of 'Fern Hill' and of Dylan Thomas' stories, of D J Williams and the poignant memories of a world on the cusp of modernity that he recorded in one of the great Welsh prose classics, *Hen Dŷ Ffarm*. This cultural and productive hinterland of modest farms and honoured traditions and industriousness and rich natural life was sustenance and succour both physical and spiritual to The Valleys, an anchor and enhancement to lives timed by glow of furnace or winding of pithead wheel. The connection implied a wider community, sense of which fed into The Valleys' political radicalism. Work, family, forebears stated the same truth – that we are all interrelated, dignified by our labour, inhabitants of a landscape profoundly human. Time and again that sense crops up here in attempts to express people and place. Look for it in the work of the Polish artist Josef Herman, who fled the persecution of the Jews in Warsaw, settled in Ystradgynlais, and recorded in images of resilience and nobility the dignity and cost of hard physical labour. Read it in the affirming comedy of the novel *William Jones*, by T Rowland Hughes from the North Walian community of Llanberis – its eponymous hero a slate quarryman from the north who moves to The Valleys to seek work in the depression of the 1930s, and finds kindness and support here too. The physical and the human landscapes are indissociable in this unique region of Wales.

Perhaps, as time winds on into a new millennium, it is appropriate to end on a watershed, and an abiding image that locates there. By the mountain road – itself following in part the Roman road Sarn Helen – that leads over from Ystradfellte to Sennybridge, on a false crest among desolate moorland, is a great standing stone, Maen Llia, enigmatic, visible from miles down valley. To the south is Glyn Neath, northwards the valley of the Usk, but this marked pass is no longer a thoroughfare for any but the weekend motorist and the occasional shepherd. The face of the stone is faintly and indecipherably inscribed – only in particular conditions of light does it give any clue to its lettering. It has stood witness here for 4,000 years, in its own place, travellers on the manifold purposes of their centuries passing by while The Valleys, through all the changes wrought upon them, endure.

4: In the Hide of the Lion

By way of a high mountain pass, I climbed up from what Gerald Brenan calls 'the harsh and tawny lion skin of Spain' and corkscrewed down through scented woods. The road brought me into Segovia in the late afternoon where I found a brusque hotel in which to stay on the Plaza Mayor. The Roman aqueduct was my first objective. In August 1838 George Borrow, plagued by dysentery and governmental persecution, had 'repaired to the aqueduct, and sat down beneath the hundred and seventh arch, where I waited the greater part of the day'. The incident's trivial, the location so precise it seemed proper to seek it out in order to pay homage to one of the great, joyful, adventurous – and nowadays scarcely read or known – books of travel. So I perched there as Borrow had done. It looked down on noisy streets with shop windows full of garlic, suckling pigs and boots of Spanish leather. A watery sunset sneaked in from under heavy clouds to infuse the aqueduct's stone with the pervasive tint of the plains. The Queen of Heaven and her infant child gazed down from a niche Minerva might once have held. I pondered the journey ahead. I'd not been to Spain in over 30 years, and then had ventured only briefly and marginally inland. When I was last here, Franco's photograph was in every post office and priest-ridden peasants shuffled about time-honoured tasks in the fields. Segovia seemed a good place to catch up on the changes. In a tapas bar on the Plaza del San Martin, a voluptuous barmaid talked gaily with women clients and poured out with measured humour the fumey red wines of Extremadura. Reticent men spoke softly in corners. A young mother on a bar stool suckled her baby. The modernity of gender-bargains were plainly on view in this renewed country. I could scarcely wait to see more of it.

Segovia's on the interior tourist itinerary, and rightly so. It has the aqueduct, the last and most vast of Europe's great Gothic cathedrals, a fairytale fortress in the Alcazar that's unconsciously echoed in the illustrations to a thousand re-tellings of Rapunzel, and a web of hill alleys and burnished cobblestone squares threaded between the three of them. Time here would be easily spent. Over breakfast in my hotel I listen to English couples plan how they would do so before discussing more crucial matters. A faded, pretty blonde woman asks what Chris Patten's current EEC role is? Advisory and non-executive, she's told by her stooped and denim-clad husband, his voice echoey with all the loud authority of the ex-pat for whom the patria no longer quite exists. 'He must be frightfully glad to have lost his seat,' muses his wife, toying with a slice of thin, dark ham, 'and not to have to associate with all the riff-raff.' 'Yes, frightfully glad,' concurs her husband, with feeling. I leave them to their imperial threnodies, recover my bike from the hotel garage, negotiate switchback ginnels of polished setts, make a quick pilgrimage to the grave of San Juan de la Cruz in the Carmelite monastery across the Rio Eresma from the Alcazar, and head on out of town.

My being here at all is down to the blandishments of two Spanish biking enthusiasts, Joe and Mary King-Nemeth. Joe's Hungarian-Canadian so space is his métier, Mary's all sunshine, and in Spain the two happily combine. They set me up with a bike from a dealership in Madrid, plotted an inland tour and sent me on my way. The bike was a big BMW boxer, an R1150 RT, in touring trim. It's the closest thing to two-wheeled bliss you'll ever swing a leg across. It behaves itself on the road impeccably. It thumps along, solid and placid, and leaves you free to enjoy the experience: the aromatic air at 6,000 feet, smelling of sage and oregano and sweet herbs warmed by the sun as we drift through the Sierra de la Morcuerra; the stony distances of the high plains, rock outcropping across them like bones breaking through old and sagging hide; the honeyed and rust-tiled towns where even the modern architecture is landscape-hued in a way that no other European country could hope to emulate. Three hundred kilometres of this go by in a Calderonian dream. I arrive in Cuenca.

Some towns almost defy description, and Cuenca is one of them. You pass from the red plains of Guadalajara to the edge of a Karst landscape of such intoxicating beauty your every sense is subsumed by delight. Cuenca is the doorway to it, the *ciudad antigua* sculpted into a limestone ridge between two deep river gorges, the only peers to its extraordinary hanging houses those that cling to cliffs 200 feet above the waves at Bonifacio on the southern tip of Corsica. Cuenca is utterly spectacular. I ride up the gorge of the Rio Huecar to the Hotel Cueva del Fraile above the town. A cold front that stretched all the way to Vienna has cleared and from my balcony a bright half-moon holds court in the Spanish sky, brilliantly expressive of the great, empty landscape that is Spain. In the restaurant, the music notates the same preoccupations that Juan de la Cruz worked with

113

400 years before: *corazon, amor, esperanza*. A post-coital couple on the next table glow and smile. The delectable simplicities of the Spanish table keep appearing in front of me, to float away on the velvet-soft country wine. *La Vida es sueno*. Life is a dream...

From which I wake next morning intent on finding my way through the Serrania de Cuenca to Albarracin. From Buenache de la Sierra to La Toba is ten miles of rattle and frail and groan. At one point among olive groves a huge flock – of plump and sedate long-eared sheep whose bells chime with a sweet redolence in irregular brisk patterns, and dapper little piebald skipping goats – fills the track. A great hound lollops baying towards us and with a nervous twist of the throttle we surge past. Hours more of this and we come suddenly on the old walled Islamic pueblo, so remote in its craggy fastnesses it seems entirely dissociated from the 21st century. It is stepped and close and alleyed, the approach to its cathedral barely a shoulder's breadth in width. Its crenellated fortifications crawl over bare limestone, and within them Albarracin is green-gardened, pink-washed, potted about with geranium and impatiens, less a village than a song in stone.

Between Cuenca and Cazorla – my next destination – stretch the plains of La Mancha, 400 kilometres of them subtly delineated in terms of tonal range: tawnies, umbers, ochres, burnt siennas, muted yellows, faded orange; long-tailed tits and thin sparrows flit among fields of ripe maize and dried sunflowers that hem the road. I navigate by the sun – a good rule in Spain where road-numbering is quirky at best. Huge birds with ragged wing-ends sail over dusty green olive groves, and the scent of the pressed oil around Villanueva de l'Arzibispo is overpowering. I turn off the highway and head down into the Parque Naturel de las Sierras de Cazorla, the largest protected landscape in Spain, its cliff- and valley- and tree-profiles exotic somehow, like classical Japanese art. The road's gravelly, inducing little back-wheel slides towards unfathomable drops. Potholes occur with unerring accuracy on blind bends round every one of which is a large Dutch camper van occupying the whole of the tarmac, forcing me on to inches of shale above almighty precipices. I've been on worse roads, but I was on four wheels and not driving then. *'La Carretera està en mal estada'* says the sign as we get back on to the good roads. A Knights Templar's castle on a soaring prow of limestone – Spaniards build on their cliffs as happily and naturally as house-martins, it seems – steps straight from the imagination of Gustave Dore into astonishing reality. Just beyond it is the hill-town of Cazorla. Under the sweet chestnuts in the Plaza de Santa Maria I sit at a pavement restaurant. A breath of wind stirs the turning leaves and the flies circle brilliantly in the lamplight. Around the tables dart and scurry a tribe of sleek cats and hopeful, ingratiating, small dogs, each species importuning after its own fashion and being variously indulged or ignored by the diners. An assertive Siamese queen, dangerously swift, and a leggy little brindled terrier prowl together, she eating the flesh from the tossed bones, he the bones she leaves. Scents of garlic and rosemary drift across the square. The sound of a flowing fountain amplifies against the shadowy ruins of a church. Heaven, I realise, is a northern hill-village in Andalucia on an autumn evening, beyond care.

Hell is leaving it in the morning rain. There is one particular and crucial junction of slick cobbles, acute, offset and inclined at 45 degrees on to a busy exit, that to attempt would be disaster. I spend a miserably wet period searching out an alternative, and many more soaking miles and hours heading north on the road to Almagro, among the endless plains of La Mancha. Only through the traverse of their cosmic tedium can you gain an understanding of the world of Don Quixote. Their passage, I considered, entitled me to an evening of pure epicureanism. I joined the late hordes of leisurely and intent diners heading for Almagro's Restaurante El Corrigedor, that has the reputation of being one of the best in Spain. Its proprietor, Juan Garcia, regaled me with mystery upon culinary mystery in warmed brown ramekins: quail eggs in tomato and garlic, strips of marinated fish, rich and smokey venison with puréed apple, and a fine, robust bottle of Valdepenas that was all blackberries and vanilla and viscous with alcohol. Spain has a knack and grace of transforming the simple into the urbane. In the restaurant you experience it; and palpably also in the Correo della Comedias, Almagro's exquisite monument to the golden age of Spanish drama – a perfectly preserved theatre of the 17th century in which the plays of Calderon and Lope de Vega have been performed for the last 400 years, affecting in its cobbled and galleried open-to-the-sky plainness, the dishes for its rush lights so steeped in oil they are unrusted still. It was one of two buildings in Spain that most impressed me.

The other I came across on a little back road through Calatrava, on a low bluff above the Rio Guadiana looking out to the Toledan mountains. On a sprawl of white rock among arid fields was the long ruin of a castle. There were no signs, no interpretation boards, no recounted history; just a twitter of small birds from scattered trees, a wind that bore a chill hint of coming winter, high walls of dressed stone and great bastions of rubble crumbling back into the plain. A chained black greyhound barked sporadically. I drifted down from the plains into Toledo, with its crowds and audio-tours and admission charges for everything, and joined a queue outside an annexe to the church of Santo Tome to view El Greco's supposed masterpiece, *El Entierro del Conde de Orgaz*. In front of it the interpreters and art historians were hard at work explaining this or that aspect of the painting (and there is much in it, and by way of facts about it, for their industry to explain), using as many words as it takes to validate a Damien Hirst. Whisper it soft, but for all the mastery in its execution the painting's a crowded and sycophantic mess – there are far more aesthetically pleasing El Grecos in the museum in Pest. I retreated for quiet into the cloisters of San Juan de los Reyes, where oranges hung from the trees and eccentric gargoyles outstared all onlookers – demons with gnarled hands clasped in prayer, a gigantic frog squatting on the head of a fish, a howling monkey, a yawning cat, its tail elegantly curled round its feet. Doves swirl past in the watery light. In the Ursuline Convent the prayer candles at 25 pesetas were electric. Quiet nuns pray behind their grille, their eyes fixed on an Annunciation beautiful in its naivety, Mary's face serious and quiet and the Holy Spirit just such a white dove as those that catch the sudden light as they wheel around the villages of the plains. Visitors on metalled heels clack over to the exit, wrest the stiff latch, let the door slam behind them and the shadowy sisters pray on.

Outside the church of San Juan brides wait to be married, restless among retinues of sleekly sexual Spanish women. Much later I leave the walled city in the dusk by the Puente de San Martin, the great river flowing beneath through its crag-rimmed gorge and on westwards to the ocean. There is a strange glimmer of white on the bridge, a flash of light as a photographer, in a scene straight from Bunuel, records the last couple of the day. Beyond its coach-tours and its coasts, Spain is not a place. It is a state of mind, an enchantment. I had not realised ...

5: 'While everybody knelt to pray,
The drifter did escape.'

There are three versions of company that I prefer in the outdoors: that of my loved one; beyond which there was that of my little dog, The Flea, who is only a poignant and ever-present memory now; and – *faute de mieux* – my own. The idea of taking part in an organised trek has always put me in mind of Dr Johnson's thoughts on going to sea. To him, gaol was both preferable and likely to offer better company. Where my fellow-Europeans are concerned, I'm not a sociable animal and I get less so as I grow older. But somehow I ended up – enlisted, conscripted, invited, pressed? – on a trek.

The rise of trekking as one of the more popular 'adventure' activities is a phenomenon I'd watched with puzzled curiosity over the last 20 years. To my ambivalent gaze, it had taken on the nature of some curiously inflated modern (and modish) counterpart to those trains – the 'Ramblers' Specials' – that ran on Sundays of my youth from Manchester's Exchange and Victoria Stations out to the Dee Valley, Derbyshire, the Yorkshire Dales or wherever. There'd be big red posters advertising them on the station approaches weeks in advance: Llangollen & Bala, Bakewell & Matlock, Skipton & Ingleborough. Pack them in and move them out, send the crocodiles, the booted and be-shorted urban hordes, out from some distant country stop over hill and ridge, moor and meadow, and don't allow them or anyone in their path a moment's solitude and reflective peace when they get there was the operative principle. You could write a social history of England around these excursions. All the sexual encounters in the English political novel of the 1930s take place on or immediately after one of them. Actually, I really liked them, and the conversations I overheard or took part in on the journeys back were one of the major formative influences of my life.

But that's by-the-bye. With regard to trekking, I judge too harshly and compare in ignorance. I needed to see what one was like. Also, even I from the grumpier depths of misanthropy had to admit that some of the destinations were appealing. Though I could counter that by reiterating the 'some', and wondering to myself what right-minded person would ever want to go to Everest, Annapurna or K2 base-camps, and who still in full possession of the faculty of reason would wish among the shit and debris of those places to seek out and suffer the company of mountaineers (a breed of sportsmen and sportswomen who in general make even tennis-players appear interesting, eloquent and modest)?

This is clearly to air a prejudice, which I should not do lest I turn into Alfred Wainwright. An invitation came. After the briefest of deliberations, and a much lengthier process of consultation with the semi-divine personage who's my domestic companion (in the course of which I had to give her my firm promise that I would not travel, as the itinerary decreed, in any ex-Soviet helicopters) I accepted. And thus I arrived on the appointed Tuesday in August at Heathrow to join the participants on a trek to the Tien Shan, the Celestial Mountains of Kyrgyzstan that run in a long rampart rising above the Takla Makhan desert and the steppes of Kazakhstan, from Urumchi in the east to Kashgar in the west.

At Heathrow I ran into Jane Westwater, the trek leader. I like women in authority. They handle it more skilfully and supportively than men, and Jane was no exception. She knew the subtler arts of control, threatened to introduce me to the other trekkies, whom I'd already identified by the monstrous red holdalls with the trekking company crest printed on them that they were trolleying round the check-ins. I demurred. Keep a wise distance and watch is the policy for me where groups are concerned. I distrust their dynamics. Because I didn't have a red bag, the woman on the check-in even gave me a separate seat with leg-room. So far so good, I thought, and no deep vein thrombosis as an added bonus. If I can stay this far detached, I might survive the proximity of my fellow men and women for two weeks. And as I've implied, it's not snobbishness on my part. It's just pure misanthropy. My dear old friend H W Tilman used regularly to quote Frederick the Great's maxim at me as a reminder:

'The more I see of humanity, the more I love my dog.'

He had an excuse for the attitude. He'd spent his 17th birthday in the trenches of the Somme. I'd not had that experience, but I could sympathise with his view even a quarter of a century ago, when all I thought about was sex and rock-climbing and 18th-century literature. Tilman said the feeling grew on you ever more intensely as the years passed. He was right. But it was because of him that I'd chosen to go on this trek. I wanted to see something of the same terrain he'd traversed in those great lone journeys 50 years ago, when his fellow explorer Eric Shipton had been British Consul in Kashgar. Maybe this whole latter-day project of trekking is an act of national homage to the two men who, in their *ad hoc*, ragamuffin, take-it-as-it-comes way were its founding fathers back in the golden age of mountain travel in the 1930s. Anyway, with such thoughts in mind I passed the hours of flight from London to Vienna to Almaty – which in all the travel literature I'd read is called Alma Ata – in reclusive ease. The hours having slipped away as we sped east, our arrival there was around midnight. Even by Asian standards, passport and customs officials were more than usually surly and slow. By the time the trekking agency had rattled us over pot-holed roads to the Otrar, Almaty's old thief-and-prostitute-frequented Intourist flagship hotel on Gorky Prospect, the hour of the wolf was upon us, sleep scarcely worthwhile. Our Leader had managed to produce a few bottles of beer, and the room even had a bottle-opener. Content only comes in brief versions, and this was one of them.

And so to logistics.

I had with me two rucksacks, one of 75 and one of 45 litre capacity. This is a very odd way of measuring the size of the most notoriously unwaterproof item of outdoor equipment. Manufacturers who use it should be sued under the Trade Descriptions Act, since everybody knows there's not a rucksack made that would hold even so much as a fluid ounce, liquid passing straight through the fabric of the thing to soak everything in its interior, or alongside it if it comes from within. If you detect a trace of irritation in this it is because every day throughout the trek I had to pack and unpack both these rucksacks. Doing it once is a difficult enough task. To have to repeat the same action 60 times is an extraordinary waste of energy and temper, and the amplification of this when done in the confines of a tent – particularly a wet tent shared with a large companion – is positively thermonuclear. I began to see a logic in those red holdalls. While the other trekkies had trooped over the road into leafy Panfilov Park opposite to inspect the fretted and gilded domes of the wooden Ascension Orthodox Cathedral, I was, to pursue the liquid analogy, cramming quarts into pint pots, working out what would and would not be needed and when. So I was not blessed, but they were, having slipped through the cathedral's warped and garish doors, chanced upon a service and had the holy water flicked across their brows. They came back radiant, and lifted up their eyes to a whole drama of hills that rise south of Almaty. My rational mind could accommodate itself to this. I reasoned that it would make it safe for them to opt for the helicopter ride, but not for me. I had both let-out and the means to keep a promise. Jane, I discovered, had neither. Her companion had wanted to insist that she didn't go in a helicopter, but of course these days a man can't do that to a woman, only a woman to a man. So I was safe, if unblessed, and she was blessed, if unsafe.

Now about this trek. We had an itinerary – detailed, impressionistic, and as it turned out, a little inaccurate. What struck me most about it in the anticipatory phase was its infantilising effect. Here, for example, is its description of the first active day:

'We drive for 1–2 hours to the [Alma-Arasan] Gorge. At the roadhead we meet our porters and trek for 3–4 hours through the forest. We camp in an idyllic alpine setting and time is then free to rest and relax. Some of the nearby peaks are snow-capped. There are forests of fir and alpine meadows.'

Little sentences. Simple images. Children's literature? Well, no – not that sophisticated – we're scarcely talking Philip Pullman here. What I didn't at first realise was that the infantilising project is not merely verbal, it extends to the way you are conducted through the environment itself. Your presence there is underpinned not by self-reliance, but by nannying. You may think I'm being critical here. Not necessarily so – I may not be attracted to the English Vice, but I can see that nannying has distinct advantages. Given a choice between taking down a wet tent yourself and carrying it for the rest of the day, or having someone else do it for you, which would you choose? Likewise with arriving at a campsite at the end of a day and having the same tents already erected and a great pot of steaming tea awaiting you? Are you really so purist as to want to refuse? I'm not. But I have to say that I don't like having a helping hand held out to me every time the angle of a slope exceeds 15 degrees. Enough of that, though. On this first day we strolled for five or six hours up a pleasant valley, the path rising steeply through spikey groves of Tien Shan Pine and slanting across alpine meadows. These were the most immediately and lastingly wonderful feature of this whole Central Asian experience for me, and I think also for most of the others on the trek. It was the day of the solar eclipse, and behind a thin veil of cloud we saw the moon roll slowly across the face of the sun, dimming momentarily the brilliance of the flowers through which our way led: edelweiss, white and blue gentians opening with imploring gestures, marigold, tormentil, aster, larkspur, cranesbill, potentilla, not ordinary and here and there in single blooms as in Britain, but spread wide in the densest carpets, and delighting us all.

Our camp that first night was above the tree-line at over 8,000 feet. We woke next morning to a grey, cold day on which we had a bleak pass to cross, made bleaker by its history. The Almaty Pass it was called, and our Russian guide Sergei explained the huge cairn of stones that marks its 11,500-foot summit. The soldiers of Tamerlaine the Great came this way in a campaign against the Chinese. Each of them added a stone to the pile. On the way back, fewer in number, they did the same again. So the cairn on its windswept col is essentially a war memorial from darker ages even than the present, and affecting despite the brutality of its instigator's reputation:

'If a man in Tamerlaine's service did something wrong, then he and a hundred of his comrades would be killed. It was a very disciplined army. Archaeologists have dated this mound to his time ...'

Beyond it was a peak-mirroring lake, and an easy long descent to another alpine-meadow campsite where we spent a cold night, snow falling, tents collapsing beneath its weight, the pack-horses standing around patient and hobbled next morning, their thick coats streaked and matted with moisture. And the group too, waking to this desolate and wintry face of landscape and with the harsh breathing of altitude asserting itself upon them, looked a little bedraggled and apprehensive as we began the long march down into the juniper-and-thyme-scented, dipper-and-eagle-haunted valley of Chong-Kemin.

It was here that the particular and identifying quality of this Tien Shan region first resolved and defined itself. Nothing else I've ever seen quite compares with its great empty width. This is the place of the horse and it was good to have our herd of pack-horses with us as help and reminder. Historically, it's home to the Great Horde, perimeter to the playing field for the Great Game. To journey here on foot is to meet unaccustomed scale.

In its way, though, it is subtle scale. A flock of sheep, a yurt, a nomads' horse-herd lend a definition at which, in their absence, you'd be hard-pressed to arrive. It is big country, and high, but in the outlying ridges that radiate from the central massif of the Tien Shan – the Celestial Mountains themselves – there is little that is spectacular. Their approach valleys have the wild spaciousness of those in the Cairngorms, say, or mid-Wales, but seldom reach the drama of Loch Avon, the Lairig Ghru or even the Teifi Pools. That doesn't matter. If there was not the oppression of grandeur, instead there was the liberty of space. Though that in itself can become a burden. The next turn in the valley might be a mile away or it might be three, and the cluster of red tents might be waiting for us round that bend or the next. We wouldn't know, until we arrived.

So for seven days we journeyed. There were sights and events along the way: the cobalt lake of Jasyl-Kul between whorled snouts of gravel the retreating ice had left behind, a little black diving duck on its unrippled surface; the bare 4,000-metre height of the Aksu Pass above its white, inviting glacier where there were tracks of deer, fox and also surely snow leopard; the frequent hilarities of stream crossings, where a slip would deposit you in raging glacial meltwater; a nomadic encampment in a forest clearing where we were given apricots, yogurt, cheese, kumis by dirty-faced, excitable children, which food we ate with polite trepidation, and the inevitable effects of which we mediated with vodka by the tumbler-full in the trekking agency's permanent valley base at Karkara, to which in a plushly upholstered former Soviet troop-transporter we were conveyed that night. (An educative aside here: you have to learn about Russian vodka, the measures in which it comes and the manner of their drinking – large, tossed back in one, another materialising immediately in its place.) 'Russian tea!' they laugh, and they suffer too, as Jane and Lena, Ian and myself – the raucous contingent – did. I have hazy recollections of crawling into a meadow and decorating a clump of delphiniums with the contents of my stomach as naturally as if it were an Ibiza pavement. The other trekkies were not so indecorous. If they disapproved, they did not show it, and it did not much matter, for we were soon to part. After a day's rest, there were another three days' travel, on the last of which we rode up one afternoon on pack ponies to a broad ridge above the camp. All across the skyline to the south were the Celestial Mountains, snowier than any I had ever seen. But I had a promise to keep, and I wasn't going to them. The others were to fly there to spend three days on the South Inylchek Glacier at the trekking agency's permanent base camp, from which mountaineers set forth to scale the high peaks of Kan Tengri and Pik Poboda.

They'd received their blessing. They were safe. I imagine the helicopter flight must have been beyond words spectacular. Instead, I borrowed a sturdy, shabby-tacked, eccentrically-bridled, wild-black-maned, lovely and independent-spirited little horse of a shade over 14 hands, and with two nomadic horsemen rode back on her like the gusting wind, 60 kilometres over ridges and down winding gorges, galloping through riparian meadows, trotting along tracks that were tributary streams to the great river of commerce which was the Silk Road, revelling in the freedom and excitement of every second, and ending up in the nomads' dwelling, on cushions at a low table spread with great wheels of fresh bread, with rich jams and buttery tea and yogurt, and little, tinking glasses of vodka too that sent a glow through every aching muscle and made me think that this one day at least had been an adventure indeed.

6: Bolivian Journey

On the flight in to Santa Cruz de la Sierra my neighbour gives me his card. 'Erick Lopez, Advocate', it reads. He tells me he's on his way to a lawyers' conference on ethics, laughs at my sardonic notion that in Britain this might be considered oxymoronic. 'Here in Bolivia,' he confides, 'everything is a little odd.' So I discover. For a start, there are the Santa Cruz telephone boxes. Some might consider standardisation a virtue. The Bolivians like to play jokes. There are catfish telephone boxes; and monkeys, parrots, flamingos, panthers, all moulded in bright fibreglass, young Bolivians chattering away excitedly within. They create a mood, in this fastest-growing city in South America, and it's light-hearted, vivacious, youthful. Fifty years ago this was a dusty cattle station among the Jesuit-mission-studded plains of eastern Bolivia; now – road, rail and air links having ended its isolation – it's a vibrant and patently wealthy metropolis with an extraordinary ethnic mix. An agricultural and economic boom has brought in colonies of Mennonites, the men straggle-bearded, the women frocked and bonneted; Japanese farmers grow rice and oriental vegetables, whilst Sikhs and Palestinians, Germans, Italians and Irish stamp their own cultural identities along the thronging alleys and shaded plazas, share their eating places with earnest American eco-activists, brash oil-workers and slick tractor-salesmen. All this intermingling and expansiveness takes place against a backdrop of bright-shawled, bowler-hatted cholas (the Indian women who are one of the characteristic sights of the country), flowered avenues, colonial-period buildings and exuberantly odd and powerful public statuary. In search of the truly strange, I head for the zoo.

Outside is a statue of the founder, a bird in his hand and a piglet under his arm. He was murdered, my guide tells me, by drug bandits whilst on a species-hunting expedition, 'but Bolivia', she adds, 'is a very safe country.' It's a recurrent refrain, amply commented upon by the numbers of soldiers and police wherever you look, on the streets, outside the public buildings, in flak jackets, carrying pistols, shotguns, sub-machine guns, teargas launchers. There is a degree of political unrest in the country, a certain amount of protest, the coca-growing campesinos clashing with a government threatened by a 50-million-dollar cut in US aid if it does not act against them. But for the tourist, it all seems rather phlegmatic and unthreatening. This is not Colombia. Bolivia feels as safe a place as any I've been – far more so than the USA in fact – and the tourist here goes on his or her way remarkably unworried and unhustled. My guide shrugs her shoulders, and we go in.

To the worst zoo and the best zoological collection I've ever seen. A giant otter splashes desultorily in a pool too small for it to turn; listless tapirs doze under a flame-tree; a Mondel wolf from the Amazon basin, rust-hued, hauntingly delicate, paces, paces, whilst strange jungle mustellidae scurry beneath the fate-enduring gaze of griffon-vultures and scruffy condors. I look around and think Edward Lear surely came to South America, for every variety that ever crawled and roosted under the Quangle Wangle's Hat is here, in the zoo, heart-rendingly: 'Perhaps they will move it to the Botanical Gardens site,' my guide tells me, 'if money can be found. Bolivia is a very poor country...'

She and I move on to these gardens, walk under hanging flowers of Heliconia, brilliant in reds, yellows and greens. Exquisite little water-rails bob and elegant, small, reddish-brown herons roost around a lagoon. A hot wind riffles through reeds. Towards evening, to escape from it, with a substantial part of the population of Santa Cruz I head down to the Rio Piray. Swifts hunt along the river where youths play and turquoise-braided kingfishers glint and dive. A silver band of good old boys drifts between thatched-roof refreshment huts beneath the bulbous-trunked boborochi trees. An ample-breasted girl canters up and down on a light-boned horse, seraphically aware of every man's eyes upon her. Something about the place speaks to the lazy hedonist in me, is prime for hanging out, drinking beer, eating vine-leaf-wrapped breads with rice, manioc, cheese. Woodsmoke from the ovens hangs in the air. I banter with children who beg for scraps of bread and omelette, admire the gorgeous young women who saunter and flirt with their eyes, and next day leave this tropical haven to fly on to Bolivia's erstwhile capital, Sucre.

The white-walled, red-roofed colonial town gleams from a ridged and textured brown landscape as the 727 slides round rocky bluffs and descends to a brief runway, its concrete streaked with burnt rubber. Later, from my hotel of shutters and courtyards and winding stairs, I stroll out to the Plaze 24 de Mayo. It's a Sunday. Under tall boborochi trees around the heroic statue of Antonio de Sucre, liberator, a marching band – three trumpets, two tubas, assorted cymbals and a couple of big bass drums – strikes up *Johnny, I Hardly Knew You* and parades exuberantly around the square, dancers twirling in front, skateboarding children weaving in and out, balloons bobbing. Finches flit among the mimosa flowers and dip across to nests in the mestizo carving on the cathedral, the pale ashlar coigns of which contrast with stained white walls and verdigrised parapets. By its west door, two scrawny, affectionate, watchful cats seek out the shade and doze. A boy sells me coca-cola. 'Habla usted Ingles?' I ask him. 'Poquito,' he beams back innocently, 'fuckyougringo...' A basset hound in the back of a pick-up roars gruff disapproval as his young mistress sways into a bar. One of the square's colony of canine indeterminates comes up, stands on hind legs, they touch noses. Pacified, the basset watches as his mistress returns with two ice creams, and licks his with intense concentration. Two policemen on Honda trailbikes consider a young ruffian who hares past on a beat-up Suzuki, scraping footrests and sending up showers of sparks, opt for preservation of dignity and return to studying the basset-owner's bottom. The Americas don't come more latin than Bolivia.

I go for a haircut. In the barber's shop, amid accoutrements of his trade my grandfather would have recognised, the barber calls his nephew, Ernesto, to keep the conversation going as he snips away with squeaking scissors and a flame-sterilized metal comb. 'Ernesto..?' I query. 'After Che,' he explains, delivering the habitual eulogy of the young for their murdered hero, telling me the final Bolivian chapter of the life. The old man's face in the mirror is rapt, murmuring the name as he puffs delicate-scented spray round my neck. Light-headed, I walk up to the Plaza Pedro de Anzures above the town. The disarming plain elegance of Spanish colonial architecture – simple porticos, paired and cupola'd bell-towers, a stepped fountain, cobblestones and Moorish-arched colonnades – show off the Spanish gift for working to perfection with an earth-toned and harmonious palette. Squat and braided cowboy-hatted Quechua women sell water from a column's slim shade. All around this high belvedere, spiky green and pinnacled ridges of the Andes tower up, cumuli massing white above them into a deep-blue high-altitude sky. Beneath, every block of the town's tilted grid has a church, the scale of it all compact, its secrecies within those squares, behind the studded doors and shuttered windows, so Spanish.

Tempting though it is to linger within the café-society of this laid-back student town, I have to get to Potosi – tragic Potosi, 'rich Potosi, the treasure of the world and the envy of kings', and perhaps the most fascinating World Heritage Site you'll ever see. No buses are running. I find a cab-driver who'll take me. We climb through a gravelly landscape of cactus, dry arroyos, mud-coloured villages and inexplicable distant ridgetop settlements. Wherever you look in the rocky, high, desert terrain there are goats, pigs, sheep, small dogs, small children, men following ox-ploughs, Quechua women with stovepipe hats carrying their burdens slung in bright red and turquoise cloths. We run the gauntlet of campesino roadblocks in an area where the Tinku tradition of ritual and bloody fighting between villages is still upheld, and arrive in Potosi, at 4,090 metres the World's highest city. I feel instantly that I've never been in a stranger place.

The yellow and terracotta city, in its richness of decoration, is quite at odds with the bleak surroundings. It stretches up to the foot of pyramidal Cerro Rico ('the rich mountain'), from which much of the wealth of the Spanish Empire was mined – eight million slaves dying in the process. I wander the town. The studs in the church door of San Francisco are of silver. Inside, painted crucifixion scenes have moustachioed Spanish nobles for Roman soldiers. The catacomb skulls bear neat holes of musket balls. I gravitate through grey tailings towards the mines, long rows of breeze-block barracks on either side. Where the track steepens to zig-zag up the face of the mountain is a small market. A chico of ten or so attaches himself to me as guide, takes me to a stall. I buy presents for the miners – a couple of kilos of coca leaves, packs of cigarettes, a bottle of 95 per cent proof liquor, ammonium nitrate, fuses, detonators, and sticks of dynamite wrapped in twists of oily brown paper, soft and malleable to the touch. The whole lot's handed over in carrier bags, casually as a corner-shop purchase, and we toil on to the entrance of a small co-operative mine called La Maria – one of maybe 500 still being worked on the mountain for silver, copper, zinc. The chico's mother gives me an acetylene lamp and a frayed nylon jacket. We crouch along a winding, tunnel into the depths of the hill, breathing hard at an altitude of over 4,500 metres. Slanting lodes rear above, shafts in the floor with hand-cranked pulleys drop to lower levels. Here and there we resort to a near crawl, the passage inches high. I'm acutely conscious of how proximous are dynamite and flaming acetylene lamp. Props and stemples are splintered by pressure in places. At times we tiptoe across precarious false floors. The chico shouts down side tunnels and along rifts, eventually gets a response, and his father joins us, takes us to the shrine of El Tio – the devil, who the miners must propitiate daily in return for extracting his riches.

He's made of clay, painted, decked with streamers, glass marbles for his eyes, his penis huge and erect, a clay frog between his goat's-horns, his cheeks pouched. 'He chews coca,' the miner explains, putting a cigarette in his mouth, lighting it, and lighting one for himself and me. 'You must smoke with the devil.' He scatters coca leaves around his feet, uncorks the flask of liquor, drenches El Tio and the walls of his niche and lights it. I hastily push the bag of explosives aside as blue flame dribbles down. He hands me the flask and I feel the fire course through me. He sips himself, and we squat and chew spinach-tasting leaves of coca that make exertion at this altitude bearable. He tells me happily of work that will kill him years before he reaches my age. I make my farewells, stagger out and wend back downhill, that night take the overnight bus across the Altiplano to Oruro, see the dawn blush behind high snow peaks of the Cordillera Real and spread across the desert, and descend to La Paz.

Nothing quite prepares you for the entry into Bolivia's administrative capital. You come from that backdrop of desert plains and mighty, snow-capped peaks to the rim of a dramatic, gouged and pinnacled canyon two miles wide, and there, a thousand feet below, hacked and terraced and tunnelled into its bed and sides, the weirdest, highest, most dramatic capital city in the World, La Ciudad de Nuestra Senora de La Paz – the city of Our Lady of Peace. I pitch off the bus at the top of the main thoroughfare, the Prado, and into what seems like a revolution. Crowds are gathered, placards are being waved about, lengthy hand-written demand-posters brandished aloft. Rockets and fireworks explode against the downtown skyscrapers, chants and shouts fill the streets. My alarm turns to bemused interest as I see the police smiling on benignly, engaging in conversation, flicking a lighter at the fuse of a proffered firework. There is, beyond all the animation of protest, a curious tranquility about it all, an onlooking wry phlegmatism. 'Teachers protesting for pay,' a young man tells me, 'and the nurses, you know – they're on hunger strike; but in four or five days they'll have lost enough weight, think how pretty they now look, start feeling hungry and they'll sign a bit of paper that gives them a fraction of what they demand. It's the Americanos, amigo – they stamp out the coca, give the government money, the government promise this and that and the money goes who knows where but not to us. Then the farmers have no coca to sell, and here in this country, where we live so high, the coca is a medicine, it helps us work. Why does America not deal with her own problems, and stop making them for us..?' Behind him, one of the cholas, of the Aymara or Quechua stock who make up over half of Bolivia's eight-million-strong population, reaches into a bulging sack and weighs out the pale green leaves in hand-held scales. My friend makes an amused inclination of his head in her direction, gestures an open palm at the sky, and suggests that I now have a grasp of the whole economic situation of Bolivia. As he finishes, a disturbingly beautiful woman with fine-drawn brows, huge dark eyes and exquisite bone-structure who has been nodding along to his every point turns her head back to the protest, and in doing so reveals a conquistadore's profile. I leave them and make my way slowly – you're at an altitude on the street here that's higher than most of the summits of the Alps – up a steep barrio lined with stalls of an Indian market. My notion of Bolivia as one of the World's poorest countries is challenged by this wealth and variety of produce – melons, green, yellow and red bananas, paw-paws, maize, grains, pulses, spices, mounds of chillies, hanging racks of meat, slabs stacked with fish, all tended by the hoop-skirted, behatted cholas squatting quietly by. The realisation dawns that this is a resource-rich country with a relatively undeveloped cash-economy. That sense is matched by a certain primitivity of superstition and belief. In the Witches' Market along Calle Sagarnaga llama foetuses are for sale, upright, desiccated, pathetic somehow, legs bound with wool, eyes that never saw life tight-closed. When by accident the farmers kill pregnant females, they smoke the foetuses and sell them to go into the foundations of new buildings. Here in Bolivia, even in its teeming capital, you are never that far from the old gods, from propitiatory magic. In the astonishingly rich baroco-mestizo carving on the eighteenth-century façade of San Francisco church at the top of the Prada there are dragons and curling vines, custard-apples, angels, saints maybe, gleeful sheelagh-na-gigs giving birth, flowers and birds and the sun. It all seems to owe more to the great Aymara deity of Pachamama – Mother Earth – than to any Christian belief, and at the centre of it all, looking thoroughly at home, weathered into belonging, a copper Saint Francis.

The festival of Alasitas, which means 'abundance' and translates literally as 'buy from me' in Aymara, is about to begin. I head down into the great fair that colonises all the open spaces of the city. There are swings, carousels, merry-go-rounds, stalls offering every kind of ethnic fast food: pastries wrapped in vine leaves, kebabs of kidneys and potatoes, of chicken, lamb, pork, beef, llama, baskets of delicious, gudgeon-sized fried fish. Beyond them row after row of stalls sell miniature everything: tractors, farms, 4WDs, Bolivian passports, kitchen ranges, washing machines with tiny packets of soap powder, wads of $100 bills, effigies of the little dwarf-god Ekeko, distributor of material possessions. They're purchased, blessed by an Aymara yatiri ('elder'), and perhaps fortune will bestow them upon their possessors in reality during the coming year. Right now the heavens open, and choose instead to bestow the torrential afternoon rain: cholas wrap their bowlers in carrier-bags and their stalls in polythene sheets; a river runs down the Prada, torrent-tributaries emptying into it from all the steep side streets; beggars' cups thrust out from under oil-cloths collect more water than coins; microbuses seethe by, sluicing waves over the kerbs, destinations yelled from open windows, would-be passengers dancing through traffic and flood to board.

By nightfall the sky has cleared, the walls of this city's lunar canyon spangled and streamered to the brim with lights. I leave in the morning for Lake Titikaka. All along the road the cholas and cholitas and chicos are selling brilliant tall bunches of gladioli, and travellers buy them to offer in front of the ornate altar of the Virgin of Copacabana, where they're bound.

We cross a narrow strait of the lake on a rickety ferry, climb over a pass only metres away from the border with Peru, and arrive in Copacabana's lovely lakeside town, white brilliance of its Moorish cathedral framed between pinnacled and calvaried rock-bluffs. In front of it, cars are being ritually blessed for the journey home with beer poured on their bonnets and tyres. On the reedy shore below is the point of embarkation for Isla del Sol – the island of the sun, and the birthplace of the Inca culture. A large modern tourist hydrofoil cruises out there. South America's largest, and at 3,810 metres above sea level the highest navigable water in the world, the lake is astonishingly beautiful, sapphire-blue, its shores terraced and wooded, its islands as those of the Aegean must have been a century ago. The hydrofoil berths by the village of Challapampa, straddling an isthmus near the north end of the island. Little friendly pigs root along the sandy shore, gorgeous Indian children in vibrantly-coloured clothing squalling and playing among them. A band strikes up by the school on the opposite side of the isthmus, and from there, rowed by one of the inhabitants, I take a small boat that bucks and battles alarmingly through the waves of this inland sea to round a promontory and land me in the rocky cove of Bahia Sabacera. By goat-tracks that lead though sweet-scented herbs and savagely-thorned shrubs I climb up to the ridge of the island. The views all around in the clear air of altitude to distant mountains and coasts, or of golden capes against slate-grey clouds, are heart-stopping in their loveliness. I descend the other side. Here, above a white-sand beach, is the Palacio del Inca – a labyrinth of thick, dry-stone walls and tiny doorways that is inscrutable, ancient, solid and unexplained.

A little way above and to the south, beyond a great flat rock that you might mistake for a picnic table before the darker purpose of human sacrifice creeps into your consciousness, a bluff of tawny rock outcrops from the backbone of the island, its form that of a crouching puma. This is Titi Khar'ka – the rock of the puma – from which the lake takes its name. I trace the natural features in it by which the Inca creation legend is delineated: the face of the puma; the four long and pronounced niches, those on the right known as the Refuge of the Sun, those on the left the Refuge of the Moon. Here, according to Inca myth, during the times of flood and darkness the sun made its first appearance; and thereafter came

Manco Kapac and his sister-wife Mama Ocllo, son and daughter of the puma-god, and they were the progenitors of the Inca empire. In the granular rock-pavement leading away from the bluff are ironstone intrusions like footprints – those of the sun, as he walked away after his birth here.

Even in the crystal light of an Andean afternoon, there is an eeriness about this remote and little-visited place – as if the rocks not only carried stories, but memories also; as if its extraordinary beauty had to be tempered and haunted with a measure of human sadness, or even tragedy. Whatever the reason, I hurried away by the little, lonely tracks that led down towards the settlement of Challabamba, an inquisitive cow leaning over the wall of its small field to greet me as I arrived, and felt glad to be back there among domesticity and cultivation and the more customary and amiable strangenesses of Bolivia again.

MEETINGS *with* REMARKABLE CREATURES

One of the chief pleasures of travel and landscape for me is that of encountering wild animals and birds in their natural habitats. Whether it's through patience and chance, by organised guidance, or intimately in one's own home territory, these experiences are among the most memorable any writer can hope for.

1: *The Wolf & the Goose*

Cooke City, Montana, just beyond the Silver Gate into the Yellowstone National Park, is a one-street town among wooded hills. Substitute horses for the 4WD pickups jagged in along the sidewalk and it could be the film set for any western you ever saw. In Martha's Diner I'm tuning in to the local wavelengths:

'If mamma's pie'd been half as good as this, Martha, I guess I'd never've left home,' fawns the guy in the 'Freemen of Montana' baseball cap, whose belly as well as his conversation proclaims expertise in the matter of pies.

'You havin' some more, Harvey?' simpers Martha, lances a 'How about you, mister?' at me from the side of her mouth, and after a squinting examination from the corner of an eye, as an afterthought adds, 'You a tourist?'

The malevolence she imparts to the last two syllables is breathtaking. Harvey's gobstopper eyes roll around above his girth, seeking a focus for Martha's enmity, finally fix on me, and reinforce it. I issue a quick denial. She's not letting me off the hook so easily.

'So what you doin' in these parts?'

'Working.'

She studies me, the notebook, the hire car outside; a slow shake of her head and the next question jabs in:

'Government ..?'

If 'tourist' came out as insult, this is uttered as curse. I exhale, answer with a vigorous shake of my head, grinning like a guilty politician. Beyond the window I can see a sign on the back of Harvey's pick-up that reads 'protected by Smith & Wesson'.

'I'm just a writer a long way from home.'

'Where's home?' presses Martha, softening.

'Wales.'

'Oh yeah, Wales – Diana! – have some more pie, honey.'

'Have some more pie,' harmonises Harvey, 'it's real good!'

'You play rugby?' pipes up a short guy with an embryonic paunch who's been spectating so far. 'I'm from Fort Worth. We play down there too. Say, you got wolves in Wales ..?'

Before I can get in a 'used-to-have-but-it-was-400-years-ago', pandemonium's broken loose. Harvey's mouthing 'dead livestock' and imprecations, Martha's talking about the business they've brought in, Fort Worth and his wife are telling how they sure hope to see some. Everyone's talking at once and I'm asking for my check and hitting the road before I get arrested for starting a riot. It seems the Yellowstone Wolves are a contentious issue in these parts.

Outside, the endless caravanserai of pantechnicon-sized Recreation Vehicles, each with its sports vehicle trailing behind on a rigid tow-rod, is rolling into the World's oldest National Park, heading along its slow road circuits through burnt forest and riverine meadow, bound for Mammoth Hot Springs or Old Faithful, its power-steered occupants intent on geyser, boiling river and volcanic vent. I pay my entrance fee at the gate and follow them in. By the travertine mound of Soda Butte ('Do not climb on this fragile feature – it is a hot spring that has been inactive for 100 years') I pull off-road. An old fisherman's standing in the river, easing the loops of his fly-line down on to the water in benign concentration, watched by his wife on the bank:

'How're you doin'?' he queries.

'Fine. Caught many fish?'

'Ain't complainin'. Are you fishin'?'

'Just looking.'

'Oh sure – it's worth looking at.' He scans round, plucking homilies from the horizon, finding one for me. 'Well now – have a nice day, and if it don't work out, don't go cryin', 'cos most of the time it does.'

I'm here looking for wolves, but then, so is almost everybody else and a few miles down the road in a lay-by there's a group of very happy people. They're watching a coyote slink warily between the river and a herd of buffalo. They're satisfied, smug even, speculating excitedly about which wolf-pack it belongs to, and if it was one of the original animals captured in Alberta and brought down four years ago to be released in wolf-extinct Yellowstone. A Ranger leans against his truck, checking the tourists don't approach the animals. I catch his eye. He gives me half a grin and his eyebrows disappear for a moment under his hairline. He's hot. He can't be bothered to explain. I know that feeling. I drive on to Old Faithful.

In the lobby of the inn ('largest log structure in the US of A!'), visitors pester staff for the time of the geyser's next eruption. 'Four, ten,' they're curtly informed, 'it's there on the board. This is a tourist attraction that arrives on time.' I loiter behind a row of pear-shapes on a bench. The women are huddling together jokily:

'How long will it last?' one of them asks.

'Depends whether it's male or female,' comes the reply. On cue the geyser huffs and puffs and blows itself out. A jet of steam swooshes 100 feet into the air, a few bloops follow and it's gone. The women look at each other knowingly and subside too, but into giggles. I walk on, past Aurum Geyser, Beech Spring and Ear Spring, look down past grey, crusted strata into rents of bubbling ultramarine that disappear from view. I'm listening to Vulcan's breath, imagining this scene of steaming craters and mounds and charred trees before the impedimenta of mass observation arrived, the chill of that vision chorused by two ravens flying above. It's contact with the magma. It's profoundly impressive. It's enough. I drive on to Mammoth Hot Springs. Herds of bulky elk rut and frisk around the car-park. A woman walking into the hotel dining room cocks an ear to their squealing and bugling. 'What's that horrible noise?' she asks of the husband who looks down silently at her side. Next morning I go to see the wolf man.

Doug Robinson's Head of the Yellowstone Wolf Project, has overseen it since the first animals arrived. He's a rangy 38-year-old from Ohio who's been interested – he stresses the word to distinguish himself from the obsessives with whom he deals on a daily basis – in wolves since he was 12. He talks me through it in his Park Service office with a calm mastery of detail and a tactical determination to win through against powerful opposing forces: present situation exceeding all expectations, a current minimum of 116 in the Park – seven breeding pairs, and another eleven breeding pairs and an even larger supporting population on Nez Perce land over in Idaho; big healthy animals too, in the best condition; a male pup he caught weighed 105 lbs – way above average adult size in most areas; perfect habitat for America's dominant natural predator, and its ecologically beneficial effect on the elk and coyote populations was already cutting in.

Doug talked on and on and the more he talked the more I wanted to see a wolf. Any chance? Not at this time of year – all up in the high country. And then he relented, smiled:

'Rick McIntyre tells me there's a big, dark young male been seen around the Lamar Valley these last few days. If you were there at the right time, maybe ...'

So I take the hint. Each dawn and dusk I drive out into the Lamar Valley, into the bleached desert rawness at the margins of the high country with swabs of white cloud drifting low across indigo sky. Nothing. Hour after hour I wait. No movement, except a flicker maybe, like a drift of grey ash, barely discernible, way over against the woods. Then it's a late October evening, my last day, the first snow powdering the rough, far sandstone peaks. I drive into the Lamar again, leave the car, walk, sit among the lemony-disinfectant scent of the sagebrush, by a rock, above the river, hidden, looking out across wide alluvial flats of the valley to the wooded bluffs beyond. The explosive green of the aspens against the dark spruce graduates to gingery tones of autumn in their crowns. Peach brilliance of sunset has faded, the russet grasses of the valley flare briefly in its afterglow, shades of landscape thicken, conifers mass into darkness, the river over its pebbles gentles out a rhythm of ripple and eddy and wash, a bright and waxing half-moon rises and sails.

Tonight, there are six Canada geese on the shingle opposite, in front of a tree-trunk brought down by the floods. They crane alert necks towards my hiding place, discuss me, peck among stones, stretch to flap wings and talk some more between themselves about the still presence across the moonlit water. A skein of mist, inches deep, resolves out of the valley flats, glimmers and swells, drift of a breeze hinting at movement in it here and there and the river shining. The geese gaze blindly into a darkness beyond. There is magic taking place in front of me and I know it by the prickling of my scalp.

The log grows ears.

A flurry of movement and five geese are in the air, wheeling and honking away, a line of swift shadows hurled across the moon. On the gleaming shingle the sixth lies still.

The wolf stands over it, dark and intense, lifts its long muzzle towards me, gives an abbreviated howl that raises the hairs on the back of my neck, picks up its prey, leaps the log and disappears back into the mist.

To see what you have come to see sometimes is to be blessed.

2: Whale-watching at Tadoussac

Some places enchant. Sometimes they even enchant despite the claims of enchantment made on their behalf. Try this, for example: 'I love Tadoussac for all the things about it that cannot be put into words, for the shiver that goes down my spine each time I see the plunging cleavage of Anse-a-l'Eau and the boats that dare venture into the turbulent waters washing around the stone nipples. At such moments, life changes pace ...'

It surely does. Maybe some subtle quality's been lost in the translation, but it sounds as though the breathing of the writer of the official guide to Tadoussac (the name means 'breast' in Algonquian) is becoming extremely rapid. It comes as a considerable relief after this introduction to find that, at the end of an easy three-hour drive east from Quebec City along the north shore of the St Lawrence Seaway and a brief crossing by ferry over the dark water of the Saguenay fjord, Tadoussac itself is such a relaxed and leisurely place. But then, this is French Canada, for which the words 'relaxed' and 'leisurely' might almost have been invented. Even at their jauntiest, the Quebecois are a pretty laid-back lot.

I'd travelled here to observe a religious ritual, but we'll be coming to that. To miss out on describing arrival at Tadoussac would be a form of sacrilege. This, after all, in 1998 was voted by the Confederation of World Tourist Organisations (maybe that wasn't the name, but it was some tourist-trade Behemoth the actual title of which no-one in Quebec seems to know, or even much care to know, which is entirely typical of the place) as one of the '30 Most Beautiful Bays in the World' – and the only one of them in North America.

It's an accolade that Tadoussac may well deserve. The village-sized town claims to be the oldest surviving settlement on the subcontinent, to the truth of which assertion archaeological evidence from the palaeo-Indian era thousands of years before the establishment of the first European fur-trading post here in 1,600 attests. What's drawn people to this shore for so long is obvious as you cross the fjord.

The ferry's warning blast ricochets between vast walls of glistening, ice-scoured granite that sheer down into water the blackness of which betokens immense depth. Where the Saguenay debouches into the St

Lawrence is a close and complex region of breast-like wooded hills, salt-bleached and tide-lined *roches moutonnées* and shelving golden dunes of sand that all cluster protectively round an exquisite little crescent of a bay. This is one of nature's perfected places, and one that man for once has not unduly despoiled or disarranged. The tiny cluster of a town, with its red tin roofs and sharp-spired churches, its veranda'd and balconied shining houses among the copses of orange-berried rowan trees and silver birches, its skeins of blue wood-smoke dispersing tangy on soft winds that drift in from a seaway the wide surface of which is banded in pewter and mercury – all these induce a particular mood of dreamy, sensual elation entirely appropriate for the observances that take place here.

My arrival at the Hotel Tadoussac coincides with that of a charabanc-load of large and loud Americans in long shorts. They congest the lobby as they queue for a lift which takes them two-by-two to their rooms. Their bulk and baggage block corridors. They roll out of the hotel onto spacious lawns and there subside, Scotch in hand, to look out over the bay from cushionless steamer chairs through the slats of which rolls of flesh extrude like elongated pale sausages. 'Les baleines!' mutters the receptionist, presuming on her guests' cultural insularity, roll of a laconic eye in their direction, 'you 'ave come to see them. 'Ere they are.'

The Hotel Tadoussac is an anachronistic delight from the era of steamship opulence. Out on lawns from which painted flights of steps descend past tennis courts and miniature golf to a beach of sifted gold, the Americans might endlessly discuss the shortcomings of Canadian civilisation; but even their complaints are tinged with an ironic appreciation of the way this place has resisted the insistent necessities of mass tourism.

'You got ice on your landing?'

'No – no ice machine – no Gideon Bibles either – an' you know what? Marlene an' I gotta share a bed. In our room we only got one double bed. Ain't bin in one o' those together in 20 years. Ain't that right, honey?'

Marlene reaches across and gives a flat-palmed friendly slap to his elephantine thigh, causing rollers of flesh to race towards his groin.

'Sure gonna be your lucky night,' she smiles.

A white apparition of a cruise liner sails into the bay, impossibly large in its intimate scale. A tiny tender buts out to it before it slides round the point into the Saguenay river and is lost to view. It is afternoon. I wander round the town. A young man in the costume of a respectable mercer of Nouvelle France emerges from the trading post reconstructed on the site of Pierre Chauvin's original one of 1,600, and so, accompanying him, does a burst of accordion music. Someone in there is having a good time. On the boardwalk above the beach a young squaw comes towards me, her hair braided, a leather thong threaded with beads round her forehead, her deerskin tunic tasselled and fringed, rough-woven decoration across every available inch of the rest of her clothing, a blanket over her shoulder, moccasins on her feet and her cheeks barred with charcoal. Too comprehensively ethnic to be real, she recognises it with a huge grin and a wink and in her turn disappears into the mysteriously musical trading post. Nearby in the excellent Marine Mammal Interpretative Centre, from the ceiling hangs the skeleton of a Minke whale found dead nearby in 1997, the skeleton of an embryo within it. With both, it is the long, expressive delicacy of finger-like bones in the flippers that affect. I drift up town, snuffing at the ubiquitous scent of resin from the surrounding forests, and end up in a room with potted geraniums on the sill of its open window, talking to Andrée Hardy, who asks me with what family I will be going out to see the whales?

'Dufour,' I tell her.

'Then you will be very comfortable and see many whales,' she responds, tossing her long chestnut hair, her lived-in warm face glowing with pleasure at the propinquities of her home place.

The southern shore, 15 miles away, glimmers above a trail of mist next morning. From the luxurious salon of Famille Dufour Deux, glass all around and the sun streaming in, I watch the Americans on the foredeck, their video-cameras pointed and primed. They press close to each other and to the rail as we heel away from the harbour. We head out into the seaway towards the reefs – submerged lateral and medial moraines left behind by the glacier that formed Saguenay – that stretch far out into the St Lawrence. The tide boils around this meeting of the waters. It's marked by a curious little red-striped asymmetrical lighthouse called 'La Toupie' – the spinning-top. On our way out to it we pass a pod of the beluga whales that hunting and pollution had brought to the brink of extinction in the St Lawrence 40 years ago. Now the discreet word is that they are securely on the increase, the population up to 1,200 from a one-time low of 80. The Americans, videos whirring, peer over the boat's side at these beautiful little white whales in their only known habitat outside the High Arctic: 'Their heads are the shape of a hare's, white as snow with no marks' wrote Jacques Cartier in 1535. The boat slows and steers a course to avoid them, obeying the strict marine mammal observation code, then tacks back towards the lighthouse.

Beyond it, along the pale strip of the seaway the freighters and container ships head down from the Great Lakes, Montreal and Quebec to the ocean. But in the dark turbulence at the reefs, a couple more cruise boats like ours and half-a-dozen Zodiacs circle slowly among the standing waves and overfalls. Over the address system our boat's biologist tells us to watch an area at three o'clock, and then raps out the curt, excited message, 'Fin whale surfacing at ten metres!' Its back of arched ebony heaves clear of the water, streamered with spray, 70 feet long and dwarfing the Zodiacs across which the spume drifts as it blows. Suddenly they are all around us, the water seething with huge shapes, bowing and plunging and soughing and sighing, minke and humpback and fin whales, the smaller dolphins and pilot whales.

Our biologist all the while intones her catalogues of facts and explanations – the proliferation of krill – the whales' food – in this stirred-up water, their long history here, their life-cycles and voyagings. But we are scarcely listening. God has left the pale heavens above and taken up residence in the deep, is glimpsed time and again here, and here again, almost within touch, before plunging back into the profound, dark and liquid matrix. They rear from our subconscious, these creatures, in all the glory of their unfathomable life. In their observation are the perfect post-Freudian mysteries and articles of faith. In their presence even the Americans are left open-mouthed and quiet.

In three hours we see hundreds of them. A cormorant veers past on stiff, rapid wings and we turn for harbour. I catch sight of Marlene hanging over the rails with her husband, gazing astern, her face contented and unlined, her hand sliding fondly down his spreading rump, her voice crooning in his ear: 'Sure they were big, but size don't matter, honey – we know that.' They press a little closer, both of them quivering with soft, affectionate laughter. His video hangs limp by his side. We reach harbour.

At twilight I walk back along the bay. White graves around the Indian Chapel down by the shore garner the last of the day, all the family names of Brisson and Morin, Tremblay and Hovington and Dufour glinting to each other as the tide ebbs with a melancholy long withdrawing roar. I hear the ferry's warning blast. In the Café Gibard assured women of a certain age with voices like wind husking through fields of ripe wheat light up another *Players' sans filtre*, drain their 20 oz glasses of *bière blonde Quebecoise*, order another and let their glances drift along with their exhaled tobacco-smoke out across the bay and the broken waters where the whales blow to the farther shore, and its lights that flicker distantly, enticingly.

3: Befriending the Raven

I dreamed last night that I returned to Wales. Not that I have ever left this country – or at least not for years. But in the dream, those familiar feelings glowed out that for me come in response to this place, and no other. So that now, sitting here at my desk, the valley filled with orange mist and peaks all around bright-morning-gold, I'm assailed by memory of emotion felt at coming back to this place, which is like no other. All roads in my life seem to have led to Wales. The images reel past like clips assembled from life's cutting-room floor, edited out from a film where the narrative always runs to evening and home and west.

All those queer, plucking emotions; all that ache within on return, having been away; all that recognition. Myself on roads outside cities years ago, setting a thumb against the red sun to beg a lift towards it; or later, and the times innumerable, behind the wheel, seeing hill-fretted horizons ahead and the clouds, fiery circles, the heather burning across the moor and smoke furling round the moon as I sped. To love is to dream, the returning miles always said. Now, there is this view – Snowdon up-valley, sea to the west, the curve of a bay, distant Holyhead. But that's just gilded frame, viewed from my window 1,100 feet up on Garnedd Elidir. It's in composition, detail, execution, you find the masterpiece that is to me this small country between Worm's Head and Holyhead.

Welshness – its root's in the Anglo-Saxon word for foreign; and there is a foreignness about this country that sets it apart from the other regions of Britain. There are those within the outdoor community who can view land as its mere carapace – these collectable and listed points reaching that height, those ridges forming their convenient physical circuit. I met one such once, by the little pass with its particular Welsh name between Moel y Cynghorion and Foel Goch, on the long ridge by which Snowdon reaches out to the sea (and what a walk that is, from Caernarfon quay by lanes, by standing stones and plover-screamed meadow-paths, to the dark moor, to the high ridges). I asked him how he was doing, where he'd been, but he didn't want to stop in his huffing, stumping round: 'Along the Big Dipper,' he threw back at me over his shoulder, in the nasal tones of South-east England. He didn't know – or couldn't be bothered using – the names of the hills he raced across, wouldn't have been aware that the hollow where he found me resting, contemplating, is called Bwlch Carreg y Gigfran, 'the pass of the raven's rock'. I feel less affection for, or indeed affinity with him than I do with the ravens, sleek and harsh, that crowd my garden each morning, take food from my hand if nothing moves, to bear back to red throats already in cold pre-spring agape in their sprawling nest. He – our hill-racer – foregoes or denies the texture of humanity, history, nature; the raven, as those who lived here in their naming recognise, embodies the spirit of its hills.

There was a summer evening months ago. I'd been recording radio pieces, left the Bangor studios and all their media-rush, passing concerns and technological impedimenta behind, walked down the road and took the path up to British Camp. It used, in my student days, to be one of my favourite places. It's discreet, hidden somehow, unsignposted, the ways of reaching it not obvious, at a remove from the city. And Bangor, for all its nestling smallness between the two ridges, is that. I don't know if British Camp ever was a British camp. Even the archaeologists seem undecided, the Royal Commission Inventory of Ancient Monuments referring ambivalently to a shale bank that might be natural, might be man-made; and the single recorded find here of a Constantinian coin. It doesn't matter to me if it isn't. The place still has distinctive character. It feels as fine and apart now as it did on spring afternoons 30 years ago when there were always bluebells in the woods of Siliwen, and at the end of long afternoons with the irregular Welsh verbs of Miss Enid Pierce Roberts or the mediaeval Scots poets with Dr David Lindsay, lovers would escape up here and look round at a landscape new then in every particular.

On this evening, sitting on one of the simple benches and gazing out over the Afon Menai to Anglesey, I was noticing what had changed, what had remained the same. The framing of the scene was much as it had ever been: the two bridges, the islands, the brocaded oakwoods and wrack-brown shorelines of the straits, the headlands receding eastwards, the pink sunset glow of Ynys Seiriol's striated rock and the way Traeth Lafan's scalloped sandflats catch the ellipses of light. The statelier incursions of humanity – those elegant terraces at Beaumaris, the 'rich man's flowering lawns' around Penrhyn and Plas Newydd, Bangor's squat pier that seems to be hobbling out over the water supported on Zimmer frames, and the tower of Top College which is so stumpy from this angle, and so much more heartening in its purpose and origin – paid for from quarrymen's pennies – than Penrhyn's quite similar one; all these seemed better groomed somehow than I remembered them, in keeping with the yachts and slipways, castellated grand houses and stark white balconied blocks of flats among the dark groves on the farther shore.

As if to compensate, a rash or blight of boxy suburbia was spreading across the ridge of Llandegfan opposite, and the pylons which strut around the limits of vision were more obvious now. More unkempt too was the immediate foreground – a tangled scrub of nettle and foxglove, spindly birch, gorse with the dry husks of its flowers split open to reveal furry black seed-pods, a litter at my feet of cigarette ends, sweet wrappers, the wire from around a celebratory champagne cork cast carelessly on the ground.

I looked up from this human detritus and what caught my eye was a bare, forked branch of sessile oak, streaked with bird droppings, barkless and dead, its skeletal-fingered gesture pointing starkly north. Just at the moment it registered on my consciousness, there alighted on it a raven.

We in our century and urban societies are so unused to encounters with wild creatures. Compare the modern Welsh poet Robert Williams Parry's taut surprise at his meeting with a fox, and the way it slips out of his sight *'megis seren wib'* ('like a shooting star') in the famous sonnet, with his great precursor Dafydd ap Gwilym's laddishly familiar apostrophising of the same animal 600 years earlier:

> *Gwr yw ef a garai iâr,*
> *A choeg edn, a chig adar.*
> (He's a fellow who loves the hens / And stupid fowl, and flesh of birds.)

So there was delight in this tamed setting at being in so close a proximity to a creature which is, for me, the apotheosis of wildness. And that sense I have of the raven is not just one of those anti-civilisation compensatory impulses like that of Williams Parry's towards the fox. It is more primitive than that. Remember the Morrigan, the shape-shifting raven-goddess of slaughter in Irish mythology, and how, in the Táin Bo Cuailnge she settles on a standing stone and tells of matters to the Brown Bull: of hosts gathering to certain slaughter; of the raven ravenous among corpses of men; of affliction and outcry and war everlasting, raging over Cuailnge with the deaths of sons, the deaths of kinsmen, death upon death, until the Bull, maddened, casts off restraint and rages uncontrollably through the land? Remember the Morrigan's temptation, in the guise of King Buan's daughter, of Cuchulain in the same epic, her seductive guiles and desire for love before his battles with Loch's brother and Loch himself? Remember them is just what I did as I watched this wildest of birds, this inhabitant of the wildest places, in perfect stillness from 20 feet away, from a distance close enough for me to see the dark brown iris of its eye, the dark grey interior of its bill. And it was aware of my presence as another creature. It began to communicate with me. At first, its gestures were aggressive, the wings drooped on either side, tail fanned, bill snapping, and a guttural, metallic note growled out at me. But its behaviour then began to relax, the ruffled feathers on legs and head smoothed down, it began to preen and peck at the branch, tilted its head straight up in a gesture of supplication or appeasement, looked away and then looked round again, squatted low on the branch with wings half open and tail feathers held straight and quivering, and all the time with a rather soft and musical rolling call to me, and by all of this I was quite entranced.

But as I watched, and as my mind drifted across the terrible images of mythology – the prophetess of slaughter, the seductress of warriors, the washer at the ford – I noticed another aspect of the bird in front of me which caused it to shift in my perception a degree away from the surprising but still understandable. For a thickness of perhaps two inches around its entire body – head, legs, wings, tail – and moving with it whenever it moved, was a bright, translucent violet aura. Just that. I have no explanation for it. I took off my glasses in case it was an effect produced by refraction through their lenses. The aura remained. I changed my angle of view. The aura persisted as the raven responded to this new game. Suddenly, behind me, a blonde-haired woman appeared. The raven flew away, taking its aura and presence with it. The woman and I exchanged greetings.

'You must be King Buan's daughter,' I said to her, and walked away in silent, puzzled laughter. But this is a prosaic ending, and beyond it came the phase of making friends with ravens. So that now, in my garden, the young of last year's brood call from the wire and feed from my hand.

We were not always so familiar, though I've always known about the place of ravens, and the presence they bring there.

There is, for example, the summit of Cadair Idris. Perhaps this is my favourite mountain, though I'm not sure: Brandon, Shivling, Rhobell Fawr – how are we to choose? Strength of association might lead me to Cadair, though. And if so, there would be the pleasure of starting from Dolgellau. It is the oddest little town, piled-up and intricate, its grey stone and plain, elegant style taken both of them from the mountain. Down on it, from 2,800 feet above, peer the summit crags of Mynydd Moel – easternmost of the trinity of great peaks which make up Cadair Idris. To procrastinate in the National Milk Bar (an institution in every North- and Mid-Wales town), listen to the playful conversation and admire the lovely faces of the local young women before setting out on a luminous winter's day maybe for the summits is one of the pleasures of life. The Reverend Francis Kilvert – surely the most amiable of all our great diarists – did exactly the same thing in 1871: 'I was very much struck and taken with the waitress at the Golden Lion. She said her name was Jane Williams and that her home was at Betws y Coed. She was a beautiful girl with blue eyes, eyes singularly lovely, the sweetest saddest most weary and most patient eyes I ever saw. It seemed as if she had a great sorrow in her heart.'

Kilvert took the Pony Track up Cadair by the Rhiw Gwredydd, but there's a better way. Fron Serth – the name means 'steep hill' and it is precisely that – on the outskirts of town leads up into an exquisite region of oakwoods, sheep pasture and little ridges at the north-eastern end of the Cadair range. Tir Stent it's called on the map – Welsh landscape at its most typical and jewelled, looking out to Rhobell Fawr which rises with an attractive symmetry from this angle above the valley of the Wnion. An old, flagged pony track runs through it over to the top of the Tal y Llyn pass, and is a good way to gain the eastern gable of the longest and finest mountain ridge south of the Scottish border. The ascent to its first summit, Gau Graig, is a merciless 1,100 feet in the space of half a mile. The view opens out to the north and east with every foot gained. There is a steep and gravelly 500 feet of ascent from Gau Graig up to the ridge's next tier at Mynydd Moel. When last here, I was dawdling up it as a friendly sheepdog came bounding down with two walkers in attendance, heading for the valley already with huge sacks on to which were strapped ice-axes and crampons, though not so much as a rag or shred of snow was to be seen even in the most northerly of gullies. They gave me a breezy, stern hello and strode off with purpose in their step after the dog, who seemed as impatient at their progress as they were dismissive of mine. Within a few minutes I was on top of Mynydd Moel, with the world and its people scattering off in all directions

If you have never been up Cadair from this eastern end then you have a delight in store. From the state of the paths by far the greater number who do climb Cadair seem never even to venture so far as Mynydd Moel, which is a great hill in its own right, massive in presence as you approach it from the east. Its top is particularly fine, with a shelter-cairn and a little cockscomb of rocks above plunging crags. You can see from it straight down on to Dolgellau, a bare two miles away, and that gives you the clue as to why, in Elizabethan times, this was considered the highest mountain in the British Isles. Penygadair – highest point of the Cadair range – may only be 2,928 feet above sea level, but sea-level is just down there. Dolgellau is at it. Ben Nevis may be half as high again but it is twice as far from the sea. Those sandflats and long, low saltings of the Mawddach estuary give Cadair its uplift, its subjective impression of height. It feels a tremendous mountain.

And I'm tempted to state that Mynydd Moel is the best part of it. Even its name suggests the effect it has, translating loosely as the mountain mountain in a deliberately intensifying way. From it, you look right along the northern escarpment, lakes flashing silver from glaciated hollows around which elegant ridges glint skywards. Walk a few yards down the southern slope and you're confronted by a view a version of which is one of the masterpieces of 18th-century art. Richard Wilson's *Cader Idris, Llyn-y-cau* of 1765 is one of those paintings which anyone with a vestige of interest in art knows. It's in the Tate in London and I go to see it there when I can – a surprisingly small canvas, not much more than 18 inches high by two feet or so wide, all russets and Payne's gray with the palest blues and greens and a touch of gold on foreground boulders which root its conceptual diagonals firmly in the landscape. It always shocks me with its capacity simultaneously to be like and yet unlike. It's less the depiction of a mountain scene than its reordering, the interpretation of its essence by a man with a kindly, respectful and loving view of nature and its power for harmony. I love it, and the place it so wonderfully expresses.

If Richard Wilson had seen it on a day like the one I was enjoying, his painting might have been even more haunting and suffused with the golden light of a Claude landscape instead of its merest suggestion. I've seldom seen so far from the hills: Snowdon seemed almost within touching distance to the north, and Snaefell hung like a cloud behind it, whilst to the south-east and the south-west the Malvern hills and the Preselis delimited the horizon, so clear their every summit was identifiable. Only to the west was the clarity compromised by an encroaching heavy front which moved inexorably in through the course of the afternoon. A blustery wind scoured the plateau between Mynydd Moel and Penygadair. Two walkers surfing along on it stopped to talk excitedly of the day's quality, their speech gasping and fragmented: 'Perfect ... the views ... can see everything ... oh!' One of them recognised me from a time we worked together on nightshifts in a Caernarfon factory nearly 30 years ago, making upholstery for cars that will all long since have gone to the scrap-heap, and neither of us knowing then of the other's passion for these enduring places. I left them to climb on to the summit, and all the memories that place holds for me. And as I arrived, the ravens grated their welcome.

These birds and their parents I have known for 40 years. This was the first mountain I climbed in Wales, in that burnished summer at the end of the 1950s, and they were there then, tumbling joyful acrobats around the summit whose flight spelt freedom, but whose presence was a stranger longing the exact words for which remain fixed only in feeling, refusing ever to succumb to our quest after definition, the birds themselves haunting the mirror tunnels of memory. Tilman is one of them now, whom I first met here, and my younger self too, soloing up the Cyfrwy Arete in the wind's exuberance. If I could never return, each bird would dance a memory there for me, memory being our slow descent from the summit-present, from the cold shelter hut I inhabit there.

Outside, wind freezes fingers and cheekbones in an instant, and I shuffle rapidly down to Cyfrwy. It must have been from here that Kilvert's guide on his ascent pointed out the place 'at the foot of an opposite precipice' where the body of the unfortunate Mr Smith had been found. He was a clerk from Newport on a walking tour of Wales in September 1865, who had disappeared whilst attempting to traverse the mountain in poor weather and darkness without a guide. He was found the following May: 'The foxes and ravens had eaten him. His eyes were gone. His teeth were dashed out by the fall and lay scattered about on the mountain ...' I was glad to pass on and race down the broad ridge over Rhiw Gwredydd, where the ponies once climbed up from the Dysynni valley, and on past Tyrau Mawr to Braich Ddu, the ridge's unvisited seaward gable, descended in the gathering dark with the light of Ynys Enlli flashing 30 miles across the bay. The vague path misled me into young spruce plantation, and on to the grimiest forestry track I've ever had the misfortune to stumble along. But by Cyfannedd a gibbous moon cast latticed shadows of branches across the road, an owl's wavering scream tore at the woods' silence, curlews descanted in the estuary. I took the footpath across the Barmouth rail-bridge with slick, black water running fast beneath, between the baulks which the shipworm gnaws, and I thought of poor Kilvert and his proper yearnings again: 'I have always had a vision of coming into a Welsh town about sunset and seeing the children playing on the bridge and this evening the dream came true.' If they had only been his, and his had been a satisfied life, sweet soul that he was. But maybe to ask for more than glimpses and memories of the perfect state is to ask too much. Maybe only in moments – as accessible in the mountains' simplicity as anywhere – does the landscape of our life approach the harmony of Richard Wilson's vision.

As with another time, beneath Clogwyn Du'r Arddu. I am listening to the raven's metallic call, echoing around the crags, and I am quite alone on a still, dry autumn day. I love this cliff – its tilting symmetries, its soar, its silvered rock. In architecture, atmosphere and detail, there's none finer in Britain. I'm in my climber's prime – strong, slim and confident so that the moves slip by – and clean my soles on the shattered boss of rock by which the White Slab starts. Slatey-smooth, fragile, creaking holds lead across. Above is grass and a little, safe corner to hide in before the long pitches start. I step in to the journey. To the left on these leaning slabs, everything falls away, but space is no more than threat and consequence, and reality's in the fingers' grip on sharp, sound tiny holds, in the careful-angled foot whose sole the same will bite. Beyond fear, so many moves to string together, the calm elation comes. You live on the brink of laughter. How ambiguous would be the falling scream? I trail a rope tied loosely round my waist, because this trip's for pleasure, not achievement. There is a lasso pitch, the alternative too hard for relaxation. But after, on the last long slab, 600 feet of air beneath, the raven perches near to me, eyeing with cocked head the trailing line as though it were some monstrous worm.

My dark and cosmic friend ...

In a churchyard, high up between rocky bluffs on a shoulder of Tal y Fan, I sit among graves. Its name is Llangelynin – the old church, not the new – and it dates from the 12th century. But it's essentially timeless, low and sturdy in its walled enclosure with the earth heaving and swelling against it. Inside, all is unerring simplicity. The North Transept is a Capel y Meibion ('men's chapel'). When I was last here a mole had thrown up a mound of soil from between the flags of the floor in chthonic jest. Painted on the east wall are Commandments and the Lord's Prayer, in Welsh and dating from the Restoration. In the churchyard, ash and hawthorn grow from a sheltering bank, the graves of the unnamed and the named mingle, the epitaphs on the latter expressing a sense of the place. The south-west corner has a well, Ffynnon Gelynin – a stone cist in a thick-walled enclosure, formerly roofed-over, which was supposed to have the power of divination. Clothes of sick children were placed in the water. If they floated, the child would live. It's scummy with algal growth and infested with pond-skaters now. Invested magic gone, nettles and ferns grow from its walls. The anxieties and miseries enacted here are forgotten and unmarked by anything but the small, harebell-crested mounds of minimal record in which the churchyard abounds, the significance of which is salutary to those who see here only peace.

There are few places I know which are more Welsh, more particular to these hills and reflective of their history, nature, community. A young woman creaks the gate, nods and smiles, goes into the church. After a while she emerges again and comes across to where I lie at rest. She talks to me:

of having lived in London, been unhappy there, thought often of this place. On a sweet-grassed grave, a greensward mattress of unnumbered bones, we lie and talk, and if desire flickers between us, as play of word and gesture intimates, it is not stated, not urgent. Even love and death's conjunctions are quieted here. At length, lingeringly, she goes, and I, who am lazy and peaceful in the sun, nestle on the greensward still, and keep so still that when his pinions hiss, as he alights and grips the edge of stone his eye fixes my immobility. He cranes his head sidelong to view. Am I his prey? He cranes his head and seems to read words written on stone:

'Who shall dwell in thy holy hill?'

Only the raven's friend ...

FELLOW TRAVELLERS

Travel-writing has been one of the popular literary genres since classical times, and every practitioner within it has his or her favourite antecedents or contemporaries. I think at times that my love of this branch of literature came from my grandfather's having taught me to read from The Pilgrim's Progress, *which is nothing if not transcendental travel. Since then, the love-affairs with authors have been incessant, from 18th-century picaresque novelists by way of Borrow and Kinglake to Robert Byron, Patrick Leigh Fermor, Edward Abbey, Peter Matthiessen and Jan Morris. I don't generally like writing about people, would myself resent the intrusion it represents, and deplore the disclosing and judgmental savageries of our national press' celebrity interviewers. But my trade insists on it, on occasion. Here, then, is a group of my favourite living authors in this field, in conversation, in the flesh; and just for variety, the account of a domestic journey undertaken with a friend.*

1: Resident Alien

Coming into Seattle by air from the east, you cross barrier after barrier, each more dramatic than the last – the high desert, the Bitterroot Mountains, the Cascades – before the plane tilts round, skids past Mount Rainier, and glides in to touch down on a narrow, citied strip of land between the Pacific and the hills. If you were on the metaphysical run, travelling the mind's boundaries, in search of an objective correlative to the defensive mentality, here's the place.

Not that it's unwelcoming. It's just set apart. It's turned its back on the Union and looks out west, across Puget Sound, over Bainbridge and the serrated skyline of the Olympic Peninsula, to the Pacific Ocean out there through the Strait of Juan de Fuca. I went looking for our resident alien here. Everybody I met in Seattle knew about him:

'Oh yeah, that Brit writer – where's he live now? Capitol Hill? Queen

Anne? Some place out there ..?'

Some of them had been to book-launches, to readings he'd given. None of them seemed to have read his books – titles, after all, suffice for cultural groupies, and they'd occasionally mouth some of these in a slightly querulous way, their unease lest they be questioned about them palpable. But there was a recurrent unvoiced question, an odd curiosity and concern, that crowded around their responses:

'What's he doing here? Why would a Brit come and settle in the Pacific Northwest of America ..?'

I could rationalise this as an aspect of the general American insecurity that seeps into exchanges with any visitor here from an old country. Except that I was asking the same question. Maybe I had an inkling of the answer – if there is an answer – from *Hunting Mister Heartbreak*, from *Coasting*, from *Foreign Land* or *Bad Land*, which are all travel-writing of a kind, but which traverse landscapes internal as much as of the objective world.

'Aged 47, I had chucked up everything and just cleared off. It wasn't a long- or well-considered move. On a visit to the Pacific Northwest, I caught a shadowy glimpse of a new life, and flung myself at it.'

Or again:

'Solitaries, sociopaths, compulsive travellers, boys who had failed to grow up found their way inevitably west, where they could pass for normal citizens. Fear of long-term attachment, to any thing or any body, was not a disability out here ...'

We arranged to meet for dinner. I was staying in a new hotel at Aurora and Denny. He didn't approve, would rather I'd been downtown: 'The Moore Hotel on 2nd and Virginia,' he'd insisted, 'that's where you need to be, in amongst it.' But he agreed to pick me up from the Holiday Inn and I went down to meet him in the lobby.

The first encounter with someone's physical presence is always so startling. Here at last are not words but the other, in white ironed shirt, off-white trousers, brown shoes and the tinted bi-focals of those who've spent too much time under the fluorescent light of libraries. To this writerly uniform he'd added a peacock-blue baseball cap he seemed never to take off, and a close-check tweed jacket. He's tall – over six feet – there's the suggestion of a paunch, he has the brisk, leaning walk of the habitually late lecturer, his eyes are dark blue and wide apart in a rather handsome face, tousle-browed, crow's-footed, straight-mouthed. He'd come in an outlandish red child's toy of a vehicle, a Jeep Cherokee – itself full of child's toys, drawings, books, un-needed shoes and clothing. In it we drove to a French restaurant on the borders of Queen Anne about which he'd read a recent review in the *Seattle Post-Intelligencer*. The review had recommended the *steak frites*, so he'd devised a test, anticipation of which seemed to delight him more than the thought of the meal itself, which in the event was left half-eaten.

We arrived at the chrome-and-minimal restaurant. We drank red wine in large glasses. Jonathan, whilst assuring me that he did not smoke, charmed a cigarette and with sensual pleasure accepted the proffered light from an obviously gay young bartender with a careful sliver of facial hair who communicated to the other staff through minimal facial gestures his opinion that we were of his sexual orientation. Jonathan either affected not to notice, or didn't notice, so immersed was he in the pleasure of tobacco. We were shown to our table. The proprietor – the unruffled preciosity of Seattle restaurateurs might have left even Molière at a loss for ridicule – took our order. *Steak frites* for Jonathan. And how done?

'*A point.*'

It was the test. The proprietor absorbed it with pointed ease. The restaurant had passed. The straight Raban mouth rippled with amusement, launched into history, explanation, justification. He rattled away, making small talk, asking about fun-filled, caring, sharing, Bibendum-dining, Millennium-Dome-building Blairite New Britain. I listened, and when I responded, some cosmic joker led me to light on and drop into the conversation the name of Kettering. I've nothing against Kettering except where it is and the way it sounds. It had flitted into my mind by entire mischance. But it was out there now, hovering between us, and it had stopped Jonathan in his tracks:

'I was in Kettering ...'

He carried on to tell me of his father's cremation there two years ago, of a surreal dash from Market Harborough where the funeral service took place, of an undertaker mouthing to him quietly about 'missing our slot, Guv' and then crawling decorous down the main street before cramming his bowler into the back of the hearse and getting his foot down once round the corner and out of sight, a cortege of elderly drivers skewing and slithering along behind. The presence of that High Anglican clergyman father, with his full grey head of hair and his assured, easy authority, haunts Jonathan's books. I asked a couple of friends who are Raban devotees what their most memorable passage from his writing was, and both, without hesitation, chose the edgy, fond encounter between father and son from *Coasting*. The father crops up throughout his books and conversation. Here he was again, laughing no doubt:

> 'It's always been one of my chief failings, that I don't take more after you.'
> 'Cheers,' my father said.

So we broke a barrier, and gossiped on: about Seattle pressmen and frontier attitudes; about those he considered the great unreads among English prose writers – Belloc, Richard Aldington, Edmund Gosse, whose *Father and Son* echoes throughout Raban's own work, throughout his own life; about his admiration for Penelope FitzGerald's and Richard Holmes' capacity and gift for bringing the past alive; about his recollection of the latter delivering in measured academic tones, bald head gleaming, a perfect extempore lecture on Shelley; about the more assured place of the miscellaneous prose writer in America and the way his own writing escapes categorisation here, as he does himself, though the downside of that appreciation is the latitude it gives to the dreadful churchiness – he, a son of the manse, speaks the word with venom – of so much American prose. How, he cries, can anyone pretend admiration or allow a place in the canon to the unreadable – his voice rises almost to a screech – John Muir? He reveals a combative insecurity when I presume to agree with his own assessment of *Hunting Mister Heartbreak* as his least successful book (a debatable fact, incidentally, that makes it neither uninteresting nor bad). He tells impish-verging-on-the-ungenerous anecdotes about writers whose authority and reputation are assured: Peter Matthiessen complacent about his zen mastery of bonefish casting in Florida; Jan Morris not quite bringing off the *grande dame* in a Cairo hotel. He reminisces about university teaching in Aberystwyth and East Anglia, winces at the memory of playing snooker at his club with Jack Longland and sharing with him equally dire and unhappy memories separated by 40 years of King's School, Worcester. He responds, when I ask him why he so dislikes England – a fair conclusion to be drawn from his writing – that he doesn't, only Margaret Thatcher and her legacy. Its 'tiresome banality,' I quote? 'Did I say that?' and he moves on to quiz further about Blair's Britain, of which he hears from his friends Amis and McEwan when they fetch up in Seattle on reading tours. There is a lot of talk of sailing, which is his crucial version of freedom and control and for which activity Seattle is perfectly provided. There are many of those facts on various themes with which his writing is so prodigally supplied. And as his writing has a default mode to metaphors of sailing and a complex personal agenda around his father ('My father was no sailor – he didn't have good sea-legs!'), so too does a default, explanatory and anchoring topic obtain in his conversation, mellow its customary acerbity and elicit a glow.

It's Julia, his six-year-old daughter, custody of whom he shares, three-and-a-half days each week, with his estranged American wife. I meet Julia a couple of days later, when he invites me to his house on the canal side of Queen Anne Hill for dinner of not-quite-unfrozen lasagne and elaborate salad. Jonathan dotes, Julia rules. She comes in at one point, arms making a bow with hands clasped above her head: 'She's telling me that I left the toilet seat up again,' he grimaces, scuttling off to make amends.

I left him in his house of varnished pine with its feral cat that drinks from the former bowl of a departed dog called Pelham – 'after P G Wodehouse', he vouchsafes me – and ambled across the bridge to meet a friend in Fremont, vividly aware of the complex self he brings to prose vibrantly alive to the human and the contingent. I liked Raban, but you can seldom approach writers. Their lives are internal, exiled. Perhaps all you can say ultimately to answer the question posed at the outset is that he's escaped, and that escape presupposes arrival in another place not of itself important. Read *Coasting* or *Bad Land* if you've not done so already. That's where you'll learn about him, intuit the reasons, come to understand his being here in another, distant country. They're tortured, haunting, attentive masterpieces. Whatever 'travel-writing' is, they sit there a little uneasily, whilst being as fine maybe as any miscellaneous prose written by an English author in the latter part of the 20th century. And I suspect that from this taut and angry private man, anchored out there in a sheltered sound of his life, barriered against rejection and the objects of a palpable detestation, there's better still to come.

2: *Drinking with Dervla*

This is a tale of three bicycles – or maybe four, if you count the Third
Policeman's, but he doesn't really come into the story except as a principle,
and we can ignore those for the moment. It takes place in Ireland – a place
to which I go frequently, especially since the alternative, going the other
way from my home in Wales, is to arrive in England and I'm not sure I'd
like that.

The first bicycle belongs to me. It has an engine. I started it up one
morning and roared off to Holyhead to catch the ferry. On board, I bought
a litre of the ten-year-old Bushmills and stowed it away in my rucksack,
because I was going visiting. Several hours later my bicycle and I disengaged
with difficulty after the long miles south through Arklow and Enniscorthy. As
Flann O'Brien sagely remarks in *The Third Policeman*, 'people who spend most
of their natural lives riding iron bicycles over the rocky roads of this parish get
their personalities mixed up with the personalities of their bicycle as a result
of the interchanging of atoms of each of them ...' In our case, this
metemcyclosis was well under way. If anyone had asked my name, I'd have
told them it was Suzuki, and as for the bicycle, well, I can't answer for her,
but I will tell you that there was a familiar at hand.

Our second bicycle – it will be some time before we get to the third –
was very slowly traversing the pavements of Lismore with an aged man
listing alongside. Would he happen to know where to find Dervla
Murphy's house? I asked. He took off his cap, folded it carefully into the
inside pocket of his gabardine coat, scratched a point not at the precise
middle of his tonsure, exhaled several deep gusts of porter, and with grave
due deliberation informed me that he did not, and was that the writer-
woman? At which point a passer-by, an alert young woman with a good-
humoured face like the Secular Mary's – all Ireland, you should
understand, is ruled by two Marys, and my preference is for Mrs Robinson
rather than the BVM – interposed herself between us: 'If it's Dervla
Murphy you're wanting, turn in the arch here, go up between the bar and
the ironmongers, round the back and you'll be grand.'

The man replaces his cap as he nods at and digests this piece of
information, adding his assurance to hers that I'll be grand. I ease myself

back into the saddle, trickle up the alleyway, and am confronted by Dervla Murphy. She's a sturdy, wiry woman in her 60s, her face tanned and very little lined, a scatter of iron-grey curls with a pronounced widow's peak, and eyes that are dark hazel, guarded beneath wild brows, piercingly intent and keen. She leads me into a book-lined room where we usurp cat-laden chairs. There's a round table, ethnic rugs, small vivid icons. I produce the whiskey, and the drinking concomitant on any visit to Ireland begins. Parameters of vocabulary are established – also important in Ireland, where every other word is a version of one not to be used in the politest company. We clash tumblers on a mutual detestation of certain politicians and all their works; and then, in a sonorous, deep voice with a high, grating, amused inflection on key words, she starts to interview me. I protest that it should be the other way round, but she presses on.

Is there otter-hunting in Britain, she asks? Not legally, I tell her, though the packs of otter-hounds still hunt mink, and as yet are capricious in distinguishing between the two. She recounts how, every morning from March to October, she goes down to the Blackwater to swim. There are otters along the bank, and if they see her approaching on foot, they disappear instantly, but if she swims round the bend in the river, they'll dive in and play around her, the whole family group sometimes within feet of her.

I tell her in response of watching badgers in a beechwood on moonlit nights, of the bounce and glisten of their coats, their innocent play and those beautiful markings accentuated in the silver light. She asks why I use the past tense. I explain that in the 1980s every badger sett I knew apart from two in the wildest places was dug, tell her the prices animals are said to fetch for baiting, conclude by commenting that though she will think it far-fetched, that seems to me the inevitable trickle-down effect of brutal and uncaring example in government. She retorts that it's the simple truth, and tragic that people are only now beginning to realise the effect of having had someone like 'T'hatcher' – she spits the word out with a glottal stop – in power for so long.

After this joint tirade, we eat – thick soup, moist soda-bread with nuts in it, crusty cheeses – and we drink a great deal – wine first, and then cider, the whiskey having gone. At two in the morning, by the cat-purred fire in the lamplight, the Guinness appears and I ask – by now not altogether coherently – about the relevance to her case of the black bicycle, which those of you who know Ireland will accept as one of the enduring symbols of the place – male, upright and motionless. All Ireland, I suggested, was contained within the frame of this bicycle, so when she mounted hers in 1963 and rode off on the solo journey to India which she describes in her first book, *Full Tilt*, had she determined to appropriate and subvert the image?

'How so?' she humoured me.

Because in her hands, I went on, the bicycle becomes female and subtle, like Irish society under the froth, it becomes the quixotic steed Rozinante, becomes a 30-year continuum of living contradictions to the society from which she grew, becomes the means of expression and travel and escape from her Catholic and finely cultured, beautiful, barbaric, narrow, circumscribed and enchanted homeland of the black bicycles. I'd just finished when the two cathedral clocks of the place began to strike an asynchronous three a.m. We reeled out into a blackness riddled with stars:

'Sure, we're very drunk tonight,' she shot after me as I swayed away to my room, 'but we'll walk it off tomorrow!'

'C'mon, wake up, wake up!'

I'm shaken out of my slumbers, ordered on my feet from where I've collapsed fully dressed the previous night, and with barely time to pull on the motor-cycling boots which are the only footwear I have with me, and no time at all to gulp down any breakfast, am marched out before eight o'clock into a morning of towering clouds and brief illumination by the sun with the explanation that if we're not on the road soon we'll spend the rest of the day feeling very ill. I'm feeling very ill anyway, and Dervla Murphy's spirited commentary on the heritage industry, on Fintan O'Toole's notion of how the Irish are being made tourists in their own land, and on the history of Lismore castle is not falling on entirely receptive ears.

Beyond the Blackwater bridge we branch off up a steep, narrow lane rising as relentlessly as Dervla's morning conversation through woods. The hill-ridge of the Knockmealdowns ahead is dull brown and faded purple under its clouds. Much of the good land around us is derelict – undrained, untilled, a square field here and there shiny olive-green with Eurograss, which rouses Dervla to vituperative comment against Maastricht and the Common Agricultural Policy. We halt by a dilapidated farmstead. She eyes ruefully the tumbledown buildings, the nettle-grown midden, the litter of fertiliser bags and the pyramid of plastic-encased Euro-silage, gestures me on up the road and, as if to pass comment, goes into a gateway to pee. I come across a black bicycle lounging in a hedge, its owner painting a fieldgate obscured by vegetation in raincloud grey. I bid him good morning as Dervla joins us:

'This land's in poor shape,' she accuses him.

'Ah yes, it's in poor shape, but there's not many of the grants now, see,' he explains.

She flashes a frame of the basilisk glare he receives at me, to let me know what she thinks, and as we continue up the road tells me of the farmer by the house where she used to live, to whom she took her jug to be filled with fresh milk every morning until the day when he told her, crying with anger and frustration, that she was no longer allowed to do it. From this – when Dervla warms to a theme the examples come tumbling out – she moves on to tell of a lift she once had, hitch-hiking from London to one of the channel ports, in a refrigerated lorry. She'd asked what was being carried; bacon, came the reply, to Denmark, to have its stamp rubbed out, replaced with a Danish one, and be re-imported to Britain.

'Can you work that one out?' she challenges me.

'No, nor that one either,' I answer, pointing away from the good, idle land towards a digger on EU grant work draining a bleak field at the margin of the bog. We carry on walking under the ridge of the Knockmealdowns with Dervla swinging her shoulders and shuffling along at a pace of five miles an hour, to keep up with which I'm forced into a loping, suppressed run. After 20 miles of this we arrive at a pub by the name of The Cats, and since it's now midday and rain dogs us, we duly go in. She orders pints of Guinness and whiskeys and taxes the barman on the abortion issue, the referendum on which is about to take place. He's called Michael, and he tiptoes delicately round the point under her withering gaze, making most clear his respect for the clergy. She passes on impatiently to an interrogation about the nearby Melleray grotto, where the statue of the Blessed Virgin had been seen to move and heard to speak a decade ago.

Again, Michael blathers, tells us how the church distanced itself from the supposed miracle and Mary's 'message', but so as not to leave us with an impression of someone devoid of wonder, recounts the experience of 'a man he knew', a sufferer from Motor Neurone Disease, who had gone to visit Father Athanasius at Mount Melleray monastery, 'and he came away entirely healed, and hasn't suffered from that day to this.' Michael left us at this dramatically opportune moment, leaving Dervla to tell me that she didn't discount the healing potential in the laying-on of hands, and insisting that I finish up the third or fourth pint that we might go to the grotto.

It was half a mile down the road. There was an information stall, a toilet block, a vast car park and an immense glass-topped collection box full of high-denomination bank-notes. At the head of a wooded gully was the statue of Mary. Groups entered, gazed up at her expectantly for three or four minutes, retreated to empty purse and wallet into the box with quick, fervent glances back over their shoulders. A continual susurrus of subdued voices followed them, phrases recurring, voiced entreaties drifting into the glade: 'Holy Mary ... intercede ... hour of our deaths ... Breeda Guiney sufferin' terrible from the rheumatics.' I'm sent to ask where the donations go whilst Dervla disappears for a pee. The woman in the information stall smiles encouragingly as I sidle up, agrees that it's a lovely place, informs me how blessed they've been with the visit from the Queen of Heaven.

'And the money?' I ask, 'Where does that go?'

I snatch my fingers out of the way as the grille descends.

'It's all ploughed back into the grotto, and we're closing now.'

Dervla shuffles over. I report back the response.

'Does it fuck,' she snorts, and taps my beret with a knowing, odd look. She hauls us disapprovingly away. We return home by a short-cut of 15 miles through Cappoquin. My feet ache but I dare not complain. After 35 miles taken at a near-run I drag off my boots, prick and drain hot blisters with a safety pin before re-joining Dervla for the anaesthesia of whiskey-talk. We drag off to bed long after midnight. Next morning at six she's at work. Long after that I emerge on to the street in search of a chemist. I ask for sticking plasters:

'What would you be wanting those for?'

'Blisters.'

'Where have you got blisters, now?'

'On my feet.'

'How did you go getting blisters on your feet?'

'I was out walking.'

'Oh, you were out walking! Who were you out walking with?'

'I was out with Dervla Murphy.'

'You were out wit' Dervla Murphy! No wonder you've got blisters – a young fella like you and her a seasoned walker. I'll sell you the plasters, and I'll give you some aspirin for the hangover, too!'

3: Nature's Intimate

Travel-writing's a bastard genre. The travel-writer slips its restrictions as easily as the traveller crosses national boundaries. The better the writer, the greater his or her range, the more true this is. You come away not with a view of a different part of the world, but with an amplified world-view. Take Barry Lopez's *Arctic Dreams* for example. It's a difficult, intense, idiosyncratic book that you have to work at – exquisitely written, deeply felt, questing. Maybe it's travel-writing, maybe not. Certainly it belongs to the wider category of literature of place. I'd wanted for a long time to meet its author, who's barely known beyond a rather arcane cult status – articles in *Resurgence* and so on – in Britain, despite being a major literary figure *(Arctic Dreams* won the National Book Award) and best-selling author in America. He's lived in Oregon for 30 years. I was in Wyoming. They're only 1,000 miles apart. In America, that's opportunity.

I drove in through Idaho and across the high desert, through Burns and Bend, over the Mackenzie Pass that threads its way among a blackened confusion of lava beds stretching all the way from the Cascades to California, and down at last to the valley of Oregon's Mackenzie River with the first rains of the fall swelling its flow. He'd given me directions: 'Look closely – you can barely see the track.' I missed it as easily as a casual reader might put aside his books. Then I looked again and it was there, unmarked, between the trees, traversing up to a jay-screamed and shaded forest ledge where his log house perches among the Douglas Firs, hidden, high above the Mackenzie River and 40 miles upstream from Eugene. He came out to greet me, a short man, still with a solid, athlete's physique despite being in his mid-50s. He's grey-bearded, forehead domed, his eyes pouched, attentive, with the brows arched in an expression of continual near-surprise. When he speaks, it's with a deep, slow, musing inflection. He invited me in to a lone man's habitation filled with books, empty wasps' nests, bleached animal skulls, collected stones, discarded correspondence, and the conversation immediately turned to ravens.

They're a good touchstone with writers about wild places – powerful, intelligent birds that inspire a respectful affection in people who know them. I mentioned that my country, Wales, has the highest-density raven population in the world. That pleased him. He asked why. I faltered through an answer, his expression alert as he listened, weighing the evidence, squaring it with his own experience, nodding as though to say 'Yes – that could be right'. Prompted by his attention, I recounted an incident that has always puzzled me. In most people it produces a pitying, sceptical response, and the sort of sidelong glances that suggest they think you not quite right in the head. But I knew from his writing the modes of response he gleans from indigenous peoples, and the quality of attention he bestows on non-human residents in a landscape. I felt safe in telling the story.

It was a couple of years ago. I'd been standing on a low hill-top near the sea. The bird had flown up from oakwoods beneath, landed on a barkless, dead branch five yards away. It spent 10, 15 minutes running through a range of call and movement so rich I would not have believed anything non-human to be capable of such expressiveness. One last thing I noticed transfixed me, was inexplicable: a shimmer of violet light, an aura, followed its every motion and contour:

'So why do you have a problem with this?' he asked. 'The raven was simply communicating with you, shifting into another mode of communication maybe, but it's not strange. Only modern cultures with an allegiance to science as the sole arbiter of truth would consider it so. You know, the idea that animals can convey meaning, can offer an attentive ...' – he gives the word a fervent stress, lets it hang between pauses – '... human being some measure of illumination is a belief commonly held by native peoples the world over. You find it wherever you travel among them. And ravens, well ...'

'... he is thorough.' I pick up, 'He will sense your peaceful intentions. Let him have the first word. Be careful: he will tell you he knows nothing.'

I'm quoting from a story, *The Raven*, in Lopez's *Desert Notes* collection. He rouses from listening, nods a quick glance at me to acknowledge the counterpoint, and begins to talk about the numinous in encounters with animals – about the reactions of indigenous peoples in these situations, and their comfort with them, their acceptance of them in a way that we who are reared in western rationalist traditions cannot easily share. He refers to the 'profound, persistent and ineluctable suspicion' confirmed by these encounters that there is more to the world than the surface appearance of things. When we accept this, it's an advent of wisdom, an expansion of our knowledge. As our talk stills down into contemplation I'm reminded of an essay in which he writes of 'the wisdom that lies in the richness and sanctity of a wild landscape, what it can mean in the unfolding of human life, the staying of a troubled human spirit.' And I'm reminded too of the whole of *Arctic Dreams*, where his travels around the near-abstract desolation that surrounds the northern polar region are lit by encounters with its animals, and by the knowledge of Inuit hunters and long-serving field biologists of those animals.

His acts of attention to the natural world, the quality of his observation, his detailed and yet unsolemn reverence, are what draw me to his books. Along with a photographic brilliance and economy of description, they have a gravity our cosmopolitan culture lacks, and which comes through in his living as well as in his writing. On the evening of our first meeting, we headed into Eugene for dinner at a sophisticated, busy restaurant. On the way in, on the opposite side of a fast dual carriageway was a dead raccoon. He turned at a junction, drove back, pulled up, lifted the warm, limp corpse, made a hollow in the long grass of the verge and laid it down. It was done without a word, and not for my benefit. He performed the ritual, and his whole presence was full of grace.

We were lingering over coffee in his house next morning. There was a green, tree-filtered morning light seeping through into a wooden-floored sitting room sparely decorated with natural objects and native artefacts. We'd drifted into seriousness, and to inject a little levity he told me about the South Pole and his dislike of flags. There are a lot there, and a hut. He took a cardboard tube with him on the plane, was asked what was in it? A fly-fishing kit, he'd replied. Raised eyebrows. When they landed at the Pole, he opened the tube, took out a kite, and was informed that if he wanted to fly it there he'd have to ask in the hut and they'd have to radio out for permission, lest it be against regulations.

He flew the kite.

Writers habitually swap tales like these, and in Barry Lopez's case find both rationale and glee in so doing. Because he explores them, sets them together in his books like gathered stones on a table, so that they spark off colour, angle, texture in each other. He discerns a serious point in this, tells of sharing breakfast at a writers' conference in Adelaide with J M Coetzee and David Malouf:

'... and we realised we were all doing the same thing.'

'Which is ..?'

A pause, tension, a searching look.

'It's the responsibility of the writer in the late 20th century to serve society. And I try to do so by expressing some sense of what's divine in nature.'

He seems almost embarrassed, darts away into an account of the heart of the mastodon in the cave-paintings at Altamira; of how, in the flickering lamplight that would have glowed across its composition, the heart beats. And he leaves it there because if I understand that, I have understood. In his conversation as in his books, the audience has to put in its own work, grasp the meaning of what's left unsaid. 'Salmon in that river,' he tells me, gesturing down at the Mackenzie, 'they go away this big' – a gesture between thumb and forefinger, 'they come back how many times that size? That's what you get from encountering the world, from going out into it and looking.'

We go out, to drive steep forest tracks above the house in his Toyota truck, for he is playful too. He talks about friends and fellow-writers, tells of how Peter Matthiessen's passion and courage as well as the perfectionism of his writing have been the greatest influence on him: 'You meet someone from whom you learn. Peter was that for me. With his background he could have been your comfortable East Coast novelist. He didn't have to endure hardship, take on the government, but he's owned the writer's crucial responsibility, and I'd say he's also one of the great versatile masters of American prose style this century.'

Writers are seldom this magnanimous to their peers. We climb out of the truck high on the hillside and he directs me to feel the branch of a tree. It's barkless, glistening, and a strangely livid colour. I grip its solidity. He sees me recoil:

'Like a thigh ..?' he laughs. 'It's called madron. You have to get intimate with nature ...'

I glance round, glimpse this stocky quiet man at ease in a forest glade, head upturned, intense eyes searching among the overarching foliage, questing after a focus for all the travelling people who look to books to guide their life-journeys.

4: *Comedian on the Tracks*

Phineas Fogg, with the aid of his Bradshaw and the incentive of a bet, may fictionally have proved the possibility of travelling round the world in 80 days when this planet, in terms of its human scale, was a rather larger entity than it is now. But even he would have been put on his mettle had he been required to get from end to end of Wales in a day with no help but that afforded by the National Rail Timetable.

It is theoretically possible to set off from Llandudno on the north coast before eight in the morning and, travelling all the way by train, with a relatively brief digression on to the English side of the border, to arrive in Swansea a little before pub closing time. With a much longer digression into England, it's possible to make the journey in an afternoon, but that's to miss the point entirely. Wales is a gorgeous country, one of the most beautiful in the world, and its railways – such few of them as remain after Dr Beeching's savagery 40 years ago – enable you to see a substantial part of the best of it.

I had a plan, which was this. I'd take three days over the trip. That would reduce the anxieties every rail-traveller feels these days around connections and timetabling. Also, I'd invite a comedian to accompany me, because Wales has a reputation in England for being a melancholy country skulking under a pall of rainclouds and chapels and slate-tips, its collective breast swelling only at the first organ chords to succeed the opening of Sankey & Moody. I knew this to be untrue, but it's best to guard against stereotypes. I asked Mike Harding along.

Now I'd been with Mike in Llandudno on two previous occasions, both marked by insobriety. To meet there early in the day was to tempt providence. Also, comedians are generally of depressive or choleric disposition. Think Lenny Bruce. Think Max Wall. I couldn't imagine Mike's temper being improved by all that slow summer thronging of Saga Holidaygoers, or the soft susurrus of their Zimmer frames as they scraped and shuffled from hotel to café to shore. For my part, I like Llandudno. It's the most perfectly unspoilt of all the great Victorian seaside resorts, uniform-crescent-hotel-façaded, wide-boulevarded inland, and its setting between cliff-tiered headlands as dramatic as any in Britain. Half the population of Liverpool was conceived here. That wouldn't raise it in Mike's estimation. I took a train of two carriages, from a Victorian station with empty platforms that stretch halfway back to Crewe, and clacked down the little spur to arrive at Llandudno Junction on the Euston-to-Holyhead line.

A minute later, Mike jumped down off the Manchester train. You could tell it was from somewhere important. It had three carriages. He was in a bad temper, just back from Barcelona where all his belongings had been stolen. 'Travel light,' I'd told him, 'steep hills, small trains.' He had four bags. I ended up carrying five – two of my own (the National Rail Timetable took up one by itself), and three of his. He leapt and I staggered on to the train for Blaenau Ffestiniog at the end of the Conwy Valley Line.

How this line survived Beeching was one of the miracles of the 20th century. There was a reason, of course. There always is when the government of the day appears to have made an oversight. Out of the terminus at Blaenau a track twists south for five or six miles to the nuclear power station at Trawsfynydd. The map would have you believe it's disused. It was built to carry radioactive waste away. So the branch line's survival is one of the few reasons to feel grateful to the nuclear power industry. This route is astonishingly lovely, running at first by the side of the River Conwy, simple old churches set against a backdrop of the Carneddau mountains on the farther shore. Beyond Betws y Coed, by means of viaducts and brief blinks of tunnels it slips into the gorge of the Afon Lledr, old oak woodland crowding the track, the river fuming and frothing beneath, salmon lazing in its pools, Snowdon itself briefly visible by Roman Bridge before a long tunnel suddenly debouches into the ruined industrial grandeur of Blaenau.

In this epicentre of one of Britain's dead industries, grey terraces of quarrymen's houses cluster together in glaciated hollows of the mountains, and down upon them from every angle spill slopes of slate-waste and spoil. The local roofs these days are repaired with tiles from Spain. Heritage tourism is the industry here now. Crowds come up from the coast on the narrow-gauge railway. They flock on to underground tramways the miners once used. They see how things used to be.

We passed on that, installed ourselves in a first-class carriage of the

Ffestiniog Railway, and drawn by a sturdy, double-headed steam locomotive, chuffed downline instead. Mike was positively beatific, imagining himself descending from some hill-station of the Raj. Stewards brought coffee. The rocky, wooded rhododendron landscape we travelled through was intimate delight, the view to Snowdon from the last embankment before Porthmadog's harbour station as sublime as when Shelley had proclaimed it the finest in Europe. We took refuge in a pub and consulted the National Rail Timetable.

This formidable volume is set in six-point type and printed on the equivalent of what used to be called fine India paper, 2,272 pages of it, very few of them relating to Wales and those few widely dispersed. After an hour with the magnifying glass we deduced that a train would shortly convey us onwards if we were to hurry to Porthmadog's other station, serving the Cambrian Coast Line, a mile across town. We caught it. Timing is everything. Its departure coincided with the daily parole of schoolchildren. They caught it too. Three stations down the line a rival horde had been released. We got off. You think soccer hooligans bad? Here's where they entrain them.

Fortuitously, we alighted at Harlech, which has a tearoom with the best view in creation. It's at the top of an exceedingly steep hill and is called the Hotel Plas. To keep Mike from thinking about muggers in Barcelona or the schoolchildren of Porthmadog, I recited him a medieval Welsh story set here on the way up to it, full of giants wading to Ireland, speaking starlings, decapitated talking heads, wronged wives and other such wonders. By the time we sat over tea on sunlit lawns, with the great Edwardian castle at our elbow, Snowdon hanging over its battlements and a bay of pure cerulean beneath, his mood had improved. It stayed that way when we resumed the coast-hugging journey. Ruskin thought there was only one finer walk than from Dolgellau to Barmouth, and that was the walk from Barmouth to Dolgellau. Crossing the Mawddach estuary bridge on a sun-flooded evening with the sculpted long ridge of Cadair Idris thrown into sumptuous relief, it's hard to disagree, and the quality of scenery diminishes hardly at all between here and Machynlleth, where we spent the night in the 18th-century Wynnstay Arms. Charles Dark, the proprietor, regaled us with the best food – all of it locally caught and grown – that I've eaten in Wales, fish, fowl and flesh punctuated by tiny, delicious sorbets and culminating in fine port and a magnificent, parochial cheeseboard. There was the ovicentric conversation of locals late into the night, too. A man called Derwen, which means oak-tree, told us a joke: 'Teacher ask boy in the class, "Caradog, there are 50 sheeps in a field and one leave through hole-in-the-wall. How many sheeps are being left in the field?" "None, Miss," says Caradog. "Now think again, Caradog." "Please, Miss – there are none in the field, because they are all been going through hole-in-the-wall after the first one."'

'And of course, he was right, wasn't he?' added Derwen, sagaciously. Charles left a bottle of Irish whiskey on the table and went to bed. The Comedian likes hotels like this. Except for the headaches, a day, a week, a decade here would slip imperceptibly by. It is the most charming and interesting of small Welsh towns. It has museums, art galleries, bookshops, eccentric cafés, nearby beaches, bird reserves, a street market, a concert hall in a mellow-wood-galleried old chapel, and the inspirational, endlessly fascinating Centre for Alternative Technology. But we had a train to catch. It goes to Shrewsbury, and beyond that with surprising regularity to Birmingham. It passes through a score of Adlestrops, each of which tempt you to stop. This is Montgomeryshire – a quiet county of scattered farms, dog rose and elder in the hedgerows, cows grazing. By way of decorative-brick-built Caersws, where a famous and still popular Welsh poet of the century before last was stationmaster, and Newtown, where Robert Owen was born, and Welshpool, where hearsay has it Hilda Murrell was held in a safe house before her murder, you dawdle through green valleys out of Wales, into the Marches with England, and down to Shrewsbury, which is the most perfectly medieval of England's cities. We allowed ourselves a couple of hours there, looking for – and finding – green men (an obsession of Mike's) in the roof of St Mary's Church, before boarding the single carriage that runs four times a day up and down the 120 miles of the Heart of Wales Line.

There are three great rail routes in Britain: from Settle to Carlisle through the Northern Pennines; the West Highland Line from Glasgow to Mallaig; and the Heart of Wales Line from Shrewsbury to Swansea. The latter is the least celebrated, the least used, and the most consistently beautiful. You could alight at a dozen whitewashed and flowerpotted station platforms for small towns and villages along its route, and end up staying forever. We chose Llandrindod Wells, where most of the population looked as though they'd done just that. The station bore a plaque commemorating its 're-Victorianisation' in 1990. Its bookstall sold manuals for Austin A40 Somersets and the nearby garage still advertised 'Commer, Hillman, Humber and Sunbeam'. We sat among the purple-rinsed in a café by the lake – round which, attended by a stooping man in a beige rainjacket, for lap upon lap waddled a plump Cardigan Corgi – and watched the rain hiss down. Mike descanted on comely waitresses with smiley faces. Chris Burton, a retired police inspector from Bristol who now runs a farm guesthouse 1,200 feet up in the nearby hills with his wife Pauline, collected us in an immaculate, elderly Volvo and drove us, with a brief visit to Disserth's exquisite, bat-adorned 13th-century church, into curlew-haunted moorland. We woke to a valley filigreed with mist, slipping away between bosomy hills patched with cloud-filtered sun. There were yellowhammers on the birdtable, red kites quartering the pasture and ravens calling from the trees behind. If Wales in general is beautiful, Radnorshire is quietly transcendent. When we re-boarded the train, that ravishing mood of landscape prevailed down to Llandeilo at least, if not quite to Swansea itself. In Llanwrtyd Wells the guard strolled though the carriage announcing that the up train was ten minutes late, being packed with golfing types for some tournament along the line and hence struggling. So if we cared to go for a stroll round and get a cup of tea, he'd count us out and count us back in again when the train was ready to go. You could count me in for a journey like this any day – there's none lovelier in Britain. I'll take a week over it next time – or maybe a month, Mike thought, muttering to himself of green men and Machynlleth and opportunities missed, and there's no higher praise, coming from a Yorkshire-dwelling Manchester Irishman. But Wales deserves it, and has that effect. And we'd not even got to Swansea yet ...

5: flibbertigibbet prose-writer

A few years ago I had a casual arrangement to meet Jan Morris in Budapest. I'd given her my address at some little Habsburg-marbled hotel, its stucco pocked with the shell-holes of '56, off Vaci Utca. She didn't turn up. I wouldn't have expected her to have phoned, because the Hungarian telephone system then was beyond Western European patience or understanding. And it didn't matter anyway. We were only going to have dinner together. When I got back to Wales, which is the country of Morris' heart and residence as well as my own, there was an apologetic message in her loopily florid hand awaiting. She'd arrived at Heathrow, had been approaching the Malev Hungarian Airlines desk, and quite suddenly was seized with an intense premonition that if she boarded the plane she would die. So she turned round and went home to Wales, where these intimations of mortality, along with corpse candles, fairies and conjunctions of the planets, are still taken most seriously.

I like to think of this story as telling, but what it tells us about its subject I'm not quite sure. Perhaps it chimes with a crucial and distinctive characteristic of her work, from the early masterpieces on Spain, Venice, Oxford, through the Pax Britannica trilogy and right down to her latest books and essays on Wales and Europe – a visceral, intuitive, rather magical quality that shimmers out from her best writing? I was pondering that, and other mildly loony Celticisms, as I drove down to meet her. She lives, with her former wife Elizabeth – since James became Jan in 1972, she's described their relationship as that of sisters-in-law – in a converted stable-block half a mile along a stoney oak-and-bluebell track near Cricieth in North Wales.

Jan hailed me from the balcony terrace where she was sunning herself, notepad and a book to review at hand. All writers pride themselves on having production targets as habitual that in reality they seldom meet, and Jan has proclaimed hers as 12 pages a day. So I chaffed her on whether her stint was complete, or would we have to wait for lunch? Peering down from her parapet with the alertness of a raptor, she brushed the impudence aside and enquired whether I was a devotee of Egyptology (in conversation as in writing she launches straight into a theme, with few preliminaries), before loosing a little torrent of words in which Morris-esque terms like 'bunkum' and 'mumbo-jumbo' and 'New Age nutters' were prominent, and which seemed to connect with the book under review. It was about Pharaonic survivals in modern Egypt. Her huffingly impatient amusement at the theme left me disinclined to pursue the 'Celtic insights' line. Ms Morris can be quite the *grande dame* on occasion. With her in this magnificent and fulminating mood, head tossing as she leaned down from her position of eminence, I was loath to try my luck, even on matters that normally might appeal to her.

This confounding of expectation is as marked in the Morrisian canon as in the manner. Encountering it again led me on to the notion that some things are so blindingly obvious we invariably ignore them – at least until a moment of realisation comes along and declares itself, to our relieved surprise. If you don't already know Jan Morris' work, you've got some reading to catch up on. Of course she's our finest living travel-writer. Who else is there? In terms of literary quality, Patrick Leigh Fermor and Jonathan Raban are the only ones who come near, but even their cases for pre-eminence, given the quality of this opposition, don't quite convince, nor do their range and bodies of work compare. Dervla Murphy? Colin Thubron? Eric Newby? All of them audacious and fascinating travellers, as writers they're simply not as good, lack the vital euphony of Morris' style, her unclouded magnanimity and curiosity, the quirkiness of her imagination, the odd and surprising perspectives of her 'well-stocked mind'. Could any of them have produced, for example, these opening sentences of *Venice*?

At 45°14'N, 12°18'E, the navigator, sailing up the Adriatic coast of Italy, discovers an opening in the long low line of the shore: and turning westward, with the race of the tide, he enters a lagoon. Instantly the boisterous sting of the sea is lost. The water around him is shallow but opaque, the atmosphere curiously translucent, the colours pallid, and over the whole wide bowl of mudbank and water there hangs a suggestion of melancholy ... It is encircled with illusory reflections, like mirages in the desert – wavering trees and blurred hillocks, ships without hulls, imaginary marshes: and among these hallucinations the water reclines in a kind of trance.

You might gather from the above that I'm a devotee of this self-styled 'flibbertigibbet prose-writer' of 'skimble-skamble stuff'. Also, she's a friend, is unfailingly accessible, encouraging and generous to others who pursue her craft. Even the Egyptian book over which she was tutting, she ended up reviewing warmly, looking for its virtues. So I didn't feel unduly threatened by all the curl-shaking animation as I clambered by a little slate staircase up to her terrace, to be confronted by a bust. Or rather two busts. One was of herself, sent by an American admirer. A sidelong glance at it, a roll of the eye, and with this brief explanation we moved on. The other was of Jacky Fisher, Admiral of the Fleet during the Great War, an idiosyncratic and loving biography of whom by Morris was published in 1995 ('Can you not see our Jacky basking in the adulation of the great ladies of the Raj, waltzing with subaltern's wives on lawns of buffalo grass, or sending acidulously biblical messages to snooty seniors of the Indian Civil Service?'). His bust made him look Neanderthal, she thought, though the raw bronze of his complexion had been improved by Elizabeth and herself frequently pouring tea over it. With that, I was led into her place of work – a book-lined loft thronged with her own drawings and stuffed owls and model boats, one of which, set in clear perspex, she picked up and turned in excited reverie to show lucid perspectives on its beautiful lines. I almost heard her mouthing to herself from Browning, 'We were sailing by Triest / Where a day or two we harboured' (she's currently working on a book about Trieste, which she claims will be the last she'll write). As her fingers traced towards the stern, she almost conjured up for me the figure of Waring from the *Dramatic Lyrics*, lounging there, 'With great grass hat and kerchief black'. She's a magician in this way, the allusive echo of literary richness hanging always on her musing, excitable speech. But then that deft, sidelong look again, humorous, self-mocking. Waring's absence from the model boat was noted, a promise made that 'we'll get him in', and we went off to a favourite restaurant for lunch.

Where she asked me about the fish.

I mention this because it was done with such mildness and traditional feminine deference. What did I think swordfish would be like? This addressed to me by a writer of exceptional distinction, and a woman of great poise who is more than 20 years older than me, more socially at ease, more gifted and acclaimed, hugely more knowledgable. And yet she deferred to my opinion on swordfish. Would it, in its Cricieth incarnation, be fresh and succulent? In *Conundrum* – her eirenic memoir of the transsexual process – she writes of just this assumed condition of secondariness:

'I discovered that even now men prefer women to be less informed, less able, less talkative and certainly less self-centred than they are themselves: so I generally obliged them.'

But why was she 'obliging' me in this way? Is it of a piece with those curiously persistent assaults on her own achievement, with which her work and talk are peppered? Refusing to be drawn on the fish, I tossed that back at her. So she considers herself to be a facile writer? 'Yes, I am,' she concurred, and began to talk about composition – a word I'd scarcely heard used in this context since school days. She talked about the fine tuning of prose; about reading it aloud in the head to perfect the necessary aural / oral dimension of it; about being a *cynghaneddwr*, and working consciously and musically with the consonantal patterning which is the presiding characteristic of Welsh verse. This, I should have responded, is anything but a facile way of working, but before I had time she was cantering into a conversation about influences and admired writers. It began with an aside about Kinglake's *Eothen*, which she claims as sole model for her writing (in her introduction to the 1982 OUP edition, she calls him 'a merry genius with an exceedingly polished style' – a description that fits the writer equally as well as her subject). She was soon raising the dust of contradiction to his being her only mentor by a brisk gallop around *Alice in Wonderland, Huckleberry Finn,* George Borrow – a wonderful show-off, but what an amiable human infirmity that is, and one he shares with Patrick Leigh-Fermor, and when would the third book in the latter's marvellous pre-war sequence appear, and despite his erudition elsewhere didn't I relish the simplicity of his West Indian book (*The Travellers' Tree*)? With which, she frisked into an anecdote about visiting Leigh-Fermor in Mani and coming across a burnt-out wreck of a car at the top of the track down to his house that was explained away – the Greeks! – as the recent result of some conflict stemming from the time on Crete when he kidnapped the German general. From that, she was on to the theme of favourite cities. Trieste, I suggested? Too melancholy, was the response, and as such a fitting subject for a last book. No, anyone who did not have San Francisco as their favourite was a hypocrite – the setting, from the north – but then, yes, it was disorderly, though did I know of any city that was orderly. Ottawa? She giggled, came back at me with an eyes-rolled-heavenwards, exclamation-marked Canada! from which she digressed into a preview of the book she and her son, the Welsh-language poet and singer Twm Morys, are currently working on – a Welsh-and-English bilingual fable entitled *Ein Llyw Cyntaf* (*Our First Leader*), in which the Nazis have invaded Britain, but to demonstrate an entirely mendacious good faith grant independence to Wales, which little country of her heart in its turn outwits them. But she is telling me too much, she suggests, spends a minute praising Twm and the pleasure of working with him, the quality of his versions in their shared projects (their first, *A Machynlleth Triad*, appeared in 1994), then veers off into qualified appreciation of Portland, Oregon, the only city where her name has been up in lights.

Jan being temporarily silent in contemplation at the incongruity of this image, I manage to slip in a question as to how the notion of travel has changed since the 1940s and 1950s, when, as foreign correspondent for the *Times* and then the *Guardian*, she first took to world-wandering? Elliptically, she responds that she's never been an adventurous traveller, has mostly written about perfectly familiar places and has always preferred to sleep comfortably in expensive hotels:

'I have always regarded myself as an outsider looking in, not as a temporary insider, and I've never felt much desire to travel in local buses knocked about by turkeys in order to establish the authenticity of what I write.'

It seems to me that she's not quite answered the question, so I press a little harder, and she admits a little wistfully that she does rather miss the loss of excitement that's come with the globalisation of things:

'I don't mean McDonaldisation – the Big Mac springs from the human heart – but rather the general ease of modern travel. I miss the occasional dangers of the foreign correspondent's life, long ago; and God forgive me, I miss the dread *frisson* of the Iron Curtain.'

So why does she continue on the road still as it leads through this tamed, changed and homogenised world? Halfway through her 74th year, it's just become a matter of footloose habit she avers: but in any case, she's never enjoyed travel just for travel's sake:

'I've hardly had a foreign holiday in my life – and have always travelled to a purpose. Nowadays it's always to write a book, the best purpose of all, although my present one will be my last.'

There is a poignant little silence at this repetition before she rouses herself to hymn book-buying at amazon.com. For which I berate her, using the local booksellers argument, celebrating the opportunity they offer to browse and choose what might not otherwise have been chosen. She counters with the observation that I probably come out with armfuls of unnecessary and unwanted books. Before she can add in the bit about swathes of forest having been felled to produce them, I suggest that she's written several of the armfuls I've carried off in my time, at which she beams happily. Looking across at her grey curls and laughter-lined eyes, at a face so animated and open and humanly warm it is impossible not to feel affection for her, I think that I do not know a more amiably intelligent and gracious woman, and we stop arguing and playing at interviewer and interviewee, and gossip on for the length of a long lunchtime about private or trivial matters, children, hotels, sudden vistas, old acquaintance and all the other clutter and texture and richness of the life-journey, as friends do and writers select from in their mysterious and solitary craft.

EASTINGS

Living in a small western-seaboard nation, I enjoy the contrast and differing atmospheres that countries and regions of or on the east bring.

1: Gaspé

I am waiting by the quay at Saint Simeon, on the north bank of the Saint Lawrence 120 miles east of Quebec City, for the boat to take me across to the Gaspé Peninsula. Out from a beach of clean sand, an osprey circles above the shallows. It stoops suddenly, there is an untidy detonation of long wings and water, and the bird rises with a large fish in its talons. It flaps leisurely back to shore, perches on a post to feed, pausing only to glance across as the dapper little ferry in sky-blue, carmine and white glides in to dock. I drive on to it, glad that I've chosen this approach to the region of Quebec least known to British travellers.

Very few ferry-crossings can be described as idyllic, but this one is. The MV *Trans-Saint-Laurent* is a little, spruce craft, nearly 40 years old, immaculately maintained, built of sound steel and varnished wood. It typifies the relaxed, bright orderliness of Quebec. A couple of its officers catch me prying around and take me on a tour – into the gleam and hiss of the engine room, up on to the bridge where they thrust a pair of binoculars into my hands as we slip past l'Ile aux Lievres and l'Ile aux Fraises, excitedly point out pods of little white beluga whales in the clear water, and seals, eider duck, razorbills on the rocks. An hour's crossing seems too short. I'm almost reluctant to leave when we arrive in Rivière du Loup, the gateway to Gaspé.

Canada is one of those countries you either love or hate, and Quebec is its quintessence. I love it, and Rivière du Loup is a perfect version of Quebecois style. It's a small and spacious well-laid-out town, full of parks and flowers, on a hill above marshes. There's a sense of playfulness and vivacity about its architectural versions of French Colonial, and that sense imbues the inhabitants too. Opposite the granite-block-and-tin-spired cathedral, from a balcony above a shop-sign that proclaims *'Erotica, Amour et Seduction'*, two weighty sexagenarian matrons exchange waves with and laughter-inducing confidences about window-shoppers, passers-by and potential customers alike. I head out of town, along narrow roads occasionally punctuated by retiree-driven recreational pantechnicons, into Gaspé proper. Marshland edging the great seaway gives place to a bladder-wrack and brown-bouldered coastline with little jutting jetties, churches with glinting spires in the settlements they serve, the dark forests crowding in behind. Two hundred miles on, at Saint-Anne-des-Monts, I turn inland along what seems at first to be a dirt track into the mountains. After 20 miles along a valley akin to that of the Duddon, say, in the Lake District or the Upper Derwent in Derbyshire, with occasional glimpses of a Cairngorms-like mountain massif vouchsafed above the encircling forest. It pitches me into the parking lot of an astonishing wooden-lapboarded French chateau with a steaming swimming-pool in front.

This is the Gite du Mont Albert in the Parc de la Gaspésie. It's Labour Day – a Canadian public holiday – and the place is uncrowded. It's not quiet, but it's certainly not over-frequented in the way British mountain venues would be at August Bank Holiday; and though there is a general air of gaiety among the visitors, it is decorous and very French. The ambience is that of a four-star hotel. Its table, I discover, is on the lofty side of haute cuisine: 'guinea fowl wrapped in vine leaves with mushrooms and blueberries in a madeira sauce; fresh and smoked salmon *effeuillade* with ginger and maple white sauce; garlic and pesto frog-leg chowder ...' The clientele sit in the bar in boots, outdoor clothing, rucksacks by their chairs, and are as relaxed as can be. A hotel of this standard in Britain would throw them out, or at least insist on a dress-code, but this is the style in which French Canada enjoys its wilderness.

From here I'm to climb Mont Jacques Cartier – Quebec's highest peak – and will be guided up it by Jean-Philippe Chartrand, a park officer for whom I wait next morning over breakfast. He arrives and hands me his card:

'Jean-Philippe Chartrand. Responsable du milieu naturel et du service à la clientele Parc de la Gaspésie.'

That's clear enough, you might think, but at this point I should give you a warning. You might be like me and think that you can get by almost anywhere in French, sustain a conversation, ask directions, order a meal, read a newspaper. If ever you visit Quebec, you're in for a surprise. For a start, French here is *de rigueur*. It's the way the province expresses its cultural resistance and separatist inclination. Wolfe may have beaten Montcalm on the Plains of Abraham in 1759, but the established Frenchness of the place was never lost. To say that English is not widely spoken is an understatement. It is properly and admirably rejected. But don't expect Quebecois French to be the same language as you find spoken on the other side of *La Manche*. Speech here is taken at a quick mutter, its vowels curved inwards, the consonants smoothed out and robbed of all their trills and peaks. Even the French, I'm told, find it incomprehensible.

Jean-Philippe's dressed in the Park's brown-shirted Ranger uniform (I avoid making the obvious joke). He's a happy-go-lucky 29-year-old from Laval near Montreal, who got out of the city, worked as a Fisheries Observation Officer first, and with the decline of the Atlantic fishing industry found himself employment here in Parc de la Gaspésie. He talks to me excitedly and at length about 'the product' and its 'development'. I would bridle at these terms, these attitudes normally, yet of all the national parks I've ever seen, none has been less commercialised than this one. We get ready to go. Jean-Philippe calls over a waitress and orders what we'd call a packed lunch. She asks – for once in perfect English – if the standard excursion menu will be acceptable to us. Of what does it consist, Jean-Philippe asks – again in English, for my benefit:

'You 'ave a litre of orange, apple or vegetable juices, an apple, a pack of trail mix, home-made cookies, a granola bar, and the "Mountain Peak" sandwich.'

'Which is ..?' I quiz, with some apprehension.

'It is a multi-grain bun this big ...' Her hands describe the circumference of a *nouvelle cuisine* dinner plate.

' ... filled with Black Forest ham, sliced turkey breast, Canadian Cheddar cheese, Canadian Emmenthaler cheese, organically grown alfalfa, sweet romaine lettuce, butter, whole grain mustard and mayonnaise.'

Five minutes later, weighed down with our 'excursion menus', we climb into Jean-Philippe's Park Service truck and set off on the 30-mile-drive along interminable rough forest tracks to the starting point of the trail up Mont Jacques Cartier. I already know something of what to expect, courtesy of the excellent *Lonely Planet Canada* guide:

'Mont Jacques Cartier (1,270m) is the highest peak ... it rises above the tree line and epitomises the conditions of the Gaspé Peninsula: cold, windy and often wet at the peak.

'Hiking it takes about three and a half hours for the return trip, and is well worthwhile – the alpine scenery and views are fantastic, and it is fairly common to see some of the herd of woodland caribou near the barren peak munching on lichen. The trail is tightly regulated in order to protect the herd from being disturbed. These are the last of the caribou found this far south and conditions are very harsh ...'

We arrive at La Galène campsite, from which a bus runs regularly between ten a.m. and four p.m. to ferry hikers the six kilometres to the start of the trail up the mountain. I take photographs of those boarding. Jean-Philippe tugs urgently at my elbow and whispers to me: 'Be careful if you publish these. The women these men are with may not be their wives.' Quebec at times is more French than France itself. We bounce up the road to the check-in point for the trail. Access to Mont Jacques Cartier is open from June to October between the hours of ten and four. In the registration shelter as we descend at the end of the day, 129 people have signed in, and this has been a busy day, the most popular holiday-time. If this were Scafell, Snowdon, Ben Nevis ..?

The path from trailhead to summit is an old army jeep-track, the granite bedrock showing through. Patches of odd-looking conglomerate here and there turn out to be concrete. Jean-Philippe jokes about the jeep-track era of geology, tells of how the path is 'healing'. In the stream alongside are beaver dams. The forest all around is encroaching and utterly impenetrable – a tangle of brushwood and fallen timber and dense-branching, small, stunted spruce and pine. The distance to the summit is about three miles, the ascent in the region of 1,500 feet, and most of this concentrated into the first mile. At frequent intervals there are signs to forbid this and that and tell how much farther you have to go. Steps lead up to the summit plateau. As wilderness experience goes, this is on the amiable and prescriptive side of gentle.

A block field covers the whole of the summit plateau, and the view flings wide. These are not spectacular mountains. Mont Jacques Cartier and its fellow Gaspésian summits all around are very much an arctic tundra plateau. The frost-patterning, the polygons and rivers of rock, are very pronounced, the coloration of hill and sky beautifully understated, muted. Here the sedums and the saxifrages grow, the ash-hued lichens and the reindeer moss nestle among the rocks and a cold wind soughs among the dwarf pines at the upper limit of the tree-line, their fallen branches blanched and undecayed and powerfully expressive of spirit of place. On the highest eminence is an extraordinary tower, the Eole. It is maybe 30 feet high, a balcony all the way round it, built of green-painted wood bolted to a strong steel frame. From its top you look across the St Lawrence to Ile Anticosti, out to Percé and Ile Bonaventure at the end of the peninsula, and behind to Mount Logan – named for one of the founding fathers of geology. All across the top are cairns like Inuit inukshuks to guide your way. There are toilets by the tower. An elegant and well-organised couple Jean-Philippe and I talk to are walking on to spend a night in a cabin ahead that they have pre-booked. My guide points out to me the ruinations of this landscape: white tailings of a copper-mine at Murdochville 40 miles away; an invisible disused copper mine of the existence of which he alone is aware on the headwaters of Rivière St Anne; a single communications mast on a distant hill. Even in sum, their violations wouldn't compare with those seen from any of Britain's hills. The place is prime.

On the way down a massively-antlered caribou ambles nearly up to us on the path, observes us quizzically for a few minutes. Jean-Philippe holds up his arms in imitation of antlers. The real creature's appeased for a while. Jean-Philippe lowers his arms. It looks up dimly, registers change, gives us a look that suggests it thinks us idiotic and possibly dangerous before drifting away downwind. At Lac René, large friendly trout suck at fingers proffered by girls perched on lakeside rocks. Farther below, a moustachioed fisherman, his rod banned from the park and his paunch quivering from exertion of the ascent, tells of seeing a fish in the lake this big – his hands measure a metre. 'A new species – the Lake Beluga, perhaps?' jokes Jean-

Philippe. The man's companion munches an apple, her eyebrows holding a conversation with us. We check back in at the registration post. 'These regulations,' I ask Jean-Philippe, 'are they observed rigorously ...'

'Well,' he smiles, 'officially ...'

Unexpectedly, I like this place. I like it even more the following day as I drive off down the majestic river valley of Cascapédia, absolutely empty for close on 100 miles apart from a few fishermen here and there. When I stop briefly, three of them on a shingle bank beckon me over:

'*Anglais?*' they ask.

'*Non – Gallois,*' I respond.

'*Ah – Quebecois et Gallois sont frères,*' they respond, and invite me to sit by the fire on which they're grilling trout fresh from the river and brewing coffee. After this unexpected second breakfast I head on along the densely-settled coastline of the Baie des Châleurs. At every little creek a jetty's been built, a harbour with small fishing boats lined against the quay. Every other house is a *poissonnerie*, a *craberie* or a *fumerie de saumon*. There are chainsaw- and snowmobile-boutiques, the advertising signs are for Stihl, Jonsered and Snow-Cat. Cape Breton Island fills the horizon to the south. The road drops suddenly down to the peninsula's end at Percé.

I find towns built around geological complexity – Salzburg for example, or Bonifacio at the southern end of Corsica – thrilling, and this tiny resort at the uttermost end of Gaspé is in their league. A craggy bluff of coarse red conglomerate dominates it, and is counterpointed by the 300-foot-high fin of pink limestone, stippled with orangey-yellow lichens, sea-sculpted into arch and stack, that juts into the steeply-shelving bay. The two enfold a once-remote fishing village – the road only arrived here 50 years ago – the lapboarded, red-shingled and dormered cottages of which have been converted into resto-bars and subsumed into a welter of motels and pizza cabins.

The fish-rich waters that aided the survival of those who came from famine-haunted margins of Europe a century-and-a-half ago to settle here have brought other colonists too. Out on Ile Bonaventure is the World's second-largest and most accessible gannet colony. I go out there with Chantal Bourget on the boat of Danny Simoneau. She takes me to the cliff-edge where these beautifully-evolved fishing machines, seven pounds in weight, six feet in their wing-spans, glanded and airbagged to rid themselves of salt, oil their feathers and give themselves buoyancy, nest. The path to it is lovely, verged with white-berried dogwood and the orange flowers of spotted touch-me-not. We emerge from a lichenous forest of spruce and pine to the stink and noise of 100,000 nesting, jostling birds. 'Arra, arra, arra,' they call, gutturally, continually, clashing beaks, fencing, stabbing, submitting, copulating. Clouds of them swirl above the sea, diving in groups, rapid-descending glints of white crosses, wings folded just before the entry, the percussive report, the plume of spray, the resurfacing with mackerel, herring, capelin in their beaks.

Later, in the Resto-Bar le Matelot, I talk over dinner with Marie Le Blanc. She's the habitual Quebecois mix of French and Irish, feisty, manuconversational, with the red of those western European seaboards in her hair. From her I have a glimpse of how tight-knit this community of Perce is: the occasional face glimpsed on the boardwalk in summer; beyond Labour Day the old bonds re-formed, music in the cafés, drama, sociability. She tells of walking out to Ile Bonaventure in winter, two miles into a searing wind, a foot of ice over water 250 feet deep, creaking and writhing with the tide. She enthuses about the Whale Festival, about the dolphin and minke she saw from her bedroom window that morning, relates legends and ghostly stories of the sea, speaks in all seriousness of the folk in New Brunswick who've seen the tall ships on the horizon consumed by fire. She's a woman in love with her home place, steeped in its mystery and aura, and that place entirely worthy of her love. As I walk back to my hotel, waves hushing in on the shingle and a scent of autumn on the wind, I can sense its appeal.

2: *The Cow's Mouth*

India both entrances and confuses me: the arrival by night in Delhi; the cacophonous manic jive of traffic on its main thoroughfares; the abject accepting plight of the dispossessed at every road margin; the weirdly circumlocutory process of train-booking and the frantic one of train-boarding; sticky heat and mingling odours of spice and ordure; methodical calm of attendants handing out patched and threadbare linen sheets in the second-class sleeper; earnest friendliness and proximity of fellow-travellers; sear of noon-heat, thrusting ferocity of auto-rickshaw drivers. Through all these I've just emerged into the cool peace and apartness of Shashank Singh's hotel on Asi Ghat at Varanasi, from the balcony of which in this night hour I look out across the great arc of the Ganga, mother-goddess river of all India, as it loops through the furnace plains of the north, watch the widows anointing the shivalinga with which the city abounds.

When the world was young and innocent, according to the myth, the Ganga rose here in Varanasi, but it retreated because of man's wickedness and retreats still. As I sit here in the stifling heat of the night, my thoughts and memories career 1,000 kilometres upriver, to the ice-caves of its present birth in the snout of the Gangotri glacier, and to the ultimate Shivalingam, the mountain of Shivling itself.

I remember the sustained immediacy of sensation in trekking to Gaumukh: the cold boil of the river from grimy fissures of grey ice; the babas and sadhus with whom only the most minimal dialogue was possible; the lemon Indian dawns; the way an old man under a tree ceremoniously spread his dhoti for his wife to sit upon; the dotterels at Bhojbasa that were surely the same birds I see each spring on my Welsh home hills; the old woman with the Brahmin family, husband fat and self-important in front and her trailing nervously along the gorgeside path, a red bag balanced on her head as she sucked nervously on the corner of her plaid shawl; the evident devotion in which these pilgrims held the river; the sweet hay-smell of a parsley-like plant; the robin-like bird at Chulobas with a rich dark-chestnut back and a carmine breast; meadowsweet – that filmy-fragrant, creamy-laced summer rose of my own country of the summer stars; the faded blue Indian sky, the drifting flight of an alpine chough at 20,000 feet, the extra-human scale and indifference of a world in the sculpting stage of process of creation, the crystal glitter of Shivling's great ridges above Tapovan at dawn.

It was two years ago. In Delhi the last monsoon rain beat down. Moist, burnt air was like a slow, clinging slap across the face. This city breaks your heart, is first stage in a process by which you enter in to the Himalayan mysteries. It's a point of disjunction, bears no relationship to your life back there. The insistent dry scrape of a beggar girl's thin fingers at your wrist, the gesture with her other hand towards her mouth, the lolling head of the infant whose mother – a shrivelled breast drooping from her sari – jabbers at you unceasingly outside the Mercedes showroom that 'this baby will die': these are not of your own country's mindscape. You reel from them into a maelstrom where all values are whirled from your grasp. Here is not a place you recognise. Here demands of you the readiness to see things, to look at them, entirely anew.

Delhi, however much of an interlude, an annoyance, a frustration it may seem to the unready, is the proper gateway to what the Himalayan traveller or climber must go through. Black kites circle lazily overhead; hoopoes flit eccentrically across the grass; pigs root in a dungheap; men and women shit in companionable groups below the walls of the Red Fort, then waddle duck-like to puddles to wash themselves. To fulfil the needs of India's Kafkaesque bureaucracy, I've come out to a decaying office in a tumbledown, filthy suburb. Above the official's head streamside willows wave through a broken window as he talks of water from the Ganga, with a permit to visit the source of which he may soon issue me: 'At holy times we put a drop on the tongue; we bathe in it before marriage and before death. This water has the property that it never corrupts. There are no germs in it. It is always pure. The scientists have tested it, but have not found what this property is.' In Varanasi two years on, I remember these words as I watch the bathers in the dawn lift their brass cups to the rising sun and drink, ten yards downstream of a sewage outlet, five from a bloated corpse. Faith!

In the capital, restricted to the hotel in readiness for departure on the instant permits are granted, I watch translucent hippies waft by, nod to white-knuckled trekkers from the north of England whose eyes semaphore panic, exchange quick glances with mysterious long women whose Indian adornments and languid gestures glide across white pages on which they incessantly write. Then we leave – trains, buses, the terror of a night-ride from Uttarkashi up 100 kilometres of road with no surface, kerbed with blackness, a rage of water infinitely far beneath. Once the bus lost traction. Peering out I saw the edge of the road crumble into the abyss. We lurched forward, somehow. But Mother Ganga's song in Gangotri soothes ...

I sit on the temple steps from which the devout bathe and listen. The high surface note is all rush and hiss, beneath it a deeper, percussive rumbling of stones and boulders pounding along the river bed that seizes on your imagination. I feel the expansion of my own lungs, become absorbed into the rhythm of the place. Above the temple in slow, steep turns the path climbs into the Deodar woods. The deep breaths that impel you onwards are themselves an elation – that your breast could swell with so much of the living air, thin and sharp here at 10,000 feet, like cold springwater after too much of civilisation's fumy wine. I learn from those who are at home in this place. The Garhwali porters, sinewy and slight, trudge past as I sit drinking *chai* in the *dhaba* at Chirbasa. They walk unconcerned, 50-pound loads secured by a twist of rope, across the log over the torrent where I balanced tentatively. I watch more closely. These distant-eyed men in sacking and flip-flops move as westerners do not move. The placing of each foot is deliberate, the transfer of weight on to it instinctive and assured. Their walking is an art that, once you have noticed, you begin to practise – too consciously and too late perhaps, and without their natural grace, but nonetheless, you have begun to learn to walk. Also, here you can begin to learn to speak, balance words, hear content and not talk merely for sound. You listen to the simplicity of porters, sadhus, cooks. Like that percussive rumbling deep in the river, you regain the gravity of your humanity.

For a few days, whilst the path's re-established post-monsoon and the brimming streams subside, I walk up and down to Chirbasa, first teashop on the way, acclimatising, returning each evening to sleep at the tourist bungalow in Gangotri. In a damp twilight Ed Douglas and myself sit on the terrace of the Hotel Ganga Niketan there. Four Korean climbers take a table by us, appraise our gear without approval except for Ed's mountain cap, which they ask to see, examine thoroughly, ask for how many dollars he would sell it? Ed, irritated, firmly reclaims it as they list their peaks as though other items of merchandise. To get away, I move next to a monk in saffron robes who's smoking Capstan cigarettes. Where does he live? Upriver beneath a rock in the summer; Varanasi, where he reads Sanskrit and Indian medicine at Benares Hindu University, in the winter. And his object in being here? To teach meditation and sexual healing, for which many students come to him. He makes an expansive gesture with the Capstan cigarette. I catch the eye of Sylvia, the trekker from Dresden who has joined us. She transmits a delicate scepticism. The monk is very beautiful, aware of it too in the way he caresses his long, brown hair and practises expressions on us. He looks like the young Krishnamurti, and like Krishnamurti there is an element of mischief and showmanship about him, and just enough suspicion of charlatanry to free him from the taint of bland piety.

I visit the temple to make *Puja*. The priest views my awkwardness with patient amusement, goes to an ornate silver statue of the goddess Ganga in the dim interior to pray, returns with water in a tiny ladle which he pours into my hands to drink, and little balls of fine-ground sugar to eat, before marking my forehead first with red and then with yellow paints. Clouds drift amongst craggy spires above the village, accentuating towers, aretes, great clefts. A lammergeier glides across, its shadow traversing the rock face. Two helicopters fly up the gorge, minute against the peaks, their engine note absorbed into the river's roar, and we start for our base camp at Tapovan.

For the unacclimatised it's two or even three days' walk from Gangotri, but I wonder if there's a more enchanting walk anywhere in the world? It has excitement. The path's forever changing. Rockfall sweeps down. Cliff-traversing sections – crazy wooden stemple-supported constructions – decay and fall into the glacier torrent beneath. Its population changes too. Pilgrims constantly move up and down between Gangotri and Gaumukh, and trekkers, mountaineers, muleteers, sadhus clad in the orange of renunciation, soldiers and the quiet porters of the hills. There is an intensely dramatic and changing beauty, the great gorge arcing east then south, into the sun with the high Bhagirathi peaks bright beneath it.

Beyond Bhojbasa – a tented hamlet with a mouse-ridden tin hut of a tourist bungalow – you leave behind the birch scrub and enter a province of gleaming stone newly emergent from beneath the retreating glacier, the route vague, slipping between moraines and silt-margined turquoise pools, its line marked here and there by eccentric flat-slabbed cairns, painted Hindi ideograms. Until a few years ago, the path to Gaumukh and Tapovan crossed the river at Bhojbasa and held to the true left bank. Massive landslides scoured it away. Now it meanders up the right. By the Cow's Mouth – the great fissures in the glacier snout from which the river bursts out – are more *dhabas*, their canvas shelters weighted by low stone surrounds, the proprietors squatting on sack-covered sleeping platforms within, blowing up the wood fires whose tang alerts you to their presence hundreds of yards away and setting on blackened kettles at your approach. Ash-covered sadhus with matted hair immerse the devout in milky water so cold it burns. The path slants beneath cliffs thousands of feet high, down which stones whine and burst like shrapnel, then debouches into the glacier. I tack inland. Glaciers! I thought they were white, gleaming places of snow and blue crevasses. This is a mile-wide highway construction site with towering hills of spoil 200 or 300 feet high. House-sized blocks rumble down them; rock-slides start at a touch; voids lipped with gravelly ice, the sound of rushing water deep within, block your path. The tributary ice-streams of Chaturangi and Kirti add to the fracture and chaos. Two thousand feet above Gaumukh, at an altitude of 14,400 feet and after a gravelly climb that leaves you gasping for breath, you reach peace and Tapovan.

I do not know in the abstract why some places are holy and others are not, but in its human and natural detail, Tapovan's distinction is palpable. You could, I suppose, question its three residents, Om Giri, Babaji and Mataji, and though just to meet the latter – a small, dark and ageless south Indian woman – alerts you to the presence of holiness – their words won't provide any better evidence than that provided by your eyes. It's a high meadow with Shivling soaring above and the strange birds, the tracks of bear and snow leopard in the mud each night and the herds of bharal. Above you, always, is the great presence of Shivling, phantasmal by moonlight, glistening in the morning sun, by turns repellent and inviting, fulfilling in its atmospheres of warm rock and furious blast, its concealments and splendours, its crystalline apartness, the notion many have that this is the World's most beautiful peak.

Somehow, I do not have an overwhelming desire to reach its summit, and I have not anyhow come on this expedition as a climber. At times in base camp, looking up at its unworldly aspire, Menlove Edwards' words steal into my head: 'This climbing. Perhaps, really, one was never made for it. I have a conceit that I was even made for more than that: more than to satisfy extremely one's own pride.'

All of the expedition members, I suspect, have mixed emotions towards the peak, from aching, anxious desire to the psychological devastation of abject fear. Some look wisely at the serac barrier at 20,500 feet, below the final snow slope, and arrive at the detached conclusion that its threat is too great and unpredictable to put oneself beneath. Others accept the risk. There is an extraordinary degree of friction between some of the climbers, their egos and ambitions spikily conflicting, their attention on self rather than scene. Competition and the idea of conquest dominate, are at odds with the ideals of those who visit here without those fixations.

Sylvia, who is rather wise, and I, who am a little older, gravitate together and when the time comes for her to start her further journey to Madras, I go down with her to Gangotri, out of the stone world, its rawness and the savage attitudes engendering there. We find a room in a pilgrims' rest-house across the river from the temple. Warm water's brought to us and we wash. Hesitantly, we approach intimacy. In my poor German and her better English we explore the ellipses of communication. After the harshness of landscape and its human correlatives, there is softness and discovery. In the nights, with the rhythm of chanting and temple bells beyond the window, our bodies on the soft bed are glimmery, melding in a grace of nakedness. A space of days passes, time which feels peculiarly blessed, and then she boards the bus for Uttarkashi. I come back to a room hollowed by her leaving, collect belongings, and return in a day, fitter now, to Tapovan. The expedition has fallen apart. I'm enlisted as a climber. Four times, by myself and with different partners, I'm drawn to Shivling's high camps and apartworld, load-carrying, feeling my way, becoming accustomed, nauseated by other expeditions' attitudes on the mountain, appalled by the sight of a Korean with cerebral oedema being dragged down, toes trailing, across the moraine of the Meru glacier in the twilight.

One morning in particular disturbs memory. Ed and I have spent a night of excruciating discomfort – my third sleepless one in a row – in the tiny tent at 19,000 feet, and set off exhausted at daybreak up the ridge above. In the blue shadow fingers and toes have no feeling. Avalanches and rock-falls are streaming down the sunlit face of Meru across the glacier. My usual reaction to our hill rations – puking and shitting, nauseous at the grease and meat that gluttony made me force down last night is taking place. When everything's come up, the discomfort intensifies as fits of vomiting and coughing coincide to ram bile into every cavity of the head before it sprays out of mouth and nostrils to marble the snow around me green and yellow – all this to a gasping refrain of laboured breath. I'm encountering the pain of Himalayan climbing, the unfamiliar gear, the weakening resolve, the stumbling incompetence.

The rock steps on the arête ahead rear up. By effort of will I relax, determine upon rhythm and control, set to the climbing and become engrossed in its subtleties and technicality. There are two of these towers and the crux is on the second – a slim groove of red granite with festoons of fixed rope, frayed and abandoned, hanging down its sides and a ribbon of hard ice in its back. The drops to hanging glaciers on either side are immense, the risks as we solo up grave, but suddenly I'm captivated by the process of climbing, enraptured by surroundings, revelling in the certain delicacy of placing crampon prongs on tiny flakes and fractures, the smooth lean of the body in making for ease. In a half-hour's climbing I find out for myself what fascination is in this game, and it is enough. I understand.

I watch from the lateral ridge abutting the seracs as Ed – young, fit and acclimatised – climbs the short ice-wall which is the last technical barrier before the summit. He hesitates, his feet slip in places, chips of ice shower down. I cannot see the fixed rope up which he jumars, assume he's still soloing, watch him join the three Czechs who are ahead of us, look ruefully at my single walking axe and conclude that what's ahead isn't for me. It is ten o'clock on a bright, still morning, the summit 1,000 feet above. I go down with only a tinge of regret.

Afterwards, by the stream through Tapovan, I rest. An avocet stalks past along the sand-flats on coppery-blue legs, upturned bill probing, pied plumage gleaming. R D Laing's acid illumination is my prayer to her: 'I have seen the bird of paradise. She has spread her wings before me and I shall never be the same again. There is nothing to be afraid of. Nothing. The Life I am trying to grasp is the me that is trying to grasp it.'

A week later, on an Agra hotel rooftop, the dome and minarets of the Taj Mahal glimmering above the haze under a bright full moon so that I ache with the evanescence of this most beautiful of human creations and finest of all monuments to human love, I have an intuition: that there are ways of approaching mountains; that properly, if your own character is to grow through contact with them, it must be by appreciation of their beauty, by respect and a concern to establish between you and your desire's object the perfection of mutual rhythm – that it must be to do with love and not the assertion of power, must be a marriage and not a rape.

Good! Know that! Kiss the joy as it flies ...

3: Fragments of Paradise

The muddy red stain bled by the Batang Rejang into the South China Sea spreads out for miles from the coast of Sarawak. From the Kapit wharf at Sibu on the river's estuary, one thing is obvious. If our planned trip to the headwaters is going to be any sort of wilderness adventure, it's not going to be so just yet. For miles upstream, timber wharves and processing plants line the banks. Huge rusting coal barges and great, lashed rafts of hardwood logs trail down in the current behind battered, rakish tugs. This waterway is an industrial thoroughfare.

'How far to Kapit, Uncle Dennis?'

'Yes, 300 kilometres, hee-hee-hee, very far, in-express-boat-be-there-Kapit-Singapore-chicken-rice-lunch-by-mid-day, hee-hee-hee.'

Uncle Dennis is our senior guide. The 'uncle' is to respect his status as an Iban tribal elder. He's a short, powerful man of 65, wears a polo shirt, thick horn-rimmed spectacles and a brown felt trilby hat. He talks incessantly in a muttering low tone punctuated by shrill giggles. If you cock an attentive ear to his discourse, a key vocabulary emerges. It consists of three words: 'Emergency', 'communists', and 'shoot'. The latter generally sets off the giggles. Also there are dates from 30 or 40 years ago, and references to tacit British approval of head-hunting in those times, so long as the heads belonged to communists. I decide not to disclose my former political affiliations.

Lemon, our other guide, looks to be in his 20s, in fact is twice that. He's a Bedayak. He and Uncle Dennis therefore are enemies, though nowadays the animosity is as covert as that between the English and the Welsh, and doesn't involve taking heads. Lemon's conversation focuses on sex and rock'n'roll (possession of drugs is punishable by death in Malaysia, so we can discount those), with occasional digressions onto bird-life, courtship rituals or tribal culture, on all of which he's admirably lucid and informed. When Redmond O'Hanlon came this way in 1983 – *Into the Heart of Borneo* describes the journey – he had a guide called Leon. Leon was a sexual obsessive in his 20s. I have a suspicion that Lemon is Leon grown up. In fact, I have a few suspicions about Redmond's book, but we'll touch on that. For the moment, the express boat is about to depart.

My travelling companion is Alex. Unlike me, Alex is a good traveller. Nothing phases her. Not even the prospect of a trip into the Sarawak rain forest where, if O'Hanlon's to be believed, every branch of every tree supports an Arsenal home-game attendance of little black slimey two-headed frill-jawed bloodsucking creatures doing a Mexican Wave in the direction of any square inch of your uncovered skin, to cope with which threat you need SAS training and equipment and a Porton Down-style chemical armoury. It hasn't yet dawned on me that Redmond stands in much the same 'wannabe' relationship to the SAS as does Michael Portillo. Ever since we left Kuching I've been chanting a particularly long word like a mantra:

'Hirudinophobia'.

Alex finally rounds on me: 'OK – What does it mean?'

I bite my lower lip, hang my head and spill the beans: 'An unreasoning and inveterate fear of leeches ...'

'Oh, is that all,' she scolds, semi-sympathetically. 'Look, Uncle Dennis assures me we can buy leech socks in Kapit, and I don't think you'll need them before we get there. Now come on ...' Without further ado, she shoulders her rucksack, jumps down onto the clangorous deck of the express boat, and lowers herself through the hatch into its cabin. Quivering, I fold my umbrella, cautiously negotiate the gangplank, and follow her into the boat.

A Borneo express boat is an extraordinary craft. *Lonely Planet*, with its usual understated acumen, gives you the picture: 'All boats are very fast, with airline seats, ultra-violent videos and freezing air-con ... the longer trips are something of an endurance test.' They're swan-necked, narrow, steel-plated things with two vast and raucous diesel engines in the back and a couple of hundred extra passengers hanging out on top as the vessel cleaves through the mulligatawny water of the Batang Rejang. They travel at phenomenal speed. The cabins are hermetically sealed, with small, awkward exits. God knows what would happen if – as often seems imminent, for the traffic code and volume here are riverine versions of Delhi's – you were in a collision. In three dinning hours you're deposited 130 kilometres upstream at Kapit (Uncle Dennis' estimate of 300 establishes what Alex and I soon come to recognise as the Sarawak Factor).

Kapit is a sprawling, busy, ugly, stinking little town above a steep, high bank of the river, for the upper reaches of which it's the administrative and trading centre. The white rajahs of Sarawak, on the cavalier history of whom volumes have been written, built a fort here in order to stop the Iban doing their own version of polling around the headwaters of the Rejang and its main tributary, the Balleh. The fort, called Sylvia, still stands behind its rifle-slitted palisade. It's now a cool and atmospheric small museum around which the town bakes and steams. Uncle Dennis bustles off to find the policeman for permits to proceed upriver, engage boatmen and buy supplies, whilst Alex, Lemon and myself end up in Fanny Nug's Cybercentre on Kapit Square, variously jetting off e-mails home or trawling the bluer depths of the internet whilst being aurally assaulted from every speaker in the place by Westlife. Global culture has hit Borneo. Come mid-afternoon, Uncle Dennis has assembled a posse of local guides, boatmen, anglers, porters and police escorts, given them their orders for meeting the following morning, and is heading out of town to pay a courtesy visit on the headman at Sebabai longhouse. We accompany him.

There's a Bob Dylan song that runs, 'He's badly built / And he walks on stilts, / Watch out he don't fall on you.' I'm put in mind of it by the longhouse. 'Tread softly, for you tread on my decay' is the golden rule. Those along the Batang Rejang resemble dilapidated versions of those holiday camps popular in the 1950s. Sebabai is even more ramshackle. 'Very-old-one-hundred-years-wood-not-good-any-more-take-care-easy-put-foot-through,' warns Uncle Dennis as we teeter across a swaying wire-and-plank bridge into the village. He's serious. These longhouses stand 20 or 30 feet above ground where everything lands that comes out of them. We take off our shoes and enter. A dozen mildewed skulls in rattan baskets hang from the rafters.

'Uncle Dennis, why do they have cigarettes and betel nut between their teeth. Isn't that disrespectful,' Alex enquires.

'This not disrespect, this appease spirit so that not become angry with tribe who take head.'

'Ah,' muses Alex, 'so if you want to propitiate the spirits you offer them cigarettes ..?'

'Yes, very good, betel nut most important. These skulls maybe

Japanese, maybe communist, in Emergency we shoot, hee hee hee. Some take heads so not to waste.'

We make it safely back to Kapit. In the square, a couple of hundred are disco-dancing at one end, at the other the same number practice Tai-Chi. Along from the wharf we notice signs that mark the height of past floods. Some of them are 60 feet above current water level. A young man comes up to us:

'You have read book about Kapit by Mr O'Hanlon? I am Tony ...'

Another, even younger man joins him and takes up the theme:

'Yes, in Mr Hanolan's book I am Tony. He and I go with Mr Hanolan and him friend to Long Singut. You want to go there we come with you.'

Alex nods graciously and pulls me to one side: 'Correct me if I'm wrong, but there isn't a Tony, is there?'

We think it's time to buy leech socks. Lemon accompanies us to a Chinese emporium where he exchanges words in Malay with the proprietess. She chuckles conspiratorially. I ask him what he's said. He grins and hands me a pair of nylon stockings. The woman shrieks with laughter, volleys words at Lemon. 'She is saying that if you want to dress like woman, you go to Miri. Many you people there.' I hand back the stockings. Alex grabs them from him and I leave without buying. She sidles up to me outside: 'Sorry about this, but I just couldn't find you the right suspender belt.'

I decide there are worse things in life than being bitten by leeches. We go to a bar and drink Malaysian Guinness to fortify ourselves. I'm taking precautions – my grandmother used to tell me she drank stout for her anaemia. Precautions for other potential ailments are on offer in the Chinese café at breakfast time. Lemon translates. I order what I hear as 'hard-boiled eggs', and so does he. They arrive in cups and look like the contents of a spittoon. One sip and you're committed to finishing. It's salmonella soup. Lemon departs hastily, looking green. I feel ill all day.

'Lemon,' I ask later, 'about those hard-boiled eggs ...'

'No, no!' he corrects me, 'half-boiled eggs. Chinese delicacy. I not try again.'

We load the canoe. It's rather an elegant craft, sharp-bowed, high-transomed, flat-bottomed and vee-shaped, built of thick planks heavily caulked and cross-membered, three feet in the beam and maybe 40 feet long. Its provenance in the Iban tribal war-canoes is obvious. On the back it has a 40-horsepower Yamaha outboard engine. Fifty-kilogram sacks of rice are stowed amidships under a tarpaulin, along with a gas cooker, tins of curried beef, bags of ginger and chillies, jerry-cans of gasoline. Lemon and Uncle Dennis, Alex and myself sit on green plastic chairs, the sun beats down, our skin blisters, Uncle Dennis' pressed men leap on at bow and stern and the boatman roars us out into the stream with a good six inches of freeboard still showing. A mile upriver he pulls in at a longhouse on the north bank. Screaming ensues. Children cascade out of the longhouse and hurl into the river, frightening away an egret as they do so. The screaming mounts. Lemon translates.

'She is saying him he should not have boat one week when his wife want market.'

We race away upstream, the boatman smiling.

'He not have mobile phone,' glosses Lemon.

Hour after hour, day after day, we thrust upriver. In the heat of noon we seek out shaded spits of sand. Abu, our accompanying policeman, casts a round, weighted net to catch small, needle-boned fish that we eat with rice. Occasional pairs of hornbills pass overhead, the great knobs prominent on their bills, a ridiculous tuft of feathers for a tail. Each dusk a horde of flying foxes, jag-winged, purposeful and the size of geese, flap silently overhead. At a great, whirling confluence pool we leave the Rejang and head up the Balleh. It's the size of the Severn below Gloucester, the secondary forest dense, every tree supporting its own hanging garden of epiphytic growth. Apart from the mud-tone of the water and an occasional illegally-constructed access-break to the river, the hardwood logging for which Sarawak is notorious becomes less obvious, and at last, beyond a whirlpool with the bow of a large freighter sticking out of it, we leave the timber-trade's water-traffic behind and gun the canoe up rapids with spray coruscating like diamonds. Towards twilight on the first day, 95 per cent humidity becomes 100 per cent humidity, a tropical downpour threatens to swamp us, we pull onto a stony strand for the night. Logs so worn, scooped and hollowed by their passage downriver that they seem more rock than wood trellis the forest 20 feet above our heads. With a plastic sheet strung out above and a mosquito net over us, in our wet clothes we lie still and listen for rising water. The forest doesn't let sleep come easily. It whoops and yammers and howls. It ticks and brays, shuffles and snores. Great Argus pheasants scream from its depths in the dark. At dawn elegant gibbons with sad black faces screech at us from high branches. Hornbills bubble away like congested curlews. Fish-eagles stoop and claw at smooth eddies; moths the size of thrushes with ribbed and cartilaginous tawny wings glide by; a silent butterfly, spotted damask with a wasp's body, settles on my hand. Lemon catches me peeing against a tree. 'You must say "Excuse me" to the fairies,' he scolds. 'What do the loggers say?' I ask. 'They leave cigarettes,' he responds. The rain has ceased, the river scarcely risen. We journey on. At our lunch-stop fishermen offer to sell us giant carp with fleshy white lips. Uncle Dennis demurs. 'Too expensive,' he tells us, 'this fish cost 200 ringit [about £40] a kilogram. Chinese buy. Good for impotencies.' A dead bird like our British nightjar lies spreadeagled on the sand, its wide beak agape. 'This bird called frogmouth,' Lemon tells us. Uncle Dennis counters by drawing our attention to slender, pale-trunked trees on the farther bank. '*Compulsia Excelsa* I think,' he recites, 'the honeybee tree. In old days timber used for making blowpipes. Very strong and hard. Loggers not like. In Emergency sometimes Iban kill communist with blowpipe, very quiet, they not expect. Poof! Dead!'

We spend the night at the trading post of Merang, headman of the Kenyh village of Long Singut, a day's riding and rapid-hauling ahead. Merang welcomes us. His every movement and gesture have a grave and absolute economy. He has extraordinary composure, an upright bearing, watchful eyes. After he has assessed, he laughs. His house is built head-high on stilts, is a boarded and corrugated-roofed loft 40 feet long by 20 wide. Puppies tumble and snap at ducks and roosters beneath. Merang asks Lemon to tell me that the dogs' mother was eaten by a python. I finger the razor-edged blade of a long spear. Merang takes it from me, assumes a wide-legged stance, demonstrates. 'This for killing wildboar,' Lemon explains, 'he stabbing boar that hide under bush.' A generator thumps outside. The only furniture within is a table, a video-player and small television set on it. Around the walls are bamboo-handled paddles, sacks of rice, bundles of tapioca, clotheslines, stacked gnarled roots about the use of which I ask Lemon. 'These we grind into powder and make drink. Very good for stress and impotence. Chinese buy ...' he tells me, then adds, 'Merang ask why you not speak Malay? You come here, you learn, he say.' We spend the evening watching Bollywood song-and-dance epics – 'Merang have other films but he polite because Alex here,' Lemon whispers – and 20 of us sleep in rows on bare boards. Our last day's journey sees the river running green and clear. There are rapids every few hundred yards now through which we have to haul the canoe. I look down after one session's wading to see a small black thing dropping off my foot, leaving a perfectly round and unfelt bleeding hole. Virgin rain-forest arches over us on either side. We arrive at Long Singut.

The valley now has opened out, the river glides shallow over stones, the village is set back a little from the bank among fields and plantations of pineapple and rice. A mile or two farther and hills, sharp-ridged and white-cliffed, rise to form the border with Kalimantan, across which the Kenyh tribe came a few decades ago to settle here at the 'river-mouth of the honey-bees'. Through the dust and savage dogs of the square in front of the padlocked Catholic church, a proud little bantam hen guards her brood. On the church door settles a butterfly whose wings are a purple that must be the colour of heaven. The longhouse extends above the main street for 300 yards. We kick off shoes and climb up to its comforts.

Later, after a meal of wild boar and forest herbs and rice, we sit out with the elders in a darkness that has cooled only marginally from the humid 100-plus of the day. Merang's wife, her arms banded with soot-and-fishbone tattoos that denote her artistry, ancestry and aristocracy, produces a small cassette player. Young men bring out plastic flagons of *tuak* – rice-wine. It tastes like scrumpy and kicks as hard at your head next morning. Our glasses are filled, we're gestured to drain them, and immediately they're filled again. A young man sets a stand in front of the elders, places on it a rattan helmet strung with turquoise and scarlet beads and plumed with hornbill feathers. Against it he props a cape made from sun-bear skin, and a parang – the heavy Sarawak jungle knife – in a belted scabbard. Wide-eyed children sit at the limits of lamplight. Self-possessed and beautiful young women walk past. Lemon is busily explaining to me the complex etiquettes by which a young man might come to sleep with them when Merang's wife, with a curt glance at him, turns on the cassette player. The *tuak* circulates and the young man who brought out the regalia dons it. 'This,' Lemon hisses, 'is the Dance of the Hunter. Everyone must do ...'

The young man begins to dance. He is graceful, muscular, finely-coordinated, but his facial expression is uninvolved, mocking even. Step-perfect and detached, he gives us his post-modern take on tribal tradition, bows to his elders, and walks smiling away. Merang's brother puts on the headdress, the cape, stills himself, and starts to dance. At first he is slow, an old man, the movement studied, cautious, stealthy, deliberate, but building into a sinuous, sure, rhythmical, intertwining ecstasy, stooping, coiling, circling, pirouetting low, low above the floor, his expression rapt, hypnotically intense, hands always describing, floating, shaping pictures for our imaginations to grasp, of his prey, conjured up for us, immanent, there.

He finishes, stamps, bows, takes my hand, raises me to my feet, dresses me in the regalia and I must dance. The headdress falls off; I jam it on, prance in drunken delighted release, frighten children, set girls screaming, cause the elders to rock and roar with laughter at my ineptitude. I survive the embarrassment, if such it is, and drink down more rice-wine. Before the night ends, like many others I lie unconscious and snoring under the stars. But in my memory some fragments of paradise are gratefully stored, against the return to civilisation beneath.

TRAVELS *with* THE FLEA
(GETTING *to* KNOW *a* SMALL COUNTRY)

If you don't know your own country, perhaps you can never expect to know in any real sense the other countries you might visit? I'm fortunate to the point of being blessed by living in a small country, 'just small enough to get to know reasonably well in the course of a lifetime', which happens to be one of the most exquisitely beautiful on earth. The following account details a walk through it – made on foot, intermittently, over a period of months, with my little dog The Flea, and with the intention of getting to know it better. The itinerary chosen will, thank God, never make the status of one of those well-trodden walkers' ways, but it gave me intense satisfaction, and I hope will alert readers unacquainted with Wales to some of its possibilities and attractions.

All along the North Wales Expressway neon reflected as shimmering gold columns on the flooding tide in each succeeding bay, and a subdued dawn was easing through the gap between hills and clouds. It was just after six on an October morning when I left the car outside Prestatyn station and set off southwards up the High Street, fumbling around in my mind for the exact words of that Philip Larkin poem about the defaced railway poster: 'Come to sunny Prestatyn'. It wasn't sunny yet, and it took a large act of faith to believe that on this day it was going to be. My small dog, The Flea, was keeping very close to heel, nonplussed by this early turn of events, stoical at having been lured from her bed before the first hint of daylight. We were setting off to walk in stages through Wales.

So what were the prompts which brought about this – to her mind inexplicable – action? Well, there's a version of seasonal affective disorder, for a start. I get restless in the autumn, want to be stirring before the leaves burn on the fires. I wanted a journey and hadn't much spare time in which to do it. But it struck me that to start, the Offa's Dyke Path from Prestatyn to Llangollen would be a fine little trek to accomplish in a day. I'd been climbing in the Eglwyseg Valley the week before, and longed to follow the lovely traversing path there between the woods and the white-tiered rocks. There were other prompts as well: a specialist I'd seen about a knee problem had told me it was wearing out and shouldn't I treat it with more respect, old chap, at my age? Which had stung me to a string of unspoken expletives that certainly won't bear repetition here, and the resolution that I'd just get up, rage against the dying of the light and make it work again; also, I was well aware of this particular designated Long Distance Footpath's reputation as a glorified, glorious pub-crawl, and The Flea likes pubs. She gets petted in them by solicitous bar-maids, admired by old men whose pockets oddly produce biscuits (how many people's secret vice is to carry biscuits in their pockets?). She has water brought to her in little bowls and is talked about, which appeals to her vanity and makes her put on the winsome expression she wears to lure people close enough to nip, which is her favourite activity. So for her entertainment as well as my own, I thought we would take a walk along the border.

I had an idea that designated Long Distance Paths were idiot-proof, that there were signposts and markers every 50 yards for the whole of this one's 168-mile length, that you would scarcely need to consult map or guide. And for the most part that's an accurate appraisal and you find the little acorn symbol scattered everywhere on stiles and posts and great baulks of timber – reach one, cast about for the next, and on you go. But some good burgher of Prestatyn had obviously taken a fancy to one of these and pinched it for his fire, and a good blaze it must have made, which perhaps warmed him up as much as the hill I climbed, after missing the turning it once marked, warmed me.

I knew after a couple of hundred yards that I'd gone wrong. I didn't turn back because I was too idle to countenance the descent, because I was hot and bothered, because I was hoping that maybe I hadn't missed it after all, and because a noisy small Ford car with spoilers on its back which doubled its length had roared past and irritated me and ruined the gently stirring peace of the morning. So I ended up in a hamlet called Gwaen Ysgor at the arrival of daylight, being viewed suspiciously by those breakfasting behind windows, and being assailed by a plethora of ferocious signs as I gave way and consulted the map to find a way back to the path.

Do you know the feeling? Have you noticed also the phenomenon by which the closer you are to so-called civilisation, the more barbaric and blood-curdling become the strictures expressed on signs against straying walkers? Dangerous dogs, prosecution, death by shooting or impalement all lie in wait for the errant rambler in the environs of Prestatyn or Beaconsfield or Killiney and are not yet encountered around Aberdaron, Renvyle or Achiltibuie (though no doubt they will be soon). Beware those places where the god of property rules seems to be the moral, and I mused on it painfully before regaining the authorised path by a post box which politely asked all walkers thereon to complete a form requesting name, address, date, duration and destination of journey before passing on.

The detour had cost me half an hour I suppose, and that oppression was matched by the dove-grey heavy cloud above contrasting with a sky the colour of robins' eggs over Snowdonia whence I'd come. I began to think this path's whole reason for existence lay in that matchless outline to the West, and it was a thought to which I kept returning throughout the day. For the moment, to set against that far skyline was the immediate perspective of a teasing serendipity through little jigging lanes and across field-paths that gave every impression of being virtually untrodden. Where it crossed the fine tilth of a ploughed and harrowed field, there was not a footmark; across a mushroomy, lush pasture not a blade of grass was bruised. Who walks the length of Offa's Dyke? The answer seems on this northernmost stretch to be few, and yet it is an ingenious piece of route-finding across pleasantly nondescript countryside – the sort you find throughout England and hardly at all in Wales. The sense of careful negotiation, of respectfully reciprocal goodwill, accumulates as you pass along, and acts as tacit critical chorus against the times where it has been refused or denied – the mile outside the forestry of Coed Cwm, for example, where speculators in timber have ruled against the public's pleasure and consigned our feet to circuitous tarmac. How tawdry that attitude seems by contrast with the graceful footbridge across the new section of expressway at Rhuallt, which you cross immediately after Coed Cwm, having passed some of the most savage dog signs (and dogs) along the whole route. I hate the vicarious savagery of a chained dog, bounding and restrained, its teeth expressing all its owner's animus towards those who encroach on what is his-or-hers and his-or-hers alone. So I was glad to be leaving it and the roar of the expressway behind as The Flea and I climbed over a gorse-blown, pretty little hill by the name of Moel Maenefa, on the far side of which a camping barn nestled under a huge electricity pylon and made me ruminate on the depression felt by some on finishing the walk's being due to external factors like spending a night under that thing. Which was an apt thought to accompany me through the village of Sodom. How did any village ever come by that name? It wasn't unappealing, either, though the bottle-dumps at the path side signified a concerted quest for oblivion and the abandoned hen-coop cars didn't invite you to look back. Not that I mind bottle-dumps and scrap cars – you might not get them in the Lake District, but generally they're a part of the British countryside. Maybe we get too precious about such things. I'm seditiously reminded of Swift taking his 'Country Walk' along the banks of Glandore Harbour and complaining all the while that he took no pleasure in the beauties of the scene, being preoccupied with not stepping in the human and animal ordure that lay all about. With this in mind, I wound down the hill to Bodfari, passing on the way a slight, worn woman being towed up by a large Airedale who was, she informed me, called Digby, and boisterous, and when I commented on his good looks and obvious breeding she countered that he, like all dogs (even The Flea, who was baring her teeth from behind my legs), and unlike any of the human race, was beautiful. Thus I arrived at the door of the Downing Arms just as the landlady was opening it. She in her turn informed me that all dogs were banned from her premises but The Flea could come in for a bowl of water if she desired, and what would I like?

I had a pint of Guinness and took it into the beer garden by the river. All foot-travellers through Wales pass in the shade of George Borrow, so I amused myself by constructing an imaginary conversation resisting his aspersions against those who preferred this papist brew to good ale. I'd passed on to some Borrovian etymological fancies around Sodom, Serendipity and Coed Efa which had me giggling into my glass – the solitary mind wanders in order to amuse itself – before I realised the butcher was listening. He made no comment on the two voices he'd been hearing. He came straight out with what was troubling him:

'That dog of yours could do with some meat.'

The Flea jumped off the bench at this, trotted across, leapt on to his lap and started to lick him under the chin. He was four feet ten inches in height and neck measurement. He sat The Flea Tom Thumb-style on a vast palm and walked over to his van, shooting back at me as he went:

'You're not one of those veggies, are you?'

I was reduced to silence, but The Flea made up for both of us as she smacked her lips and crunched her teeth on the scraps and bones he'd given her, whilst the butcher wedged himself behind the steering wheel of his van and rolled out. Thus fortified – and in my case chastened – we made for the Clwydian Hills.

It's a long step from Prestatyn to Bodfari, but the Clwydian range that follows is a walker's dream. 'The bracken hill at its best,' declares Patrick Monkhouse, and you know exactly what he means the minute you set foot on these rounded, alluring heights. For 12 miles they swell and heave away southwards, dark with heather and glowing with the autumn fern. The northern end is curiously quiet and unvisited, farms lying silent and deserted under its flanks. On top of Penycloddiau The Flea and I came across a dog fox stretched out on its back sunning itself, and a merlin scudded round the flank of Moel Arthur as we crossed. The tops of this range hurry by, the walking as broad and easy as the hill shapes, the route so logical you merely follow your own momentum. Moel Fammau, with its squat stump of a memorial tower ('It was built in 1810 to commemorate the 50th year of the reign of George the Third, and at one time sported a spire nearly 200 feet high. This has mercifully crashed, but what remains is bad enough.' Monkhouse), is one of the great and enduringly popular viewpoints in Wales, from which on a clear day you can see from the Derbyshire Peak to Snowdonia, from Cadair Idris to the Lake District and the Shropshire Hills. Half of the population of Merseyside crowds up here on fine Sundays. Today it was deserted and I raced on down over Foel Fenlli, with its abrupt ascent from the Bwlch Pen Barras, and on past Clwyd Gate and over Moel Llanfair with the sun westering behind Eryri and the knowledge of a dreary tract of countryside between Llandegla and World's End ahead – squelchy forestry, tussocky moor with grouse exploding away, and then the open road from Minera in the twilight, bats flickering past a half moon rising over the long ridge of the Berwyn, its glimmer on the tree-sentried white rocks of Craig Arthur.

If you walk through the fading of the light, it never really becomes dark until you hit the artificial illumination of the town. I descended into Borrow's old Llangollen in thick dusk, past the shop window sign that read 'Taxidermist – Closed for Renovation', pondered on the burden of getting back to my car through post-deregulation border country, and pondered also on the pleasure of where the next stage in a journey from Llangollen might take me? The Flea sat on the kerb and looked her most appealing to solve the one problem. Two lifts and a bus and we were back in Prestatyn. I ached, and The Flea snored peacefully on my knee. And as to the way on from Llangollen, we shall see ...

Following Borrow

Llangollen is a difficult place to leave behind: bookshops, cafés, music on the streets, bustle, its river-and-hill setting, and all the Borrovian association too. Time passes easily in a town like this. I've been a devotee of George Borrow's eccentric personality and writing since my earliest teens, when I set out in 1960 with a copy of *Wild Wales*, bought from the bookshop on the Chester side of the bridge, in my rucksack. Throughout the next fortnight, by candle or streetlight, in the barns, telephone boxes and bus shelters in which I slept, I laughed at his prejudices, warmed to his enthusiasms, thought his vividly-sketched characters and ranting perorations entirely wonderful. Forty years on, I still reread him, though I prefer now the vigour and verbal portraiture of *The Bible in Spain*, or the gypsy lore and vagrant life in *Lavengro*. By the time he made his 1854 Welsh tour there'd been a severe hardening of the prejudicial arteries. But *Wild Wales*, for all its dogmatic authorial persona, is still the best regional British travel book ever written. The idea appealed to me of following a stretch of the route it describes, to see how things had fared in the years between.

At about eleven o'clock on the morning of the 21 October, 1854 – a fine, cold morning with a rime frost on the ground – Borrow took leave of his wife, daughter and the church cat (the story of which latter I suspect is pure invention) and 'started on my journey for South Wales, intending that my first stage should be Llan Rhyadr'. At about 11o'clock on the November 11 a century-and-a-half later – a morning so cloudy and dark it scarcely had the energy to rouse itself into daylight – I set off from the same place on the same route and with the same initial destination, 20 miles away, in mind. Llangollen's marginal embroidery of new bungalows and spruce cottages with lamp-posts, white-painted wagon-wheels and torrents of aubrieta down garden walls soon receded. The bed of the sunken lane I followed was stony, running with water between dams of fallen leaves. On the OS 1:25,000 map it's called Allt y Badi, and is clearly one and the same with Paddy's Dingle, which Borrow's Welsh guide John Jones feared to descend in the dark lest he be robbed of the money in his pocket as he passed the Irish tinkers' encampment.

There were no tinkers in camp today, nor have been, I suppose, for years. The sheaf of propertied prejudice which masquerades under the title of the Criminal Justice Act has outlawed anything resembling their (or Borrow's own early and late gypsy) lifestyle. The view as I climbed was blinkered, sodden and dull. Mist hung thick among gorse and heather at the hill's summit, as it did when Borrow passed this way. He uses it in *Wild Wales* to foist on the reader the first of his long translations from Welsh poetry – a gabbling, exclamatory version of Dafydd ap Gwilym's cywydd on the mist. Borrow's translations from Welsh poetry are for the most part an embarrassment and this one's no exception:

Pass off with speed, thou prowler pale,
Holding along o'er hill and dale,
Spilling a noxious spittle around,
Spoiling the fairies' sporting ground!

That bears not the slightest resemblance in meaning or verbal music to Dafydd's original. I could wish to tax George with the conundrum of how someone who professes such affection for a subject can produce such doggerel in its praise. Though perhaps if it came to the point, and you kept company with his shade for a fast-striding mile or two along the dusk of a Welsh road, the criticism would only manifest itself in a degree of ironic mockery, and his vast enthusiasm for Welsh poetry would prevail. So with a more charitable view on this particular shortcoming, The Flea – her low-slung belly thoroughly bemired – and I took the road slanting down out of the mist into Glyn Ceiriog, recalling with fellow feeling the effect of the descent on his knees too.

Glyn Ceiriog is a sprawling old quarry village, not notably pretty but with an air of vitality about it. There are bakers and weavers and a Christian coffee shop (born-again, no doubt – all instant caffeine-and-redemption) where I would have stopped had I not been in haste on this short day to get to Pont y Meibion. So I hurried along the road for a while before branching on to the Glyn Valley Tramway, restored as a riverside path by the National Trust and dedicated to public use. After a wooded, pleasant mile by the brown, flooding river the tramway crossed a track, and down to the right was 'a small bridge of one arch which crosses the brook Ceiriog – it is built of rough moor stone; it is mossy, broken, and ... there is a little parapet to it about two feet high.' I crossed the river by it and sat on the parapet, along which, mewing frantically, came a black-and-white long-haired cat, which sat on my lap and butted moistly under my chin, much to The Flea's annoyance. A woman came by with two blonde children, one of them in a pram, the other pointing and laughing at the cat's antics:

'Are these the *meibion* of the *pont*?' I asked the woman.

'I'm sorry, I don't speak Welsh,' she replied.

Feeling vaguely embarrassed, I asked her if she knew where Huw Morus' Chair was.

'Oh, it's up here by the bend in the road.'

I sat a while longer on the parapet with the friendly cat, then made my way to the road, a few yards up which, at the entrance to a farmyard, was an ugly modern obelisk in memory of Huw Morus. Not what I wanted at all, so I went to knock on the door of the house, which is where he had lived though not, as Borrow was misinformed, where he was born. The woman from the bridge opened it. No, she didn't know where the chair was, but if I went down to Erw Gerrig, Ann Kynaston might be able to tell me. She could:

'Oh yes, it's in my garden. You're welcome to see it. Just go through the gate there and it's on your right in the top wall.'

This was easier than Borrow had experienced. He had been led through nettles and dripping shrubs by a serving-girl for half an hour before the woman of the house had come out to find it for him. Whereupon he'd installed himself in it and held forth on Huw Morus, recited his verses to the assembled company, 'all of whom listened patiently and approvingly, though the rain was pouring down upon them, and the branches of the trees and the tops of the tall nettles, agitated by the gusts, were beating in their faces, for enthusiasm is never scoffed at by the noble, simple-minded, genuine Welsh, whatever treatment it may receive from the coarse-hearted, sensual, selfish Saxon'.

The chair is set in a wall at the end of a short avenue of box and yew – a single seat between blocks of dull pink stone diagonally veined with quartz, and overarched with ivy. The slate slab which forms its back, and into which formerly were carved the initials H M B (Huw Morus, Bardd), is delaminating now, with no lettering evident upon it. The whole runs with moisture, and is as dirty still as it was in Borrow's day, when the woman of that time offered to wipe the seat for him before he sat in it. I perched gingerly on its edge and talked with Ann Kynaston. No, I wasn't from Cadw – the Welsh ancient monuments agency by whom it was listed. Yes, it did look to me as if it needed urgent restoration work. She went back in to her lunch and left me looking out east – Borrow describes it as 'fronting to the west' – over her tidy garden to broken rocks on the opposite side of the valley, a peregrine sporting around them: 'He read the songs of the Nightingale of Ceiriog when he was a brown-haired boy, and now that he is a grey-haired man he is come to say in this place that they frequently made his eyes overflow with tears of rapture,' was how Borrow described his feelings to his listeners that day in 1854. Huw Morus, who lived from 1622 to 1709, has the sweet assonance and sentimentality of Burns (both men's work was written to be sung) at his most facile, but with little of the Scots poet's emotional range or intensity. His work is a triumph of form in concealing lack of content. I don't share Borrow's estimate of it, felt a distance as well as a closeness on this mutual seat over the gap between our times.

Thanking Ann Kynaston, I stepped back to the road just as a bus came straining up the hill. It lazed The Flea and myself over the three miles to Llanarmon Dyffryn Ceiriog, a small village with a self-possessed air of its own prettiness in a wide strath where the River Ceiriog starts to sweep round north-westwards to its source in the Berwyn moorland. There were two pubs. The car-park of one was full of Jaguars, Rovers and Mercedes, so I entered the other, The West Arms, the car-park of which was empty. This was, I suppose – being the older of the two pubs – the one in which Borrow had encountered the illiterate wagoner studying a newspaper: 'By looking at the letters I hope in time to make them out.' Go to an evening school, Borrow had told him, before passing on to an exchange of opinions about the Crimean War then in progress.

The conversation that took place during my visit, though less edifying, was equally representative of its time. The Flea and I sat in a corner with my book and pint whilst two women of a certain age talked. Ginny and Trish, from Putney and Barnes, were dressed in oatmeal knitwear, silk scarves, slacks, and with highlights in their sculpted hair. They discussed tactics to secure property on divorce, how to enact insurance frauds, and the beachwear one might buy for cruises from Debenham's store in Telford. What, I mused, would Llanarmon's own poet – John Ceiriog Hughes, writer of three lyrics in particular that any Welsh person over the age of 40 can happily quote to you, and who left the farm of Penybryn above the bend in the river six years before Borrow passed through here – have thought of their conversation? Narrow-minded and Anglophile in his later life, how disillusioning would he have found this sorry drift of talk (no doubt that of the respective husbands would be equally, if differently, dire)? I set myself to imagining the themes and quality of discourse he might have enjoyed in his Manchester exile with his fellow Welshmen R J Derfel, Creuddynfab and Idris Fychan. Ceiriog was a railway clerk, Derfel a preacher, dramatist, early Socialist and commercial traveller, Creuddynfab a literary critic and railway navvy whilst Idris Fychan was a harpist. Picture them together at the time, say, of Borrow's visit to the West Arms – a group of four young men conversing excitedly in a language not of their country of residence. Perhaps they're walking up and down Ardwick Green, factories and warehouses silent for once all around them. It's a warm Sunday, their talk even warmer on the subject of the Blue Books that have damned educational standards in the country of their birth and desired their native language's demise. (Why does Borrow never once allude to a subject paramount among the Welsh

212

intelligentsia of his day? Did he never meet a schoolmaster or a Sunday school teacher?) R J is satirising, as he did forcefully in his 1854 play *Brad y Llyfrau Gleision*, the 'traitors' who have sold out their own language for a mess of Gradgrindian advancement. Ceiriog and Creuddynfab set forth from this topic on to a vigorous exploration of the merits and limitations of writing poetry in the strict metres, and Idris Fychan steps in with special pleading for lyrics to be composed with the harp's musical accompaniment in mind. I've no doubt this conversation or similar would have taken place, in that setting and others on scores of occasions between these men. And now the place of birth of their most eminent has to listen to how a husband can be incited to violence before a witness, the manner in which burglaries can be faked, and what factor sun cream to take to the Caribbean.

Back in the real world, I stole another look at the women from the South, gulped down my beer in rapid disgust and set forth. Mist was down on Cefn Hir Fynydd. A raven harassed a heron along its margin and flocks of fieldfares soughed past, windblown Maltese crosses. Lowing cows guided me down to Cae Hir along a track deep in mire. I thought of Borrow knocking on the door of the house and asking of the woman who answered whether she was alone there: 'Quite alone,' said she, 'but my husband and people will soon be home from the field, for it is getting dusk.' Nowadays a question like that would get you arrested. The woman's response suggests it unnerved her a little too. The farm-linking footpaths I'd intended following were policed by every kind of hissing, yapping, cackling, bellowing animal antagonism, all of which served to raise The Flea's hackles and curl her lip. I gave up on them, and followed Borrow's four long miles by lanes, where yellow leaves seemed to give out their own light and white streaks of lime mortar glowed from the collapsing chimney breasts of ruined cottages, to Llanrhaeadr ym Mochnant, where good fortune led me to the door of the Plas yn Llan guest house of Mrs Sheila Fleming, who took The Flea and myself in unannounced, bemired and bedraggled, installed us among her dogs (upon whom The Flea politely and wisely refrained from making war) with a pot of tea by the stove whilst she made up a bed; who fed me, entertained me and directed us on a tour of the town's amusements that evening which ended at an undisclosably late hour in a particularly friendly pub in heated agreement with the socialist Mayor of Llanrhaeadr.

She turned us out next morning rested, Berwyn-bound and breakfasted with the laughing comment that I shouldn't interpret too anatomically Housman's description of this area as 'A country for easy livers, / The quietest under the sun.'

That sally alone made me grateful I'd lit upon her establishment rather than the Wynnstay Arms, where Borrow had stayed and to which I did have brief recourse during the evening. He noted that it 'seemed very large, but did not look very cheerful. No other guest than myself seemed to be in it.' The present licensee has that text framed on the wall as advertisement. I had a brief talk with a moustachioed 82-year-old who looked to be a fly-fisherman but vouchsafed that he'd scarcely missed a Liverpool game at The Kop in 60 years. At the next pub they were watching – and discussing in beautifully clear Welsh, the first I'd heard that day – the Manchester United game played that evening. For the rest of the night's talk, it and the beer flowed, and in the course of it I learnt a great deal about the economy of Llanrhaeadr, which is apparently based on an egg-packing factory and something that's 'green, gets you drunk, and comes on a Thursday'. Unpretentious little mellow brick town that it is, the most amusing incident in the whole of Borrow's long book happens during his two-night stay here. (On his excursion to Sycharth he meets two flaxen-haired Saxons whom he quizzes solemnly about church-going. They respond that they like ale. When he presses them further on what they like, he unwittingly describes them simulating sexual intercourse, and roaring with laughter at his mystified response. It's an astonishing escapee from the book's presiding morality.) There is about Borrow's visit to Llanrhaeadr a puzzle. It was here that William Morgan between 1578 and 1587 worked on his translation of the Welsh Bible – a work of scholarship and linguistic power that more than any other single factor ensured the survival of the Welsh language. Yet Borrow records only an inaccurate comment about Morgan by the clerk who shows him Llanrhaiadr church.

It is the seventh-wonder-of-Wales cataract that draws people to Llanrhaeadr and from which the town gets its name. Borrow's often-quoted 'long tail of a grey courser at furious speed' description of it is as loosely impressionistic as his poetic translations. The fall is rather complex. A stream of no great volume spills in three columns that pulse and mingle down a blocky, dark cliff of perhaps 120 feet, efflorescing on the strata, rosetting white against the black rock before a right-hand mossy ridge obscures the water from view and it tumbles into an unseen pool, from which it jets out sideways through a remarkable round hole in the foot of the ridge to a series of lesser cascades beneath, the general impression being of less than the 240 feet that is the fall's total height. The hole and the strange spirit-bridge spanning it Borrow, as a critic of scenery, deplored, yet it gives Pistyll Rhaiadr its uniqueness and oddly disquieting atmosphere. In the valley above the fall, by the little Afon Disgynfa, I saw a stone circle and alignment that Borrow had passed unaware; I saw black grouse too, a peregrine chase a skylark, the immediate texture of crystalled, frondy tussocks, red-bladed moor-grass and quartz pebbles among the peat as I navigated by compass in thick mist up to and across the high summits of the Berwyn; and I thought him a man who did not notice such things.

But as I waded through the morass that motor-cyclists and latterly mountain bikers have left all along the commodity-crest of these their smooth, high hills, as I collected their discarded high-energy drink-cans and chocolate-wrappers, I knew that Borrow's disregard is not as their disregard. And when I reached the Wayfarer Plaque to 'one who loved these hills' at the Nant Rhydwilym, and looked inside the metal log-box to find it overflowing with mementoes, business cards, status reference ('Fourtrak', 'Frontera', 'Trooper') and language of the 4WD fraternity, I turned down towards Cynwyd with a sense that 'Wayfarer' would be ashamed of the changes wrought in his name. In this ruined, magical country Borrow's sense that landscape is also to do with lives and histories, is more fitting, more respectful, more aware than the uses we make of it.

Waun y Griafolen

Just beyond a bridge over the Afon Fwy the path that had been nagging at my curiosity on the map for months assumed reality in the form of a break running in the wrong direction into a thick plantation of spruce. Within a few yards it swung round to the required compass reading and mounted the hillside. Worn rocks, fragments of broken-down wall among the trees spoke its age. It was pleasing to see how the Forestry Commission had preserved the route, and surprising too, for Coed y Brenin, of which this woodland is an outlier, is dire country for rights-of-way closures and obstacles. Perhaps the planting of spruce hereabouts is a sufficient sin. I'd have far less quarrel with forest planters if the trees were larch, with its dusty-ginger autumn tones, and vivid feathery green of spring that always reminds me of Marty South's epitaph for Giles Winterborne in *The Woodlanders* – the most moving passage maybe in the whole of Hardy's fiction, and in its mood of quiet desolation and murmured remembrance perfectly suited to the landscape beyond this wood.

Something about journeying – not only on foot, but perhaps particularly then – directs you into metaphorical thought. As you travel, the ideas work their way inchoate into your mind and your observation of things in the natural world enriches and amplifies them until they resonate out into themes, excitements, images. A sort of rapture is accessible to those who walk alone. It was working for me along the path after the wood. It ran through a marshy bwlch with Arenig Fawr and Moel Llyfnant dominating the scene, rising from a cloud-filled valley to the north, the immediate texture of landscape – light-stippled moor-grass and shattered outcrops – counterpointing their simpler forms. In front, Dduallt – long a favourite of mine among Welsh peaks – was lifting into view, between us one of the great and powerful places in the Welsh hills, and one to which few go. I reached the gate before the descent into Waun y Griafolen, leant on it looking out, and wondered what it is about this place that I find so affecting.

The name means 'moor of the rowan tree' but there are none here now, though down among the peat groughs their embedded remains are clear enough. Its surface area is two miles long by a mile wide, a basin surrounded – on all sides but the one on which Dduallt rears up – by low ridges. It has a quite astonishing sense of space about it, and of emptiness. The vegetation – the heathers, rushes, mosses and grasses, have simply taken over, wiped the slate clean, started again in their slow way and produced a tabula rasa. There seems to have been an attempt made to drain it – ditches cross it regularly, for more forestry, no doubt, the presence of which here would be a manifest obscenity. But they too, futile as they are, are being filled in as frond, tendril, blossom uncurl, straighten toward the sun, bend in the wind, fall, rot and compact down to raise up this breathing organism, this simple place. The path marked on the map as crossing it is conceptual rather than actual. Down among the preserved rowan stumps are doubtless the smoothed rocks of old passage, but it has been erased, its line on the map now a dangerous one to follow. The Afon Mawddach drains out in deep canals from reed-choked Llyn Crych y Waen. Better to describe a prudent ellipse, avoiding the brightest green moss and heading for an obvious step low on the north ridge of Dduallt. The cloud from which I'd been freed spread down the valley of the Dee to England to keep chill the heart of the Tory shires. Peaks were islanded among it, and all around were the hills of Wales, clear and identifiable. Frost flowered the moss beneath the summit, where two grey falcons perched on rocks, watching. I ate lunch by the cairn whilst The Flea crept into the rucksack for warmth. There is one finer viewpoint in this region than Dduallt and we were bound for it – the neighbouring peak of Rhobell Fawr, from which on a clear day you can see from Snowdon to Pumlumon, from Garn Fadryn to Caer Caradoc. We climbed it, and made our way sunwise down this 'noble mountain', as Patrick Monkhouse terms it, after half a mile picking up the path that runs down to the Bwlch Goriwared. The sun set in the estuary of the river whose birthplace we'd traversed, and in the afterlight the long bulk of Cader Idris in front acid-etched against a tangerine-and-eggshell sky.

Gloywlyn

When you are still in a landscape, and become an object temporarily fixed there, the landscape itself starts to come to life around you. Those who have written about the Rhinog comment on what they see as its sterile and lifeless quality. Perhaps they were too busy passing through, too intent on destination to see what's here. I begin to be aware of how much is moving around my bed in the heather. From a rock behind me there is a fierce fluttering and chipping of small birds, as pipit and wren argue over territory, take up aggressive stances on prominent boulders before joining brief flurries of battle in the spaces between.

On the shining lake-levels there is a convergence which threatens more trouble. I see it all from this vantage point. A drake teal – a lovely small duck made shy and fearful by the depredations of the wildfowling fraternity – is gliding round the margin of a reed-bed, whilst unseen to him in the next inlet a moorhen jerks and bobs along. They meet in an explosion of wings, clattering away across the water, the teal airborne and wheeling back to alight in a clearing amongst the reeds before the more aggressive moorhen has even raised her trailing legs from ripples that follow her. A bemused fox comes down to the farther shore to drink, watches with one foreleg held aloft, points delicately to where the teal has landed, pricks its ears at the metallic call of a snipe that rises from the sedge.

The accent of light falls differently now. Carreg y Saeth has become black, the stoney detail of its crags entirely gone. Its ridges serve as dark frame for the peak of Yr Wyddfa, 20 miles away and purple with coming night. The bright lake itself is a map, its countries sketched out in quicksilver, in wavering lines of rushes, reeds and sedge, in undisciplined clumps of bushy heather and the stirring, tawny grasses that catch the last rays. These also light up rock strata that dip at a steep angle into the water, bearing the scars of glaciation, erratics scattered across them from the yesterday of geological time. It catches too and glitters on the rings which surface tension has pulled up the brittle grey stems of reeds furred underwater by green algae and standing in soldierly groups. The hillsides, hitherto plain and dark, are glowing with rich greens of plaited bell-heather stems, and the dusty pink husks of last year's flowering in the common heather. Two ravens creak across the indigo sky. I imagine them as the 'twa corbies' of the old ballad, discussing in this stately progress their next meal:

> The one of them said to his make,
> Where shall we our breakfast take?
> Down in yonder greene field,
> There lies a Knight slain under his shield
> His hounds they lie down at his feete,
> So well they can their master keepe,
> His haukes they flie so eagerly
> There's no fowle dare him come nie.

A scimitar-winged peregrine flashes by. Colour ebbs away, then suddenly surges above the horizon again. An arc of palest turquoise in the west modulates down through sunset's palette to a glisten of sea beneath. Above the rim of the cwm the lights of Cricieth and Pwllheli register, and beyond them the beam from Ynys Enlli pierces the haze. The moon is up, climbing above Rhinog Fawr, the lake still bright with its reflection. I watch the stars come out one by one, as though switched on. Across from my tent snipe are still drumming in the marsh. The sound is eerie and yet comforting. Noises of the stream mingle, stilled momentarily by a breeze. As it traverses the hillside, on the farthermost ridge scarlet flames where the heather is burning leap as vivid and temporary within this landscape as our lives, tugging as they do so at the most primitive emotions. Streamers of livid smoke furl round the moon, extinguishing in their short sway the brightness of the lake.

Dyffryn Dysynni

I climbed the stile-like entrance to the enclosure and memorial on the site of the family home of Mari Jones at the head of Dyffryn Dysynni. It is a curious kind of memorial to a small event, a small human interchange, that had in its day considerable resonance. The roadside cottage of which it is built must have fallen into decay, but the walls were made good to shoulder height, the chimney-breast and hearth – the aelwyd which has meaning among any nation of exiles – rendered sound, and the floor paved evenly with slate, on which has been erected, above a plinth of native stone, a squat pillar of polished brown granite with an open-book motif carved on it. A plaque records the following detail in English and Welsh: 'In memory of Mari Jones, who in the year 1800 at the age of 18 walked from here to Bala to procure from the Reverend Thomas Charles BA a copy of the Welsh Bible. This incident was the occasion of the formation of the British and Foreign Bible Society.'

It also became part of the folklore – the Reverend Charles taking pity on the girl after her 25-mile walk across the mountains, giving her his own copy of the first cheap edition of the Welsh Bible, the rest having been sold. It was still part of the propaganda in the Sunday schools of my own

Manchester childhood. I remember a print of the barefoot girl poised against the mountain wind, black curls cascading from beneath the hood of her cloak and looking to my ten-year-old eyes just as Kathleen Williams did, whom I sat next to in school and with whom I held hands sometimes in the playground. The extent to which the story has been pared down is striking. Its narrative detail is all moralistic – the girl's arduous devotion, the minister's charity. There is nothing by which to grasp an understanding of her life. That part of the story has been left hollow and empty as the hearth at which she read her Book. You learn more about her from her grave in Bryncrug chapelyard, a few miles down valley, than you do from the shell of Ty'n Ddol; that she married Thomas Lewis, a weaver, died in Bryncrug on the 28th December, 1864 aged 82, and was buried above the flood plain of the river by which she grew up, her grave paid for by the Calvinistic Methodists. Bar memory in the region's pubs adds more – an unreliable sense of a woman whom celebrity had turned unpleasant and vain. I prefer to think of her, if indeed she was the agent by which the B&FBS came to be formed, as the instrument of Borrow's creation as a writer, for it was his experiences on behalf of the Society in Russia and Spain that gave us his masterpiece, *The Bible in Spain*.

I left Ty'n Ddol, its beech-shaded stream and the old track over the mountain that had taken Mari Jones to unenviable symbolic celebrity behind and set off down the Dysynni. The valley's most intriguing site is Castell y Bere – the Kite's Castle, built by Llywelyn Fawr in 1221. It was to here that Dafydd ap Gruffydd retreated, after the death of his brother Llywelyn ('Ein Llyw Olaf') in December 1282 had spelt the beginning of the end for the Welsh stand for independence against Edward I. The castle was sieged by 3,000 men. The imminence of its fall obvious, Dafydd escaped – apparently to Dolbadarn – and Castell y Bere fell to the English on 25 April, 1283. Dafydd himself was taken prisoner on the slopes of Cadair Idris on 28 June and put to death in the unspeakable manner the English inflicted on those they deemed traitors at Shrewsbury Cross, where a plaque still marks the spot, on 3 October.

Nowadays, no trace remaining of the atrocities of that time, the broken walls of Castell y Bere trail haphazardly around the summit of this surprising rocky outcrop, with its well from the mortared joints of which the ubiquitous spleenwort grows. A cool wind from the mountain was drifting through the gaps in them as I entered its green curtilage. Thyme was spreading and violets discreetly blooming. In months to come the delicate harebells would wave here. It is so still. Seven hundred springs having passed since the murderous commotions of war, since the siege and the fall, the blood and the cries at noon. Cloudshadow has passed over, the rain, snow and hail fallen. There have been mornings when the valley has been white with frost or filled with mist. Seven hundred times the woods have put forth green leaves, seven hundred times they have grown tired, faded, burst suddenly into autumn glory and declined into dank miseries of winter. There has been human labour and mortality, birth pangs in the cottage by the church down there, in the garden of which today a brown-haired woman sits playing a guitar. The first mewling cries of infants have been heard tenderly or with resignation, and the last breaths of old men whose bodies putrefied and returned to earth to enrich the graveyard loam. The jittering wrens have nested in cracked walls throughout these years, cuckoos called and the cormorants returned to roost on their inland rock as the sea retreated from the valley. The dial on which this valley's time is told has subsumed, rendered insignificant, my time, Mari Jones' time, the time of those who worked, died, were betrayed here, and its hands still sweep on, so that time itself becomes insignificant, and there is only the great calm beauty of process, renewal, decay, the impersonal force and urge of nature in which all of us have our part.

Market Day in Machynlleth

The Wednesday market was in progress along Heol Maengwyn, as it has been every Wednesday since the 13th century, its traders outnumbering the town's population by all appearances, and on this hot day doing little business in their various wares. There were dapper Pakistanis with vivid, cheap clothes from Bradford, refrigerated counters of cheese and home-cured bacon from beyond Aberystwyth, a bookstall of the Welsh Christian Evangelical Fellowship, Hong Kong toys and Taiwan tools shouted up by strident Liverpudlians, long-haired women of faded beauty down from the valley sides where they'd been holed up and earth-mothering, digging

221

potatoes and The Grateful Dead since 1967, presiding over jumbles of carved boxes, incense sticks, Indian scarves and packets of henna whilst sharing surreptitious, fat, sweet-scented cigarettes. I slipped aside from all this bustle into the Quarry Café, behind the bright primary colours of the façade, which is one of the singular institutions of the new Wales.

Thick soup with thick bread thickly buttered, and thick coffee in thick mugs that you eat and drink sitting on thick benches at tables made of thick boards – it's all designed, I think, to ground the place, introduce an air of solidity to offset the metaphysical yearnings of notices which line its walls. Taken together, they make an intriguing index to the preoccupations of the other Wales that's grown up in the last 30 years, beyond the confines of chapel, eisteddfod, and Cynddylan-on-a-tractor bleakness of the communitarian-past-seeking Anglo-Welsh literary coterie.

My eye roves over sheet upon sheet of photocopied A4, lighting promiscuously on phrase, slogan, advertisement: 'Love isn't plastic – it's natural'; 'Drumming and Sweat Lodge'; 'Learn organic gardening'; 'a dynamic martial art based on co-ordination of mind and body'; 'Self-heal events summer-autumn 1995' (Selfheal is a beautiful little purple flower, underfoot everywhere); 'Peace Pilgrimage in Britain 1995'; 'Free Gendun Richen'; 'Come rock-climbing with other women'; 'Gandhi Foundation (Nurturing Ourselves and Others)'; 'Shelters, teepees, Celtic Huts, domes, yurts, made to order'; 'Ancient Pathways and New Directions – a residential weekend with Rob Lind of the Kwakiutl Tribe from West Coast Canada. Teachings on use of herbs and role of animals in Kwakiutl Healing. For information contact Jenni'.

The part of my mind not engaged on this odyssey through the alternative was picking up meanwhile on a conversation between the two women behind the wholefood counter about the effect of floods in South America on the price of walnuts. It would be so easy to mock the culture represented here, to scorn its frenetic reachings after new (and ancient) directions. My inclination is towards the sceptical – I'm quite sure the dupes and tricksters, the charlatans, hypocrites and spiritual materialists cluster as thickly among the exponents of alternative culture as they do in society's mainstreams. But I'm still left somehow with a sense of the good-heartedness and reverential nature of the enterprise, of its rejection (discussions on the price of walnuts aside) of materialism and its implicit acts of rebellion.

Hyddgen

Once you climb out of Glaspwll and reach the ridge of Esgair an easy grass track, acrid with the smell of sheep and undulating through hummocks, carries you three swift miles south to where a path, the marking of which across high ground by quartz boulders suggests its age, veers down eastwards to the old tyddyn of Hyddgen. Its former house is now a nettle-infested pile of boulders, of fallen roof-trees crumbling to tawny dust, but alongside it is a complex of wintering sheds crowned by a crazy-angled chimney and built of corrugated iron sheets, rust-red, surprisingly mellow and suited to the moorland colouring of grass and moss, stream, mine-spoil and peat all around. As a place to live, it is remote in a way few places are south of the Scottish Border, the nearest habitation perhaps four miles away. But then, no-one has lived here for years. At shearing and dipping, lambing and gathering, the farmers and shepherds converge by Landrover and scrambles bike. The stove flames and smokes, the kettle sings, sheep protest and the men laugh and curse until the work's done. Their vehicles sway off along the tracks, ash flakes and cools in the grate, a bat flickers from the shed's rafters, solitude orchestrates its adagios again. Thus Hyddgen, but there is another aspect to this name. Here's an account from the manuscript known as Peniarth 135, transcribed in the 16th century but from its language clearly dating to the first part of the 15th century:

'The following summer [ie 1401] Owain rose with 120 reckless men and robbers and he brought them in warlike fashion to the uplands of Ceredigion; and 1,500 men of the lowlands of Ceredigion and of Rhos and Penfro assembled there and came to the mountain with the intent to seize Owain. The encounter between them was on Hyddgen Mountain, and no sooner did the English troops turn their backs in flight than 200 of them were slain. Owain now won great fame, and a great number of youths and fighting men from every part of Wales rose and joined him, until he had a great host at his back.'

Walk the track from Hyddgen with the gleam of the Nant y Moch reservoir in front and you come in a mile or so to a little meadow of tussocky grass where the Afon Hengwm and the Afon Hyddgen join together. Its grass is spear-like, carmine-tipped. On the bank above, perhaps 80 feet apart, are two white blocks of quartz, the southerly one a four-foot cube, its neighbour a little smaller. '*Cerrig Cyfamod Owain Glyndwr*' they are called – the Covenant Stones of Owain Glyndwr – perches now for the hawk and the quartering crow.

From outside the tent on the bank of the Afon Hengwm, The Flea and I looked across to them as the gold disc of a full moon rose from behind Pumlumon. They glimmered a little, the grass waved in a fitful breeze, a peregrine traversed the dusk, stooped half-heartedly and sheered away. The Flea growled softly. The bare facts recounted above are all we know from contemporary accounts of a day nearly 600 years ago when the longbowmen and spearmen of Glyndwr prevailed against terrifying odds. What the covenant commemorated in those death-symbolising stones entailed is obvious: the terrible ferocity of warriors with nothing left to lose but life; the grim determination of their cause's last stand; recognition, slaughter, and the raven's profit.

The vegetable life rises round the stones and my mind, running on this theme, turns to a historical curiosity. There is, in Kentchurch Court on the border between Herefordshire and Wales, a panel painting of an old priest called Sion Kent. If widely known it would be recognised as one of the finest portraits from its time – the early 15th century. The representation of an old man, it is a work of exceptional power, is of an artistry far greater than would have been expended then on a mere parish priest. The house in which it's to be found was that of Glyndwr's son-in-law, Sir John Scudamore.

Tradition has it that Glyndwr, whose rebellion ultimately and inevitably was contained but who himself was never captured, came to the Scudamore estates of Herefordshire's Golden Valley in his old age, and died there. I believe he did. I believe 'Sion Kent' is Glyndwr, the skin puckered and lined, the hair on his high forehead receding now, the eyes sunk deep within the strong bones of his face. It's the same face as on the Great Seal. You cannot look into those eyes, that face, without understanding how, here, by this upland stream, desperately

outnumbered, by force of spirit and will he prevailed. And you cannot but
see the suffering endured and the waste of it all too, beneath the
unchanging outline of the ridge from which his enemies descended, by
the constancy of the stream's flow, among these now-quiet hills.

Pumlumon

The high summer sun had sucked the marshes dry, baked quaking bogs
into immobility, desiccated even the floating foliage of bogbean as I walked
by little pools which bejewel Fainc Ddu above the north-eastern arm of
Nant y Moch reservoir – a geological curiosity by which a track curves
round to the lake of Llygad Rheidol below Pumlumon's summit. As I
rounded the spur into the cwm, two ravens flew overhead, making for a
rocky bluff around which they revelled in a pouncing, tumbling,
pirouetting aerial dance to the screaming distraction of a peregrine nesting
there to whom their play was mischievous taunt. The lake itself glittered
beneath sombre, heathery crags. Llygad Rheidol is tucked neatly beneath
the dome of Pen Pumlumon Fawr, not much more than a quarter of a mile
distant from the summit itself, but almost 1,000 feet beneath. In 1854
George Borrow, in the course of his pilgrimage to the springs of the three
rivers that have their sources on Pumlumon, descended this slope, and a
memorable experience he found it:

> 'Yes, sir,' said my guide, 'that is the ffynnon of the Rheidol.'
> 'Well,' said I, 'is there no getting to it?'
> 'Oh yes! But the path, sir, as you see, is rather steep and dangerous ...
> more fit for sheep or shepherds than gentlefolk.'
> And a truly bad path I found it; so bad indeed that before I had
> descended 20 yards I almost repented having ventured.

Borrow must have made a very direct descent of the slopes above the
lake from the ridge, for a brief detour round their western rim leads on to
the smooth and swelling summit dome. The recurrent theme of these hills
of mid-Wales is spaciousness, and Pumlumon expresses it to perfection.
The quality derives from a general levelness of the mid-Wales plateau, the

way it stretches away in rolling solitude, the tucked-awayness into deeply-incised valleys of human habitation, the fewness of the roads, the way soft outlines lead your eye inevitably into distances. On this fine day, despite cloud to the east and an overall haze, I could still see the Longmynd and Brown Clee Hill in the Marches with England, and Cadair Idris stretched and reclined along the horizon to the north. Nearer at hand, little flashes of silver were the lakes of Bugeilyn and Glaslyn, around whose margins bog-oak starts from the peat. The valleys of Severn and Wye thread away along their different routes toward England; I followed mine to the dilapidated Ordnance Survey pillar and shelter cairn.

Borrow's description from 1854 is interesting. He scans round, reporting on the wilderness, the 'waste of russet-coloured hills', the lack of trees, and remarks to his guide that 'This does not seem to be a country of much society.' The guide's reported answer runs thus:

'It is not, sir. The nearest house is the inn we came from, which is now three miles behind us. Straight before you, there is not one for at least ten ... Pumlumon is not a sociable country, sir; nothing to be found in it, but here and there a few sheep and a shepherd.'

It's a puzzling exaggeration. There were more farms and shepherds' dwellings in the valleys immediately to the north in Borrow's time than there are now. Hyddgen, for example, which Borrow may well have visited and drunk buttermilk at, was inhabited at his time, and on a clear day – which that of Borrow's visit was – would have been clearly visible less than three miles to the north. I wonder if, for all his physical prowess and perhaps as a result of his exceptional childhood reading, Borrow was short-sighted? That would explain the clarity of his close description and the extreme vagueness of his accounts of hill-shapes and distant views? If so, he might have found fellow feeling with the son whose conversation with his father I overheard as I sheltered in the cairn: 'So you see, Robert, there to the north is Snowdon and Cadair Idris, and out west, across the sea, the hills of Ireland. The Preselis are in that direction, and you can just make out the Brecon Beacons to the south.'

'But father,' the boy stated, with phlegmatic emphasis, 'I can't see any of them.'

Ystrad Fflur

I came out of the woods to the village of Cwm Ystwyth – half its houses for sale, some of the main ones in ruin, a sheep gathering in progress – and ran on over smoother slopes as yet unplanted to the complex landscape of the Teifi pools, from which a footpath leads along the bank of the Afon Egnant and through a valley of haunting loveliness to Ystrad Fflur. The nearer I approached to Ystrad Fflur, the more excited I became. It has always been, throughout the years I've known it, 'one dear perpetual place'. I've sheltered from the sun beneath its graveyard yews, slept the length of summer nights on its green monastic turf, dreamed afternoons away with friends and lovers on my way from here to there. And so, in expectation, I arrived ...

Plastic canopies, interpretation boards, admission fees, displays, galvanised steps – here ..!

Ystrad Fflur, a Cistercian monastery founded in 1164, has claims on our attention other than the beauty of its setting. The main one's that it is reputed to be the burial place of Dafydd ap Gwilym, whom tradition claims to be buried underneath a majestic yew tree. Of all the lyric poets of late-medieval Europe, Dafydd ap Gwilym has the finest ear, the surest grasp of language's capacity for music. And he has also, as far as comes through in his poetry, an endearing, mischievous, sensual nature. On romantic love and natural beauty, on sexual play and cosmic jokery, he writes as well as any poet ever has written. For all my adult life I've loved his work, had him as one of the dozen poets I would not be without. Which made it the more wonderful when, as a teenager, I first came to this place, and found it so plainly lovely, so unstatedly holy. The heritage industry has now destroyed it – another example of the trend Robert Minhinnick defined in his fine recent essay, 'A Postcard Home'. Tourism, 'now the most important Welsh industry,' he suggested, 'is doing its level best to destroy what many people consider the two essential characteristics of Wales – its environment and its culture.' At Ystrad Fflur, the environment has been degraded, the culture reduced to slogans. Is that as much refinement and sensitivity as *Cadw* and the Welsh Tourist Board are capable of in their Cardiff tower block by the main line to Paddington?

Tregaron

I met a woman and she drove me away from the ruins to Tregaron, where we sat outside the Talbot Arms in the main square drinking excellent beer and watching the sun set behind the church's weathercock and cypress trees. The older Georgian houses had UPVC windows and the old cattlemen's bank was covered in ultramarine plastic signs. People next to us, up from London, talked about Maestros and Citroëns with a second-hand car-dealer who had left the police force there. By the war memorial, old men in shorts, sunning themselves, shouted at youths in baseball caps whose ghetto-blaster was the size of a large suitcase and turned up to thudding volume. They sauntered away to a safe distance before tweaking the sound again, so that the gangsta rap of Snoop Doggy Dog thudded against the grey walls of the chapel. Black American street culture in the square of a Welsh market town! Laughing, I half-expected to see the walls fall. If these were vandals, what words are adequate to the foresters and heritage police, of whose insensitive thighs their generation was conceived?

Drygarn Fawr

Beyond Ty'n Rhos the track climbs north of the land ruined by conifers, past the moorland pool of Llyn Gynon the stream from which feeds into the Claerwen reservoir, and on to the long ridge of Esgair Garthen above it to the south. This is truly the great wilderness. The headwaters of the Claerwen drain the most extensive tract of wild country south of the Scottish border. The rough traverse of this Elan and Claerwen headwater country is the most satisfying (and arduous) approach to one of the best, strangest and most remote of Welsh hills, the taunting presence of which teases at your topographical sense from miles away. It is centrepoint, focus and definition of the Elenydd, presiding spirit of the once and future wilderness, and its name is Drygarn Fawr.

It's always intrigued me, the way in which some hills have a character out of all proportion to their height. Drygarn Fawr is a mere 2,115 feet above sea-level yet it still ranks with the finest hills. Height isn't the primal quality here, and the lift of its ridge above the surrounding moorland is by

228

no means remarkable. It has a rocky spine running north-east and south-west – attractive rock, too; a rough, stony conglomerate with quartz pebbles and seams – that rises just high enough to command. Bronze Age man augmented the feeling of the place by building two huge burial cairns, perhaps a quarter of a mile apart (the third of the cairn that give the hill its Welsh name is a mile away to the south on the ridge-gable of Drygarn Fach). They are visible for miles around, beckoning, and when you arrive at them, neither of them disappoint. The one on the higher summit is perhaps 10 feet tall and 60 in circumference, squat and powerful, dwarfing and looking down on the decayed Ordnance Survey pillar on a stump a few yards away. Beautifully built in drystone blocks, it's immaculately preserved.

The northern cairn is less well cared for, has an old Brecknock county concrete boundary post stuck into it irreverently, but has one striking feature. Its top is crowned with white, glittering quartz, and the effect is quite magical. To the south and east deeply incised valleys lead off to the lush country. Their sides are blotched with heather and patched with outcrops of pink-tinged scree. Beyond are glimpses of the border hills: villages in a folded landscape, fields of ripening wheat and barley, hedgerows, copses, half-timbered cottages. But this is not the land Drygarn Fawr inhabits. The carpet around its throne is of peat, seamed and cliffed and stratified, dark chocolate against sage, tawny and purple moor-shades. The whole of a 90-degree arc to the north appears featureless, but the map is rich in names. For 10 or 15 miles there is no sign of habitation or human activity other than the impinging forestry. It appears entirely featureless, but if you were to follow these vague long depressions where the streams start, there would be rocks with smooth green turf around them, pools of green or of bright ochre, emerald patches of sphagnum, and the sound of skylark, curlew and grouse. The skyline, lacking in striking individual notation, curves round in a slow, powerful, melodic sweep, very fluid, and across the whole scene there is the constant play of light and shade. As I look, it is khaki, but where the cloudshadow has passed, from amongst it glimmers a burnt-out, faint green that is almost grey. The cliffs above Claerwen are red. Suddenly, in the heart of the moor, a long streak of sun sketches in the underside of a ridge so that it looks like the belly of a recumbent animal. I'm reminded of prehistoric cave paintings. When the electric light goes out the guide holds a candle to them, your eyes accustom to the dark and because of the primitive artist's use of relief in the rock they flicker into magical life. That thought in turn reminds me that 2,000 years ago this moor was inhabited. Five hundred years ago people lived here. Now it is empty. But as Hilaire Belloc wrote of a not too distant hill, it is 'like the continual experience of this life wherein the wise firmly admit vast Presences to stand in what is an apparent emptiness, unperceived by any sense.'

Llandod Café

The mid-Wales line is a miraculous survivor in the modern railway age. It serves a vast hinterland, runs through sublime countryside, and has the argument of social amenity as the main reason for its anachronistic existence. Four trains a day run each way between Swansea and Shrewsbury, passing through Llandovery and Llanwrtyd, Llangunllo and Knighton. There was an old woman I knew – widow of a railwayman – who used to travel on it every year from Pontarddulais to take her annual week's holiday in Llandrindod Wells.

'Oh, Llandod,' she used to tell me. ' 'Eaven on earth!'

When I first knew Llandrindod, in the latter half of the 60s, this old spa town, administrative centre for the old county of Radnorshire, was distinctly run-down. I used to come to the cinema here when I worked in Glasbury-on-Wye. It was called the Grand Pavilion – decaying Victoriana perfectly described by its name and opulent enough to have been an opera house. I saw *Woodstock* here when it first came out. There were three people in the audience and one of them was so stoned he fell off the balcony when Jimi Hendrix came on. The music caused pieces of plaster to fall from the roof. The usherette was in her 80s. She slept through it. You could make love on the double seats of the back row unnoticed during the film's longueurs. I don't think it stood a chance. Last time I saw it, it was boarded up, notices everywhere to tell you it was unsafe. Perhaps the usherette's sleeping in there still, waiting and dreaming on the Valentino kiss that will restore her youth.

Nowadays the town is cosmopolitan, bustling, upbeat. Its large, redbrick Victorian terraces and pump-rooms still feel incongruous among the low green hills of Radnorshire, but it's manifestly more opulent now. The electronic cottage, in connecting people throughout the world, has liberated them from the cities and enabled them to move back into these dreamy places away from the world. The grocers and ironmongers may have gone, but there are the usual glut of delicatessens, antique shops and business consultancies along the high street, signifying new prosperity.

The old Llandrindod, meanwhile, maintains its presence as interested observer of this change. I went into a coffee shop for breakfast and – where else in untrusting Britain would this still happen? – was joined at my table by Joan from the Elan Valley, who told me she was in town because her husband was away with the lambs at Rhayader market:

'He used to work on an experimental farm, increasing stock and improving yields,' she told me, 'but now it's all going back the other way to nature, isn't it? The farmers of my husband's generation, well, they don't know what to think, but the young ones now are talking to the very old ones for the knowledge they have, and that's a good thing, isn't it? He's from Llanddewi Brefi, you know – they speak good Welsh there, but there wasn't much Welsh where I was brought up. But that's coming back too. My son, he learnt it at school, so now I'm learning it too, and it's easy for us – classes in every village, and friendly, isn't it? But it's all changing, and some things won't come back. The farm where I was born, well, that was sold for houses to people from Birmingham, and a company bought the land.'

As soon as Joan, a good-humoured, elegant middle-aged woman, had left, Alice came and sat in her place. She was under five feet in height and over 80 years old, but her eyes were the brightest blue. In an accent two parts cream to one of apple juice, she asked me if I was here for the convention at the Baptist chapel, told me that it had been going on since the revival of 1903, very popular, and the singing ..! She was given a lift in every day from her home in Newbridge by a relative who worked in the council offices, and came in here for a cup of tea and a sandwich before visiting friends or sitting in the park. Was I on holiday? She never went away, except sometimes for a few days to her sister in Shrewbury, on the train of course, oh yes, the train, what would we do in Llandod without the train?

I left her there pondering that question, a distant smile on her face as though every remembered clack of its wheels along the line revived old memories. Llandod! Yes, time and the train still stop there ...

Kilvert Country

There are some groups of hills of which memory never loses the sense. They needn't be high or grand, but they root themselves so as to call you back time and again. They are the places to which you return, in mind and body too, as a character in a romantic novel might turn at the story's end from obsession with beauty's drama to the plain, quiet charm of constancy. In my life, I always come back to The Begwns.

They are – or rather it is – a scarp of brackeny slopes, steep to the north, rising gently from the south to an altitude of barely 1,300 feet to swell out the rectangle of land enclosed south and west by the River Wye, to the north by its tributary the Bach Howey, and to the east by the border with England. It is an area that in itself you might pass a dozen times and disregard – just such another piece of high common pasture as you find throughout the middle parts of Wales, with the mountain ponies, sheep and the ranging crows, scattered rowans and thorns and the buzzard screaming overhead.

After an autumn in India I came back to exchange cacophonies of Delhi – the street-noise and traffic, the beggars' heart-breaking importunities – for those of the Mawn Pool: seagulls and moorhens and the 'tsi-tsip' of the tits among the branches of dying pine trees. The night was bitterly cold, with a cracking frost and insistent east wind. I cut a hearth and soon had a small fire crackling and leaping. There are few things quite so comforting as a fire in night's solitude. I sat by it for hours with the moon flitting and glowing among rags of mist and my thoughts all quiet and fixed upon the man who'd brought me here, and whose personality infuses this landscape with complex and subtle blends of observation, sentimentality, personal tragedy, disturbing sensuality and profound human concern.

Maybe, I thought, there might once have been processions here as there were to his 'Wild Duck Pool' over at Newbuilding, to which 'the people used to come on Easter morning to see the sun dance and play in the water and the angels who were at the Resurrection playing backwards and forwards before the sun.' What, I wondered, would they do on a frozen night? Would they skate across in the moonlight under the pricking stars? On the glimmer of the ice-bound lake out there beyond the firelight, if I believed sufficiently, would I see them too?

Or the fairies, for fear of whom 'boys would wear their hats the wrong way round lest they should be enticed into fairy rings and made to dance'. I might not believe in them, but then, 'Walter Brown of the Marsh says that his grandfather once saw some fairies in a hedge. But before he could get down out of his cart they were gone.'

My own grandmother, born on the Welsh borders in the lifetime of the recordist of that memory, told me similar stories with complete conviction, and as I walked out of the fire's illumination and looked back from silvered shadows on my camp, as I observed a hare's leisurely staccato across the opposite slope, I would have to say that in me too, beneath the sceptical overlay of 20th-century consciousness there is a yearning after the irrational and the magical that gnaws at this safety in times and places like this. And a yearning, too, for something at least of the – for us at times disturbing and difficult – innocence of the Reverend Francis Kilvert:

The right conquered, the sin was repented and put away and the rustle of the wind and melodious murmurs of innumerable bees ... suddenly seemed to me to take the sound of distant music, organs. And I thought I heard the harps of the angels rejoicing ... I thought I saw an angel in an azure robe coming towards me across the lawn, but it was only the blue sky through the feathering branches of the lime.

The Begwns, Clyro, Hay, Chapel Dingle, Rhosgoch, Colva and Bryngwyn Hill as they were in the 1870s, as the lives and concerns of the inhabitants of these wooded hillsides and secretive valleys were, are stitched through the tapestry of his daily record in the most vital and vivid colours. There is more of Victorian rural life and belief in the pages of Kilvert than can be gleaned from any other source I know.

Y Gelli Gandryll

From behind the house where Kilvert lived in Clyro you can cross the road and follow field paths most of the way to Hay, which you enter across a bridge over a stretch of the Wye where riverbank poplars are reflected in its unrippled waters. Hay is an idiosyncratic little town. It has a Welsh name, and an odd, evocative one at that – Y Gelli Gandryll – the shattered grove. Musing on it bookishly – and how can you not muse so in a town comprised entirely these days of second-hand bookshops? – it put me in mind of the agonising delicacies among the bombarded wood with which David Jones concludes his semi-autobiographical masterpiece, *In Parenthesis*, about trench-life in the Great War:

> The trees are very high in the wan signal beam, for whose slow
> gyration their wounded boughs seem as malignant limbs,
> manoeuvring for advantage.
> The trees of the wood beware each other
>   and under each a man sitting;
> Their seemly faces as carved in a sardonyx stone; as undiademed
> princes turn their gracious profiles in a hidden seal, so did
> these appear, under the changing light.

Sitting in Oscar's Café in the upper part of the town, I thought to go to Capel y Ffin in the Black Mountains, to make an excursion to it as Kilvert had done in 1870 – he to see (and pass censure upon) the monks brought there by 'Father Ignatius', myself to visit the place where Eric Gill had set up the bizarre artistic community to which David Jones – whose poetry, prose and character I love more than those of any other Modernist writer, and the mystery and magic of whose paintings and engravings I'd urge everyone to see – came to work in the mid-20s.

It was a wet day for a pilgrimage, and I like idling hours away in cafés, particularly when they have good coffee and engaging, bright waitresses. A café is often the best index of its community. Oscar's was a fine expression of the embourgeoisement Wales has undergone in the last 10 or 15 years. There were prints of Moorish villas in the Spanish interior, of Citroën Light Fifteens in French provincial squares. There was a poster for Newlyn

Art Gallery's last exhibition. There was much varnished pine, a soot-free spot-lit inglenook with vases of colour-coordinated dried vegetation, and blackboards with the menus chalk-written on them: Hot bacon & crouton salad: crevettes in a wine and garlic sauce; toasted brie with walnuts and orange: sorry, no elderflower pressé today. And then there were the women, two of them (do women in cafés and pubs always come in pairs?), who'd swept in from the rainswept street with a swirl of oiled cotton coats, a flourish of knitted scarves and a shake of broad-brimmed hats. They had sat down, they had patted their hair into place, they had run the index finger of each hand along delicately plucked eyebrows and flicked off the drops, they had loftily called for Earl Grey tea; and then, in a surprising London twang, they had begun to converse:

'She's got a hyperactive child – God he wears me out – excess energy basically – he lives near Chippenham with his new partner – you know what he did in Kilburn? – that's why he's called the butcher of Kilburn – half the teachers in the school gone – he was active in the Labour Party, of course, though he's rather taken a back seat now – Tufnell Park – that's North London, isn't it – yeah, but you know, the pits, the real pits actually ...'

In 50 years' time a snatch of conversation like that will have become social history.

Black Mountains

All the way up from Hay I'd been scouring my brain for the names carved on two stones on a ridge of the Black Mountains that I'd seen for the first and last time nearly 30 years ago and the recollection of which, because of some conjectural romance, had inexactly stuck there.

'The first one,' I explained to Bill Bowker, 'was to an Irishwoman – Mrs O'Shea, Mrs O'Grady – something like that. And the second to a squire. And it's my belief that she was his mistress and they had natural children together and when she died he was so devoted to her that, because their relationship was illicit, he had her buried up there and himself close by her when his time came, in the wild, away from propriety and prying eyes.'

'That's just the sort of romantic gush you would believe, isn't it, Jim?

Anyhow, I've never seen these stones, but I tell you where they'll be. They'll be on the Rhos Dirion ridge, and I don't fancy our chances of finding them today, but we'll have a look. Or at least we'll go as far as The Twmpa and see how we get on.'

'When you say The Twmpa, are you referring to what the OS one-inch seventh series map used to refer to as Lord Hereford's Knob, but which the 1:50,000 first series decided should go under a name without any such apparent – ah – oddity?'

'Ah, well, if you look at the map I have, which is the Landranger second series, you'll see that what your dirty mind insists upon and which the Ordnance Survey expurgated has been reinstated, to the delight, no doubt, of you and every giggling schoolchild west of Hereford.'

'I've got it! It was Mrs MacNamara,' I butted in, before Bill could launch into one of his lengthier tirades against my character and personal morality.

'What was Mrs MacNamara?'

'The name on the stone ...'

'There you are, you see – obsessed by Irishwomen! What you need is a long, cold shower, and that's just what you're going to get.'

With that, Bill turned south into the gale and I – grateful for full waterproofs, feet sodden already – plashed alongside him, snapping and sniping and chaffing away in the full, friendly flow of old acquaintance. For two miles we tacked along the whaleback ridge at 20 degrees to the wind, surfing a solid wall of rain with nothing to be seen beyond it.

'Good job I'm with a holder of the Mountaineering Instructor's Advanced Certificate, Bill, otherwise I might get lost.'

'Pity they didn't make them waterproof is all I've got to say to that.'

Occasionally we passed forlorn groups of ponies, long manes hanging sodden and string-like across their withers. Sometimes we veered yards wide from the path to avoid trampled bog. We entered into a disquisition upon why we both liked the Black Mountains but felt no similar affection for the Brecon Beacons. And then we came upon the stone.

It's a small slab of the local sandstone, its top rounded like a gravestone, heavily encrusted with lichens, measuring perhaps 18 inches wide by 30 tall. Mrs MacNamara's name is still legible upon it, and a date, which appears to be 1825 but is difficult to decipher, and in this weather we were not inclined to study it for long. Thirty years ago, I remember the stone as being intact and firmly rooted in the greensward. Now, it has apparently been vandalised, a large corner of it broken away, and it lists, supported by a heap of stones, in a mirey pool. I know nothing about it. I wonder if Raymond Williams was constructing a story around it for the ambitious novel, *People of the Black Mountains* – a novel structured in part around a grandson's search for his grandfather in a storm along this actual ridge of Tarren yr Esgob? I wonder if this stone was part of his meaning in the last words he wrote for publication: 'Press your fingers close on this lichened sandstone. With this stone and this grass, with this red earth, this place was received and made and re-made. Its generations are distinct, but all suddenly present.'

That, I think, has something of the essence of this wonderful hill area's appeal. The long, high ridges and lovely valleys between are aesthetically appealing in themselves, but in their associative texture they pass beyond the merely recreational into a density of spiritual resonance. This is not just country of the geographical border – it is one of the rare places where time and historical moment shiver into concurrency. For our part we shivered too, and hastened along to Chwarel y Fan, too damp and dispirited to search for the partner to Mrs MacNamara's stone, before dropping off the ridge by the oddly-shaped stone called the Blacksmith's Anvil down a desperately steep and slippery hillside sentried with thorn, yew and whitebeam trees into the valley of the Honddu, or as Giraldus describes it, 'the deep vale of Ewias, which is shut in on all sides by a circle of lofty mountains and which is no more than three arrow-shots in width.' The aptness and reality of his image became even more strong as we turned north along the road and came to the tiny church of Capel y Ffin.

Kilvert, on his two visits here, describes this 'chapel of the boundary' – the church of St Mary here is in fact a chapel of ease for the church at Llanigon, over the scarp to the north-west – as 'squatting like a stout grey owl among its seven great black yews'. The trees and the raised, circular churchyard are obviously older than the church that stands amongst them, and dates from 1762. It's easy to imagine the Welsh archers cutting their longbows here before departure for Crecy and Agincourt. And yet, despite so much of the association being of belligerence and war – the Third Crusade, border skirmishes, Sir John Oldcastle, Henry the Fifth, David Jones' masterpiece – the atmosphere is of simplicity and peace – an interior of whitewash and wood, without ornament apart from an east window that bears, in one of Eric Gill's elegant scripts, the text 'I will lift up mine eyes unto the hills, whence cometh my help'. It is a church that has about it not the expression of power and aspiration through stone – the sort of architecture, as at Tewkesbury, Exeter or Chartres, to which I thrilled in earlier years – but the yearning for oneness and harmony that in a more true and unsullied way is at the root of religious experience. In one of his late fragments, *The Roman Quarry*, set on the hillside above, David Jones wrote of the 'place of questioning where you must ask the / question and the answer questions you'. Capel y Ffin, with its simplicity and lack of pretension or guile, turns your own outlook and desire back upon you to reconcile you with the elemental world of which you are inescapably and most happily a part.

Glasbury-on-Wye

There's a comfort in returning to a rural community in which you once lived to spend a night in its pub. I first arrived in Glasbury over 30 years ago, as an instructor at the Woodlands Outdoor Pursuits Centre run by Oxford Education Committee. In the time I spent here, I came to know the paths and farms and hills of this discreet country. It remains one of my favourite areas, and because I once knew it so well, the changes register the more starkly. An evening's conversation in the slow, warm drawl that belongs more to Herefordshire than to Wales brought them powerfully home. In my time here there were three shops and two garages in the village, a dairy, a score of small family farms and a population infused with tradition and local knowledge and possessed of countless skills. I do not find it so now. Prairies spread across the Wye's flood-plain. Death's taken some of the old faces. Progress has dispossessed many of those who remain.

I don't suppose many these days read the books of George Sturt ('George Bourne'), which is a pity, for his anatomy of social progress and change in titles like *Change in the Village* (1912) and *The Wheelwright's Shop*

(1923) seems as applicable to present-day Radnorshire as it was to turn-of-the-century Surrey:

'We are shocked to think of the unenlightened peasants who broke up machines in the riots of the 1820s, but we are only now beginning to see fully what cruel havoc the victorious machines played with the defeated peasants. Living men were 'scrapped'; and not only living men. What really was demolished in that struggle was the country skill, the country lore, the country outlook; so that now, though we have no smashed machinery, we have a people in whom the pride of life is broken down; a shattered section of the community; a living engine whose fly-wheel of tradition is in fragments and will not revolve again ...'

Of course there is sentimentality and limitation in that view, but there is also truth and value. As for Farnham after the Great War, so for Glasbury in the 1960s. For my own part, I'm grateful for having been witness to a former way and a fading tradition, for having been able to learn from it and be affected (often in retrospect) by its attitudes:

> ... no higher wage, no income, will buy for men that satisfaction which of old – until machinery made drudges of them – streamed into their muscles all day long from close contact with iron, timber, clay, wind and wave, horse-strength. It tingled up in the niceties of touch, sight, scent. The very ears unawares received it, as when the plane went singing over the wood, or the exact chisel went tapping in (under the mallet) to the hard ash with gentle sound. But these intimacies are over ...'

Gun Hill

One of the delights about walking with Bill Bowker is the gift he has to explain with graphic simplicity the plan and detail of a landscape. He has no training other than his own reading and acquired knowledge, but he's still the best teacher I know – as on a wet morning, standing on the banks of the Wye, picking up a stone and explaining its oddity here – limestone, fossils showing, not from anywhere along the river; or again, pointing out to me the evidence for the process of river-capture, but going beyond its mere mechanics when he tells of how, on crisp, blue-skied mornings, he's looked down from the slopes of the Black Mountains into the cloud-filled valleys to see all the former courses filled and flowing again. Listening to Bill at times like this, I'm reminded continually of the profound simplicities of Krishnamurti:

> A complex mind cannot find out the truth of anything, it cannot find out what is real – and that is our difficulty. From childhood we are trained to conform, and we do not know how to reduce complexity to simplicity. It is only the very simple and direct mind that can find the real, the true. We know more and more, but our minds are never simple; and it is only the simple mind that is creative.

But to turn again to the river, it strikes me that such is its range and variety that I cannot begin to describe it except in terms of the power of feeling it elicits: 'The river is within us,' wrote T S Eliot. It's our awareness of time, of beauty, of process made actual in flooding green water, in a roar. Its course is memory, its time-scheme concurrency. My mind still bears the imprint of the pebbles beneath my feet in the summer bathing-place beyond Rhayader years ago; on my lips the sense of drops from when I drank at its source; the heron still stabs at eddies my canoe left behind coming down from Builth, and the rippling shallows keep the rhythm of Wordsworth's poem I learnt in my schooldays:

> Oh sylvan Wye! Thou wanderer through the woods,
> How often has my spirit turned to thee.

This reverie was sharply despatched when we came to the Wye's confluence with the Bach Howey, and chanced upon this sign: 'This has been designated a Site of Special Scientific Interest. Please do not walk up the stream nor disturb the area in any way. Thank you.'

Why should I not 'walk up the stream', as I have done hundreds of times in the past? Are my steps less careful, less reverential, less aware than those of the landowners and ecologists who collude in this prohibition, and whose unholy alliance is one of the most disturbing developments in the outdoors post-1979 (in which year the first Thatcher government began its campaign to bring to heel and corrupt the environmental agencies and curb by all manner of insidious means our legitimate rights responsibly to enjoy the countryside)?

It is not exclusion that is required to protect these holy places, but education, and an unoppressed populace whose spirit can appreciate them. Bill and I climbed in irritation past the sign to the top of Twyn y Garth – locally known as Gun Hill. It is barely 1,000 feet high, its top circled with a fine Bronze Age fortification, the views up the Wye, across to the Beacons and into Epynt majestically wide. It possesses a remarkable oddity – a 25-pounder field gun from the Great War. The story goes that it was bought jointly by the villagers of Erwood and Llanstephan as a war memorial and placed on the village green of the former. Night raids and thefts of the gun by the youths of the two villages ensued until the compromise was reached of towing it to the top of the hill that looks down on both of them, and here it still stands, rusting, the wood-spoked wheels rotting away, pointing at the military ranges of Epynt across the Wye. I find it quietly moving, more poignant in its position and decay than all the phallic God-King-and-Country tokens to the same purpose across the land.

A squall of rain drove us from the hill's summit, and Bill and I became separated on the descent. I made my way down by the farm of Ciliau, curious to see whether this untouched 17th-century farmhouse had been gentrified in the quarter-century since I'd last enjoyed summer-evening hospitality here. It had not. A tortoiseshell cat sitting on the doorstep gave me brief hope, but no smoke came from the listing chimneys, no light from the kitchen within. Decayed machinery littered the yard, the cat fled to the barns at my approach. As I looked closely, I saw cracked window-glass and fissured walls. In the orchard, fruit trees grew mossy and unpruned. Round the front, where bean-frames still stood in the kitchen garden, the outer course of a gable had fallen away. These shales and mudstones are poor building material, do not long survive neglect. All will be ruin soon, where there was hospitality and warmth of human interest. I had stories here from the old man, mingling folk-tale and history: water-sprites on a green rock at Craig Pwll Du, cavaliers jingling two abreast along the Painscastle lanes. Not for the first time in these Welsh travels, I was reminded of the great lament, Stafell Gynddylan, from the ninth-century Heledd cycle:

Stauell Gyndylan a'm erwan pob awr,
Gwedy mawr ymgyuyrdan
A weleis ar dy benntan.

('Hall of Cynddylan each moment pierces me / With memory of great talk / I witnessed at your hearth'.)

Had it been restored, over what subjects would the hearth-talk – the dinner-table conversation – range now? 'Reality' television programmes? Property prices? The National Lottery? Serial murderers? The Cardiff Opera House? I'm glad I knew it in a former time ...

Epynt

Opposite the inn at Erwood, steps lead to a steep green lane, sunken and celandine-carpeted beneath its sheltering oaks, that climbs out of the Wye valley on to the long ridge called Twmpath. There was spring sunlight flickering fitfully across the bark of an oak trunk, the grains of apple-green lichen luminous upon it and a drift of crisp leaves around its foot. Resting my back against it, I relaxed down into the lane's repose to catch at its former usage. The beef cattle from the green straths of Cothi and Tywi, from Llanddewi Brefi and Llanybydder, from all the rich pastureland between the Elenydd and Cardigan Bay once streamed and funnelled this way, bullocks bellowing, tar-shod geese hissing, boys yelling, dogs snarling and yapping, drovers hallooing *'Buwch! buwch!'* as the whole furious precipitate tribe plunged and slithered down towards the crossing of the Wye and the tracks out to the smithfields of England. This was one of the main trade routes, one of the arteries of the West Wales economy for perhaps 400 years, its livestock heading out by tens of thousands from the soft fields of their rearing to sharp steel and the town's appetite. Here's how one regional historian from the early years of the century, looking back on a way of life only recently defunct, pictured the scene:

'The track was ploughed by the hoofs of the cattle in the damp weather, and manured by the cattle as they passed over it. In the dry weather it would be harrowed by the hoofs of the cattle again. No bracken or fern has grown on it since and it is still today a green sward which has not been used since the black cattle went over it.'

The echoes of the last beasts' bellowings have long since dissipated across these long horizons. You breast the ridge of the Twmpath and come into a subtle-featured country of buzzard-mewed skies below the moors of Epynt. I followed little roads with cropped hedgerows, fields with wattle fencing and fat Kerry sheep, a continual dipping scurry of flycatchers, most characteristic of Welsh birds, in front of me. By way of the Nant yr Offeiriaid – the priest's dingle – dusty with the spring budding of hazel and willow and a place of so calm and unremarkable a loveliness that it puts you quite at peace (which is as well in view of what's to come) I came to the Griffin Inn at the head of Cwm Owen.

It's 1,200 feet up, dark-beamed and gas-lit, and I went in for a sandwich and a glass of beer to fortify myself against the next stage of this journey. I remember nights here 30 years ago when the farmers would drink through to the dawn, singing, telling stories, a prickling tension coming from them whenever any brash young soldier chanced this way pining for his lager. Now the landlord talked gratefully of the business from REME last month, the Paras last week. I kept my mouth tight-sealed, acknowledging economic necessity, and all the time the sound of gunfire beyond the door, for Mynydd Epynt, since the early years of the last war, has been the largest military range in Wales, the map spatched with red lettering: Artillery Range, Danger Area, Rifle Range ...

You cannot move anywhere in the Elenydd or the valleys that intersect it without being conscious of the great hill-barrier of Epynt to the south. It has presence, and its name carries a talismanic charge, standing almost for the type of these Welsh hills. Its 1,000-foot-high slope runs in a long wall from Llanfair ym Muallt almost to Llanymddyfri. I love the lines from Cynddelw Brydydd Mawr's Rhieingerdd Efa (maidensong of Efa) on Epynt:

> *Cyfleuer gwawr ddydd pan ddwyre hynt,*
> *Cyfliw eiry gorwyn Gorwydd Epynt*
> ('Bright like daybreak in the moment of its arriving,
> So bright is the snow-gleam on the wooded scarp of Epynt.')

But you cannot now walk freely along the crest of that scarp. From the brown moors above which Bronze Age man made his burial mounds, among which he placed the mysterious permutations of his stone circles, there comes the thud of howitzer shells, the stutter of automatic weapons, the ragged punctuation of rifle fire. There are rights-of-way, of course, used since prehistory, and you may still use them by the book. The battle-range ordinances tell you that you may pass here when the red flags are not flying. That's a sour joke. The knots of their lanyards are sealed with moss and algae, the gates' hinges rusted shut. These scarlet prohibitions are never taken down. For the public good, no doubt, but to me it seems dishonesty and sleight of hand.

If you imagine that there will ever be any change in this situation, then you are more sanguine about it than I would ever dare to be. I cannot see the Ministry of Defence ever being prepared to relinquish its tenure here. In the history of its land acquisitions, which generally take place in the heightened emotional climate of wartime, often as not there are promises stated or implied that the land will be returned to its rightful occupants on cessation of hostilities. Invariably, that contract is dishonoured. It is justified, of course, in the interests of national security and defence. Training is necessary, especially as other countries grow increasingly sceptical about our military presence on their soil. It's also, you'll be pleased to learn, environmentally friendly. All manner of plants, birds, animals, are grateful for the respect accorded them by the army during its training routines, its live firing across these landscapes. The case for this was argued in the MoD's tasteful and persuasive study of its own impact on the landscape published several years ago – to near-universal scepticism among concerned bodies – as *Defence and the Environment*. The arguments go back and forth: the *Report of the Defence Lands Committee* (the Nugent Report) of 1973; the Countryside Commission's study of *The Cambrian Mountains Landscape* and the UK Centre for Economic & Environmental Development's extended discussion paper on *Military Live Firing in National Parks*, both from 1990. In all this languishing verbiage, Epynt is the ghost at the feast. It is a huge hill area, and a forgotten one:

'Let's ignore Epynt, and then we can get on with the more popular and significant campaigns to be fought for access to Dartmoor, to Castlemartin on the Pembrokeshire Coast, to Otterburn in Northumberland,' goes the argument. I'm not inclined to accept it, nor the idea that Epynt is barren, dreary, treeless, insignificant. It is not. It is one of the key places in the Welsh uplands, and if it were not for the surly presence and dishonest prohibitions of the military, it would widely be recognised as such. What I would like to see in the short term, and what I cannot imagine anyone might reasonably oppose, is the reaching of an accommodation with the army: at weekends and holiday periods, in accordance with its own ordinances, the flags are taken down, the public rights-of-way which have existed for millennia opened up, the Drovers Arms up there on the Upper Chapel to Garth road which the MoD land agent hereabouts, to his credit, has recently restored, turned into a café and perhaps even an exhibition centre on the history of these moors. Let them lease it out to private enterprise, let them put in for lottery money for the project, but above all, remove the barriers, let the public in.

I do not believe that individuals within the armed forces are unaware of the amenity value of this land. On the contrary, as I walked across it recently, I came across a touching example of just that. At the Drovers Arms an old woman and her daughter drew up in a car, climbed out, bunches of snowdrop plants in their hands. We talked. She was the widow of a REME officer who'd driven the first military roads across the ranges on their acquisition in 1940: 'After he'd retired, he often used to say to me, "Let's drive up on to Epynt." He loved it up here. When he died last year we scattered his ashes from that knoll, which is where I'm going to plant the snowdrops now.'

I hope they flourish for her. I hope the army opens its heart a little too, and abandons its harshly exclusive deceits. Meanwhile, obviously I cannot advise you to trespass there. But let's conjecture. If, in the course of this journey, I had found myself, having made a four-mile detour by road down from the Griffin and back up to the Drovers Arms, able to sneak round the cordon of soldiers – Dutch in this case, on a training exercise – and had managed, furtively, camouflaged, hiding in hollows, hunted by Landrovers and buzzed by helicopters, to traverse this great moor where there was once school, chapel, community, but where the houses now are blind-windowed shells; if – and I must stress that this is conjectural, because I don't wish to get anyone into trouble with the MoD – I'd been able to rise above the fear and threat to walk this finest of moorland crests along from the Drovers' Arms to Tri Chrugiau (which cairns, I'm sad to say, the army have treated with scant respect – how interesting it would be to have some properly independent archaeological and environmental studies carried out on the army's impact here), what would I – or you, whom I cannot possibly recommend to follow my conjectural example – have found, before dropping down to that last outpost of empire which is Llangammarch Wells? I'll tell you: despoiled land; a sad absence of peace and freedom in a place where those qualities alone are the rightful inhabitants.

Llangamarch Wells

The first living creature I set eyes on as I came down off Epynt and into Llangamarch Wells was, I think, made of steel. She had steel-rimmed glasses and steely-grey curls, wore stockings of worsted steel wire which glinted up and down as, steel-spined, she pedalled her steel bike uphill. It was a Raleigh. In its front carrier, proudly displayed, was a copy of the *Daily Mail*. I looked down, to register what I'd just seen, and when I looked round she'd gone. I felt I'd been accorded a glimpse into the soul of the place, and went looking for a café to ponder it.

There wasn't one, nor a pub either, it seemed, unless you counted the bars of grand hotels on the outskirts of town. There was an odd and ungainly church, into which the steel lady may have disappeared to arrange *immortelle*s on the altar and read her *Daily Mail*. There was a bookshop. I looked in the rack outside: *The Story of the British Empire in Pictures; Painting as a Pastime* by Winston Churchill, and a volume of Patience Strong. Inside, the proprietress and a customer who was so dusty and foxed he might almost have been part of the stock were having fun with an English-Hindustani dictionary. I would have liked to have bought it, but it seemed rude to intrude. There was a distant rumble of gunfire from beyond the hill. The military were active on their ranges again. The colonels pensioned back after '47 to a country they'd not known since their schooldays would have felt at home. Not so much as a B-road runs to Llangamarch Wells. It exists in lane-obscured oblivion somewhere to the west of Llanfair ym Muallt. In the window of one of the shops is a picture of a station on the mid-Wales line with a platform, a poster and a cat. 'The station in 1936,' read the caption, 'Not many more people about in those days!'

Even then, I'm sure most of them were colonels. The countryside writer and broadcaster S P B Mais, when he stayed across the valley in grander and more popular Llanwrtyd Wells just after the Second World War, mentions hiring a Welsh cob from a former colonel of the Gurkhas. It fits perfectly, but the nearest I saw to it was a lithe young woman washing a small red car on the main street with the same brisk strokes by which, in an earlier decade, she'd surely have groomed her cob. Mais refers to the misuse of Epynt as well:

> Shooting on the big range at Mynydd Epynt all day at minute intervals was a sharp reminder of the rate at which the Government spend my income tax. I'd rather they let people have petrol. It would bring more cheerfulness into their hearts.

The bookshop proprietess and her customer had finished their discourse on Hindustani and for purposes of comparative study were looking for a dictionary of Gujerati. I bought a copy of *The Siege of Krishnapur* – giggling at the notion of how Farrell's ironies would have raised the colonels' eyebrows – and headed out of town.

Cefn Brith

I'd come out of curiosity to Llangamarch to see the house where John Penry – the Blessed John Penry, Presbyterian martyr – had been born in either 1559 or 1563. I've long admired Penry for the colour and vigour of the abuse he employed in what was, in its time, a righteous cause. In tract upon tract he excoriated the venery of the absentee clergy of Elizabeth's reign, and its consequences in the backwardness of his fellow-countrymen, their idolatrous beliefs, as he saw them, in fairies and magic, their ignorance of the Gospel. His publications bear snappy titles like 'An Exhortation unto the Governours and people of his Majestie's country of Wales, to labour earnestly to have the preaching of the Gospell planted amongst them.' Or again: 'A Treatise addressed to the Queen and Parliament containing the Aequity of an humble supplication in the behalfe of the countrey of Wales, that some order may be taken for the preaching of the Gospel among those people. Wherein is also set downe as much of the estate of our people as without offence could be made known, to the end (if it please God) that it may be pitied by them who are not of this assembly and so they also may be driven to labour on our behalfe.'

Don't be misled by those genteel and deferential forms of address. What lay within these and also the famous 'Martin Mar-Prelate' tracts, for the printing if not the authorship of which Penry was responsible, was biting rancour, savage sarcasm, crude wit at the expense particularly of the bishops, and the bishops bit back. His books were banned, he was arrested, released, fled to Scotland, returned after three years, was rearrested, tried, refused to recant and was sentenced to death by a court that did not have the power to impose that penalty, for an offence that did not carry it. A week later, whilst at dinner, he was ordered to prepare for execution. He spent his last hours writing to his four young daughters, the eldest of whom was only four years old, and to Lord Burghley, to whom he describes himself as 'a poor young man born and bred in the mountains of Wales ... the first since the last springing up of the Gospel in this latter age that publicly laboured to have the blessed seed thereof sown in these barren mountains.' At five p.m. in the churchyard of St Thomas-a-Watering in Surrey, Archbishop Whitgift, the brutal incumbent of Canterbury, had his revenge for the slights and insults visited on his gracious personage by the Mar-Prelate tracts, and Penry was hanged.

It seems at odds with the peace of the place that one of the fiercest chapters of religious dispute from the Reformation should locate here, under the scarp of Epynt. I made my way up to Cefn Brith, his birthplace. It's two miles from Llangamarch by the Tirabad road – a long, low, whitewashed building, still primitive, the byre next to the house, rock strata breaking through the mire of the yard and a lowing of bullocks from barns where they await the order for their slaughter from a higher authority. The great beech trees that surround the house are bowed away from the west, the wind blusters along the mountain wall. I'm reminded of what the educationalist Owen Morgan Edwards wrote of the atmosphere of Cefn Brith: 'To look at the beautiful ridges of Mynydd Epynt was rest for the mind, not the rest that leads to idleness but the rest that leads to activity. This is rest like that of heaven, rest that awakens the mind and strengthens it for work. No wonder that John Penry's mind was alert and active ...'

The incantatory rhythms have little in common with the harshness of Penry's own utterance. I suspect 'O M' is simply trying to resolve in his own mind the indecipherable enigma of land's power over mind: 'How could a scene as soft, mellow and lush as that of Cefn Brith produce so fiery and intransigent a character, so firm and convinced an idealist?'

Maybe that's simply to misinterpret. Look again, beyond the greenness of this spring afternoon, at the beeches' testimony, at the lowness of the house on its rock foundations. There's force in plenty beneath the softness – the latter just a title, like those of Penry, that belies the underlying text. Look north and west across the Irfon into the kite-country and the headwater gorges of Pysgotwr and Cothi, up to the bare prominence of Drygarn Fawr behind which the midsummer sun sets. There's wildness in abundance here. How much, anyway, would Penry have known of the place where he first drew breath? The carefree child gambolling through the meadows whom we'd like to place here, imbibing peace, harmony and a sense of beauty, is a later, post-industrial social construct. Perhaps it's more realistic to construe his character as modelled by cottagers' poverty and the pedagogue's lash in the 17 years before he left for the fens of Cambridge and the crises of conscience around the spiritual puberty of ordination. I don't find the religious tenets to which Penry held particularly attractive. Divorced from historical context, they have a narrowness and a pungency which alienates. But to honour is not necessarily to agree, and as a Welshman whose strength of character was forged, whether by landscape or heredity, amongst these hills, who came to fear no earthly power or title, whose steely witness to individual conscience was paid for at the highest price, he is one of this small nation's great exemplars.

As I rested against the stone-and-turf wall of the farmyard, the door of the byre opened and the farmer came out. We exchanged greetings. His dog circled round behind me, manoeuvring for the nip to the calf. I picked up The Flea lest she engage in hostilities and, teeth bared, she craned down towards the adversary:

'*Dos adre'r diawl uffern*,' I hissed at it – very useful vocabulary, this, for Welsh farmyards, and at least as effective as a stick.

'She don't speak Welsh, don't Fly,' the farmer smiled, offering me a cigarette and calling her off in the rich, amused drawl of the border country.

'Where are you from, then?'

We got to talking – an intense conversation about BSE to the accompaniment of the bellowings of his Hereford beef herd from barn and byre, of which the main exchanges certainly can't be reproduced here and the mildest were animadversions against a 'Teflon-coated bloody Government every member of which deserved John Penry's fate'. We talked about Penry himself. Many visitors to see his birthplace? Very few, but they were welcome. Was he of the family? No, his forebears only went back here into the last century, but his descendants would hold on if they could. Only beef cattle? Sheep as well, on the ranges, but you could only get up there to tend them on Sundays, and not every Sunday at that. His cattle looked healthy and well-cared-for, and the yard, beyond the inevitable mire, was tidy and clean. He was a big man, face weather-beaten under a cap and with a direct gaze. Large hands, very strong, unlatched the gate for me and invited me into the yard with a surprisingly delicate gesture:

'Oh, don't worry, it's not deep,' he said, catching my grimace at the mire. 'We're on rock here.'

Campers

I've nothing against Llanwrtyd Wells. It's an admirable little town, enterprising, entrepreneurial, thriving. The pony trekkers and the mountain bikers and even a few gregarious hill-walkers throng in every weekend to its cafés and pubs and excellent independent hostels. It feels youthful, brimming with life and energy. Its temporary residents rush around excitedly at their fashionable exertions in their shiny clothes, and I, in consequence, feeling myself to be a shabby, quiet man of a certain age in this brilliant company, am obliged to leave town by the fastest mode available and head into calmer pastures. So I took the train through the tunnel and a stop down the line to Cynghordy, whence it's a couple of footpath miles over the hill to Rhandirmwyn, where I made for the campsite of the Camping and Caravanning Club. Campers and caravanners! I'd never been at close quarters with these people before. An anthropologist would have a field day amongst them. Witchcraft among the Azande pales into insignificance alongside caravanning at Cilycwm.

As far as I know, such rules as there are on C&CC sites are pretty understated, to do with courtesies and consideration, and are faultlessly adhered to in an affable way. It's not the rules, it's the tribal rituals that are startling. There is, for example, the question of regalia. I had imagined a certain gaudiness would be the vogue in matters of equipage. I was wrong. Every trailer (I gather this is the experts' name for caravans), every pavilion, every piece of bunting adorning the latter, and candy-stripe on a folding chair and glimpse of a zip-together sleeping bag on an inflatable double mattress is of one or other of the two sole hues – a sort of light, muted tan or subdued sage green.

The habits of the people too are equally reticent and understated. Foremost is the occupation of territory, between which and that of the neighbour a clockwork gap of 20 feet. Within the territory, activity – or rather inactivity – takes place. There are three phases to this. The first lasts from early morning to early evening and – breakfast and ablutions apart – is characterised by complete motionlessness. At seven o'clock this ends. It's followed by ritual charring of flesh – steaks, sausages, other things on the provenance of which I dare not speculate – on collapsible braziers. These are allowed to be black, and the men officiate at the ceremony with long silver forks. Thereafter, handicaps increased, it's back to the collapsible-chair endurance test, though playing Scrabble and drinking wine are now allowed. Each territory is guarded by a dog. These also come in two colours. There are black labradors and golden retrievers. They enter into the spirit of the inactivities and sleep all day. The signal for the end of the daylong competition is for the dog to wake up and take the winning male of the group – the chief supine – on patrol along a fenced perimeter footpath round the whole site, after which darkness and silence supervene.

On Sunday mornings those who have lost the motionlessness competitions go to church, five minutes' walk up the hill. It is exactly halfway between the campsite and the pub. The latter is very good, called the Royal Oak, has a terrace looking out over the valley, serves excellent food, keeps its beer well, stands among a grove of laburnum trees, and introduces us to new factions amongst the valley visitors. Firstly, there are defaulters from the ongoing campsite competitions. They are for the most part heavy men with heavy Birmingham accents, their heaviness accentuated by the t-shirts and long shorts they wear. They trail up the hill behind worn, slender women in cotton print dresses with Empire waistlines, drink several pints of Burton ale, and in the mothy twilight roll back down again. They do not say much, but sit at tables on the terrace quietly, and the breathing peace, the breeze in the chestnut trees, the rustling of oak-leaves, the stream's sound, seeps in to them and now and then they intone little prayers to it in the rounded nasalities of their native town. I've seen the same effect, as of a congregation waiting on the immanent, at the Taj Mahal. It is here. It is undefinable. It makes you wistful-happy. So, silently within yourself, you celebrate.

The second faction comes in garrulous, intense groups, eyes quick and darting. They wear trousers with an infinity of zips, and waistcoats multi-pocketed, and their conversations are catalogues of species and places. These are the 'twitchers' – the travelling fraternity of bird-watchers. Not many sisters among this brotherhood, whose talk is as seriously competitive and self-unaware as any body of salesmen discussing the lettering on their company cars. Ever since the days when Rhandirmwyn was the last British stronghold of the Red Kite, the valley has been a lodestone to them. The kite is now more numerous almost everywhere else in the Elenydd than here, yet still the birders come. I saw a trio of them by the Doethie. A kite soared over the ridge and never was activity more fervid and agitated than these three displayed. A clashing of tripod legs and swinging of astronomical telescopes and raising of binoculars and waving and gesticulating and hallooing must have terrified every shy brown hedgerow bird within 100 yards. The kite sailed serenely back behind its ridge. The birders performed a shaking, uncoordinated dance like post mortem muscular involuntaries. I don't think they take up residence on the campsite, being too unquiet.

Finally, there are the locals, and once you have come through that tunnel to Cynghordy, you cross a linguistic watershed as clearly defined as the physical one from which the rivers now drain not eastwards to England but west into the Celtic Sea. On the lips of the men and women in the pub – the solid stratum of permanent residents with their easy manner, farming talk and allotted seats – there is the good Welsh of Carmarthenshire, *Iaith pur Pantycelyn*, exotic, resistant and wonderful to hear after the long miles of Anglicisation.

Ystafell Twm

The *Dictionary of Welsh Biography*, in the stuffy manner characteristic of such publications, notes of Twm Shon Catti that 'apocryphal tales have been associated with his name, but his manuscripts show that he was not devoid of scholarship, and official records accord him the status of a country gentleman'. In *Wild Wales*, Borrow has a memorable conversation with a cattle drover as he walks into Tregaron. The drover introduces Tregaron's most famous son to Borrow with a catalogue of folk-tale roguery and drollery that has Borrow intrigued, and when he finds in Tregaron a copy of 'a kind of novel called *The Adventures of Twm Shon Catty, a Wild Wag of Wales*,' he's captivated. The episode germane to the Tywi valley is given thus by the drover. Twm has rescued and charmed a rich lady, returned her to her husband, and extracted a promise that on the latter's death she will become his wife. In due course the news comes that this sad event has taken place:

> ... but the lady, who finds herself one great and independent lady, and moreover does not quite like the idea of marrying one thief, for she had learnt who Tom was, does hum and hah, and at length begs to be excused because she has changed her mind. Tom begs and entreats, but quite in vain, till at last she tells him to go away and not trouble her any more. Tom does go away, but does not yet lose hope. He takes up his quarters in one strange little cave, nearly at the top of one wild hill, very much like Sugar Loaf, which does rise above the Towey, just within Shire Car. I have seen the hill myself which is still called Ystafell Twm Shone Catty. Very queer cave it is, in strange situation: steep rock just above it, Towey river roaring below. There Tom takes up his quarters ...

He manages to trick the lady, who retains a sneaking fondness for him, on the pretext of going away forever to fight in France, into extending her arm through the iron bars of her window that he might bestow on her hand one last kiss. When she does so, he seizes her by the wrist, draws his sword, and threatens to sever her arm if she doesn't hold to her promise – hardly politically correct behaviour, but the lady succumbs, Twm's fortune is made and his character reformed.

It has to be said that the facts known about the life of Twm Shon Catti don't lend much credence to the story. The lady in question was the widow of Thomas Rhys Williams of Ystradffin. Twm married her in his 70s – hardly an age for passionate adventurism or fighting wars in France. Still, the cave was surely worth finding, and on the old one-inch map I used when I first came to this area, it was clearly marked as Ystafell Twm Shon Catti, in Gothic lettering, on the north-west side of Dinas, above the confluence of the Afonnydd Tywi and Doethie. So I thought to look for it. On current 1:25,000 and 1:50,000 maps, in plain lettering, the word cave appears – no mention at all of Twm. Since Dinas is now an RSPB reserve, I have the shadow of a suspicion that the link is being played down to discourage frivolous visitors – myself for example – who are attracted by the suggestion of villainy and venery. However, I set off along the path to see what I could find. It runs through a bluebell wood above the river. Wood warblers were singing in the trees, but only the first trilling run of notes, not the plaintive diminuendo of its conclusion. Occasionally I caught sight of a flash of bright yellow high amongst the oak leaves. There were signs along the river bank warning of the coming perils of the path above its gorge, but these only consisted of a step or two over boulders, a descent here and there. At length I saw a fainter path rising into the trees. I followed it, and came to the cave.

It's a landslip among the silurian rocks of the hill's summit. You squeeze through a narrow cleft to arrive in a chamber – the ystafell – perhaps 12 feet long by 8 feet wide, a skylight leading up out of it, the rocks polished by the passage of decades of visitors, initials carved into every square inch. The earliest date is from shortly after publication (1828) of the book Borrow saw, which leads me to suspect an element of fabrication – of story-location to tease the tourist imagination – similar to that of Gelert's grave. But it would certainly be a fine hideout for an outlaw, and as I came down from the hill to the deep confluence pool beneath, a lovely young woman with long blonde hair and a black bathing costume stretched her limbs in the sun before plunging into cool water, and I imagined the ghost of old Twm looking on from his hill-top and smiling in approval.

The Drowned & the Saved

There are many places in Wales of which I am fond, all of them entrancing in their different ways and at their proper seasons. But if I were asked by a stranger to this loveliest of all countries which place is the most beautiful, then I would tell of the pleasure in walking up the valley of the Afon Doethie on a fine day in the high spring of May or June when hawthorn blossom beacons the hillsides and bluebells shimmer like low flame amongst the woods.

It's reached from Rhandirmwyn by walking up towards the new reservoir of Llyn Brianne, the disfigured hand-shape of which grasped too much of Wales' beauty when it drowned the infant streams of Camddwr and Craflwyn, Tywi and Nant Gwrach. Those culpable surveyors looked, no doubt, at the adjacent valleys of the Doethie and the Pysgotwr, and I don't for a moment disbelieve that they are capable of looking there again (at Blaen Doethie currently, there are plans to install a huge wind-farm development, which would be desecration here). The Pysgotwr, from Pwll Uffern where Pysgotwr Fawr and Fach meet down to where it joins the Doethie, has been ruined by insensitive plantation of conifers. Miraculously, the Doethie, apart from a marginal encroachment of dark trees over the brow of one ridge and the slash across a low-down hillside of a Eurotrack, remains unmarred. It has its source in the forest pool – lonelier and sourer now than it ever was when it shone across the wide moorland – of Llyn Berwyn, five miles up from Tregaron in the Great Wilderness. From there it zig-zags crooked as a snipe's trajectory eight miles in direct map-distance before, in the great dark pool under Dinas, it calms the rage of the Tywi and together they flow down to Llandeilo.

You enter its valley by lanes beneath Gallt y Bere, their verges flowery with red and white stars of stitchwort and campion, walls braided with herb robert, a musky scent of hawthorn on the air and a heavier, richer one too of rowan blossom. At first the road is metalled, but after the farm of Troed Rhiw Ruddwen it becomes a rutted track from which, purposefully, an old green path sheers off round the shoulder of a hill, contouring, alluring, beckoning you into the delights of its own secret place. There is an excitement about this valley of the Doethie. It plays on your anticipation. You see just so far into it, and then a bend obscures, a craggy bluff juts out above the stream and you follow ledges above the falls and pools, the mountain ash, the holly and the small, twisted oaks that cling to their riparian steeps. Beyond, there is the haven to which your curiosity has led: a bushing of sweet ash and oak woodland between these valley thighs, distance too in the sight, that takes beauty beyond its admirers; and there is old memory – in the broken-down walls of those who lived here, in the summer pastures of years ago.

The ache of it can be unbearable. Camus wrote of the Aegean that 'If the Greeks knew despair, they did so through beauty and its stifling quality.' Perhaps it's here, in the nexus of emotions when faced with temporal heavens, that you find cause for the developers' urge to destroy the loveliest places. Do we, as human beings, lack the magnanimity to stand back and love? Must we always give in to the urge to possess, and if that proves impossible, through envy to destroy the essential nature of what we cannot possess?

I escaped over the hill to the Nant Llwyd, the grey stream – the name of which inconsiderable tributary of the Camddwr is taken by a small hill farm where old brothers still follow their sheep on horseback, and from which today they were absent, ponies grazing the inbye land and oiled saddles hanging in the stable, for there was a service a mile away at Soar y Mynydd.

Soar y Mynydd is one of those places it astonishes you to come across. The whitewashed simplicity of chapel and chapel house are so congruent here with plainness of stream and green hill. Chaste front of the house harmonises with the chapel's two doors, high windows between them rounded and lancet-framed, three red panes through which the sun shone at the back warming those inside. I went through the gate, and from open doors into the blue brightness of the day, these words of Pantycelyn's:

> *Pererin wyf mewn anial dir*
> *Yn crwydro yma a thraw,*
> *Ac yn rhyw ddisgwyl bob yr awr*
> *Fod ty fy Nhad gerllaw.*
> ('I am a pilgrim in the wilderness / Wandering near and wide /
> Watching, hoping every hour / To be at my Father's side.')

A woman came out. She wore a floral print dress and the frames of her glasses swept ornately heavenwards. She offered me an order of service and asked kindly, in high, fluting Welsh, if I would step inside. I excused myself, ' *'sgidiau budr,*' I told her, with a shrug – dirty shoes.

But really, it was because I could not – not even into the fine honesty of that place and company. Because if I had gone inside, what would I have done but gaze out through the high windows, watch the mottled light on the trunks of tall pines and the tree creepers in their intense search across them, and my attention, praise and love would be directed on to them. If I could only have told her so that she would not have been offended, I would have let her know that my chapel is not Soar of the mountain, not some Carmel or Hebron transplanted here, but the mist on the mountain and the fitful sunlight and the star-vaulted sky and all things that move innocently beneath it. These are the things in which I exult; and to Calvinism I can accord only an anxious respect.

So instead I sat amongst the small and unremembered graves, the tiny mounds among the tree roots that bespeak a harsh former reality, and watched the house martins' vibrant rhythm of wing-beat, fold and glide.

Yet inside, where the old brown varnish is thick over the wood's living grain, the minister's strong voice sings out too, his congregation listens to him with full and proper respect, and behind them the sun streams through the coloured lights and its rays, transformed to bright artificiality of garnet and amethyst, fall on grey curls and bald heads alike; and where one red pane broke and its shade could not be matched, a clear shaft slants down. They are His flock, attentive, hopeful, welcoming, though their breeding seasons are past.

And I, I suppose, have strayed and gone wild, and am too mistrustful of civilisation, congregation, society, ever to want to come back. Yet I cannot hear these old hymns, of Pantycelyn's in particular, without an irresistible surge of uncritical emotion, and at times like this in the chapel yard of Soar y Mynydd, it brings me close to tears. There is an essay by D H Lawrence entitled 'Hymns in a Man's Life', in which he writes that 'all these lovely poems which after all give the ultimate shape to one's life; all these lovely poems woven deep into a man's consciousness, are still not woven so deep in me as the rather banal Nonconformist hymns that penetrated through and through my childhood ...They live and glisten in the depths of the man's consciousness in undimmed wonder ...'

I remember myself the wonder listening to hymns as a child induced in me: the swelling rhythms, the fervour of the singers, the mystery of language and name, for these were Welsh hymns in my grandmother's Manchester chapel, and in the memory of them, the distance from mid-century Chorlton-on-Medlock to Soar y Mynydd at the millenium's end becomes in the moment of recollection only a sounding board to the echo's intensity. And I'd take issue with Lawrence, too, over the idea that there is a necessary banality in these hymns. Is he willing to dismiss Isaac Watts or Charles Wesley so easily? Certainly, the Welsh hymns of my childhood, of Ieuan Glan Geirionydd or Ann Griffiths or William Williams Pantycelyn, even in the light of the growth of intellect, do not seem to me thus. They seem – and none more so than Pantycelyn's – suffused with passion, sensuality, the desire for knowledge and an ardent social commitment, and I cannot hear them without being moved by them still.

I walked at length a little way from the chapel and sat on the edge of a marsh for some time, very still, with the music permeating the air, and one of those small miracles that come to us only when our being is thus quietened then happened. From the clumps of brown sedge on stiff legs darted a snipe, shyest of birds, slender, long-billed. In a brief flurry of sharp wings, it alighted on my palm, upturned on a knee, its feet a pricking roughness soon lost in moist warmth of its down as it nestled there. I scarcely dared breathe, and have never felt more blessed.

After this communion, I made my way back to Rhandirmwyn by way of dead pastures in the Nant Coll and Banc Ddu – lost rill, black bank; past Pwll Uffern and Cors Pwll y Ci – the hell pool and the marsh of the dog's pool. Lonely Drygarn Fawr lent her cairned presence eastwards to keep me company, and low diagonals of the sun across Allt Maesymeddygon made incandescent the fields of bluebells – so late and burning still this spring. To welcome me back to the secular world, at the Tywi Bridge Inn where I stopped for beer a bold peacock with a dry rustle shook out his tail feathers in vain and alien display.

Afon Cothi

It's difficult to imagine a place more agrarian than the valley of the Cothi. As I came down from the hill a huge tractor with all the contrivances and safety equipment of modern agriculture was ploughing a field of astonishing steepness on Banc Maes yr Haidd, and looking in need of a wizard's protection. In former times the ploughman, without legislation and roll-cages to safeguard him, would no doubt have had it from the inhabitants of the fine old farm of Pant-coy that I passed on my way to Cwrt y Cadno. For this place was home to the most famous of all Welsh conjurers, astrologers, medicine men.

John Harries and his son Henry died respectively in 1839 and 1862, and before those dates both of them had been renowned as wise, mysterious doctors, conning their knowledge from an extensive library that ranged from all the medical text-books of the day to Latin and Greek authors. The collection's now in the National Library of Wales. Their working methods are less accessible to us, though the content of Henry's prospectus of 1838 suggests they'd have plenty of takers, and not just amongst society's alternative sectors, if they were still plying their trade today: '... to calculate nativity; to tell fortunes; to tell friends and enemies the trade or profession best to follow; whether fortune will attend in speculation, viz lottery, dealing in foreign markets, etc etc.'

It sounds to me a profession perfectly suited to the new Dark Ages of post-Thatcher Britain, with its commodity brokers, futures marketeers, management-and-consultancy cohorts, and Mystic Meg. Perhaps some business school should run a course in it alongside their more usual curricular schemes: mastery of acquisitiveness & greed, language abuse, snout-alignment & trough-draining, nativity-calculation and lottery-prediction ..? Other modern professions might jib, however, at some of John Harries' cures. In his 'water treatment', for example, for the nervously afflicted, he would take the patient to the bank of the river above a deep pool, discharge a flintlock pistol by their ear and cause them to fall in. It sounds only a mite less barbaric, and was probably as effective in cowing the patient, as electro-convulsive therapy. Then as now, the wisest course of action is probably to stay away from society's self-styled healers.

The walk along farm lanes by the Afon Cothi is anyway healing enough. This is one of the loveliest of Welsh rivers, and to rest by it in a field-verge fragrant and filmy with meadowsweet, watching dippers work their way against the current between mossy boulders pearled with wood anemones, is to hold for a moment to the paradise place. I love the delicate complexity of meadowsweet. *Blodau'r mel* it's called in Welsh – honey-flowers – and the name's so apt for this elegant field-rose, creamy-coloured and heavily aromatic, the defining flower of Wales and summer.

The Cothi itself may appear pastoral and idyllic, yet 2,000 years ago the Romans tapped its waters and channelled them by way of a seven-mile leat that's now a scheduled ancient monument, clearly discernible on the southern slopes of the valley, to fill washing tanks for the crushed ore extracted from the goldmines of Dolaucothi. I remember years ago climbing the upper gorge of the Cothi, a mysterious place of waterfalls, sculpted rocks, rare ferns jewelled with spray and green, dappling light, to arrive at the point from which the leat takes water – Pwll Uffern Cothi, the Cothi hell-pool – deep, circular and bell-like, with the moorland stream dropping vertically into it. It's one of those landscapes-in-miniature that imprint on the consciousness, and to which you should perhaps never return lest you disturb the power of the retained image.

Caio

An old dog slept in the sun on a mat in front of the former post office, whilst another slunk away panting into the shade. Petunias trailed from hanging baskets. The notice board offered a *Noson Carioci* – Japan, after all, sustains the culture of South Wales – in Rhydaman on behalf of Plaid Cymru. As I looked at it – notice-boards, village shops and local papers are good indices to any community – a woman of 30 or so with a sharp, amused face came out of one of the neat cottages opposite to pin on it yet another notice – the party had a monopoly here across the board – advertising a Plaid Cymru event. 'Are you from India, then?' she asked, and without waiting for a reply and in the singing accent of her native place lilted on, 'of course we don't get many from your part of the world down by 'ere, still it's very nice to see you, I'd be inviting you in for a cup of tea but I'm down to Llandeilo to pick up the children from their nain. This chap 'ere, of course, 'e knew a thing or two about India,' and with a gesture at the church porch and a plaque she sped off, leaving me to puzzle over this newly ascribed nationality.

This was less easily solved than the identity of the man who 'knew a thing or two about India'. The plaque revealed him as General Sir James Hills-Johnes, a formidable old India hand of Victorian times who fought in the Indian Mutiny, won his VC at the siege of Delhi, served in Abyssinia, in the bloodbath of the Second Afghan War of 1878-1881 was second-in-command to General Roberts at the battle of Kandahar against Ayub Khan ('although weakened by illness, Roberts commanded the entire operation from the saddle, taking occasional sips of champagne to keep up his strength'), and was briefly appointed military governor of Kabul before returning home laden with honours in 1881 to marry the heiress of the Dolaucothi estate and spend the four decades left to him as a Welsh country gentleman. After the rigours of playing the Great Game on behalf of Empire in the wilder regions of Asia, Caio must have been balm to his dauntless old soul.

I went in to the yard of the double-naved church, where inscriptions on the grander marble monuments were in English, on the humbler ones in Welsh. One angel with raised finger and trumpet at the ready above a child's grave reminded me that somewhere in the vicinity of Caio was born the 15th-century poet Lewys Glyn Cothi, whom Borrow mentions as 'the greatest poet after Ab Gwilym of all Wales'. We're spared in *Wild Wales* one of Borrow's doggerel translations, and that was something for which I was profoundly grateful as I stood by this child's tomb and there came into my mind lines from *Marwnad Sion y Glyn* – the poet's elegy for his five-year-old son which is one of the most profoundly poignant and unexpected – because expressive of personal emotion in an age of stylised tribute – achievements of medieval Welsh literature. Here's an extract:

Afal per ac aderyn
A garai'r gwas, a gro gwyn;
Bwa o flaen y ddraenen,
Cleddau digon brau o bren.
Ofni'r bib, ofni'r bwbach,
Ymbil a'i fam am bel fach.

Canu i bawb acen o'i ben,
Canu 'wo' er cneuen.
Gwneuthur moethau, gwenieithio,
Sorri wrthyf fi wnai fo,
A chymod er ysglod
Ac er dis a garai'r dyn.

A literal translation might run: 'A sweet apple and a bird / The little fellow loved, and white pebbles; / A thorn-twig bow, / A frail wooden sword. / Frightened of the pipe and scarecrow, / Pleading with his mother for a little ball, / Singing out every inflection of his thought, / Crying 'Oh!' for a nut, / Playing sweet, flattering, / Turning sulky with me, / Reconciled by a bit of wood / Or a dice the little man loved.'

But in instances like the elegy for Sion y Glyn, translation underlines the untranslatable dimension of the poem, literal meaning underwrites mystery and suggestion, the rhythm of thought is the native tongue's alone. Yes, the transcribed meaning does convey some aspects of the whole. It evokes character and fragility, the father's awed sense of childhood's vulnerability, his watchful love and fastening grief. But when that meaning comes through in the tremulous conjunctions of the original, it achieves something more achingly complete. The lines I whispered on the warm Carmarthenshire breeze were the echo of too common a pain and longing down the centuries – of the agonised comfort of recollection that resonates from so many sparse epitaphs, and to which, in honouring this bright, brief flame of life extinguished over five centuries ago, Lewys Glyn Cothi gave the solace of brave memory and heartfelt expression.

Llansawel

I'd walked down lanes from Esgairdawe and was in a pub in Llansawel. It was The Angel on Pen Cnwc Square – for its very small size Llansawel has a lot of pubs – the shelter of which had helped temper the wind for the Carier Bach, on his way back from selling the neighbourhood's butter and eggs at Neath market, with his black mare tethered outside, a century ago. I was listening to the Monday lunchtime conversation whilst the sun baked the deserted street. Two old-timers, one weighty, the other a meagre scholar, were at a corner-table lamenting the changes at the Arms Park, bewailing the politics of it and the way rugby had gone. I caught the scholar's drift first: 'Nowadays, it's just a man coming in, taking 'is coat off, and doing a job of work. There's a spark 'as gone from the game, 'e's not fighting on 'is own territory any more, and when 'e climbs into 'is Jaguar to drive the 'undred miles 'ome, 'ow much money 'as 'e got in his boots these days?'

That last question prompted the fat man into his own threnody for the scrum on the five-yard line, with the Welsh pack attacking, the inside-half poised, waiting. And since I was poised and waiting too, as he drifted off into contemplation of his golden-age sporting dream I came flying in with a question of my own: 'Since you two gentlemen are so fond of the old ways, I wonder if you might be able to tell me where I'd find Penrhiw Fawr, which is the Hen Dŷ Ffarm around his early life in which D J Williams wrote the sharpest and loveliest expression of nostalgia, the clearest statement of the value of community, in the whole of the prose literature of Wales?'

Like a true Borrovian, I thought that convoluted formality would be likely to produce a positive response from this scholar and his poetic friend, but no such luck. They looked at me askance; they shook their heads; they appealed to the landlord, who was from Surrey; they implied that even the smallest detail I might wish to know about the sporting career, on or off the field, of J P R Williams was within their gift. But D J Williams ..? Sorry – never 'eard of him.

I didn't have a map, so I thought that if I were to go into Llansawel's only shop, even if they couldn't provide that commodity they would be able to give me the information I needed. They could have supplied a map of Shrewsbury or the Lleyn Peninsula, or even a motorist's map to take me from John O'Groats to Land's End, but a large scale map of Llansawel – no, they had no such thing. Galvanised buckets, hen-coops, vanilla slices, wellington boots, cattle-drench, chocolate ice-creams or four-star petrol – Llansawel's combined general store, petrol station, agricultural merchants and medicinal dispensary could supply them all, but not the plan of the region that makes use of its comprehensive facilities. I asked the woman who seemed to be in sole charge of this great barn behind its rusting metal-framed windows. Did she know of a farm by the name of Penrhiw Fawr? She cocked a careful ear: 'Penrhiw Fawr,' she repeated, 'I wonder if that's the same as Penrhiw? If it is, then go back to the end of the road, turn up for Esgairdawe, and it's first on the left at the top of the hill after you've left the village.'

I bought an orange lolly and thanked her, walked out into the furnace of the street sucking on the ice and thinking myself in luck. The right track was surely the road to Esgairdawe, where his mother had been a member before her marriage of the Congregational Chapel, and where D J himself had not often been taken, because for short young legs it was *dwy filltir faith dros gaeau serth, a gweundir ac afon y rhan gyntaf o'r ffordd* – two long miles across steep fields, with a moor and a river on the first part of the way. At Penrhiw a cascade of puppies and assorted other friendly dogs lapped, deluged, tumbled and yapped around my lower legs. A dark, plump, pretty young woman in a bathing costume came through the gate of the yard, and they frothed and foamed round her legs instead. No, this wasn't Penrhiw Fawr. That was on Maesycoed land, but it was no use my going there because the place was in ruins now, nothing left of it. Yes, it was the place about which D J Williams had written his book, but no, she hadn't read it – too much to do in running a farm, you know. The sound of tractors throbbed down from the hayfields. She gave me directions for Maesycoed.

There were starlings in the wires and honeysuckle hanging sweet and rich-scented in every hedgerow. I descended the lane to Maesycoed, past a new bungalow into the empty yard. I knocked on the door of the farmhouse. No reply. I looked into the sheds. Nobody. As though from the heart of the valley, the steady rhythm of haymaking pulsed on. I heard an engine approaching, and soon a small Daihatsu jeep whined into the yard. I went over to greet the driver. He was in his 70s, his shirt collarless, his braces red and his eyes cornflower-blue. His wife sat beside him with a couple of young children on her lap, a riot of older ones in the back of the jeep: 'Grandchildren,' she explained, 'we've been down by the river.'

The old man, after we'd exchanged pleasantries on the good weather for sileaging and I'd told him why I was there, climbed out. 'Come by 'ere,' he beckoned me, walking slowly over to the fence, 'I'll show you where Penrhiw Fawr was.' We stood looking west across the valley of the Marlais brook: 'See the roofs by those tall trees, up at the top of the red field – that's where you'll find it. But it's down now – it's down – just the barns left.'

Was it on his land? Might I go there?

'You're welcome, boy. Walk down by the river. Shut the gates. It's good that it's not forgotten, the old place.'

Hen Dŷ Ffarm

I struck down the hill beneath a spruce plantation, passed an incongruous renovated cottage where a lonely cavalier spaniel howled from behind satin-aluminium double-glazed windows, and wondered if I was on the right track. At length it curved round to reach the Marlais brook, which I crossed on stepping stones. A grey heron, surprised in its fishing, lumbered into the air and flapped slowly away. At the top of the steep field above were the trees. I climbed towards them in mounting excitement. For this was the red field of Cae Dan Ty, as a result of running down which on hearing that a cow was stuck in the bog of Cae Du when her time was near, D J's mother's first-born was delivered still-born, his tiny corpse for over a century now under one of those unmarked mounds which stipple the margins of the chapelyard at Esgairdawe. Rutted and grassed-over, the approach slants across then steeply round the barns in a final twist before entering the top of the sloping farmyard. I had arrived at Penrhiw Fawr, at Hen Dŷ Ffarm.

Generally, the visiting of literary monuments doesn't much appeal to me. I'd no more wish to seek out Chawton or Abbotsford or Haworth parsonage than I'd desire to go to Disneyland or Alton Towers. Penrhiw Fawr is somehow different. In a sense, it's the main character in the book for which it provides a title. Within its walls, across its fields, on excursions from its secure base, all the action of *Hen Dŷ Ffarm* takes place. If you asked what this book is about, I could tell you that it's an account of life on an up-country Carmarthenshire farm towards the end of the 19th century. But that's as informative as saying that *Paradise Lost* is about the big boss sacking an under-manager. *Hen Dŷ Ffarm* is one of those uncategorisable masterpieces which discomfit academics because they refuse steadfastly to fit into their neat schemes of things, and are hard to teach, but which the reading public of Wales (an English translation by the great modern Welsh poet Waldo Williams was published 40 years ago, and has just been reissued) continues rightly and instinctively to love. The nearest equivalent in English, and from a very similar period, is Flora Thompson's *Lark Rise to Candleford*, but D J Williams' is the more complex, witty and accomplished piece of writing. Its working premise is that the eye of the child is of the utmost clarity. As D J – it's a measure of the affection in which he's held in Wales that he is always referred to by his initials – writes early in his book, 'I've long been of the opinion – quite apart from everything the psychologists say to confirm it – that a child's memory and observation of what's going on around him in his earliest days are very much deeper and more intense than people in general have believed them to be.'

The remembered child-observer of *Hen Dŷ Ffarm* becomes recorder of community, society, individuality and entrenched value and belief. At one level this is a self-deprecating stratagem that attempts to conceal the gathered wisdom of a man's life and the developed skill of his art. This book is not the work of a child of six-and-a-quarter-years-old – D J's age when he left Penrhiw Fawr. When it first appeared in the October of 1953, its author was 68 and-a-quarter years of age and had been gone from Penrhiw Fawr for a decade more than the century was old. But the record he recreated from those earliest memories, and the values he underpinned by them, are extraordinarily vivid and persuasive. It teems with anecdote, oratory, folklore, song, incident, character of women and men and horses – if you wish to understand the importance of the horse in agrarian societies before the invention of the internal combustion engine, here's your source-text. Most of all, though, it shines with the character of its author.

There is a phrase in Welsh, *dyn ei filltir sgwar* – 'a man of his own square mile' – that in a sense defines D J Williams' literary project. It might sound simple, but the web of interdependence, knowledge, role and responsibility implicit in that phrase is intricate and profound. Its design is comprehensible, the individual's relationship to it defined. It's not some website you can log in and out of at will, gaining information, understanding – what? As a literary work *Hen Dŷ Ffarm* was the expression of a historical moment and a nation where scale was human and appropriate – where the *filltir sgwar* could both contain and satisfy aspiration. Perhaps the reason why I so passionately love this small country is that the diminishing echo of that moment remains.

No doubt but that D J knew it was passing. And as I walked down through the farmyard, the evidence was all too plain that in the material manifestation D J knew, it had gone. I looked in the barns: an axle, an old, steel-tyred hay-rake, a three-bladed plough; an undershot water-wheel made by T Jones, Priory Foundry, Carmarthen, the leat feeding which had entirely collapsed; a roofless hayloft where rotten floorboards were ribbed and latticed with sunlight. Of the house, the only traces were a mound of rubble where nettles and foxgloves grew, a pile of slates stacked against a tree. And yet – this fallen place, looking up the valley to Esgairdawe where his parents worshipped, is real in a way that the Roman cartoons, say, for the tourists at the goldmines of Dolaucothi can never be real. Because of D J's attention and memory, we know the specifics of work and thought, words and values that directed and defined this place. Because of his writing and his example, something still adheres. Because, out of a selfless and communitarian moral conviction, he wrote *Hen Dŷ Ffarm*, for all its ruin and neglect Penrhiw Fawr remains a place resonant with meaning.

Look – high up in the ash tree's bole! Is that the scar from where Uncle James the idler and joker, tolerated, loved for his gift of song, mocked for his unsteadiness, tried to shoot the dancing squirrel and succeeded only in raising white splinters from the living bark, so bad was his aim, with a gun, in life ..? Maybe I like to think it is – as indeed it may be – because it gives me something tangible, some actuality to reconcile myself to the subtle, quiet force of D J 's moral convictions. This was, after all, the man who so passionately believed his cultural web to be worthy of preservation that he served a sentence in Wormwood Scrubs in 1937 for burning sheds at an RAF bombing range on the Lleyn peninsula, the construction of which had caused the destruction of Penyberth – a house, in the words of another Welsh icon, Saunders Lewis, that 'belonged to the story of Welsh literature ... a thing of hallowed and secular majesty ... taken down and utterly destroyed a week before we burnt on its fields the timbers of the vandals ...'

As I sat among the ruins of Penrhiw Fawr, there came to me W J Gruffydd's definition of the cultured man as *'y dyn sy'n cyffwrdd a bywyd yn y nifer luosocaf o fannau'* – the man who touches life in the greatest number of places – and of D J Williams' variation on that theme: 'I do not think there is any occupation in as favourable a position to answer this requirement as that of those who dwell on the land and obtain their living out of it. In this work one has to do daily with one's fellow creatures, man and animal, and with nature herself in every aspect. From cradle to grave, the inheritors of the earth are in closest touch with all the secret powers of life.'

I left Penrhiw Fawr regretfully, knowing that the life of its day had passed into the words, the logos of the man who was born here over a century ago, where its perceptive lovingkindness will endure as long as we give it attention and understanding. I crossed over Cwmcoedifor Bank, came down to Rhydcymerau where D J and his wife Sian are buried in the chapelyard. By chance, as I rested amongst warm graves, eating lunch, scanning the day's paper, I read of the acquittal of the heroic women in Lancashire who'd rendered temporarily harmless the Harrier jets destined for use against the innocent people of East Timor. And I knew in that moment the strength of the community of the spirit, among whom D J Williams is an honoured guest.

Rhydcymerau

D J had stood up and spoken here at a meeting before returning to his pew, where the life had passed from him as he sat among his own people to whom his last words had been addressed. Realising he'd gone, the congregation offered up a prayer and sang a hymn before his body was taken away. There's something about this story that, to me, is both affecting and satisfying – the return to the native place, the peace, the respect. It has an atmosphere of deep-rootedness that few of us can identify in our lives. Here in Rhydcymerau, taking up the journey again in a raw wind and the shortening days, the spruce plantations were darker under a dark sky and only the dulled ginger of the larches lightened the gloom. The gimcrack portico of the Red Dragon caravan site, rotting wood and faded paint of the chapel windows, tell the usual tale from unvisited rural Wales, of change and neglect.

This is not country through which the recreational walker often passes. From Rhandirmwyn to Aberteifi and Caerfyrddin, no ways, no trails, few paths. It is a sort of waste land, its few small towns – Llanybydder, Llansawel, Llandysul – workaday little places with a scattering of taverns, a butcher and baker, banks, a cattle mart maybe, hardware stores with goods spilling out across unhurried pavements. It's not picturesque landscape. Nor is it entirely nondescript and nor was it entirely useless. In *Hen Dŷ Ffarm*, D J Williams described the genesis of the rural scene of his time, the loving and unremitting activity those like his father, who lies in a nearby grave in Rhydcymerau chapelyard, put into rendering productive the rough land that had lain fallow since the first settlers whose cairns star the hill-tops and moorland ridges had turned the sod and manured the ground millennia ago:

> ... in their day these made a cultivated land out of the steep hillbreasts of the north of Carmarthenshire, turning them into grassland and cornland and into a hedgerow-knitted net of tamed country up as far as the mountain heather.

In 1951 a government spokesman made the following comment: 'We intend to plant 800,000 acres in Wales. We intend to change the face of Wales. We know there will be opposition but we intend to force this thing through.' The effect of this chilling assertion's enactment upon the Welsh landscape has been the biggest environmental catastrophe in Britain this past century, and one that is only now – as the conifers approach maturity – becoming apparent. Unthinkably large tracts of land in the upland areas of the most beautiful region in Britain have been laid waste. From viable, if marginal, agricultural land that, properly managed, was a national resource and in human terms was far more than that, a future desert has been created, its onset assured by tax concessions to the most wealthy in our society, its reality concealed for the moment beneath dense coverage of trees, its occurrence showing that we've learnt nothing from the examples of Oklahoma, the Amazon, the Himalaya. Once these trees, dark-suited, upright and mutually indistinguishable as Tory politicians, and as dire in their effect on the land, have been clear-felled, the true extent of damage is revealed. The ground beneath is soured, its earth washed away down the ditches by which it was first drained to cloud the rivers and silt the lakes. A law of diminishing returns operates. If it can be planted again, it is with less success, and less again beyond that. Conifer plantation apart, it is rendered unusable. Do the wealthy few of our species have any right in the pursuit of short-term financial gain to treat the planet we must share with our descendants in this manner? For in 50 years time those descendants will view what our generations have allowed to be done with outrage. A new Mercedes, life membership of the local golf-club, or whatever else these self-centred gentlemen desire are not worth the merest fraction of the cost at which they were bought.

That cost was made entirely clear in one of the great Welsh poems of the century, published in the same year as the infamous pronouncement of the government spokesman quoted above. It's from the collection *Eples* (*Ferment*) by Gwenallt – the bardic name of the poet David James Jones (1899–1968). He was a cousin of D J Williams, one whose family, like many others, moved from rural Carmarthenshire to the industrial towns of south-west Wales. His father was incinerated by molten metal spilt in an accident at the steel-mill where he worked. Gwenallt himself rebelled against the Calvinism and industrial brutalisation of his background, was imprisoned in Dartmoor for his pacifism, faltered his way through Christian Socialism and Marxism, on a visit to the Irish Gaeltacht encountered the idea of nationhood, and emerged to a reconciliation between Christianity and social justice as radical as it is rare. A profoundly interesting writer in many genres, his organic perception of the nation as cultural entity – not properly subservient to the requirements of the state but often, and most particularly in its stress on individual human creativity, superior to the latter's mechanical uniformity – strikes me as being of crucial importance within our society. The poem, on its most obvious level, is about the effect on a small rural Welsh commmunity of that 1951 government spokesman's infamous edict. I was in Hungary recently, lecturing at the university in Budapest on the tradition of political dissent in Britain, and read this poem – both in Welsh, where the language builds from grave, calm, humorous recall to spitting, apocalyptic ferocity – and in English to the audience. The response to it, from students in a country conquered and subject throughout much of its recent history that has yet managed stubbornly to practice the forms of cultural resistance and maintain cultural identity, was heartening, overwhelming. I hope you, as readers, understand that the project of cultural nationalism (as opposed to its political version, about which I am far more ambivalent), around which hovers much of the material I've presented you with in this journey through Wales, has a singularly effective and enabling dimension. It takes from the past, without being unaware of the past's shortcomings, in order to apply the worthwhile aspects it finds there as critique of the uniformity and exploitative basis of the culture of the present. This visit to Rhydcymerau for me was a dual pilgrimage – if a nation's culture is the root, the act of pilgrimage is one a flowering of respect – to the place that produced two texts the coming-to-terms with which has taken me many years. Both generate complex resonance from apparent simplicity. With both, the character and history of the writer adds immeasurably to the depth of the writing. The first was *Hen Dŷ Ffarm*. Here, in my inadequate translation, is the second, Gwenallt's *Rhydcymerau*:

They have planted saplings for the third war
On the land of Esgeir-ceir and the fields of Tir-bach
By Rhydcymerau.
I remember my grandmother in Esgeir-ceir,
Pleating her apron as she sat by the fire,
Skin of her face yellowy-dry as a Peniarth manuscript
And on her old lips the Welsh of Pantycelyn.
A piece of last century's puritan Wales she was.
My grandfather, though I never saw him,
Was a character – small, vital, tough, lame,
Fond of his pint;
He'd wandered in from the eighteenth century.
They brought up nine children,
Poets, deacons, Sunday School teachers,
Leaders each of them in their little sphere.

My Uncle Dafydd farmed Tir-bach,
A country poet, a local rhymester,
His song to the bantam cockerel famous around:
'The bantam cock goes scratching
Round and round the garden ...'
I went to him each summer holiday
Of shepherding and sketching lines of cynghanedd,
Englynion and eight-line stanzas in 8-7 measure.
He too brought up eight children,
The oldest son a Calvinist minister
Who also wrote poetry –
In our family a nestful of bards.

And now there is nothing there but trees,
And their insolent roots sucking the ancient earth –
Conifers where once was community,
Forest in place of farms,
Corrupt whine of the southern English where once was poetry, was divinity,
A barking of foxes where lambs and children cried,
And in the central darkness
Is the den of the English Minotaur,
And on the branches, as on crosses,
Corpses of poets, deacons, ministers, Sunday School teachers,
Bleaching, rain-washed, desiccated in the wind.

It is a good thing, I mused, as I made my way up the lanes which led once to Tir-bach and Esgeir-ceir, that within proper limits desecration of the land and its community can rouse this strength of feeling. Up on Llanllwni mountain in a clawing, steel-cold wind, the cairns from 4,000 years ago nestled beneath the police masts and Wales hunched its patient shoulders under the burden of time. I ran down to Llanybydder, caught a bus, sat on the back seat and at some rainswept spot Sheba jumped aboard, on her way to sign on in Llandysul. She had hair of bright henna hue and rings in eyebrow, ear and nose. She huddled into a parka on the back of which was scrawled 'New Model Army', and rolled up small herbal cigarettes, shared them with me in conspiratorial ritual as we bumped along. I couldn't help but smile at the thought of what one puritan sect might make of its precursors, or the other of its supplanters. But she was a pleasant, dreamy young woman who smelt faintly of woodsmoke and goats. Her conversation was ripe with vague, sweet ideals, and before she caught her return bus we idled away some time over food and a beer in Llandysul, which was home to another writer – in English this time – of entirely different complexion.

Llandysul

'Sheba' gave me a discomfitingly frank and garlic-hued kiss on the lips in thanks for lunch, and with a shake of henna plaits boarded the bus back to Llanllwni, leaving me alone to contemplate the delights of Llandysul. It has them, too, though readers and admirers – if any still exist – of the works of the town's most famous ('Infamous!' contends time's whisper) son might have been led to doubt it. It's a pretty little place stacked up above its battlemented church and looking down on to water meadows through which the Teifi flows. Beloved of anglers, it seems more suited to Izaak Walton's century than to ours – footpaths along green banks, kingfishers I'm told, trout rising – and it still feels curiously remote and lapsed from time's rattling needs and pieties. The cultural texture of the place suggests this sense of peace to have been illusory. At one time it was epicentre to an early form of football hooliganism. On *Dydd Calan Hen* (Old New Year's Day – the day on which New Year fell before the calendar change of 1752), a football match called Y Bel Ddu was played between the youths of Llandysul and those of Llanwenog, eight miles away. The goals were the two parish churches. The local historian W J Davies, writing in 1896, tells that 'they began early in the morning and by nightfall the lads were drunk and had given each other many clouts and nasty kicks. Many a lad came near to being killed too.' When, in 1833, the Llandysul vicar decided to set up a Church Sunday School festival in quiet competition, local opinion was deeply divided, and didn't swing behind the new event until a fatality finally did occur in the football match, which the religious festival had caused to be pursued with even more fervour. The latter still follows its catechising, choir-singing course, whilst the football has long been defunct.

Despite its demise, the Llandysul area this past century has been a fruitful gathering ground for students of folklore and folk-customs: harvest customs, Valentines, divination – Llandysul has supplied its oddities in each, none more striking than the marriage-prophecy ritual where a contestant was blindfolded, had to dip her hand into one of three bowls, each of different import. If she chose the one filled with soil, a death would follow; dirty water signified a vexed relationship; pure water success through life. When I'd told Sheba of this, she'd held up a grubby hand, wryly.

The Bereft Lunatic's Embrace

These customs which survived among rural people in the secret, unvisited country along the borders of Cardiganshire and Carmarthenshire until at least the close of the last century bring us inevitably to one of the most startling and bizarre works of literature in English of the 20th century. When *My People: Stories of the Peasantry of West Wales* was published in 1915, its author was duly elevated to the rank of 'most hated man in Wales' – a position he held secure until ousted by Winston Churchill in 1926. Even today, Caradoc Evans' first book retains its power to shock and disturb, its psychotic presence. Glyn Jones, in *The Dragon Has Two Tongues*, wrote of its author that 'He was regarded in Wales as the enemy of everything people of my upbringing and generation had been taught to revere, a blasphemer and mocker, a derider of our religion, one who by the distortions of his paraphrasings and his wilful mistranslations had made our language and ourselves appear ridiculous and contemptible in the eyes of the world outside Wales.' So who was he, and what did he write about, that so angered this forbearing country and community?

He was born David Evans in the village of Llanfihangel ar Arth, east of Llandysul, in 1878. His father died when he was quite young, leaving his mother to bring up five children. They moved to Rhydlewis, just to the west of Llandysul, where he spent what appears to have been a poor (his mother was expelled from chapel for not paying her dues) and unhappy childhood, falling foul of the Cymrophobic education system of the time. He was apprenticed to a draper in Carmarthen, moved on to London where he spent years in poverty and servitude before breaking into journalism and finding eventual literary fame at the age of 37, when *My People* was published – after which he became malignant icon to the emergent modernism of Anglo-Welsh literature. Dylan Thomas made a pilgrimage to visit him in 1934, when he was living in relative affluence in Aberystwyth, and has one of his characters refer to him as 'the great Caradoc Evans'. His influence, mediated through Thomas' more genial character, is pervasive in the latter's play for voices, *Under Milk Wood*. Even today, among the Welsh literary establishment he causes discomfort – a necessary and unloved footnote.

The root problem is a profound misanthropy that finds expression through the grotesque and malevolent characters who drive his stories. Essentially, these are horror stories of a peculiar psychological bent, claustrophobic and sadistic, unredeemed by any glimmer of humanity, recounted in parodic Bible rhythms and a sneering, lisping patois which is one of the author's most extraordinary achievements. They're at once utterly distasteful and comically, horribly fascinating, their theme religious hypocrisy, and no author ever flayed the souls of his characters more completely than did Caradoc Evans. The plot of the first story in the collection, *A Father in Sion*, gives the flavour. Its main character is Sadrach Danyrefail: 'He was a man whose thoughts were continually employed on sacred subjects. He began the day and ended the day with the words of a chapter from the Book and a prayer on his lips.' He marries an older woman, Achsah for her good farm, sires eight children on her, she appears to lose her sanity and he locks her in the saddle-loft: 'Once a week when the household was asleep he ... threw a cow's halter over her shoulders, and drove her out into the fields for an airing.' He moves another woman into the house, is elected to the Big Seat of Capel Sion. Six of Achsah's children die: 'Rachel developed fits; while hoeing turnips in the twilight of an afternoon she shivered and fell, her head resting in the water-ditch that is alongside the hedge. In the morning Sadrach came that way with a load of manure ... Rachel was silent. Death had come before the milking of the cows. Sadrach went to the end of the field and emptied his cart of manure. Then he turned and cast Rachel's body into the cart, and covered it with a sack, and drove home singing the hymn which begins 'Safely, safely gathered in ...' On the wedding day of Sadrach and Achsah's first-born, the wife escapes her loft, watches the marriage procession go by, wonders at the absence of six of her children, finds their graves in the chapelyard. When the son returns with his wife to Danyrefail, the latter is embraced by a lunatic.

Caradoc Evans country! He's the Hieronymus Bosch of the printed word, and Wales still rightly shivers at mention of his name – as I shivered next morning on the outskirts of town, glaring vacantly upon the map in a state of indecision as to which route I might take onwards. At which point there drew up alongside me the small blue Peugeot car belonging to Mr Harri Pritchard Williams, retired schoolteacher, on his way to Synod Inn if I wanted a lift. Which is how I came to be regaled with stories of Rebecca: 'If you'd been passing Pont Tyweli down by 'ere, boy, 150 years ago, you'd have run into a rough gang of women, if women they were. You 'eard of the 'osts of Rebecca?' he demanded of me, and without waiting for reply went on, 'because this is the place they got up to their mischief, if mischief it was. They pulled it down twice, the toll-gate there, and the second time who d'you think they got to do it but the constables 'ad been set to guard it. Of course they arrested this boy on suspicion of being Rebecca, but he got off. Doesn't change, does it boy? Rebecca, Meibion Glyndwr – nobody knows 'o they are, in a country where everybody knows everything. What do you think ..?'

With this shot, he wheezed into coughing spasms of laughter that left me in no doubt where his sympathies lay and lasted most of the way to Synod Inn, where I thanked him and climbed out just as a bus arrived to take me on to Cei Newydd – Newquay, Welsh version, and not entirely unlike its Cornish cousin. It's more clustered, less bleak, but there are the same red-brick-and-white-render bungalows with pampas grass in the gardens; the same names – Sparkie, Artemis, Hurlybird, Bojangles – on the sterns of the summer boats drawn up and draped on the quay; the same obsessive recording on menu-boards outside hotels of the weight of what you might eat and the novelty of what you might eat it with: 'Twelve-ounce chicken breast in a garlic and black cherry sauce', 'Four-ounce gammon steak with peach, madeira and cream'. I had a glass of bitter and a cheese sandwich amidst the electrified antique lamps, framed shipwreck posters and Admiralty charts of an off-season pub where a bored and querulous barmaid who'd drifted ashore here from Ongar engaged me in conversation about the responsibilities of child-rearing (' ... I don't care what she wears, so long as it's not indecent, because the fashion's not going to last, but I tell her it's her responsibility and if it gets her into trouble she'll have to pay the consequences and she can't look to me for help though of course I would if it came to that because you can't turn your own daughter out can you but she's got to learn ... '). From this cascade of moralising – Heaven knows what Caradoc Evans' venom would have made of it – I escaped to a noon of mist and buoys and apricot clouds, walked round the headland past the fish-freezing plant and arrived on one of the least-known and best stretches of coastline for walking in Britain, running down south-west for 25 miles from Cei Newydd to Aberteifi.

Like most British landscapes it's significantly marred – in this case through electro-optical tracking stations to monitor commercial weaponry trials taking place on the 2,600-square-mile range of the Royal Aircraft Establishment at Aberporth. There were objections to their installation and its effect on land newly acquired through the Enterprise Neptune appeal, and newly designated as Heritage Coastline, in the 1980s. Their installation went ahead – Margaret Thatcher, after all, couldn't allow anything to stand in the way of her son making his millions or Saddam getting his hands on decent weapons. They fit ill with the beauty and peace of the place and the most prominent of them is sited within the ramparts of a promontory fort, Pendinaslochdyn, dating from about the time of the birth of Christ. If you divert a little from the path which traverses this gorse-flamed coast, and from the more discreet promontory fort of Castell Bach climb up through lanes bordered by corbelled banks and wind-angled thorns, you arrive at a little church dedicated to St Tysilio.

It's one of those rare locations where you can imagine the life of former centuries taking place. The church is 12th-century in origin, but restored. Two sections of semi-circular bank delineate the former round churchyard, outside which to the north on sloping ground is a tiny stone well. Lingering here in the fading light, I can almost feel the activity of the *clas*. A fence of wattles resolves out of holly and hawthorn, sheep call, pigs grunt, children laugh, women banter, the crow wings past and it falls silent again, bent oaks in the valley brooding down into night and the sea running beneath. According to tradition, St Tysilio spent seven years of solitude here, praying. Across the headlands, the last sun glints on a dome of white perspex, monitoring tamed oceans with a savage heart. Perhaps Caradoc Evans was right? Insufficient and self-interested in the vitality of our love for the land, some of us conscience-stricken, others graspingly unaware, hypocrites all, we endure the bereft lunatic's embrace.

Gwbert in the Gale of the World

From Llantysilio down to Gwbert and Aberteifi there are 20 miles of coast that, had they been left unspoilt, would have given as fine and interesting a coastal walk as any in Britain. But there is the presence here of the Royal Aircraft Establishment weapons testing range based at Aberporth. I could rant more about this, but won't. The argument anyway is an impossible one. Objectors to the presence of the base are always characterised as mere visitors; the great shibboleth of local employment in an area where it's scarce raised; and the officers of the National Trust would hurl their customary vitriol against anyone with the insolence and temerity to question the degrees of responsibility and allegiance that body has instinctively shown in its holdings hereabouts. Here's Wales' finest natural history writer William Condry, at his best in making what he can of what's left, defilements aside, along this gorgeous unknown coast:

> These long stretches of cliffland, flowery slopes and pebbly shore have kept a great deal of their wildness. There are miles of yellow gorse and heather, and elegant, tall grasses; and even woods of ancient cliff-edge oaks, kept dwarf by salty tempests off the sea. Buzzards, ravens, choughs and sea-birds nest in safety along the precipices. Seals lie out on flat wet rocks, asleep and undisturbed. And everywhere there is the beauty of shape and colour that comes with time and rain, frost and sun and sea-winds.

Those salty tempests were scouring wildly into the sheltered cove of Mwnt when I came back in the gales of February. They were wailing like demons round the resistant, low walls of its plain, medieval church where medieval pilgrims prayed before embarcation on the hazardous crossing to Ynys Enlli, 40 miles across the bay off the tip of the drooping arm of Lleyn. A mile or two west from Mwnt, along greensward clifftops that in the May month will be azured with spring squills, crested green waves were surging through the narrow sound between Cardigan Island and the shore and the spray from its windward rocks was hurled and spiralled hundreds of feet into the air. Of the herd of Soay sheep introduced on to the island by the West Wales Naturalists' Trust there was no sign. They were doubtless cowed and sheltering behind the cloddiau left here by the first settlers in time beyond record. This whole coastline is Condry country, and in his last essay collection (*Welsh Country Essays*, Gomer Press 1996) there's a moving piece from our most Thoreau-esque writer about a night spent on the island:

> I lay awake under the stars watching the play of grasses close to my face
> and hearing the very softest swish of wind through grass, the very
> slightest rustle of water against rock ...

That was in midsummer. Had he been there now the noise would have been deafening on this shelterless meadow atop its sea-bound rock. At Gwbert, sand-wraiths streamed across the beach to blast the bungalows and empty boarding houses above, and a confusion of white horses milled across Cardigan bar. The Flea, her ears flapping wildly, and I retreated to the town to find café, relief and shelter.

It was full of schoolgirls, comparing notes on Blur and Oasis and berating their mothers' enthusiasm for a singer called June Tabor, who'd just been performing or was about to perform in the town ('What d'you expect? She's just an old hippy. It's sad, really ...'), over their spun-out lunchtime cappuccinos. We left by the Teifi bridge, where brown water raced high beneath and nearby houses had sandbags piled against the doors. The same houses testified to a river trade as past and dismissed as the mothers' enthusiasms had been by these girls. The feel of the land was changing again. Pembrokeshire – a county which exists now only in name but exerts an entirely distinctive influence, asserts a real individuality of character – was making its presence felt already as we reached the border village of

Llandudoch (St Dogmael's). The idiosyncratic stuccoed houses, the ornate window frames, the occasional Flemish gable pointed to differing cultural influence as surely as the luminous white lichen and pennywort on corbelled field-banks revealed geological change.

St Dogmael is one of those mysterious early-Dark-Age Welsh, or possibly in this case Breton, saints whose identities and stories fade in and out of each other to the exclusion of all certitude. The Welsh name suggests an association with Saint Tydecho, about whom more substantial and elaborate folk-tale traditions remain, but whose main location was at Llanymawdddwy, 100 miles to the north in Meirionnydd. The elaborate monastic ruins in the village have no connection with either character apart from the Sagranus Ogam stone in the Victorian parish church, which perhaps dates from the time of the original clas here and through its joint Ogam / Latin inscription gave the basis to the interpretation of Ogam script.

The monastery was of much later foundation. For over 400 years, until the dissolution of the monasteries, the Tironensian way of life (a suborder of the Cistercian – one of many attempts by the latter to reinvent itself and return to first principles) flourished here. The monastic groundplan is laid naked now among the clutter of the later village. The sole clue to the nature of the former regime is a crude stone cadaver, a skeletal carving which takes you to the heart of the Cistercian outlook on life, to St Bernard's tortured conceit of tears as the wine of angels. The modern travel writer Patrick Leigh Fermor, with characteristic brilliance, describes the Cistercian project as follows:

> The overwhelming sadness ... is no fortuitous by-product of the
> Cistercian way of life but one of its vital preconditions. A Cistercian
> cloister is a workshop of intercession and a bitter cactus-land of expiation
> for the mountains of sin which have accumulated since the Fall ... a long-
> drawn-out atonement, a protracted imitation of the Wilderness, the
> Passion, the Agony in the Garden, the Way of the Cross, and the final
> sacrifice of Golgotha. By fierce asceticism, cloistered incarceration,
> sleeping on straw and rising in darkness after a few hours sleep,
> by abstinence, fasting, humiliation, the hair shirt, the scourge, the
> extremes of heat and cold, and the unbroken cycle of contemplation,

prayer and back-breaking toil, they seek to take the sins of others on to their own shoulders, to lighten the burden of mankind.

If it would be a touch blasphemous to say that The Flea and I were beginning to identify with Cistercian rigour as we arrived in Poppit Sands, at the start of the Pembrokeshire Coastal Path, it would be no exaggeration to state that setting out on it in the hope of reaching Newport, in the drenching rain of a February afternoon with a southerly gale blowing, was to don the metaphorical hair shirt, however well protected from the elements by modern waterproofs that garment might have been. There are times when you cannot find any justification for your own actions, and yet you still go ahead with them. By the time we reached Cemaes Head and the path swung round to the south, our project had become utter madness.

The wind was gusting and howling offshore, plunging down the cliffs, whirling up again, creating vortices, tornadoes, waterspouts, plucking up the spray and hurling it up 300 feet like sheaves of needles into our faces. I had not been out in such wild weather for years. The seal bay of Traeth Godir Coch beneath, spectacular at calving time when the grey seals gather here in hundreds, was a raging turmoil of water, of white noise and spume. The folded and contorted cliffs seemed from stasis to have evolved their own reflection of the storm. We retreated for respite into the old coastguard station on the clifftop, its walls shuddering violently. After a while we emerged again and pressed on past Pen yr Afr. At times I was bodily borne aloft and flung down again – all this on top of huge cliffs dropping into a tortured sea. The Flea did her crocodile walk that she usually reserves to express guilt when caught eating the cat's food. I was reduced in places to crawling on all fours, at other times I must have looked as though wrestling with invisible maniacs. Each time I stole a glance into the wind from beneath my hood I thought of lines from Richard Murphy's poem on the Cleggan disaster, 'Spears in hundreds are hurtling / Against my head', and of the blinded boatman guided by the boy's directions, his eyeballs pierced and riddled by hail.

As we dropped down into Pwllygranant, with one accord we set our faces to the badger-traversed paths and lanes that would lead us safely inland. Some days, in rueful delight, you have to give best to nature and let be.

The Glittering Sea

By paths, by lanes, sheltering from the gale that was blowing from the west, creeping along behind bank and hedge, we threaded our way through the anonymous country between the tor-capped moors of Preseli and the fractured slopes north of Gethsemane that fall – often quite literally – into the sea. At nightfall we came to Trefdraeth – Newport, but let's keep to the descriptive Welsh name (it means 'beachtown'), to distinguish this attractive, quiet old place from a dozen other 'Newports' throughout the country. I had that sapping weariness of the end-of-winter-not-quite-turned-to-spring upon me, needed a place to stay:

> Downhill I came, hungry, and yet not starved;
> Cold, yet had heat within me that was proof
> Against the North wind; tired, yet so that rest
> Had seemed the sweetest thing under a roof.

I walked up and down the main street – three or four pubs of all degrees, but the inside of *Y Llew Aur* – the Golden Lion – looked warmest, friendliest. Yes, they could give me a bed. And my dog? What sort of dog? A Jack Russell – oh, well, I could bring a dozen of those in, now there's a proper dog, a real unpretentious (lovely South Walian pronunciation, full of warm summits and dips) sort of a dog for you. And soon my rucksack's contents were strewn around a room and The Flea and I were downstairs in the bar, she fed and with her nose warming at a great log fire and me with a plate of good food and a pint of good beer in front of me, and a barmaid leaning on her elbows and addressing this or that sally on life and the trouble with men and on having sons and the tedium of football and the everlasting philosophies that enable you to rise above these trials in my direction, to none of which warm-hearted stuff I was under any constraint to reply:

> Then at the inn I had food, fire, and rest,
> Knowing how hungry, cold, and tired was I.
> All of the night was quite barred out except
> An owl's cry, a most melancholy cry.

You should know how the poem ends. I always think of it as set in Wales, and perhaps it is. The man who wrote it died on Easter Monday 1917. I travel with him often, puzzling away at his lines as they run through my head, understanding something of his character through them. You can so love those who speak honestly and unguardedly to you:

Shaken out long and clear upon the hill,
No merry note, nor cause of merriment,
But one telling me plain what I escaped
And others could not, that night, as in I went.

It was written by Edward Thomas in 1915, before he enlisted and went to France. It's called 'The Owl':

And salted was my food, and my repose,
Salted and sobered, too, by the bird's voice
Speaking for all who lay under the stars,
Soldiers and poor, unable to rejoice.

Salted it may have been, but sobered scarcely describes the conversation. The Flea and I enjoyed for the rest of a long evening in *Y Llew Aur*. This part of North Pembrokeshire is still very Welsh, its language softer than in the north, and with a mellow rolling inflection. There was a sharp-featured man in his middle years with a mischievous expression and a grave voice. He wore a flat cap, might have been a farmer in a small way. He was talking to a young woman who was still at school and doing a project on folklore, so the conversation hovered round topics like the *canwyll corff* and the *tylwyth teg* – corpse candles, that were believed to predict a death in tracing the corpse's funeral route, and the fairies (literally the fair people, since they could hear whatever humans said about them and it behoved us thus to be complimentary). It was an intriguing, intense conversation, but its frame of reference was not that of belief, rather to the collected and the anthropological – not to old Gwilym or Rhiannon who had had their milk turned by uttering a bad word against the fairies, or who'd seen the candles travelling the route Gwenno's corpse had been carried after dying in childbed, but to the numerous works of the region's excellent local historian Dr Brian John.

When this conversation had finished, I tuned in to an engaging interchange between an eccentric character with long white hair who'd hobbled in on sticks and was crustily supporting one end of the bar whilst chaffing a young sailor about his attachment to the coasts of Pembroke:

'Do you know what you've got here in this countryside of yours you're so attached to? I'll tell you what you've got – hundreds of miles of fuck-all, that's what. I think it's really boring. I'll tell you where the best place you could live is – it's Hampstead – there you can have this dreary open air stuff if you must, and you've still got the city.'

I stole a look to check that it wasn't that good adoptive Welshman Michael Foot who was talking, from whom the same sentiments, more elegantly expressed, wouldn't have surprised me, and then listened to the sailor's reply:

'I know places like this can be boring, but I like the trees ...'

We were back with Edward Thomas again: 'For the life in them he loved most living things / But a tree chiefly.' The sailor went on to explain that for him the best thing about a city was the road out of it, told of heavy, exotic nights' drinking in Liverpool, rested there at the bar, heavy, young and rooted while the old man goaded him and he patiently explained about his elder brother who was away to Cardiff for college 24 years ago, an educated man now, but he'd be back here at the drop of a hat if the opportunity for work arose. The evening's tempo rose, men laughing and shouting, young women shrieking round the pool table, country and western music on the jukebox sugaring life's pill. Standing against the optics looking out, the weary barmaid rubbed her belly and struggled with resignation. I had a brief, sharp sense that – as corollary to Edward Thomas' poem – there's as much sadness within as without, and without any more eavesdropping, took myself off to bed.

Next morning dawned brightly on the streets of Trefdraeth. I idled my way through a huge and delicious breakfast, paid a very modest reckoning, and took the road down to the sea, where I picked up the coastal path, and turned west along the 12 or so miles for Abergwaun. It was a clear, bright day in early spring. The wind had abated but was still a powerful, gusting presence. Parrog was all colour-wash, stepped gables and halyard music. Lines of white rollers streamed in, thudding against the cliffs and recoiling in turmoils of spray, from which blanched petals of foam were torn and whirled into the clifftop air, catching among the dry branches of elder in early leaf. The way stretched out ahead, mile upon mile of it, featured, headlanded and coved, alluring. There were daffodils – the low, lacy daffodils of Wales – thronging the path, violets stitching new life into the dead litter of last year's growth and primroses starring the turf. In coming months this same turf would be backcloth to the most vivid floral displays: bluebells and vernal squills, thrift, campion, bugloss, scurvy-grass. Rock-doves clattered from bent thorns, the nut-scent of the gorse filled my nostrils, and always there was the roar and glitter of the sea. At Cwm yr Eglwys, with its little, sandy cove and sea-wrecked church claimed in the great northerly of October 1859, I took a short-cut through Cwm Dewi, where the green blades of flags speared out of the marsh, preparing to burst into lipped, bright bloom. I was hoping that the Sailor's Safety Inn at Pwllgwaelod would be open, but it was too early in the season. 'Every distance is not near,' runs the line from the Dylan song, and I couldn't get it out of my head along the miles between Pwll Gwaelod and Abergwaun. As far as distance goes – and sometimes it's far farther than you imagine – the force of the subjective greatly exceeds that of the objective. Miles on the map can double or reduce on the ground. These miles doubled. Maybe it was the windings in and out, the descents into coves and the pulling out on the other side of them that got to me. Or maybe I just didn't want to arrive in Abergwaun. Eventually I did, the five miles having taken forever, and then searched high and low for a decent café. I'm particular in the matter of cafés. I like them to serve good ground coffee, decent tea, and have character. If they also have an interesting clientele, luscious cakes and talkative waitresses, so much the better (this is patently unreconstructed, but I'm of a generation to whom biology spoke louder than dogma). Anyway, my brief survey of Abergwaun – Fishguard if you must – failed to reveal anything up to this standard. A bus was standng in the square with its engine thrumming, so I caught it back to where I'd left my car. The hourly Richards brothers bus service between Aberteifi and Abergwaun is a godsend for anyone wanting to walk this coast in stages, though I can't entirely recommend catching the four o'clock out of Abergwaun if you have with you a psychopathic Jack Russell with a suspicion of the human race in general and a detestation of the younger members of the species in particular. The scenario runs thus: syrupy effusions preface the extending towards her of an unsuspecting hand; lips curl back to reveal wicked fangs and a shudder of a growl rasps out. I clamp a hasty hand over her muzzle and explain that she's a bit old and cross-tempered, and another poor innocent's received a lesson in not judging a book by its cover.

Having missed out on a café this time, I was determined to stick with the reliable and the known. So I went back to the Fronlas Café in Trefdraeth, which is a very good and obliging café, and one I'd previously visited and even written about. I was just congratulating myself on having wheedled eggs on toast on to its ornate and wholefoodsome menu when the proprietess sidled up and slipped into conversation with me, started quizzing me – in a friendly manner, but nonetheless distinctly interrogative. Oh, I was a writer, was I? There'd been an article written about Newport – or should it be Trefdraeth, she teased? – just appeared in a magazine. It had implied that the café's habitués were rather elderly – not really the impression she cared to project. I looked round the other tables with their – mature – occupants, and back at her. She smiled, cocked her head on one side. I'd been rumbled. I slid my notebook underneath the table in case it was confiscated, and in the course of the ensuing conversation had my coffee cup re-filled five times by the proprietor, who complained in wry amusement that since the article had appeared his profit margins on coffee had been cut drastically. By the time I left I was buzzing with caffeine and guilt, in possession of considerably more information about its residents, and convinced that the angels had made a sensible choice in choosing as their roost, and giving it their name too, the dramatic tor above the town. Carn Ingli – the rock of the angels – was where they kept the early Christian saint Brynach company in his retreat. Brynach is an intriguing saint, contemporary with the more famous Dewi (David) and source of a wealth of regional tradition. His church is at Nanhwyfern, but his hermitage was up here in this more spectacular location. His well is here too. Giraldus tells the story of a man who dreamed three times that if he were to put his hand under the stone overhanging it, he would find golden torques there. So he did, was bitten by a viper, and died. There's so much evidence of Bronze Age and Iron Age occupation on this dramatic hill-top that it's hard not to wonder whether an older story still underpins this tale.

Much as I would have liked to linger on one of Wales' most exciting minor summits, I had other objectives in view, so I raced off down through Cilgwyn, up Banc Ddu, and on to the ridge of Preseli proper – dour and unwelcoming under grey cloud, its dolerite tors looming suddenly out of the mist. Damp and breathless, I had no intention of reaching the high point of Foel Cwmcerwyn today, and was grateful to drop down the contour path before Carn Bica and arrive at my destination. The Reverend Done Bushell, writing in 1911, has this to say of the scattered parish of Mynachlogddu, which hugs the southern scarp of Preseli:

> ... three or four thousand years ago, about the time that Israel came out
> of Egypt, and the circle-dwellers lived in Britain, this barren but
> delightful region was the sanctuary of Dyfed. The numerous dolmens,
> maenhirs, circles, cromlechs and the like bear witness to its former
> sanctity.

Most people are dimly aware of Preseli as the source for the bluestone megaliths of Stonehenge, and every few years a new theory emerges as to how they were transported from Pembrokeshire to Wiltshire. From glacial deposition to the motive power of earth energy along ley-lines, most of them have been canvassed. Dyfed County Council have even sponsored a recent venture to replicate the journey. It foundered (literally, when the supporting leather canoes sank in Milford Haven, a year having been taken over getting a single four-foot monolith that far), in the words of one participant, 'because they didn't have so many field-walls and hedges in neolithic times'. Whatever the truth of the matter, you don't need to travel to Wiltshire to see antiquities. As the Reverend Bushell noted, they are everywhere to be seen around Mynachlogddu. The finest of them is perhaps the Bronze Age stone circle of Cors Fawr, intimate and atmospheric on the boulder-strewn, gorsey common under Preseli. But I hadn't come here for monuments from prehistory. My search was for a monument of much more recent date, and I found it on the common land south of the little road that runs west from Mynachlogddu to Maenclochog.

It's a great flake of Preseli bluestone, ten feet tall, upright among outcropping boulders, with a plaque of polished marble bolted to it on which is carved this inscription:

> Waldo
>
> 1904–1971
>
> Mur fy mebyd,
>
> Foel Drigarn, Carn Gyfrwy, Tal Mynydd,
>
> Wrth fy nghefn
>
> ym mhob annibyniaeth barn.

The lines are from a poem entitled *'Preseli'*, the names those of the ridge's summits, the homage to the mountain wall of the poet's childhood and the underpinning of his every independent thought. 'Waldo' is Waldo Williams – whom we've met before as translator of *Hen Dŷ Ffarm*, and who is to my mind the finest poet, and one of the great exemplary figures, of modern Wales. I'd come here in grateful acknowledgement of his art and political example.

I'm confronted again with the problem of explaining to a predominantly English-speaking audience why a Welsh writer is important, what he speaks of, and why it is of continuing significance to our world. I should say at the outset that Waldo Williams deserves the gratitude of all lovers of wild places for it was he, more than anyone, who averted the post-war threat of 16,000 acres of Preseli being commandeered for an artillery range by the Ministry of Defence, with all the prohibitions and mindless vandalism that would have ensured. Without his principled, eloquent and spirited opposition, this ancient and beautiful landscape would have become as tawdry and ruined as that of Epynt is today. Imagine Ted Hughes having run the military off Dartmoor, and you might grasp the magnitude of Waldo's achievement. But this is not what Waldo is chiefly remembered for. There is about him a sense of benignly committed and altruistic character that comes across in the single name on the memorial. Could you conceive of a poet's monument in England with Alfred or Edward, Wystan or Thomas or George written on it?

Does 'Waldo' tell us something of the status of a poet within a society? And yet he only published one full collection of poems, *Dail Pren – Leaves of a Tree* – which came out from the quintessential Welsh press of Gwasg Gomer in 1956, when the poet was 52 years of age.

At his outstanding best, his verse has a mystical intensity and a calm beauty of vision that are powerfully sustaining and memorable. Its musicality is allied so nearly to an amelioristic urgency of meaning that, divorced from his own echoing language, Waldo is virtually untranslatable. If you want fully to appreciate the greatest British mystic of the 20th century, you have no real option but to learn Britain's oldest surviving language. For those who don't have time or inclination for that, here's a stanza from one of his most celebrated poems, 'Mewn Dau Gae' ('In Two Fields') to give a hint of what he can achieve:

And when the great clouds were flying and pilgrim,
Red with the late sun of stormy November,
Down where the ash and the maple partition the field
The song of the wind was deep as deep silence.
Who was it, dividing authority and excess?
Who, standing and embracing?
Witness to all witness, memory of memory, life-principle,
Peace-bringer to the vexed self.

As I turned away from Waldo's memoral, having recited to the landscape that inspired it and conjured up for myself its spirit through the words of his poem, I noticed another stone across the road, towards the ridge of Preseli. It was a smaller bluestone, upright, rather scarred and hacked about. A smaller plaque recorded that it had been transported there by an RAF Chinook helicopter – no point to the description beyond that. If I'd had a sledgehammer, I'd have set about it there and then. It is so heedless an affront, so vacuous, so irreverent in its proximity, a careless insult to the memory of one of Wales' great figures and most devout pacifists. How can officialdom be so ignorant and insensitive as not to see the import of its actions, even where no ill intention is held? Some distances, perhaps, are too near ...

Martial Arts

There was a skyscraper visible in Goodwick harbour as I stood by the burial cairn on Cerrig Lladron – or is it Foel Eryr? Actually, it turned out when I looked closely to be the new ferry, dwarfing the little port village, so with one anomaly solved I turned to the other oddity of this hill with two names. There are plenty of hills with alternative names scattered throughout Britain, but this westernmost point of Preseli must have one of the most romantic pairings. Stones of the Robbers or Hill of the Eagle – I wonder which is the older? And who the robbers were and when there were last eagles on this ridge, and where they would have nested – eagles and robbers both? These were the diverting thoughts and speculations that accompanied me as I dropped down to Penlanwynt and the path along Allt Cwm Du, which skirts oak woodland where the floor is mossy-cushioned and pearled with anemones, to reach Pontfaen in Cwm Gwaun. If heaven exists, I think it is a long, quiet road winding downwards maybe with a glimpse of sea or more hills beyond and us glad-hearted upon it:

> Roads go on
> While we forget, and are
> Forgotten like a star
> That shoots and is gone.

It's one of the 'mountain ways of Wales' and it's April and the oak leaves are bronzy and alive with the flycatchers' simple song, and they dip along in front of you, back from Africa to rear their young, impelled by their own mysteries, revelling in the cool green of a Welsh spring. It was along this valley-road, if legend's to be believed, that St Brynach shunned the temporary heavens of the flesh. Looking for a site on which to establish a church he came across a group of women bathing in the river, naked, shameless and teasing – at which the saint (in defence of this country it should be noted that he was not a Welsh saint) fled over the hill and ever after pronounced the people of Cwm Gwaun irredeemably wicked. It's a curious story. Its prudishness and implicit misogyny are not remotely typical of Celtic Christianity. Anyway, no similar spectacle assailed my eyes, my purity of thought, word and deed was put to no such monkish test, as I made my way down once more by lanes to Abergwaun. This was the setting for the film starring Richard Burton of Dylan Thomas' *Under Milk Wood*. I'm fond enough of this soft-hearted, sing-song survey of the suburban vices, but I have to say that I prefer the grotesque comedy of its astringent and misanthropic source in the stories of Caradog Evans. The one's unknown, the other celebrated worldwide. The one's theatrical pap, the other moral comedy of the most intense gravity. It's a curious thing, the world's acclaim. All that aside, Abergwaun seemed more congenial than on the previous afternoon, and I even found a decent café in Goodwick, after which I straggled up through housing estates above the harbour to the hamlet of Llanwnda with its tiny Celtic church of St Gwyndaf. The lanes hereabouts are banked on either side with white, bobbing flowerheads of a spectacularly proliferating and attractive little plant that bears the name of common scurvygrass. Its Latin tag is *cochlearia officinalis*, which alerts you to the name's origin and the plant's use. Richard Mabey, in his fascinating *Flora Britannica* – sums it up thus:

> The leaves have a high Vitamin C content, and before the availability of citrus fruit were widely used in the prevention of scurvy on board ship, as recommended by, for example, Captain Cook. Even inland, they were sometimes included in spring tonics, mixed up into a bitter infusion with fruits and other herbs.

It never ceases to amaze me that there existed so precise a body of medical knowledge about the effect of herbs and plants in previous centuries, when there was only practical sampling and application and not scientific analysis to establish use. And conversely, the way in which modern analysis has so frequently underwritten the efficacy of these traditional medicines is curiously heartening in the way it connects us back to the everyday or arcane folk-knowledge of our forebears. I'm curious as to how the leaves of this plant of the salt-marsh and the maritime wind were stored for long voyages? They don't look as though they'd keep well.

I wonder if they were dried? One thing I am sure about is that they wouldn't have been popular – their taste is even more bitter and astringent than feverfew, or the comedies of Caradog Evans for that matter.

Beyond Llanwnda, which is a place of sleeping dogs and idle old cars and ramshackle farm machinery strewn haphazardly around a little patch of common ground, a path dips down into an exquisite dell where a small stream flows through a birchwood, the filtered sunlight beneath the trees bright with primrose and celandine, and then climbs up through the most incandescent ramparts of gorse I've ever seen to arrive very swiftly at the memorial stone on Carreg Wastad Point.

There was a general hubbub in Pembroke recently that focused on the 200th Anniversary of the Last Invasion of Britain. It's an apt reflection on British xenophobia that such great play be made of an historical event that was characterised above all by an element of farce. The so-called invasion consisted of the landing at Carregwastad Point from two frigates of a force – it took the name of the Legion Noire and was a sort of 18th-century Dirty Dozen – comprising 600 troops and 800 convicts under the command of William Tate, a violently Anglophobe Irish American, a century-late straggler from the 'Wild Geese' and a friend of Wolfe Tone's.

After a tempestuous six-days' crossing from Brest, the unwilling little army, seasick and demoralised, clad in English uniforms captured during the disastrous English raid on Quiberon in 1795, made an unlikely landfall on the rocks of Carregwastad. They shambled up this same wooded primrose chine I'd crossed to reach their memorial stone, commandeered as headquarters the farm of Trehowel and ransacked the neighbouring dwellings for supplies. Fortunately or unfortunately, depending on your allegiance, the area was well-stocked at the time with wine and brandy looted from a recent shipwreck, and that, combined with the indiscipline of the rabble army, was their undoing. Tradition has it that next day they were too bleary-eyed and hungover to recognise red garments lined along nearby hilltops as the shawls of local women and children. A baker's dozen or so were rounded up by one local woman, Jemima Nicholas, armed only with a pitchfork. Within a day or two Tate had surrendered, and that was the end of the affair, apart from the arraigning for treason of a few Welsh dissenters who had supposedly conspired in the invasion.

I stood by the memorial stone on Carregwastad Point, with its simple inscription recording the landing of the French, and wondered what cause there was here for triumphalism, and beyond that, why too frequently we cannot celebrate, lack the emotional vocabulary to praise and understand the value of, the truly fine: the rippling of the dark sea among the cliffs' strata; soft burnish of the gorse; the feel of the velvet spring wind and the flower scents, the mother's delight in the smell of her child's skin, the love of our own kind and more than that of all human kind. Competition? Victory? I look over the fields, Dinas Head phantasmal in the distance. Nothing moves in the landscape. Speck of a hawk climbs and towers; unwitting dove clatters from its tree; talons strike in the necessity of a grace not ours.

Strumble & Thrum

The sea was stretching and pawing lazily at the cliffs, sluicing and hissing on barnacled rock and pebbled beach. Offshore, rafts of seabirds cackled and preened. The sun shone on the bright gorse and the gull's harsh diminuendo sent a note of melancholic longing into the composition:

'Like as the waves make towards the pebbled shore,
So do our minutes hasten to their end.'

But it seemed impossible to be unhappy – Strumble Head and flowers and a wind like velvet and the day's miles ahead. There are times when the world around you is so beautiful you feel it within. Maybe that is the only way properly to experience beauty. If you see it at all, then in Coleridge's phrase you 'see it feelingly'. On some days, everything conspires in the plot. Beyond Carreg Wastad I came to a National Trust sign-post, and the name it carried was 'Good Hope'.

'Jog on, jog on the footpath way
And merrily hent the stile-a.'
I sang out cheerily:
'A merry heart goes all the day,
One sad tires in a mile-a.'

The mood was infectious. Even The Flea had caught it and was bouncing along like a puppy again. She had every right. They obviously care for dogs in Pembroke. They even provide them with special stiles on this Strumble Head-Penbwchdy section of the coastal path – odd little contrivances at which dog and owner look askance until their use is puzzled out. We met a man sitting by a rock just beyond one of them, reading his map:

'Better than a newspaper!' I called out to him, and he looked up, his face all lit with good humour.

'Any day! Any day!' he responded. 'Not so many lies set down here – you can rely on a map to tell the truth.'

I sat down with him and we philosophised in the spring sunshine for a quarter-hour or so on the nature of truth, on subjectivity and illusion, but really, on this sublime day, it was no more than a brief conspiracy of unspoken joy, expressing itself in good-hearted banter and communication. I left him there, still sitting on his rock, still reading his map and looking up from time to time, his smile shining across the sea, bright as the Strumble light.

Strumble is a remarkable headland – indented, islanded, bridged and arched, its lighthouse – a relatively recent addition in the early years of this century – an imposing presence. Fishermen were down on the wave-washed rocks, rods jaunty as they sat in contemplation. On the surface, nothing stirred, though who knows what writhings and dashings and wavings of antennae and mouthings of fishy lips and clawings and trackings of predatory eye went on in the submarine unseen. To us, it was calm, repose, peace. The little waves waltzed with the inlets, seaweed skirts of the latter swaying. Down there, no doubt, the life-and-death struggles, the cataclysmic moments, the snatch and the prey and the hunt were all taking place as the quiet fishermen dangled synthetic lures.

Maybe they knew the motions of life beneath them, were preternaturally alert, intuitively aware? Or more likely they were just relaxed and happy in the sun, waiting, hoping, not minding overmuch if nothing happened at all, such was the appeal of the place. I remember from the years I walked the hills at night how sensitised I became to the presence of animals, so that when intuition led me to flash the lamp, it would catch always in its beam the fox, the badger or the hare. We are more primitive than we know. When we lose that instinctual response, we lose too much. As I walked along, I heard a low resonant sound, growing sharper, listened, it thrummed closer, louder, and out of the haze there resolved the shape of the new Irish catamaran surging into Goodwick harbour. I was reminded of one of Krishnamurti's dialogues. The sage is in conversation with an engineer, who tells him that though he is told things are beautiful, he does not feel them so:

> Those modern jet planes are functional machines. When you pointed them out to me and said they were beautiful, I somehow felt they were things to be used and wondered why you got so excited about them. That yellow flower on the walk didn't give me at all the same quality of feeling as it gave you. I dare say I am rather crude. Your mind is much sharper than mine. I've never bothered to look at my feelings or cultivate them. I've had children and the pleasure of sex, but even that has been rather dull and heavy. And now I wonder if I am not being deprived of something you call beauty ..?

In Krishnamurti's response is the recognition that the man, if he could but see it, is supplying the answers to his own questions:

> First, sir, one has to sharpen the senses by looking, touching, observing, listening not only to the birds, to the rustle of the leaves, but also to the words that you use yourself, the feeling you have – however small and petty – for all the secret intimations of your own mind. Listen to them and don't suppress them, don't control or try to sublimate them. Just listen to them. The sensitivity to the senses doesn't mean their indulgence, doesn't mean yielding to urges or resisting those urges, but means simply observing so that the mind is always watchful ... so the whole organism becomes alive, sensitive, intelligent, balanced, taut.

However profound the intention of passages like that may be, the sceptic in me often wonders if their abstraction and generality isn't itself a sign of inadequate observation rather than the wholehearted attentiveness it proclaims. I'm not sure that the detailed eye of the great naturalists, the discipline of whose study is itself an immersion in the wonder of creation, isn't the purest instrument of praise. Certainly, when I read writers on natural history like Condry and Matthiessen and Gilbert White and Edwin Way Teale, the overriding impression I take away from them is of complex, wondering reverence.

That thought saw me happily round Strumble Head and on to the wild stretch of broken, rocky coast ahead, where off-shore islets were mysterious and backlit amongst the waves. There was a cliff-bound cove with dramatic steps into it that looked as though it harboured plenty of mysteries from down the storm-swept years. A house on the cliff-top faced enigmatically away from the apparent reason for its presence there. At Pwll Deri, a gleaming Youth Hostel sighted along the craggy miles of Penbwchdy. A lovely small butterfly alighted on my knee as I rested on top of them, a distinct black comma marked on the underside of each wing.

Beyond Penbwchdy the cliffs, and also the flowers, are less spectacular, the ground a dull, heavy clay. The guidebooks point to plenty of local interest, but the atmosphere is unenlivening by contrast with what's gone before. I hurried along it, and with some relief came at evening to the extraordinary little settlement of Porthgain, where, thirst by now raging, I made at once to the Sloop Inn.

Porthgain is the sort of place that initially takes you aback, seems incongruous in its setting. But the more you look, the more appropriate it appears. The great bulwarks and hoppers of the old quarrying and brick-making industries, the little quays from which stone and brick were exported to build the houses and metal the roads of London, the unpretentious low cottages are all scheduled monuments now, and the place has stoutly resisted being prettified. But its functionalism and homogeneity has the same appeal as New Lanark, say, or Saltaire, though in miniature, and more than that, it belongs to its inhabitants. They bought the village when the opportunity arose in 1980, with financial backing from the Pembrokeshire National Park Authority – a heartening and enlightened attitude displayed there! – and the documents to prove it are proudly displayed in the pub at the village's heart.

The Sloop Inn is as fine a pub to rest your limbs in at the end of a strenuous day as you'll find. There's good, plain food – cheap, as well – excellent beer, and devastatingly pretty barmaids. The conversation of the drinkers was enlightening too. One old fellow with white hair and a pipe was jabbing the air furiously with the latter as he held forth on the 17 wind turbines on Mathry Hill, which were not at all to his fancy:

'Once you have an industrial intrusion into an ancient landscape, it's gone!'

From that premise, he went on to marshal his facts with military precision and a certitude that his devoted female audience betrayed no sign of finding overbearing. Or at least, not until I raised an eyebrow at one of them, who was studying the stranger in their midst as the lecturer gave out that it's possible to handle unused fuel elements in nuclear power stations with no risk to oneself at all. After that she was consumed with a fit of suppressed gigles, and the pipe-bearer, feeling the focus upon him soften, was soon ushering his flock out of the door. I was forced after that to eavesdrop on some outdoor pursuitists from a nearby centre, who were discussing the price of their mountain bikes – apparently it's possible to pay £1,800 for one – and the various treatments they'd recently received from their acupuncturists, reflexologists and chiropractors. My eye travelled out from this scene of preening materialism, competition and self-obsession to the industrial landscape outside: the simple houses, the evidence of lives devoted to labour, the museumisation of it all. We are such a strange race. We live alongside the past, perhaps notionally we understand it, but there has been such change that the gap yawns wider than any mere gap of years might suggest.

Time and Void

Expectation is the ruination of experience. As this traverse of Wales approaches the westernmost point of its itinerary, I was keeping that truth firmly in mind, was determined to avoid as far as possible the blighted venues and not to let richness of historical and spiritual texture arouse unrealistic anticipation of continuing distinction. I kept away from the holidaymakers at the peninsula's end, stayed on the campsite at Cwmwdig, which is quiet and uncluttered in fields behind the black beach of Abereiddy. But when I resumed the journey, I was coming from a stranger place and its echoes were a disturbing counterpoint to the green comforts of Britain. Ray Wood and myself had been in Varanasi, the Hindus' holy city on the Ganges, for some weeks, in the heat and dust of a high Indian summer, observing that nation's way of death at the closest quarters, and we had come back chastened, humbled, and more than a little shocked by the experience, so that the joy of fine days in Wales was salted by consciousness of their luxury, and western self-indulgence was thrown into more than usually sharp relief. This, though, is the longer perspective, and as every photographer knows, the foreground is of crucial importance to the overall picture.

The foreground for the next stage of the journey was the deeply indented coastline of Ynys Barri – Barry Island, but not as noisy and populous as its southerly counterpart, except when great green rollers streamered with spray surge into the narrow, west-facing inlets of Porth Dwfn and Porth Egr to explode against shattered and contorted cliffs and send fusillades of spume across the fields. It gave a wonderful cliff-walk, with the dramatic little hills of the peninsula's end in front and the clear sea surging beneath. I ambled back along it to the campsite in the evening, after another visit to the Sloop Inn at Porthgain. The sun was setting way round to the north, sinking slowly into the sea, rays jetting out under a bank of black cloud as though they were sparks thrown out from the fireball's sizzling immersion. I descended to Traeth Llyfn, from which secluded and steep-sided cove two of the great saints of the early Celtic Church are supposed by a curious local tradition to have departed in penitence after a ferocious disputation. St Finbar is reputed to have gone to Cork, and St Columba to Iona. The story appears to derive from a late and extremely political account of the life of Dewi – Saint David of Wales, who was certainly contemporary with both men. Its detail doesn't come from the great *Vita Columbae* written by Adamnan, which is far more nearly contemporary, nor is it mentioned in any of the written records of St Finbar. But it's a nice picture – two ferocious young brawlers despatched in shame from this wild and lonely beach by the local holy man to lead lives of devotion and pious regret at the farthermost corners of the realm. And historical accuracy aside, it does give an impression of the ardour, the wandering lives, the presence of these crucial names from the earliest phase of British Christianity on these western coasts. So, casting verisimilitude to the mild sea-breeze, I sat on boulders and dreamed the episode through as the light faded from the cliffs opposite and the tide rippled up the beach.

There's far more interest in the imaginative dimensions of a history like that than you'll find in the romanticised Blue Lagoon at Abereiddi, which for all its swoon-swoon name – expectations again! – is nothing more than a flooded and abandoned quarry hole, around the top of which in the gathering summer dark I picked my way to the road leading back to the campsite.

In the bright morning I raced along the close-turfed, badger-haunted, chough-screamed five-mile stretch of coast from Abereiddi to Gesail Fawr, Carn Llidi's rocky crest beckoning me on, in the knowledge that along the last two miles of this marvellous coastline of north Pembrokeshire I'd encounter old memory and some of the most alluring coastal scenery I know. At Garnedd Gwian I diverted up to the summit of Carn Llidi – the highest in this little group of hills, and with a terrific atmosphere out of all proportion to its actual height of 595 feet above sea level. The slopes leading up to it were a greenness of low gorse, velvety, spangled with tormentil and kidney vetch, hemmed and brocaded with lousewort and thyme. On the way back down I lay among the blooming heather. There's a late and quite beautiful little love poem by Tennyson called 'June Bracken and Heather' that describes 'the green of the bracken amid the gloom of the heather', but here in late June on the cliff tops the heather was in vibrant flower, gloom the last word you could associate with it. Rocks and flowers and sky were bright as if new-made that day, a gull alighted on a honey-coloured rock and eyed me in imperious anticipation of food – tame and expectant gulls are a sure sign of tourist country – so I shared my lunch with it, conversed back in the low chuckling notes by which it had demanded food of me, tried out a few lines on it from Dafydd ab Gwilym's poem, '*Yr Wylan*':

> *Yr wylan deg ar lanw dioer*
> *Unlliw ag eiry neu wenlloer,*
> *Dilwch yw dy degwch di,*
> *Darn fel haul, dyrnfol heli ...*
> ('A fine gull on the warm tide-flow / One colour with snow or the white moon / Faultless is your beauty / Sun's fragment, sea's gauntlet').

It seemed to like it, relaxed, preened itself with fierce stabbing motions, looked at me wonderingly, and as two people approached from behind, took to its wings and glided out over the cliff-tops with a wild exultant scream. Or so it seemed to me, who feels no antipathy towards anthropomorphism and would anyway as happily converse with animals and birds at times as with fellow human beings. ('I think I could turn and live with animals,' wrote Walt Whitman, 'they are so placid and self-contained'.) Though the two walkers, six days out from Poppit Sands and lathered in sweat, who'd frightened the gull away were pleasant enough individuals, rejoicing in the scene, lamenting only at the 70-pound weight of the man's sack, and rueful in their agreement with my suggestion that in spiritual places like this the shedding of material possessions was the proper course to follow. They left me sitting there and headed off to Porth Meigan, where they were determined at least to shed their clothes and bathe in the cool sea instead of the salt trickle of their own sweat.

Eventually, I roused myself and went on my way too, increasingly conscious of the voids opening up beneath me along the coastal path. I used to climb along this coast occasionally 25 or 30 years ago, though the main area in the exploration of which I took part was the limestone in the south of the county. So there drifted into my mind, as I idled along and recognised cliff-profiles and the exits from routes up them, distant memories of times on them. Curious how grateful I feel for the consciousness of that void beneath and the knowledge of those lines and attitudes which lead out of it, and by which we can be changed. As if to reinforce the lesson, on top of Craig Coetan, over the rough red rock of which I'd ambled at will on summer evenings long ago, texture of its sound gabbro imprinted as tangibly in my mind as it then was on my finger-tips, two climbers were coiling ropes. I went over to talk to them. One was from Llechryd, one from Cas'Newydd Emlyn. The latter dozed in the sun as his friend and I talked. His face was sunburnt, quite serene and radiant. He'd lived in Guildford, had escaped to West Wales. There on the clifftop, as we looked across to the visible hills of Ireland, he gave me an impromptu lesson in an exercise and meditation system called Chi Keung, which made me think that perhaps I will drift peacefully over the rocks of Craig Coetan in the evening sunshine again. Who knows?

Bleak Moments in David's House

There is a plaque down on the last rocks of Penmaen Dewi, from which on the rough red tidal platforms you look across to the bulk of Ynys Ddewi – Ramsey its Norse name, Ramsey Island the holidaymakers' preferred tautological alternative, and as much of an irritant as it would be if people referred continually to Anglesey Island. After years as an offshore farm, it's now a nature reserve owned by the RSPB, and visitors who are allowed to land are limited to 40 a day. So it now suffers the even greater disturbance of circumnavigation by fast rubber boats – 'rigid inflatables' – whose proprietors promise all manner of adventure, exploration, unique experience to be shared with a couple of thousand gawping others the course of every summer's day. They surge out and round it, penetrate its clefts, caves and inlets and rouse its colonies of basking grey seals to groan sleepily at the frantic clicking of camera shutters. You can watch all this going on from Penmaen Dewi – for my part without the least desire to become involved – as time floods and ebbs, slack water sluices lazily then gathers itself into the tidestream fast running and roaring across The Bitches which mark the entrance to the island harbour. I sloped off instead past Coetan Arthur, one of the great and evocative sites chosen by Neolithic people for the burial of their dead, boulder-hopping down and round the little sandy cove of Porth Melgan, the great capstone silhouetted behind me. The more active and spirited of Pembroke holidaymakers wend their way here from the car-park at Porth Mawr ('Whitesands Bay') a half-mile away, and it has a genial, friendly atmosphere, in marked contrast to what lies in wait at the latter – as I was to discover as I ambled down to it past banks of tall-stemmed campion.

I wonder what a visitor from another planet would make of the typical venue of the British holidaymaker – and Porth Mawr is surely just that? What would they think of the milling cars with all manner of fibreglass sailed and finned things strapped to their roofs and shibboleth-numbers on their boots proclaiming the desired identity and size of the male drivers: Cavalier, Escort, Probe, 220 SEi 16v? How would they hear the characteristic music of the place – wailing children, hissing and guffawing adults, soughing waves, tinny stereos, the metallic 'tink' of a driven golf-ball from the slopes above? Would they be oppressed by the strutting aggression of the mirror-glassed and long-shorted males, by the heavy, surly hopelessness of the women? Sitting among them by the margins of the beach, I was surrounded and appalled by an overwhelming sense of frustration, unhappiness, barely suppressed rage rising from these stolid seasiders at the end of a long, hot Saturday, consoling themselves with ice-cream cone, hamburger, melting chocolate or greasy hot-dog and contending with time's vacancies as the young men on their water-machines rutted and roared.

The last beach I'd rested on, a month before in the fierce heat of the Indian plains, had been on the bank of the Ganges at Varanasi, where I'd received hospitality from, had curious, intelligent contact with, people who had nothing – a clay stove, maybe, in which they burnt dried dung to cook the daily handful of rice on which they lived, a rush mat for a bed which they'd spread across the sand for me to sit on. At Porth Mawr, one particularly sour-faced and whale-like chain-smoking woman who'd waddled the few yards to the beach from a white Ford Granada parked nearby was berating her children in the strident tones of Rochdale as they made timid, friendly overtures to those of a Sikh family already established there:

'Don't you play wi' them fuckin' Pakis now.'

I caught the man's eye, shook my head, went across to squat on the sand with him and his family. He was an accountant from Slough. We talked of India, where he'd never been. I told him of visiting the Sikh temple in Old Delhi, and the impressions I'd taken away of the energy and charity of the community there, of which one of his uncles, he told me, was a member. I recounted the tricks of a Sikh fortune-teller on Janpath, at which he laughed aloud and said he'd try them out on his clients in Slough. After a while I took my leave and walked past the woman, who'd subsided in tight clothes and sweating misery on to a collapsible chair. She mouthed the word 'scum' quite audibly as I passed her by – probably addressed at my old, faded shirt and sandals. I felt only pity for the abject discontent she displayed – the fear, greed, hatred, material obsession which for her were occluding so many of life's possibilities. She was handing out money for ice-creams to get rid of her children for a while so that she might sleep. Down at the water's edge her husband was still meticulously assembling his sail-board. I walked away, and when I rocked on my heels and looked back down from a few hundred yards up the hill, he was heading out unsteadily across the waves. Where he'd prepared for the voyage of escape, the young Sikh was building a sandcastle with his children whilst his wife, brilliantly clad, splashed him happily with her bare feet from the canal he'd dug around it. The children of the whale and the windsurfer, ice-creams finished, were looking on from a safe and yearning distance. So much for 'Whitesands Bay'! I headed for Ty Ddewi, feeling more than usually saddened, hoping and perhaps even unwisely expecting some form of spiritual solace and relief.

Ty Ddewi – David's House – is called St David's in English, and it's probably right that it is so, for Welsh is very little in evidence on the streets and in the pubs of this tiny city. Jackdaws were flying raucously in and out of the great wheel window in the King's Hall of the Bishop's Palace, and in the cathedral Evensong was taking place. The cool, grey ashlar inside is touched with pink, and though the building's not particularly grand, there's a lovely sense of the improvisational genius of medieval architecture here. Strengthening pillars at each side of the west door look like afterthoughts, and the north side of the nave appears sensationally off -perpendicular. Maybe it was the singing that caused it. The sharpness of that was counterbalanced by the flatness of the lesson, read from the New English Bible – a text that I wholeheartedly detest, and to which I found myself muttering in counterpoint from the Authorised Version (how strange the extent to which the rhythm and content of our childhood lives on in us!) to exorcise its dullness as the clergyman drawled his way through the story of Jairus' daughter from St Mark's Gospel:

'And he took the damsel by the hand, and said unto her, Talitha cumi; which is, being interpreted, Damsel, I say unto thee, arise. And straightway the damsel arose and walked.'

Afterwards I emerged into the town square, went into a supermarket where a surly fat girl slammed down short change in abrupt dismissal. So even more disconsolately – and convinced by now of how inevitably expectation of a place is traduced – I sidled into an appealing pub, where the barmaid smiled as she undercharged me, and joked too.

At this point a cosmic joke occurs. I encounter the objective correlative of my growing black mood. The beer garden of the pub, where I go to sit and drink beer and eat in the evening sun, is quite crowded, so I find myself sharing a table with a stranger. He's of a certain age, wears dark glasses, and despite the heat of the day is dressed entirely in black. A sardonic half-smile plays continually over saturnine features. The Flea regards him warily, ready to nip. I study him surreptitiously from behind my newspaper, of which activity he's probably aware, but is himself too busy observing the newly arrived occupants of the garden much to mind.

These consist of a film-crew and a bunch of heroes. The former is setting up reflectors and tripods, ushering people brusquely out of their way, and preparing to interview the boss-hero, whom I suddenly recognise as the man directing the conversation on the price of mountain bikes in the Sloop Inn at Porthgain a few miles back on this journey. Lean and fleece-clad, square-jawed, white teeth flashing, he fields the questions:

'The kids come down here because we're here. They've never been here before in their lives. They're surprised how beautiful it is compared to Devon and Cornwall. We're a pretty active bunch of people – we get them down to sea-level and it's just brilliant – they see a different Pembrokeshire.'

The designer shades glint, the designer-stubbled jaw juts a little farther for the camera to catch the carefully-turned profile, my table companion eases forwards on his elbows, a wolfish, expectant grin spreading across his face.

'We gain their confidence and let them do all the things their parents told them they never should.'

The man in black snorts derision, whispers loudly to me, a stranger:

'Listen to that! The justification of the child-abuser down the ages ..! Don't they ever hear what they're saying?'

Alarmed by his vehemence, I retreat behind my paper, whilst cocking an ear to the hero and his acolytes, to the conversation being filmed:

'If work isn't fun, it isn't worth doing ... we travel ... when the surf's up, I tell them, "Drop your typewriter, your word-processor, do what's important ..!"'

The hero smiles winningly at the camera, looking like a hero, directs one of the production assistants to go outside and fetch something from his car:

'If you go into the street, you'll see a white XR2i ...'

White Fords are becoming theme for the day. My sombre neighbour, meanwhile, has been putting on a fair impression of a pressure-cooker, disconnected phrases steaming out from between furiously working lips:

'Tosh ... glib inanities ... confusion of appearance with depth ... as much to do with adventure as New Labour has with Socialism ... masquerades ... duping the innocent for personal gain and acclaim.'

He's so animated I begin to fear a scene, and without having addressed a single word to him make my way out into the empty streets of the town. A long crocodile of schoolchildren, perhaps associated with those males who are advertising themselves in the pub, is being shushed along by a lone young instructress. They seem curiously subdued, vacant, leaderless. I walk past whistling *Tomorrow Belongs to Us*, catching as I do so something of my chance acquaintance's daemonic, excoriating glee.

Leaving Wales

'It is a country that is just small enough to get to know reasonably well in the course of a lifetime,' is how a radio producer I work with once described Wales. And I agree with him. The greater part of my life has been spent in this small country, and yet I still feel that I've scarcely come to know it, barely begun to discover what lies hidden beneath preconception, obvious attraction and hackneyed expectation. On this journey I've tried to avoid the frequented places and to lead you through the ones that for me reflect most clearly the essence of a nation and a landscape that I love above all others. Even so, I'm left with a feeling of frustration, a sense of how inadequately such a project bodies forth the place it describes. I wish at times that I could just turn round and take you through the land again, by a different route this time that would reflect different facets, that would tell you stories crucial to the understanding of the place that I've left untold.

I left Ty Ddewi by the road that leads down to Porthclais, where a climbing club from the north of England were actively and noisily engaged with the rock climbs on the small and accessible cliff here. Escaping from all their shout of encouragement, chink of equipment, scraping and grasping of limbs and shrieks of achievement with a certain sense of relief, I padded quietly round the cliff path with islands offshore sleek as seals in a calm sea to arrive at St Non's Chapel and Well.

For the first time in this immediate landscape of old piety, I felt here a sense of real holiness. There were bullocks huffing round the broken walls of the chapel and a great peace hovering. I sat down where St Non had given birth to St David over 1,500 years ago, the site of her cottage marked by this edifice itself now run to ruin, and felt the calm come upon me. In a corner of the old chapel is a stone – a rough-hewn block of the local violet-tinged Cambrian sandstone – with a ringed cross crudely and plainly cut into it. That extraordinary symbol began to work its magic upon me, figuring forth its depth and breadth, flashing out the electrical connection of its transept, reaching back across time and place to bring to mind all the places and moods of this traverse of the holy land of Wales, so that I became a quiet soul in contemplation at tierce in the treasure-house of history. These moments, it seems to me, are when we become most human, most removed from the petty concerns of ego and commerce and most finely attuned to the essential condition of our lives. At times like this, stilled in ourselves even to the extent of our breathing and our heartbeat becoming no more than the gentlest motions barely felt, we connect and are somehow at one, assets of the great peace which is maybe what God is, and appreciative of its goodness and beauty.

At length, people passing, I sank down from reverie into the body again and left the chapel, in its field falling away to the sea, a freshet with cresses running through and odd shapes of handled stones poised here and there, to climb to the source of the stream at St Non's Well. There were fuchsias and hydrangeas, pale-papery-flowered, in the garden beyond it, and friesias in a jar, coins in the well, too, and cockleshells to tell of continuing tradition and superstition. The statue of the Blessed Virgin nearby was garlanded, looking towards the well, which has its own story. Its first issue was in the night of storm on which St David was born in 462. Its level is said to fluctuate with the tide, its property formerly deemed curative to the sight. Perhaps faith can heal? I climb steps beyond it that lead me to the new chapel of St Non and Our Lady, built of retrieved ecclesiastical stone in the old Pembrokeshire style as recently as 1934, and beautifully light and peaceful within. There was a table with candles burning, and cards there for prayers to be said – curiously self-centred for the most part. I paid for two candles, lit them, and wrote a card asking for prayers for the poor people of the riverbank in India.

Outside, the gaunt grey Retreat of the Passionist Fathers was empty and cold. I descended back to the coastal path and hurried away in the direction of Solva. I'd spent time here in past years in its many pubs, drunkenly more often than not in the company of a friend, the Welsh singer Meic Stephens, who's from the village. So The Ship and The Cambrian and The Harbour Inn were no strangers to me as I passed them by – remembering this lyrically angry Welsh protester and poetic rebel husking and thrashing out verse and chord in the bar corners of years ago, wondering too whether his considerable talent and sensitivity had been diluting and atrophying with the froth of each glass, or whether, like *Der Leiermann* of Schubert's greatest song-cycle, I should most admire his jaunty courage in the face of contingency.

Today, by the Harbour Inn, a father and son were fishing in the brown stream, disconsolately waiting for time to pass. On the other bank a couple walked by, she long-dressed and lithe, twining round her husband, her hand fondly on his rounding belly as his no doubt would soon be on hers. A little dog, at whom The Flea uttered a reflex growl, trotted along behind, keeping them in sight.

'We'll find an ice-cream shop,' said the father to the boy.

'I've got lots of pocket money.'

'You have got quite a lot, haven't you!'

They walked off hand in hand, toy rod trailing, and I headed off along the coast and across the Landsker – the castles-marked line that separates Welsh-speaking north Pembrokeshire from the 'Little England beyond Wales' of the south of the county. This is the part that I know best, and into which I was bound, even though that meant having to ignore the fascinations of inland Pembrokeshire and the wealth of story to be found in places like Narberth:

Once upon a time Pwyll was at Narberth his chief palace, where a feast had been prepared for him, and with him was a great host of men. And after the first meal, Pwyll arose to walk, and he went to the top of a mound that was above the palace and was called Gorsedd Arberth.

'Lord,' said one of the court, 'it is peculiar to the mound that whosoever sits upon it cannot go thence, without either receiving wounds or blows, or else seeing a wonder.'

That's from the first of the *Four Branches of the Mabinogi* – the great medieval collation of folk-tale, legend and dimly remembered historical source which is one of the ornaments of Welsh or indeed European literature, and the stories from which permeate the mood and landscape of Wales. But there's no time for more than glancing reference even to these jewels. We must press on to a conclusion.

For me, that's to be found along the south coast of the county, and on the sheer cliffs of the Castlemartin peninsula where for so many years I practised the craft of climbing, sought danger there, and relief and perhaps even acclaim. Standing on the Green Bridge of Wales – that outstanding point of a coastline where the remarkable is commonplace – I look east and view vertical feature and line, scan detail as though reviewing vignettes from my own history. So many dead friends with whom I climbed here, with whom I followed the narrow roads, passed through the strait gates of control and mastery that are yet far wider than the lessons we must come to thereafter. I remember them and honour them, see even the rock-cairn that my dear, dead friend Peter Biven and myself raised 27 years ago on the summit of the offshore stack of the Elegug Tower, and know that I have grown beyond, feel thankful to have left behind, to have survived, to have come through to an appreciation of the World's beauty and substance.

In the stillness of an autumn evening I walk across the bridges by the unrippled lovely lily-ponds of Bosherston, hidden from the west-facing fire of those cliffs, out to the naked, joyful beach of Broad Haven and its curling, soft waves. All journeys have an end, and in each ending, for those who look, is a new beginning. And so I came to start a new phase of this travelling, with a full and grateful heart.

POSTSCRIPT

AN ABSENCE
BOUNDING *at our* SIDE

The Flea, who had been an integral part of my life for 17 years, died in the spring of 1999. I wrote the following piece to commemorate her, and include it here in gratitude for all the love and companionship and entertainment that she brought me throughout a life long in canine terms, but far too short for the depth of affection I felt for her. Dozens of kind, and kindly intentioned, letters arrived after it was published, telling me that she would be waiting for me 'on the other side', urging me to 'get another dog as soon as possible'. I wish I had faith to believe in the former, could not have done the latter, which would have felt like an infidelity. The Flea, for all her quirks, was unique and utterly irreplaceable. Here then is her obituary, which is the most heartfelt I've ever written:

You may or may not bear with me on this, may or may not understand. But I'm going to tell you, both because it has been a significant part of my life for a very long time, and because, apparent sentimentality aside, I believe that there are educative and humane aspects to what I have now to come to terms with that it is proper to communicate.

My little dog, The Flea, has died at the age of 17. Even just to set those words down brings the tears and the anguish flooding back. I look out at the dyke by the house where I live and along which she took her last walk, and on this harsh April day of sleet and rain and fitful sunshine the world momentarily seems again as desolate as it did in the time of her departure three long weeks ago. That Friday morning we walked down as we did most mornings (the scent then would have cleared by evening when the animals emerge) to leave food by the badger sett alongside the old sunken way. I chided her as usual when she went too close to the openings –

terriers and badgers do not mix – and she trotted off phlegmatically to sniff at rabbit burrows instead. Returning, I looked back and whistled as I reached the garden wall her legs would once have had spring and elasticity to leap her over, but on to which she now had to be lifted. A light wind stirred the blackthorn blossom and the hazel catkins. The grass of the field where the sunlight touched was shot through with a brilliant emergent green and she came lolloping, panting, eager, black ears flapping and her little white body apparently vigorous and muscular even in the extremity of canine age.

She sat on the wall for a moment after I had lifted her there and attempted to lick my face. Her eyes, cloudy with cataracts, were fixed on me. Then she jumped down, stumbling a little as she landed, and took to her basket for the rest of the day, ignoring even the chicken in her bowl with which we had been trying recently to tempt her increasingly erratic appetite. She made a few forays for water over the next few hours, panting and uncomfortable. Her belly looked full – of the bones she'd stored in caches around the garden I'd presumed. Or maybe she'd been thieving the cats' food again, or that left out for the badgers. When I picked her up to cuddle her at the end of the afternoon, though, she yelped in agony as I rubbed her distended abdomen. I phoned and took her to the vet, who diagnosed a massive malignant tumour on the liver, inoperable at her age. And so the inevitable, and the only proper thing, sparing her further pain. I brought her home in her basket and buried her in it, wrapped in a blanket of fine Indian wool, with her bowls and her toys by her side. F, from her medical knowledge, explained the suddenness of her ending, and she – who was as fond of her as I was – and I clung together in grief and mourning.

You may not like dogs, or even animals at all, and if so, that's your business and I have no desire to criticise. This account may leave you quite cold. My point in writing it is not self-indulgence or maudlin sentimentality but a need to express this: wherever and in whatever sphere our response to the world is predicated on love, we are increased in our dignity of sentient being, and the world is enhanced. If you desire to counter that by pointing out that a love of animals is easy by comparison with love for our fellow human beings or our abused planet, I wouldn't necessarily disagree with you, but questions of degree do not discount the essential point. Love in its every form, so long as it's possessed at root of a pure and disinterested concern for the other's welfare – whoever or whatever that other may be – is our truest point of connection into the world we inhabit.

And as I implied, my little dog, who shared my life for 17 years to the day, was one of those who taught me this lesson. Maybe it is nothing more complex than empathy for a small and helpless dependent creature and the threats that existence poses to it. I'm sure I felt that at first when I brought her home as an assertive, six-weeks-old, hamster-sized puppy from Llansannan. She was intended for my son, but like most pets bought for children, duty of care fast devolved upon the parent after the first excitement was over. I remember a walk with her on Kinder Scout in her first winter, in the snow, and how pitiful she looked and tired she became, sunk through on her short legs to her hairless puppy's belly; and how, wrapped in a duvet jacket, she rode inside my rucksack with her head sticking out; and how always thereafter on the rare occasions when fatigue overtook her or in periods of rest, my rucksack became her habitual nesting place, and its contents would be dragged out by her to make room if necessary. I told myself at the outset that I didn't like little dogs – too yappy, too uncertain of temper. She won me round. She had qualities that may not have been entirely admirable, but were certainly worthy of respect. Any dog larger than herself, for example – and that meant most of the canine population – she disliked with a sly and dangerous intensity. Once, in Sefton Park in Liverpool, she saw two Dobermann Pinschers belonging to a burly Scouser, and set off at a pace towards them, deaf to my command to return. At a distance of four or five yards from the first one she became 12 pounds of projectile teeth that clamped on to its throat. The second Dobermann fled, whilst I had to run up and prise her jaws from the first terrified animal to an accompanying tirade from its owner about dangerous dogs, disgrace, control, police and all the rest. Her sheer courage was frequently as much source of embarrassment as admiration to me.

But in the outdoors, where she was my constant companion throughout her life, she came into her own. I look through my transparencies and always she is there, sneaking into the frame, peeping from behind a cairn, curled up on or in a rucksack, finding a friendly lap to sit on. She was a good mountain dog. On scrambling sections where she couldn't find her own way round she was so light and agile she could be carried, or thrown up steep and difficult bits, and once over them she'd make her way to some vantage point and look down panting with excitement, ready to lick furiously at the first face that might arrive at her ledge. Maybe this will stir mountain rescuers to paroxysms of rage about irresponsible outdoor behaviour, or animal rights people to fret about cruelty. Both would be wide of the mark. I never risked her safety, and she never prejudiced mine. Over her long life she added immeasurably to every hill and mountain, countryside and coastal experience we shared. It is the way a dog's behaviour leads your attention that most stands out in my memory. They frisk and brisk about the life in so alert a way, ready for every new scent and chase and experience, so wholeheartedly given to them that you cannot but follow them in the process, and through them your own senses become more finely attuned. Being outdoors with a dog teaches you more alertly to see. It is as simple as that: the hedgehog in the drift of leaves; the other path, branching off through a thicket in the wood, that her instinct hunted out and that led where you wanted to go; the badger sett below the coastal path, all sign of it hidden from above, that her nostrils quivered at; the stalking fox she saw first at Gloywlyn, that a chance move might have sent slinking away. She gave me things to see …

Also, she brought as well as kept me company. Everywhere I went, her daintiness and reserve, her idiosyncrasies were looked on with affectionate interest – or if there were rare places where they were not, we did not go to those places again. There was the butcher in Bodfari at the beginning of this Welsh journey. On Inishbofin, Brian, the hotel proprietor from Clifden, fed her smoked salmon. How she could charm … When Cameron McNeish invited me on one of his Wilderness Walks for television, we went to County Mayo to film it. The fan mail flooded in for her. She was the star of the show and Cameron and myself just the supporting acts. The people of Inishturk were at least as glad to see her back again as they were me, and talked of the little dog, her nose sticking out from my jacket, who'd ridden in on a force eight gale the first time we'd gone to the island. One of the fan letters sent to me for her protested at my cruelty in not letting her into my sleeping bag. She had her own that I carried everywhere for her, though she seldom let a night go by without attempting to burrow to the bottom of mine. These memories …

It's evening now. F and I have been walking through the spring woods where the badgers live, and in the fields we've not ventured in since she went. Everywhere, nature burgeoning. There was the thinnest crescent moon in a pale sky, a single star rising, and an absence bounding at our side, reminding us, insisting upon how empty a world we inhabit when we lack the capacity to notice, to care, to love.